*325.00 (5 vols)

1-30-98

39765339
v4

Encyclopedia of Family Life

Encyclopedia of Family Life

Volume 4
Mental health – Single life

Editor

Carl L. Bankston III
University of Southwestern Louisiana

Project Editor

R. Kent Rasmussen

SALEM PRESS, INC.
Pasadena, California   Hackensack, New Jersey

Managing Editor: Christina J. Moose
Project Editor: R. Kent Rasmussen
Manuscript Editor: Robert Michaels
Development Editor: Wendy Sacket
Research Supervisor: Jeffry Jensen
Acquisitions Editor: Mark Rehn
Photograph Editor: Karrie Hyatt
Production Editor: Joyce I. Buchea
Design and Layout: James Hutson
Indexer: Robert Michaels

Frontispiece: James L. Shaffer

Library of Congress Cataloging-in-Publication Data

Encyclopedia of Family Life / editor, Carl L. Bankston III; project editor, R. Kent Rasmussen.
   p. ; cm.
Includes bibliographical references (p.   ) and index.
ISBN 0-89356-940-2 (set)
ISBN 0-89356-992-5 (vol. 4)
   1. Family—North America—Encyclopedias. 2. Domestic relations—North America—Encyclopedias. 3. Family services—North America—Encyclopedias. I. Bankston, Carl L. (Carl Leon), 1952-   . II. Rasmussen, R. Kent.
HQ534.E53   1999
306.85'097'03—dc21   98-42491
                                                         CIP

First Printing

PRINTED IN THE UNITED STATES OF AMERICA

Contents

Encyclopedia of Family Life

Mental health

RELEVANT ISSUES: Children and child development; Health and medicine; Kinship and genealogy; Parenting and family relationships

SIGNIFICANCE: In 1993 it was estimated that 2.8 percent of the adult population of the United States suffered from severe mental illness, requiring that they receive extensive support from professionals and family members

The importance of families in determining mental health is widely accepted, but the role of the family in mental illness is not clearly understood. Historically family members have been depicted as the causes of mental illnesses ranging from alcoholism to "schizophrenia." The nagging wife who "drives him to drink" is a well-established stereotype. Less familiar, but equally damning, is the "schizophrenogenic mother," who causes her child's disorder through her inconsistent and inadequate parenting. Family interaction patterns have also been charged with triggering mental illness.

Modern views of the role of family in mental illness suggest a more complex situation. Far from being blamed for causing mental illness, modern families are typically seen as important supports for their mentally ill members, providing daily care and engaging in advocacy with mental-health providers as well as policymakers. National organizations such as the National Alliance for the Mentally Ill in the United States and the Canadian Mental Health Association have engaged families in advocacy efforts on behalf of those suffering from severe mental illness. Another national organization, the American Association of Marriage and Family Therapists, engages in a wide range of activities designed to strengthen families' ability to promote mental health.

What Is Mental Illness? Thomas Szasz argued that mental illness is a cultural construction—with sets of labels and rules that guide interactions with those whose behavior is deviant. His views run counter to the vast majority of therapists, who view mental illness as symptoms with their origins in the physiological, cognitive, and social lives of individuals. The American Psychiatric Association has identified fourteen broad categories of mental illness with at least 83 specific diagnoses. Each is described in careful detail in the Diagnostic and Statistical Manual of Mental Disorders (DSM).

The DSM-IV is widely used and is periodically revised to reflect emerging trends in the field. In the manual, major diagnostic categories are grouped along two axes. Axis I categories include disorders usually first diagnosed in infancy, childhood, or adolescence; delirium, dementia, amnesic, and other cognitive disorders; substance-related disorders; schizophrenia and other psychotic disorders; mood disorders; anxiety disorders; somatoform disorders; factitious disorders; dissociative disorders; sexual and gender identity disorders; eating disorders; sleep disorders; impulse control disorders not elsewhere classified; and adjustment disorders. Axis II categories include mental retardation, personality disorders, and other conditions that may be a focus of clinical attention.

As E. Fuller Torrey has argued, it is important to distinguish severe mental illness from mental discomfort. Most people pass through periods of difficulty or unhappiness in life. Many experience difficulty adjusting to loss or change. These might be termed the "worried well," persons suffering from a diminished quality of life.

The National Advisory Mental Health Council for the National Institute of Mental Health has characterized severe mental illness as "disorders with psychotic symptoms such as schizophrenia, schizo-affective disorder, manic-depressive disorder, autism, as well as severe forms of other disorders such as major depression, panic disorder, and obsessive-compulsive disorder." In 1993, an estimated 2.8 percent of the adult population in the United States were affected. In contrast to the worried well, the severely mentally ill often suffer from neurological dysfunction that renders ludicrous the expression "quality of life." These individuals require extensive support from professionals and family members to maintain a viable existence.

Families as Causes of Mental Illness. Although they are largely discredited among professionals, theories that attribute mental illness to families remain popular with the general public. They are based on widespread observations that certain mental illnesses, like certain physical illnesses, run in families. Historically, these observations led to careful scrutiny of the families themselves. For example, in 1911 Sigmund Freud published his analysis of Daniel Schreber, a paranoid schizophrenic. Freud attributed Schreber's disorder to a "conflict over unconscious homosexuality" which stemmed from an inverted Oedipus complex. In a nutshell, Freud suggested that Schreber became attached to his father instead of his mother and this, with its attendant implications for the patient's psychosexual development, was the cause of the disease.

Subsequent psychoanalytic theorists, among them Carl Jung, Melanie Klein, and Karl Abraham, went on to elaborate and debate causes of schizophrenia. Some of their efforts focused on identifying a critical period, possibly between three and six months of age, when developmental failures produced the disease. It was not until after World War II, however, that mothers became identified as the primary causal agents. Several in-depth (but not controlled) studies of mothers of schizophrenics described them as "overanxious," "obsessive," and especially "domineering"; thus, the concept of the "schizophrenogenic mother" was born.

Later, more general patterns of family interaction became the focus of concern, and the now-famous "double-bind" emerged. A leading proponent of this view, Gregory Bateson, argued that schizophrenia is the result of confused and misleading communications between parent and child in which the child simply cannot win.

Biological Explanations. Because many mental illnesses run in families, most biological explanations refer to genetic abnormalities. Indeed, researchers believe that the genes associated with manic-depressive psychosis have been isolated. However, simple genetic explanations are insufficient to explain the pattern of occurrence. Some people become ill with no apparent family history of their disorder, while others with extensive family histories remain free of mental disorders. Thus, while there is consensus that most mental illness has a genetic component, what is inherited must not be the disease itself, but a predisposition toward developing the illness.

Biochemical explanations of mental illness typically focus on neurotransmitters that transport information between nerve cells. Substances such as dopamine, serotonin and norepinephrine in either deficit or excess may produce the symptoms of mental illness. Some biochemical theories suggest that abnormalities in the receptors for these neurotransmitters are responsible. Still others consider chemical changes in neurotransmitters. For example, dopamine might be changed into a compound like mescaline, which causes hallucinations.

There are three other types of biological explanations. Some researchers have argued that a viral infection produces mental illness. Others focus on nutritional deficits. Still others have argued that schizophrenia in particular may be caused by a failure of the body's immune system.

Institutionalization and Deinstitutionalization. Institutional placement of the mentally ill was developed as a humane alternative to earlier practices. In his classic work *Madness and Civilization*, Michel Foucault described treatment of the insane during the Renaissance in vivid detail. Foucault noted that the mentally ill replaced lepers as a group to be expelled from polite society. One method of expulsion stemmed from the Renaissance view that madness and the sea had affinity for each other. The insane were forced onto "Ships of Fools" that crisscrossed the seas and canals of Europe. These ships relieved families and local authorities of responsibility for their cargo and offered entertaining sideshows when they stopped at foreign ports.

Conditions were little improved in seventeenth century America. In 1843 Dorothea Dix appeared before the Massachusetts Legislature to decry "the state of insane persons confined within this Commonwealth in cages, closets, cellars, stalls, pens, chained, naked, beaten with rods, and lashed into obedience." Partly as a result of her efforts, public funds were allocated to establish thirty hospitals to care for the "mentally defective." Expansion of state-funded hospitals for the insane continued, with most applying the principles of "moral treatment" originally articulated by Philippe Pinel in France and brought to the United States by William Tuke. During this era, mental hospitals seldom had more than a few hundred patients; the use of physical restraints or seclusion were kept to a minimum, and diet and exercise were stressed. Kindness, firmness, and structure were integral parts of moral treatment.

Between 1880 and 1955 the population in U.S. mental hospitals increased dramatically, rising from 41,000 to 559,000. This growth overwhelmed hospitals' capacity to provide humane treatment.

A pivotal case illustrated the appalling conditions in many state mental hospitals. In mid-1944 a grand jury was appointed to investigate conditions in Cleveland State Hospital. Its findings revealed a "case history of brutality and social criminal neglect."

Concern with the high cost and poor quality of institutional care, coupled with the development of the effective antipsychotic drug Thorazine, set the stage for the release of large numbers of mentally ill from state hospitals in a policy known as "deinstitutionalization." In the mid-1960's Congress gave impetus to this movement through passage of the Community Mental Health Centers (CMHC) Act, designed to ensure outpatient care. Under this act federal seed money was provided to establish community mental-health centers with the expectation that states and local authorities would then fund their operation.

Deinstitutionalization dramatically increased the number of mentally ill individuals living in the community. In 1955 there were 558,239 patients in the nation's public psychiatric hospitals. By 1994 the figure had been reduced to 71,619. In the late 1990's the failures of deinstitutionalization can be seen in the number of severely mentally ill persons who are homeless and incarcerated in jails and prisons. Although it is difficult to conclusively determine the number in each group, estimates are available. In 1990 a task force of the American Psychiatric Association concluded that individuals with severe mental illness constitute from 28 to 37 percent of the homeless. Surveys of jails and prisons suggest that 10 percent of those incarcerated suffer from serious mental disorders. This has led many to conclude that the outpatient care provided under the CMHC Act is insufficient to meet the needs of the severely mentally ill.

Families as Caregivers and Advocates for the Mentally Ill. With growing numbers of mentally ill persons living in the community, more families are called upon to provide daily care and supervision. The impact of family members' illnesses varies tremendously. Nonetheless it is possible to identify factors that influence families' experience. Perhaps most significant is residential proximity. Those who live with victims of mental illness often find the demands on them to be never-ending. The extent to which symptoms are stabilized by medication is also important. For a variety of reasons persons with mental illness often fail to comply with their medication regimens. The resulting symptoms can dramatically disrupt family life. A family's experience is also influenced by the meaning they ascribe to the mental illness. For parents who feel responsible for their children's disorders, guilt is a daily companion. The presence of other children is another important factor. Siblings of the mentally ill often report feeling neglected by their parents, with all family attention directed toward management of afflicted members. Finally, families' experience with the mental-health system can either help or interfere with efforts to cope with mental illness.

In the 1970's families of the mentally ill began to organize in self-help groups and advocacy or-

Mental Health Facilities in the United States in 1992

Type of facility	Number of facilities	Total inpatient beds (1,000)	Average daily inpatients (1,000)	Total Expenditures (million dollars)	Patient care staff (1,000)
Total	**5,498**	**271.1**	**216.9**	**29,765**	**432.2**
Mental hospitals: State and county	273	93.1	83.9	7,970	110.9
Private	972	73.8	52.7	7,469	99.7
General hospitals	1,616	52.1	36.3	5,193	72.9
Veterans Administration	162	22.5	18.1	1,530	20.8
Free-standing psychiatric outpatient clinics	862	—	—	821	13.2
Other	1,613	29.6	25.9	6,782	114.7

Source: U.S. Bureau of the Census, *Statistical Abstract of the United States: 1997.* Washington, D.C.: GPO, 1997.

ganizations. The National Alliance for the Mentally Ill (NAMI) was founded in 1979. This grass roots organization mobilizes the mentally ill and their families in self-help and advocacy efforts designed to reduce the stigma of mental illness and eliminate discrimination in employment, housing, health insurance, and social contact. NAMI has more than 1,100 affiliated groups with chapters in all fifty states in the United States The Canadian Mental Health Association is a national network with 135 branches across Canada. It predates NAMI, with at least one branch founded in Toronto in 1953. Like NAMI, the Canadian Association involves the mentally ill and their families in mutual support, education, and advocacy activities.

Family Violence and Intervention Efforts. As a group, persons with severe mental illness have a greater tendency to commit violent acts than do those without mental illness. This is especially true of those who have a history of past violence, who abuse drugs or alcohol, and who fail to take their medications. Violence by the mentally ill might involve random acts against strangers, but more often family members are the victims. Dramatic and brutal incidents are well publicized, but equally poignant are unreported cases of abuse that leave family caregivers torn between love and fear in their daily interactions with the mentally ill.

Interventions for families of the mentally ill vary in their goals. Some psychoeducational programs aim to shore up families' coping abilities by pro-

Efforts to destigmatize mental illness have made it possible for treatment centers openly to invite persons who suspect they have problems to seek care. (James L. Shaffer)

viding information and advice on daily life and decision making. Often psychotherapeutic programs attempt to provide insight into the causes of aberrant behavior in the hopes of generating empathy among family members and enabling them to prevent relapses. Finally, collaborative programs attempt to engage families in partnership with professionals.

Three well-established intervention models offers benefits to the mentally ill and their families. First, the Program in Assertive Community Treatment (PACT) is based on an intervention strategy developed in Madison, Wisconsin, in 1972. A team of eight to ten professionals assumes full responsibility for 100 to 150 patients twenty-four hours a day. This program has given patients and families great satisfaction and has been applied in other nations. Second, the clubhouse model was pioneered by Fountain House in New York City in 1948. A clubhouse offers social and educational activities to mentally ill members seven days a week. Vocational rehabilitation and work teams are integral components. Finally, the Fairweather Lodge Model developed by George Fairweather at the Palo Alto, California, Veteran's Administration in 1963 integrates housing and rehabilitation. Each lodge houses six to eight persons with mental illness who jointly operate a business. A home coordinator supervises the lodge but does not live there.

Ideally, interventions for families of the mentally ill should benefit both patients and their families. However, often the interests and needs of family members conflict with those of the mentally ill. Such is the case when patients consistently refuse treatment and abuse family members, when siblings develop behavioral problems in response to parental inattention, or when patients refuse inpatient treatment against families' wishes and insist on the freedom of life on the street. Thus, professionals in this field often struggle to identify the best interests of families as a whole. Some have gone so far as to argue that the severely mentally ill should not be cared for at home.

Promotion of Mental Health: The Role of Families. In the mid-1950's, mental health professionals began to focus on families and their implications for the mental health of individuals. Some date this "family movement" in mental health to the 1957 meetings of the American Orthopsychia-

tric and American Psychiatric Association. There, several researchers suggested that theories of mental health based on individuals might be replaced by theories based on family dynamics. Family therapists began to explore the practical implications of this notion.

Virginia Satir was a pioneer among family therapists, focusing on strengths and capacities in families instead of illness and pathology. With Don Jackson, Jules Ruskin, and Gregory Bateson, she founded the Mental Research Institute in Palo Alto, California, and established the first formal program in family therapy in the United States. Drawing primarily on the principles of Gestalt psychology, Satir suggested that functional families (those that promote mental health) can be distinguished by four features: productivity, leadership patterns, expression of conflict, and clarity of communication.

As the field of family therapy has matured, a professional association, the American Association for Marriage and Family Therapy (AAMFT) has grown. AAMFT accredits training programs throughout the United States and Canada, works to influence public policy, and promotes research and education in the field. The association publishes the quarterly *Journal of Marriage and Family Therapy* and maintains a register of licensed family-therapy providers. —*Amanda Smith Barusch*

BIBLIOGRAPHY

Foucault, Michel. *Madness and Civilization: A History of Insanity in the Age of Reason.* Translated from the French by Richard Howard. New York: Vintage Books, 1965. Foucault used original documents to re-create mental illness as it was experienced during the Renaissance, resulting in a rich descriptive exposition.

Satir, Virginia. *Peoplemaking.* Palo Alto, Calif.: Science and Behavior Books, 1972. Classic in the field of family therapy, this work draws from sensitivity awareness, encounter, and especially Gestalt psychology to describe family processes and their implications for the mental health of individuals.

Szasz, Thomas. *The Myth of Mental Illness: Foundations of a Theory of Personal Conduct.* New York: Hoeber-Harper, 1961. Controversial work arguing that from a nucleus of neurological dysfunction society has constructed an elaborate set of roles and games that define relationships between those labeled mentally ill and others with whom they come into contact.

Torrey, E. Fuller. *Out of the Shadows: Confronting America's Mental Illness Crisis.* New York: John Wiley & Sons, 1997. Compelling indictment of the modern approach to mental illness in the United States and a clear approach to solving the problems created by the deinstitutionalization of severely mentally ill persons.

Wilson, L. *This Stranger, My Son.* New York: Putnam Books, 1968. Written by the mother of a man who developed schizophrenia as a young child, this story emphasizes the guilt generated by theories of causality that attribute mental illness to parental failures.

See also Alcoholism and drug abuse; Alzheimer's disease; Americans with Disabilities Act (ADA); Behavior disorders; Birth defects; Child abuse; Childhood fears and anxieties; Emotional abuse; Family counseling; Health problems; Learning disorders.

Middle Easterners

RELEVANT ISSUES: Demographics; Divorce; Kinship and genealogy; Parenting and family relationships

SIGNIFICANCE: In a tradition-bound region such as the Middle East, the family, despite the evolving social, economic, and political context, continues to be an important, all-pervasive institution

Despite great differences among the approximately two dozen Arab and non-Arab countries in the Middle East, they are all strongly affected by the family. The older generation shapes family life for the younger generation and strict family codes govern the relations between the sexes.

Middle Eastern family members generally place greater value on the integrity, pride, and prestige of the family than is true of family members in the West. Thus, there is more respect for parents by children, and family ties are stronger. Sex roles of family members are more clearly defined, and greater stress is placed on both premarital chastity for girls and postmarital fidelity for women. Premarital sex among girls is seen as dishonoring girls' families, while marital infidelity is seen as dishonoring husbands' as well as wives' families. Traditionally, it has behooved girls' fathers or older brothers to sanction female family members whom they believe to be wayward—in extreme cases, by killing them. Such immutable family tradition is often reinforced by a strict interpretation of Qur'anic law, such as that followed by Muslim fundamentalists.

The fact that marriage in Middle Eastern countries is a union of two families rather than of two individuals, as in the West, is demonstrated at every step: in the selection of brides, which is often performed by parents to maintain families' status; in the determination of the bride-price; in betrothal and wedding ceremonies; and in the raising of children. Obviously, these traditional family attitudes and rituals have weakened among modernized, often Westernized, well-educated, upper-income, urban families and their emancipated women family members.

Kinship and Genealogy. As in the West, descent among Middle Eastern families is patrilineal—that is, it is determined through the male line. Middle Eastern societies are both patrimonial and distinctly male dominated. Especially in rural areas, they are also patrilocal—that is, married couples traditionally go to live in husbands' fathers' households. In such an extended family arrangement, households often consist of a man, his wife, his unmarried sons and daughters, and his married sons with their wives and children. In more evolved city environments, the nuclear family, as in the West, has become more commonplace.

While the extended family satisfies some of the economic, security, and emotional needs of its members, it also creates occasions for intergenerational conflict. Despite the fact that Islam tolerates polygamy, cases of polygamy in the late twentieth century have become rare, eliminating this potential additional source of tension. As the outer world impinges increasingly on traditional family values, young people try to elude the stifling patriarchal grip by migrating to a distant, anonymous, and more liberal urban environment and, in many cases, abroad.

The birth of male children is marked by elaborate celebrations, because they are expected to perpetuate family tradition and are considered greater and more secure economic assets than girls. Despite some changes, women are still gener-

A Canadian Middle Eastern family. (Dick Hemingway)

ally subordinate to men. Family judgment, especially in the villages, is severe, and deeds considered improper often weigh more heavily than meritorious acts.

The Evolving Family. Under the impact of some industrialization, urbanization, conscription and army life, improved communications, and the provision of some kind of social security by governments or other organizations—no matter how rudimentary—individuals are no longer as willing to be subordinated to parents, uncles, aunts, and other older family members as they were pre-

viously. Moreover, with the centralization of governmental power, persons are beginning to show greater loyalties to the nation and perhaps less to families. Mobility, the demands of revolution and war, and the emergence of the modern interdependent world are increasingly propelling individuals in this direction.

Finally, the changing status of Middle Eastern women, who are now better educated and more likely to work outside the home and participate in economic and even political life than in earlier times, also helps to explain the changes in traditional family values. Thus, more women now have a say in the choice of their spouses, as parents' unilateral determination of spouses for their children has become less common. Divorce, which has become widespread, is no longer the exclusively male prerogative that it once was. In short, the Middle Eastern family is in a state of transition.

Family Values. Changes in the Middle Eastern family should not be exaggerated. Generally speaking, the family is still the premier institution in society. Consequently, family values continue to involve the frequently unquestioned authority of male heads of households as well as the lingering practice of endogamous marriage—that is, marriage within the extended family. Even the payment of a bride-price by grooms or their families, while less frequent, is still practiced. Most important, while fundamental values of North Americans include individualism, freedom, equal rights and equal opportunities, and the chance to realize individual goals, Middle Easterners focus on the importance of the group and hierarchy. Respect for elders, the separateness of sex roles, the complementariness of social roles, and the ethic of sacrifice to the family are still strong. Such cohesive kinship relations have often given Middle Eastern communities a relatively unified view of the outside world.

In this scheme of things, Islam has contributed to the strengthening of family institutions through its detailed guidance of family practice and its legal and moral authority. Islam and the family have, in fact, helped to stabilize Middle Eastern societies, which have witnessed much turmoil since World War II.

In the United States, with more than two million immigrant families from the Middle East, and Canada, with more than a hundred thousand, family values continue to be strong among the first resettled generation. However, as the second and subsequent generations have become more assimilated as they learn English in the schools and experience other socializing factors, original family values have tended to become diluted among Middle Easterners. Thus, the younger generation, whose members are more "Americanized" than their parents and who are concerned with their individuality and rights, no longer tend to return to the Middle East to marry spouses selected for them by their families. Moreover, they often marry

spouses from outside their ethnic groups. Among the younger generation, the nuclear family has become the norm. Young people are also not as wont to send remittances to family members in the Middle East as earlier generations of immigrants have been. Such fund transfers, whether their purpose is to buy land, build a home, purchase appliances, or cover the bride-price, have in some cases been a significant source of revenue for recipient local economies.

A somewhat analogous impact of environment on family may be found among the fifty thousand or so Ethiopian Jews (Falashas) who were airlifted to Israel in the 1980's. The changes that have taken place among the Falashas are twofold. The internal structure of the family has been reorganized, as parental authority, age, and gender have all acquired new contexts and meaning, and the family's external borders have been redrawn, as many of its functions have been taken over by other religious and secular institutions.

The predominance of Muslim families among Middle Eastern immigrants in North America is essentially a post-World War II phenomenon. Earlier groups of immigrants, which included large groups of people who belonged to an array of Middle Eastern Christian sects and a few Jews who came to North America in the late nineteenth and first half of the twentieth centuries, tended to be more Westernized than modern emigrants, bilingual from the start, and subject to less stringent family rules. They therefore found it less difficult to assimilate than the later waves of Muslim immigrants.

—*Peter B. Heller*

BIBLIOGRAPHY

Abdo-Zubi, Nahla. *Family, Women and Social Change in the Middle East: The Palestinian Case.* Toronto: Canadian Scholars' Press, 1987.

Fathi, Ashgar, ed. *Women and the Family in Iran.* Leiden, the Netherlands: E. J. Brill, 1985.

Fernea, Elizabeth W., ed. *Women and the Family in the Middle East: New Voices of Change.* Austin: University of Texas Press, 1985.

Makhlouf-Obermeyer, Carla, ed. *Family, Gender, and Population in the Middle East: Policies in Context.* Cairo: American University in Cairo Press, 1995.

Rugh, Andrea B. *Family in Contemporary Egypt.* Syracuse, N.Y.: Syracuse University Press, 1984.

Tadros, Helmi R. *Social Security and the Family in Egypt*. New York: American University in Cairo Press, 1984.

Westheimer, Ruth, and Steven Kaplan. *Surviving Salvation: The Ethiopian Jewish Family in Transition*. New York: New York University Press, 1992.

See also Arranged marriages; Bride-price; East Indians and Pakistanis; Endogamy; Extended families; Family values; Jews; Men's roles; Muslims; Patrilineal descent.

Midlife crises

RELEVANT ISSUES: Aging; Health and medicine; Sociology

SIGNIFICANCE: As a stage in adult development, midlife for some men and women is a time for major changes with potential for profound impact on the family

Midlife crisis refers to the psychological distress encountered by some people in their middle age. There is little consensus on what time period in an individual's life constitutes middle age. Some consider forty-five as the beginning of middle age, while others place it as early as thirty. The end of middle age is also uncertain because of the difficulty in determining the onset of old age. U.S. Census reports define middle age as beginning at forty-five and ending at sixty-four. Most social scientists believe that middle age is more a function of the developmental milestones in persons' lives than a function of their associated chronology.

The concept of midlife crisis was first proposed by Elliott Jaques in a 1965 article published in the *International Journal of Psychoanalysis*. In this article Jaques held that in midlife people experience a crisis or distress caused by the awareness of their own mortality. This crisis happens because a definite shift occurs in their awareness of time. Such persons no longer reckon their lives in terms of how long they have lived but in terms of how long they have left to live. Ever since Jaques proposed this idea, theorists and researchers of adult development have used the term "midlife crisis" to explain a variety of behavior patterns and psychological problems faced by people in middle age.

Midlife Crisis as a Cultural Myth. Whether or not midlife crisis is real is still an open question. Peoples' developmental stages and life circumstances vary so greatly that it is difficult to determine whether or not the distress persons experience is actually midlife crisis. Findings of empirical studies have yielded only mixed results to support the hypothesis that people in midlife are more likely than those in other age groups to experience acute psychological distress or critical life events. Some dismiss midlife crisis as a cultural myth created by relatively affluent middle-class people in Western societies.

Real or not, the concept of midlife crisis has come to be an integral part of our collective beliefs. Cinema, dramas, novels, songs, and television talk shows have helped to cement the theory that the problems that people in midlife experience are symptoms of major crises. The concept has become so entrenched in modern social consciousness that it has been applied to explain not only the problems of individuals but also of organizations and institutions ranging from the United Nations to computer firms.

Prevalence and Symptoms. To the extent that it is real, midlife crisis is best understood as a multidimensional concept that is useful to describe some of the problems that accompany the dramatic psychological and social transformations that some individuals undergo between the ages of thirty-five and fifty-five. Developmental psychologists suggest that people in midlife, although they not always have feelings of crisis, become aware of the limited amount of time they have left to live. This awareness leads them to reevaluate their accomplishments, marriage, families, careers, and overall quality of life. Nearly half of all middle-aged men and women weigh their choices calmly and rationally to make needed changes, which are often minor, without precipitating crises for themselves or their families. For approximately 10 percent of this age group, however, such self-evaluation can trigger acute distress. The typical symptoms of this distress are anxiety about aging, exaggerated health fears, changes in sexual interest or drive, dissatisfaction with one's marriage, an intense desire to meet former lovers, deep regrets about missed opportunities to marry someone else, fear of impotence, painful realization of the gap between one's aspirations and accomplishments, a sense of urgency to do something very different with the remaining years of one's life, and an acute awareness of one's own mortality.

Impact on Family Life. As their careers peak and their salaries level off, middle-aged men increasingly feel the gap between their aspirations and their actual accomplishments. During periods of economic restructuring, corporate downsizing, and technological changes, many middle-aged men either become victims of layoffs or they fear layoffs. The resulting displacement and insecurity may spill over into personal and family life. In cases where wives are still climbing the career ladder, husband's fear that their wives may outdo them in accomplishments can make some men even more insecure. The expanded social contacts and assertive behaviors that women develop as a result of their career advancement or continuing educational attainment sometimes produce mutual distrust and misunderstanding between husbands and wives, playing havoc with their marriages. Husbands who have been accustomed to being nurtured by their wives may perceive their relative unavailability and assertiveness as signs of rejection. In sexual life, middle-aged men may experience occasional impotence or longer refractory periods (the time in which they cannot have another erection), causing them to feel anxious and inadequate.

Parents' middle-age is usually the time when children reach adolescence or young adulthood. Children's developmental needs for independence and autonomy coincide with middle-aged parents' need to feel acknowledged and appreciated. Conflicts also arise when parents compare themselves with their children. They may become jealous of their children's health, beauty, and energy level. On the other hand, children's social, educational, legal, and other problems can cause strains in family life, causing parents to blame themselves or each other.

Midlife and Sexuality. As children leave home, parents' sexuality and intimacy are affected in various ways. While opportunities for togetherness increase, there is the realization that the fire of romance may need rekindling. For some, the time for undisturbed togetherness, which they have long awaited, becomes a problem. As the passion and fantasies of youthful sexuality become difficult to revive, some men feel disillusioned. In an attempt to recapture lost romance, they may regress to an adolescent mental state and become infatuated with younger women. Cases of success-ful and happy businessmen suddenly abandoning their careers, wives, and children to elope with nineteen-year-old women to exotic places are extreme examples of midlife crisis. Usually, such impulsive and ill-conceived relationships falter very quickly, deepening the crisis even further.

Marital crisis may eventually lead to separation, divorce, or prolonged extramarital affairs. In rare instances, middle-aged men rediscover their homosexual tendencies and may move in with a male friend. Such dramatic lifestyle changes are, however, the end result of prolonged and gradual transformations rather than sudden decisions.

It is perhaps true that no other age group feels the same level of pressure as do middle-aged persons. Middle-aged persons are sometimes described as caught or "sandwiched" between the demands of the young and the expectations of the old. They may feel unappreciated by their own children and unable to live up to the expectations of their parents.

Many middle-aged persons face the prolonged illness or death of their parents or that of their older siblings. The burden of caring for their elderly and sick parents may prove to be too heavy a burden for them. It may strain their limited financial resources and time. Parents' serious illness and eventual death also take on personal meaning for them as they contemplate their own mortality.

Midlife Crisis and Women. Although the concept of midlife crisis was first coined to describe a male developmental stage, women are also believed to encounter midlife crisis. The nature and the course of the crisis are significantly different for men and women. While the source of men's crisis is primarily the world of work, women's crisis originates from the developmental cycle of the family and the launching of children. Furthermore, compared to men, women tend to see their crisis as an opportunity for personal and career development and are psychologically less distressed by the challenges that they face.

An obvious change that middle-aged women undergo is the menopause. Some consider the menopause a clear marker of women's midlife. About 10 percent of women experience physical symptoms associated with the menopause, such as hot flashes, and psychological problems, such as extreme mood swings. What makes the menopause a matter of crisis for some women is that it puts an end to their potential to conceive children. Women who have spent their years climbing the career ladder and who have postponed starting a family may feel an urgent need to exercise their potential for motherhood, except when their decision to forgo motherhood was made deliberately. Increasingly larger numbers of women face the dilemma of choosing between career success and motherhood as they approach the menopause. The effects of the menopause, however, are exaggerated when it is used to explain all changes women undergo during midlife.

Another issue that confronts women more so than men is the "empty nest" syndrome. Although many modern parents look forward to the time when the youngest child leaves home, mothers who have not found satisfying roles outside the home are likely to feel lonely, depressed, and empty when children go off to college or get married. These feelings generally pass as they adjust to their new stage of life and expand their spheres of social and career interests. Some women who did not work outside the home when their children were young return to full-time or part-time employment, pursue more education, or perform public service. The pursuit of these positive alternatives is generally welcomed by their spouses. Unfortunately, for many persons, spouses' support often remains at the verbal level. The perceived lack of real support from spouses becomes another source of marital conflicts.

Some women develop a negative body image at midlife. They subject themselves to the cultural pressures to remain thin, wrinkle-free, and attractive. Some women who have failed to cultivate a positive self-image and who have not found alternative ways of making a smooth transition to old age resort to unhealthy behavior patterns. However, compared to men, most women manage their midlife crisis more creatively with fewer disastrous consequences.   —*Mathew J. Kanjirathinkal*

BIBLIOGRAPHY
Gallagher, Winifred. "Midlife Myths." *Atlantic* 271 (May, 1993).
Jaques, Elliott. "Death and the Mid-life Crisis." *International Journal of Psychoanalysis* 46 (1965).
Kaye, Elizabeth. *Midlife: Notes from the Halfway Mark.* Reading, Mass.: Addison-Wesley, 1995.
Sheehy, Gail. *New Passages: Mapping Your Life Across Time.* New York: Random House, 1995.
_____. *Passages: Predictable Crises of Adult Life.* New York: E. P. Dutton, 1974.
Shek, Daniel T. L. "Midlife Crisis in Chinese Men and Women." *Journal of Psychology* 130 (1996).
Tamir, Lois M. *Men in Their Forties: The Transition to Middle Age.* New York: Springer, 1982.

See also Adultery; Ageism; Baby boomers; Childlessness; Cultural influences; Divorce; Empty nest syndrome; Family crises; Family life cycle; Gender longevity; Generational relationships; Menopause; Retirement; Sandwich generation; Sheehy, Gail; Widowhood.

Military families

RELEVANT ISSUES: Children and child development; Parenting and family relationships
SIGNIFICANCE: Increases in the number and value of social benefits available to American military families have been dramatic since the All-Volunteer Force was established in 1973

Prior to World War II and also during the Korean and Vietnam Wars most American military servicemen were single, especially those in the lower enlisted ranks. Although they were usually not forbidden to marry, there was pressure on them to remain single or to delay marriage until after leaving the military. It was tacitly assumed that a wife and children would weaken, or at least compromise, the serviceman's allegiance to his primary responsibility: the nation's defense.

The huge number of men required for military service during World War II effectively eliminated restrictions on marriages during that conflict. However, during the Korean and Vietnam Wars the supply of single men for the draft was more than enough to minimize the need to conscript married men.

The debilitating outcome of the war in Vietnam prompted a significant change in the armed forces by ending conscription and instituting the All-Volunteer Force (AVF) in 1973. The intent was to recruit and train a more highly educated and more deeply committed complement of men, and later women, by offering incentives that competed with those available in the civilian business sector. The taboo against marriage and family was dropped entirely. In fact, a complete turnabout took place. Extensive and expensive family-oriented social programs were either expanded or inaugurated to attract the type of prospective recruit who previously had paid scant attention to becoming a member of the armed forces.

By the mid-1990's the results were mixed. The quality of recruits increased but retention was disappointing. Ironically, although perhaps not surprisingly, it seemed to some that the men and women enticed into the armed forces by offers of family and financial perquisites were more committed to the military for occupational rather than for idealistic reasons. The armed forces became for many a job rather than a calling.

Families During the American Revolution. With a few notable exceptions, the American military had lacked for its first two hundred years a genuine social concern, extending beyond its immediate active-duty members. Service members were honored, respected, and eulogized for risking or giving up their lives for the nation's cause. However, virtually no attention had been given to the related hardships suffered by their wives and families.

During the Revolutionary War (1775-1783) wives and families were not prevented from joining their military husbands; but without financial subsidy and moral support it was impossible for many military families to remain intact, especially those among the lower ranks. If a serviceman was married, he either left his wife and family at home or attempted to provide for their well-being while they followed him from camp to camp. As camp followers, wives might have been hired as laundresses earning a half ration for themselves and a quarter ration for each child. Her task was to wash and mend soldiers' clothes. Otherwise, she had to provide for herself and her children.

George Washington's wife, Martha, accompanied her husband at one time or another throughout the Revolutionary War, but she was an exception. Continental Army officers' wives often joined their husbands when the army was in winter camp and inactive. Also, there were occasions when battles were fought or camps were established near soldiers' homes, thereby allowing opportunities for military fathers and their families to be together. Some progress in the military's support for families was made after the war, when in 1794 cash payments to widows and orphans of officers killed in battle were authorized. Eight years later, pay-

ments were extended to the families of noncommissioned officers.

Throughout the nineteenth century and the first four decades of the twentieth century, the military continued to discourage its members from marrying. Enlisted men were required to gain the permission of their superior officers before they were permitted to marry. Most often, the strictness of the ban depended more on the temperament of the fort, post, or camp commander or his designate than on specific regulations.

From the Civil War to the World Wars. From the Civil War to the Vietnam War, with the important exception of World War II, the probability that married men with dependents would be drafted was remote. In the North married men with families were not officially exempt from the Civil War draft from 1861 to 1865, but those between the ages of thirty-five and forty-five were placed on a Class Two list and were not eligible to be drafted until the Class One list was exhausted. Young men who provided the sole financial support for either or both parents or for motherless children were exempt. Every draft-eligible young man, single or married, could pay a commutation fee of three hundred dollars or provide a substitute in lieu of serving in the military. Just 8 percent of the 2,100,000 men who served in the Union Army were drafted and few of them were married. On the other hand, 700,000 married men enlisted as volunteers in the Union Army.

Reflecting the Victorian values surrounding motherhood during the last half of the nineteenth century, the separation between family and military service deepened. The major and sole responsibility of mothers was to raise their children at home. The military agreed. For example, in 1883 the army continued to obstruct marriage by refusing to permit separate housing for couples and families; in 1887 it vetoed free family transportation; in 1901 it discouraged married soldiers from reenlisting; and later it even formally prohibited the reenlistment of men with wives and minor children. Any exceptions were carried out informally for the most part and were restricted to officers and noncommissioned officers.

The draft reappeared in 1917 when the U.S. joined the Allies during World War I. Close to 75 percent of the married men who registered for the draft were deferred, and 90 percent of those who were drafted were single. Also, wives and families were not allowed to join their husbands overseas. The implication was: single men only. The adage "If the army had wanted you to have a wife, it would have issued you one" seemed to be the order of the day.

Recognizing the need for a huge expansion of the military during the early months of American participation in World War II Congress passed the Servicemen's Dependents Allowance Act, which augmented the monthly salaries of enlisted men, amounting to twenty-eight dollars for a wife, forty dollars for a wife and child, plus ten dollars for each additional child. After the war ended in 1945,

however, allowances for dependents were eliminated, although as a goodwill gesture converted troop transports carried 25,000 wives and children to join their husbands and fathers in occupied Europe in May, 1946. Private, nonprofit family assistance programs were also available. The Army Emergency Relief program helped to relieve distress in military families. The Red Cross was another valuable source of relief.

Although the armed services promoted a return to a single-man's military during the 1950's and 1960's, they also had to face reality. By 1960 military dependents outnumbered active-duty military personnel. Retention of expensively trained men

An Air Force family watching a special armed service television program service during the 1950's. (AP/Wide World Photos)

was down. Failure to win the Vietnam War lowered American military prestige. One response was an increase in on-base housing for military families. Another was the Civilian Health and Medical Program of the Uniformed Service (CHAMPUS) passed by Congress in 1966. This program guaranteed medical care for military families stationed in locales where military treatment facilities were nonexistent.

POWs and Families. Although military families enjoy a number of perquisites that match and go beyond those available to civilians, they are also susceptible to more traumatic experiences. Wives of prisoners of war (POWs) in Vietnam, for example, had to make emotional and psychological adjustments in their attempts to overcome severe loneliness and depression. One third of POW wives required psychotherapy to cope with their problems. The military services became more assertive in these cases; instead of waiting for wives to seek help, they took the initiative by encouraging wives to accept psychological help.

After husbands' return from captivity, adjustment remained difficult. Many wives found it necessary to become more independent during their husbands' absence. They were unwilling to resume their previous roles. Children were also affected by their fathers' return. Behavior problems both at home and at school were a result. If husbands were willing and able to accept a more egalitarian family arrangement, family adjustment stood a better chance of succeeding. Evidence suggests that husbands and fathers who had most strongly resisted their captors were more authoritarian in disciplining their children; such men therefore found it more difficult to share responsibility with their wives, who had been the principal disciplinarians during the fathers' absence.

The All-Volunteer Force. Opposition to the draft during the Vietnam War was a major reason for the signal change to the All-Volunteer Force in 1973. To attract and retain volunteers, the armed services had to contribute more generously than in the past to the quality of life of their recruits, and in particular, of recruits' families. However, from 1985 to 1997 the annual budget of the Department of Defense was reduced 38 percent from $400 billion to $250 billion, causing considerable program curtailment. Downsizing the military was not accompanied by a commensurate decrease in

workload responsibilities. In fact, in many cases the "personnel tempo," or rate of performance expected from officers and enlisted men, was either maintained or increased to fulfill the expectations of the All-Volunteer Force. The armed services were required to do more with less. For example, in September, 1994, air force personnel were away from their home bases four times more often than in 1989. Periodic and frequent family separations often either caused or exacerbated family disharmony.

Nonetheless, numerous programs were expanded or initiated for the purpose of raising the quality of life of military families. By the mid-1990's, $25 billion was being spent annually on family-related programs. In 1985 base commanders were authorized to establish child-care facilities. Four years later the U.S. Congress passed the Military Child Care Act to improve the availability of child care on military sites. The need was genuine, since children under five years of age numbered more than two million, while 65 percent of military spouses were employed. Child care was implemented through two venues. The Child Development Center (CDC) offered trained provider care at a lower cost than the private sector. The Family Child Care (FCC) alternative consisted of military spouses who were trained to care for up to six children in their government quarters. Total capacity for CDC and FCC homes worldwide was 166,600 in 1993. Yet, by 1996 an additional 144,000 child-care spaces were needed.

Housing and Health Care for Families. The military was also determined to provide high quality housing facilities and services to all eligible military personnel and their families. Housing was available in government-owned or government-leased quarters, or housing allowances were granted covering partial living costs in civilian communities. In 1996, 35 percent of military families lived in 387,000 homes owned or leased by the Department of Defense. The average age of these homes was thirty-three years; 64 percent were deemed unsuitable. The cost of needed maintenance, repairs, revitalization, and replacement was estimated at $20 billion. Progress was made in 1996 with the passage of the Military Family Housing Act, permitting army bases to form partnerships with private companies. The family housing shortfall was expected to be eliminated by 2006.

Budget restraints helped to bring about necessary changes in health care delivery, including a greater reliance on civilian medical care. CHAMPUS became Tricare in 1997. As a health care program similar in structure to civilian health maintenance organizations (HMOs), Tricare has been managed by the military, even though medical services were provided by contract with civilian doctors and facilities, as well as by military medical personnel. Active duty and retiree families must choose one of three Tricare options: Prime, Standard, or Extra. Differences among them have included enrollment requirements and costs, copayment fees, deductible amounts, availability, provider choice, claim filing, paperwork, and informational assistance.

During the 1980's additional programs supporting military families were established, including a special effort to accommodate those in the lower enlisted ranks. More attention was paid to families in which both parents were members of the military and to single-parent military families headed by females. Family-support programs providing relocation assistance, personal financial management, counseling, and other family-related services have been established on many military bases. Special attention has been paid to family-violence programs stressing identification and treatment of child and spousal abuse. Spousal employment centers were authorized in 1982 to provide information about and assistance with job opportunities. Youth programs have been expanded and subsidies for education made available. The profile of the military and its families has changed dramatically since 1973.

—John Quinn Imholte

BIBLIOGRAPHY

Alb, Betty S., and Bonnie Stone. *Campfollowing: A History of the Military Wife.* New York: Praeger, 1991. Short, popular account of the roles played by military wives from the Revolutionary War to Vietnam that is a mixture of historical research and anecdotal information written with journalistic flair.

Cohen, Eliot A. *Citizens and Soldiers: The Dilemmas of Military Service.* Ithaca, N.Y.: Cornell University Press, 1985. Scholarly and readable critique of the military manpower debate during the mid-1980's that devotes a brief chapter to the origin and quality of the All-Volunteer Force and provides a context leading to a deeper understanding of the place of families in the military.

Eitelberg, Mark J., and Stephen L. Mehay, eds. *Marching Toward the Twenty-first Century: Military Manpower and Recruiting.* Westport, Conn.: Greenwood Press, 1994. Focuses on American societal trends and changes that may determine the nature of the armed forces in the early twenty-first century, demonstrating the impact of social and demographic forces upon Army families and discussing the effectiveness of the all-volunteer force in an environment in which funding for the military has been reduced.

Hunter, Edna J., and D. Stephen Nice, eds. *Military Families: Adaptation to Change.* New York: Praeger, 1978. One of the groundbreaking works on military families, this book is a compilation of papers presented at a 1977 conference on Current Trends and Directions in Military Family Research that emphasizes the many changes in the lifestyles of military families, such as alternative styles of marriage and the growing number of single-parent and dual-military career families.

Kaslow, Florence W., ed. *The Military Family in Peace and War.* New York: Springer Publishing Company, 1993. Emphasizes mental health care for military families, discussing family centers on military bases that provide information and referral services, marriage and family counseling, money-management assistance, a family relocation program to assist in making the numerous moves required of military families, and support for family members after duty separations.

Kirby, Sheila N., and Harry J. Thie. *Enlisted Personnel Management: A Historical Perspective.* Santa Monica, Calif.: Rank, 1966. Deals with the effects of military personnel policies on enlisted men, describes and interprets personnel recruitment and retention policies, reviews the increased emphasis on family matters, and analyzes retirement reform, women in the military, and the impact of downsizing.

Schwarzkopf, H. Norman. *It Doesn't Take a Hero.* New York: Bantam, 1992. Numerous references throughout Schwarzkopf's autobiography express his deep and genuine concern over the separation of military men and women from their families.

See also Corporate families; Death; Grief counseling; War brides.

Missing Children's Assistance Act

DATE: Enacted on October 12, 1984
RELEVANT ISSUES: Children and child development; Law; Parenting and family relationships; Violence
SIGNIFICANCE: This act focused national attention on the approximately one million cases of missing, abducted, and runaway children in the United States

On October 12, 1984, Congress passed the Missing Children's Assistance Act, leading to establishment of the National Center for Missing and Exploited Children (NCMEC) in Arlington, Virginia. The center was established under the auspices of the Justice Department. A 1982 bill known as the Missing Children's Act had been sponsored by Representative Paul Simon, a Democrat from Illinois, and Senator Paul Hawkins, a Republican from Florida. This bill mandated the entry of data on missing children into the national crime computer maintained by the Federal Bureau of Investigation (FBI). The 1984 law focused further attention on a serious national problem: the growing population of missing, abducted, runaway, and exploited children. According to a somewhat conservative estimate, some one million children fall within this definition.

While media attention has focused on high-profile cases of abduction, sexual molestation, and murder, such as the Adam Walsh case in Florida and the Polly Klaas case in California, the majority of cases that fall under the jurisdiction of the Missing Children's Assistance Act of 1984 involve abductions by family members, particularly in child-custody battles; short-term abduction by strangers, often involving sexual abuse and violence; runaways; and lost or missing children who may have been injured.

The NCMEC is aided by the FBI's crime computer and by other technological advances, including age-progression computer programs that can create images of missing children as they might look many months or years after their initial disappearance. Other techniques, such as infant footprinting, are also invaluable in tracking abducted children. Ongoing school and community-based programs aimed at educating children and parents about the dangers of abduction have contributed to greater social awareness of the problem of missing children, while enthusiastic support from private and corporate donors, including IBM and Intel, have helped safeguard children and youths.

—Jo Manning

See also Child abduction; Juvenile delinquency; National Center for Missing and Exploited Children (NCMEC); Parental Kidnapping Prevention Act (PKPA).

Moiety

RELEVANT ISSUES: Kinship and genealogy; Parenting and family relationships; Religious beliefs and practices
SIGNIFICANCE: Many small societies are divided into complementary dual halves of exogamous clans or phratries, with the clans of each half fulfilling onerous tasks, ritual ceremonies, and socioeconomic and political activities for its counterpart

Moieties (from the French word *moitié*, meaning half) are always exogamous and are either patrilineally or matrilineally named, formally organized groups. They are often named to complement contrasting elements in the universe, such as sun-moon, war-peace, earth-sky, or summer-winter. A moiety, in a sense, is a structural mirror image of its counterpart, because each moiety has the same number of named clans, which have a definite affiliation and the same ultimate ancestor. Many moiety-structured villages are divided into two halves, which are made up of clans that reciprocally marry, perform initiation rituals, bury the dead, perform curing ceremonies, and kill favored domesticated animals.

Moieties are significant because the clan of one moiety supports the same-named clan of the other moiety. Despite instances of conflict between moieties, same-named clans are closely affiliated to each other. Persons can never marry within their moiety. A member of the whale clan, for example, cannot marry a member of other whale clans, regardless of moiety affiliation, but they can marry a member of the eagle clan belonging to another moiety.

—John Alan Ross

See also Clans; Cross-cousins; Exogamy; Kinship systems; Lineage; Matrilineal descent; Patrilineal descent; Tribes.

Mommy track

RELEVANT ISSUES: Economics and work; Marriage and dating; Parenting and family relationships

SIGNIFICANCE: Proposed by Felice N. Schwartz, mommy track was one of two career tracks for women, the purpose of which was to differentiate working mothers (the mommy track) from career-primary women, to protect companies against personnel upsets caused by women who go on maternity leave, and to encourage companies to promote career women

The phrase "mommy track" is commonly used in contrast to the concept of the "fast track" or "success track." These terms reflect a cultural tradition in which women are not seen as necessary to providing primary financial support to their families but are either expected to leave the workforce in order to have children or be more costly to their employers because they are their children's primary caregivers. Such assumptions hold that women, being less committed to pursuing careers in the workplace than men, should be regarded by employers as temporary or peripheral. According to this view, women should be placed on a special "career track" that provides lesser pay and fewer opportunities to them than to men, who are considered to be more committed to work outside the family.

In 1988 Felice N. Schwartz, the president of Catalyst, an organization that promotes women's career and leadership development and

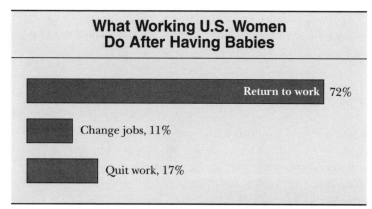

What Working U.S. Women Do After Having Babies

Return to work 72%

Change jobs, 11%

Quit work, 17%

Source: Christian Science Monitor (May 9, 1997)

Felice Schwartz, inventor of the phrase "mommy track," in 1993. (AP/Wide World Photos)

works closely with businesses on issues concerning women in the workplace, wrote an article for the *Harvard Business Review* advocating that employers create a "two-track" system. Her article and the letters and editorials that responded to it highlighted the controversy surrounding the concept of the "mommy track." Some economists, social scientists, and feminists suggest that because the majority of U.S. and Canadian women work outside the home, with more young women than men attending college and some men assuming more responsibility for child care, it has become economically advantageous for employers to create a more family-friendly atmosphere at the workplace. In the absence of such an atmosphere, a parental or family-oriented career track is more appropriate than the discriminatory mommy track.

—*Erika E. Pilver*

See also Dual-earner families; Family-friendly programs; Maternity leave; Motherhood; Second shift; Single-parent families; Women's roles; Work.

Monogamy

RELEVANT ISSUES: Marriage and dating; Parenting and family relationships; Sociology

SIGNIFICANCE: The dynamics of monogamy affect many of the world's religions, cultures, sexual attitudes, and family environments

A dedicated monogamist, Mark Twain (pictured with family) wrote: "People talk about beautiful friendships between two persons of the same sex. What is the best of that sort, as compared with the friendship of man and wife . . . ?" (Arkent Archive)

Monogamy implies sexual exclusivity between two partners. It appears in two general forms: as a temporary commitment to exclusivity, sometimes called serial monogamy, and as a life-long contract between two individuals that may be ended only when the terms of the agreement have been broken.

Marriage represents a common method of formalizing partners' commitment to a monogamous relationship. In modern secular states monogamous marriage is the only form granted legal recognition. Generally, this bond is only recognized between heterosexual partners. In some countries, such as the U.S., if a man and a woman have lived monogamously for a specified number of years, they will be considered married under common law. Serial monogamy through divorce and remarriage is widely accepted in such states. According to some belief systems, such as the Roman Catholic and Hindu religions, individuals must remain faithful to a single partner, even after that partner's death. The obligation to maintain the monogamous relationship can only be lifted when one partner violates the terms of the marriage contract.

The widespread practice of monogamy in many cultures has been attributed to personal and social desires, such as the desire to provide a stable environment for the nurturing of children, the establishment and regulation of family lines, the division of labor, economic stability, social status, and psychological and physical pleasure. Anthropologists have found monogamy especially prevalent in societies in which men and women contribute equally to the economic livelihood of the family and in which small families are equally as efficient as large ones or even more efficient. Hunter-gatherer and industrialized societies exemplify this phenomenon.

Polygamy, which involves marriage between three or more partners, is widely practiced throughout the world, especially in Africa and Asia. In a study of 565 cultures, 75 percent favored polygyny, marriage between one man and more than one woman; 24 percent favored monogamy; and 1 percent favored polyandry, marriage between one woman and more than one man. Despite these numbers, however, most of the world's marriages are monogamous due to the generally equal ratio of males to females.

Monogamy plays a profound role in family life. Psychologists recommend monogamy as an environment in which couples can develop highly intimate bonds, noting the substantial practical limitations of establishing equivalent relationships with more than one person. Child development theorists suggest that a stable family with positive role models is essential for successful child rearing and that monogamy encourages such stability in both the immediate and extended family, providing children with a network of resources for support and guidance.   —*H. C. Aubrey*

See also Adultery; Bigamy; Cohabitation; Common-law marriage; Communal living; Couples; Endogamy; Family: concept and history; Group marriage; Marriage; Polygyny; Serial monogamy.

Moral education

RELEVANT ISSUES: Children and child development; Education; Parenting and family relationships; Religious beliefs and practices

SIGNIFICANCE: Philosophers such as Aristotle, Jean-Jacques Rousseau, Confucius, Buddha, John Dewey, and others have been concerned with the role of education in the development of moral character

In his writings on ethics the ancient Greek philosopher Aristotle reflected on moral education and character development. He wrote that although individuals might disagree on the definition of virtue, those who practice it tend to become ethically responsible members of society. The French Enlightenment philosopher Jean-Jacques Rousseau believed that humans are basically good but that environment and communities can nurture or corrupt individuals. An elder from a Central African society once explained that young people exhibit good behavior because it is the honorable thing to do, not because they fear punishment.

In his 1997 work on raising morally literate children, Robert Coles argued that moral development is not acquired through memorization, rules, and regulations; it occurs as a result of persons' lives in the community. Expressed actions and experiences help shape character and guide persons toward moral intelligence and the development of values. Thus, a good person is usually compassionate, caring, and unpretentious. Other scholars have identified courage, self-discipline, integrity, creativity, playfulness, loyalty, generosity, empathy, honesty, and adaptability as values that encourage moral decisions. Some have used literature and storytelling as a means of helping children to understand the importance of becoming moral decision makers.

Cultural Diversity. In pluralistic democracies such as Canada and the United States, the notion of moral and ethical values and character development are not always clear-cut. Although most people agree that there are some shared values within immigrant nations, ethnic, linguistic, and religious pluralism permits individual choices within cultural groups and families. Concepts of family also vary among cultures; nuclear families are not the only family units. For many immigrants, the concept of family includes grandparents and aunts or uncles living under the same roof as extended families. Many families are headed by single parents.

The values and practices of families in some cultures are occasionally in conflict with those of the larger society. In some Latino families, for example, boys are allowed more social privileges than girls—a practice that may conflict with teenage expectations in mainstream American culture. In many families, fathers, reinforced by the church community, are responsible for promoting values and character development within the family unit.

Defining Moral Education. Many Americans believe that parents and families, not the schools, are centrally responsible for the moral education and character development of children. Historically, however, American schools have always been instrumental in their students' moral and ethical development. John Dewey and the progressive education movement held that schooling must empower students to become full participants in a democratic society. Participatory citizenship implies responsibility and the ability to make appropriate decisions within the moral and ethical context of religious values that claim to be universal.

The essence of morality is a philosophical concept grounded in the notions of justice, freedom, and dignity. Although the study of moral awareness is rooted in philosophy, the study of values, ethics, and morals became a concern for psychologists. A moral sense is considered integral to personality and character development. The pioneering Swiss psychologist Jean Piaget defined morality as a set of rules that children between the ages of six and twelve internalize as autonomous morality.

The study of moral development continued with the American educator Lawrence Kohlberg, who identified six sequential stages of moral reasoning that are consistent with moral philosophy and ethical behavior. At the preconventional stage, moral decisions are seen as good or bad, right or wrong, rewards and punishment. There are two levels at this stage: punishment and obedience, linked to physical consequences of actions, whereby persons respect power and try to avoid punishment; and personal usefulness, whereby moral decisions are made to satisfy persons' needs with occasional regard for the feelings of others.

At the conventional stage, persons value the rights of family, community, or nation, regardless of individual needs. Moral choices are usually conformist, acquiescing to the rules and expectations of the group. There are two levels at the conventional stage: conforming to the will of the group and earning approval from others.

In the stage of law and order, moral judgement is justified by fixed rules and the maintenance of social order. At a high level of maturity this leads to independent judgements based on general principles of behavior. Moral decisions are based on generally accepted universal values that may exist separately from the authority of the groups with which persons identify. At this stage, there are two levels: social contracts, constitutionalism, and higher law; and personal conscience. At the level of social contracts, persons' notions of right actions are usually defined by general values within society, such as freedom, equality, and justice. What is right is often a matter of personal values under the umbrella of democratic, constitutional laws—the "greatest good for the largest number of people."

For Kohlberg, the highest stage is that of personal conscience, whereby persons make moral decisions based on universal, abstract principles of justice, reciprocity, and human rights. These ethical and moral principles are not necessarily tied to particular cultures or societies. According to Kohlberg, the highest stages of moral development are the "more defensible forms of moral reasoning and ethical behavior."

Many advocates of what have been called "traditional" families see religion as central in the moral education of children. (James L. Shaffer)

The Role of Schools. In private religious schools the study of morals and values has always been integrated into curricula and has been taught in specific courses on religion. The question of teaching moral education in public schools has been controversial. Until the mid-twentieth century, most educators believed that schools were

vehicles for instilling Judeo-Christian values "for training up youth in wisdom and virtue." Thus, ethical character was included as one of the Seven Cardinal Principles of Education in 1918.

In 1963 the National Education Association acknowledged the importance of separation of church and state, while continuing to stress that

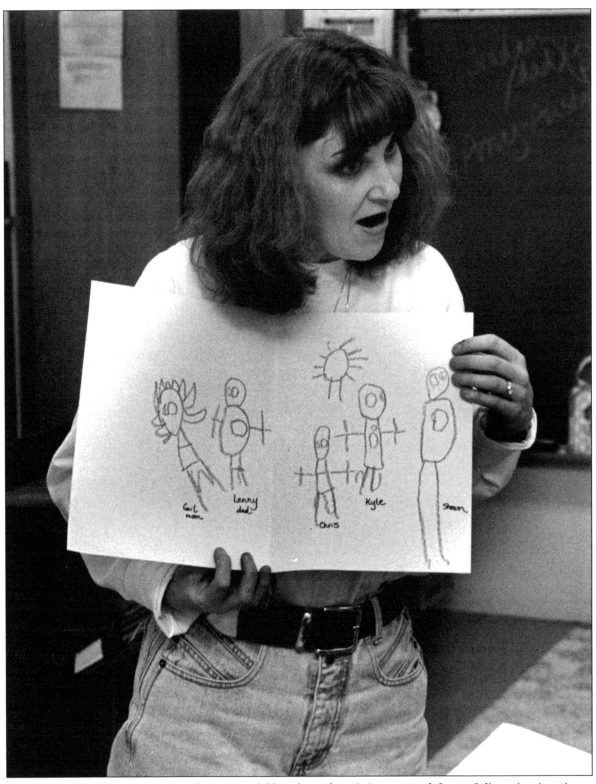

Because family is one of the things that young children know best, it is a natural focus of discussion in primary grades. (James L. Shaffer)

"public schools can and should teach the moral and social ideals of conduct that contribute to harmonious human relations." In the 1960's and 1970's the concept of "values clarification" was introduced into the schools. This approach seemed to deemphasize moral content and rely primarily on student opinion without a specific standard for evaluation.

The 1980's saw renewed interest in moral development and character education. The California State Board of Education, for example, published a booklet on moral and civic responsibility and expected public-school educators to teach about religion and moral character. School personnel, it was argued, must foster in students an understanding of moral values and habits that reveal a commitment to citizenship and responsibility. Moral values, in the California framework, included respect for cultural differences; the significance of religion (not indoctrination), including Judeo-Christian beliefs, in shaping moral and ethical behavior; the search for truth and commitment to fairness and justice; patriotism and citizenship; self-esteem and empathy; and persistence and courage in the face of adversity. Teachers were encouraged to engage students in discussions that foster moral interaction and ethical reflection and asked to model appropriate ethical conduct.

Several schools have woven character education programs into their curricula in conjunction with parents and other community organizations. Curricular options have often included selections from multicultural literature exhibiting exemplary moral values and character education. In addition, many students have also been required to perform community service as a means of developing commitment to social action and responsibility to the community. Character education programs have often included conflict resolution strategies and skills to facilitate intercultural communication, understanding, and respect.

Teaching Values and Character Education. The components of good character have been identified by some scholars as moral knowing (in values, reasoning, and decision making) and moral feeling (conscience, self-esteem, empathy). Both moral knowing and moral feeling lead to moral action. Based on these principles, a holistic, methodological approach for teaching values and character education has been designed. This approach

calls for teachers to create a moral, democratic classroom environment that nurtures respect and responsibility. This moral community helps create a school culture and reaches out to parents and the community. Scholars adhering to this schema see teachers as caregivers, mentors, and models who guide learners in developing critical consciousness and moral reflection. Ethical issues are woven into curricula and discussed through cooperative learning. Students learn to listen and mediate conflicts in ways that respect the democratic process.

Another view deals with responsible, moral, character development, envisioning school curricula that integrate narratives (stories) on themes of inclusion such as family, religion, and virtue and describing moral attitudes as "voices of conscience." Such voices of conscience include prudence (good judgement, dialogue, discernment), justice (fairness, equity, inclusion), courage (resourcefulness, loyalty, sacrifice), and temperance (discipline, balance, proportion). This view further identifies three theological virtues—faith, hope, and love—as essential in attaining "responsible self-hood" in a participatory democracy.

Other scholars have proposed that moral literacy be taught through literature by focusing learners' attention on the ethical dimensions of stories, engaging them in discourse and teaching them to apply moral lessons to their own lives. At the same time, such scholars argue that the analysis and discussion of historical events should be encouraged from multiple perspectives and that skills of moral discourse should be built that go beyond casual argumentation. Part of being an adept educator requires a variety of materials and strategies that are effective with diverse students. Still other scholars argue that multicultural curricula, based on social transformation, aid learners and citizens in developing a critical consciousness of moral choices in personal and public life. These scholars offer suggestions for incorporating multicultural literature in curricula as a means of teaching values and moral literacy.

The Role of Curricula. Another view on moral education holds that ethics and morals are rooted in the cumulative development of specific beliefs about appropriate human behavior. A large commitment to citizenship is the ability to make moral, ethical choices in decision-making situations. These moral and ethical choices are based on the values of community, societal, family, and religious institutions. Schools, as societal institutions, have a responsibility to integrate moral and character education in their curricula. Curricula, however, should be inclusive, respectful, and affirming of the diversity of modern pluralistic democracies, such as those of Canada and the United States, whose immigrant populations come from diverse ethnic, linguistic, and religious backgrounds.

Moral education is an important part of schooling, according to other specialists, who believe that schools should be designed to support and nurture the ethic of caring that can only emerge through spiritual connectedness and responsiveness. Thus, students should be exposed to various religions and religious practices as the basis of values across cultures. Moral education and ethical character development should be integrated intoschoolcurricula.

Finally, others hold that effective school leadership must be viewed as stewardship, which involves a civic and moral reciprocal relationship between schools and the communities they serve. This relationship requires that all members of the community be treated with dignity and respect and that every parent, teacher, student, and administrator should be viewed as an interdependent member of schools' covenantal community and that every action taken in the schools must seek to advance the welfare of this community. The virtuous school is a community of learners in which every student can learn; it fosters respect and works cooperatively with parents, understanding that collaborative decision making is beneficial to the moral dimension of the community. In a democracy, students become the foundation of school curricula that foster creativity and diversity, while strengthening moral and civic responsibility.

—*Maria A. Pacino*

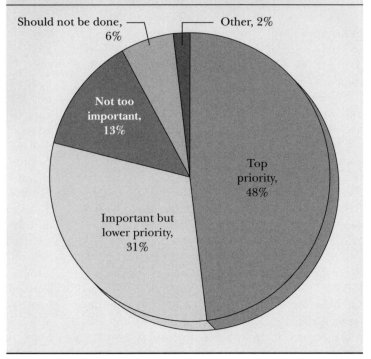

U.S. Public Opinion on Moral Reform as a Government Priority in 1998

Should not be done, 6%

Other, 2%

Not too important, 13%

Top priority, 48%

Important but lower priority, 31%

Source: The Pew Research Center (1998)

Note: In early 1998 the PEW Research Center conducted a nationwide survey in which 1,200 adults were asked how high a priority dealing with the "moral breakdown in the country" should be for federal government leaders during the coming year. This chart summarizes responses.

BIBLIOGRAPHY

Brooks, B. David, and Frank G. Goble. *The Case for Character Education: The Role of the School in Teaching Values and Virtue.* Northridge, Calif.: Studio 4 Productions, 1997. Offers practical suggestions and examples of programs in moral education and character development.

Coles, Robert. *The Moral Intelligence of Children.* New York: Random House, 1997. Using case studies, Coles develops a definition of moral intelligence and appeals to parents and teachers to collaborate in educating morally conscious children.

Greer, Colin, and Herbert Kohl, eds. *A Call to Character: A Family Treasury of Stories, Poems, Plays, Proverbs, and Fables to Guide the Development of Values for You and Your Children.* New York: HarperCollins, 1995. Collection of various forms of literature designed to strengthen families and rear children.

Hekman, Susan J. *Moral Voices, Moral Selves: Carol Gilligan and Feminist Moral Theory.* University Park: Pennsylvania State University Press, 1995. Addresses moral issues from a feminist perspective, arguing that moral values are relational rather than autonomous.

Killpatrick, William, Gregory Wolfe, and Suzanne Wolfe. *Books That Build Character: A Guide to Teaching Your Child Moral Values Through Stories.* New York: Simon & Schuster, 1995. Suggests book titles that prompt discussion of moral values and character development.

Lickona, Thomas. *Educating for Character: How Our Schools Can Teach Respect and Responsibility.* New York: Bantam Books, 1992. Makes a case for teaching values and offers a twelve-point program for implementation that includes creating moral classrooms with the cooperation of parents, educators, and communities.

Noddings, Nel. *Caring: A Feminine Approach to Ethics and Moral Education.* Berkeley: University of California Press, 1984. Draws on ample examples to build an argument for an ethics based on natural caring.

Sergiovanni, Thomas J. *Moral Leadership: Getting to the Heart of School Improvement.* San Francisco, Calif.: Jossey-Bass, 1992. Attempts to create a new leadership practice with a moral dimension that inspires commitment, devotion, and service.

Wynne, Edward A., and Kevin Ryan. *Reclaiming Our Schools: A Handbook on Teaching Character, Academics, and Discipline.* New York: Merrill Publishing, 1993. Aids educators and parents in understanding and exploring strategies for teaching moral values and character development, which will guide students in developing self-discipline in their academic and personal lives.

See also Coles, Robert; Comer, James P.; Educating children; Entertainment; Family life education; Family values; Home schooling; Kohlberg, Lawrence; Myths and storytelling; Nuclear family; Pornography; Religion; Sex education.

Mormon polygamy

RELEVANT ISSUES: Marriage and dating; Parenting and family relationships; Religious beliefs and practices

SIGNIFICANCE: Mormonism experimented with polygamy during the nineteenth century

Joseph Smith, the founder and president of the Church of Jesus Christ of Latter-day Saints (Mormons), introduced polygamy to only a few trusted followers, because he knew that others would oppose the practice and because it was illegal in his state of Illinois. His successor, Brigham Young, publicly sanctioned polygamy in 1852, after the Mormon Church had established itself outside the United States in the Utah Territory. A large number of Americans, however, regarded polygamy as unfair to women and children, un-Christian, and immoral. Under increasing pressure, the Mormon Church reversed itself in the 1890's and officially forbade the practice. Mormons who regarded the reversal as caving in to secular pressure broke away and formed polygamist splinter groups, some of which still survived in the late twentieth century. The stress that polygamy brought many families was compounded by the church's changing public and private stances. These changing stances, a source of friction between the Mormon Church and society, demonstrated American society's firm commitment to monogamy.

Roots of Mormon Polygamy. By the mid-1830's rumors abounded within the Mormon community that church founder Joseph Smith was intimately involved with women other than his wife, Emma. He strenuously denied all such charges throughout his life, condemning them as lies invented by his enemies to discredit him. There is extensive evidence, however, that he advocated polygamy and secretly married many women himself. It is believed that he had between twenty-four and fifty wives. His first polygamous relationship probably began in 1835 with a seventeen-year-old live-in domestic helper named Fanny Alger. Eventually, his youngest plural wife was fifteen years old and the oldest fifty-nine. In all, he married five pairs of sisters, as well as a mother and daughter. About a dozen of the women also had living husbands, some of whom were Smith's close associates. His relationships appear to have been more sexual than spiritual. Upon his death in 1844, a number of his wives became the spouses of other church leaders.

Polygamy fit into Smith's evolving theology, according to which Christianity, soon after its founding, had become corrupted in its teachings and practice. He proclaimed himself to be God's only living prophet, whose job it was to restore the church in its latter days, bringing new scripture and ordaining apostles. He came to view civil marriages as invalid because they were not based on the true priesthood, which he had come to restore. Such loosening of marriage bonds as well as the acceptance of the polygamy practiced by some Old Testament figures no doubt strengthened his rationale for multiple marriages. Adding ceremonies closely paralleling those of the Freemasons, in which he was involved, he gave Mormonism secret rituals, transforming the movement into a modern mystery religion. Accordingly, ritual marriage in a Mormon temple ensures that couples will continue to be married in the "next" life. Since the amount of glory in the next life is related to the "assets" acquired on Earth, polygamy fits naturally into the goal of ever-increasing exaltation and the objective of populating and ruling future worlds.

Polygamy in Early Mormonism. Many who were secretly introduced to polygamy were initially shocked. When Smith told Apostle Heber C. Kimball that he wanted to marry Kimball's wife, Kimball did not eat or drink for three days. Seeing the couple's torment, Smith said he wanted only to test their loyalty. They instead gave him their fifteen-year-old daughter, whom Smith persuaded to marry him only by promising that it would ensure salvation and exaltation for her and her family. She later confided to a friend that she had been deceived into thinking that it was only a ceremony and regretted the marriage. Some Mormons, such as Orson Pratt, initially resisted polygamy but later embraced it enthusiastically. After an initial suicidal episode, he eventually married ten women and had forty-five children. Others accepted polygamy out of sheer faith in their prophet. When Smith told his bodyguard that he wanted to marry the man's sister, the latter agreed but said he would kill Smith if he found out that his real purpose was to "debauch" her.

Many plural wives felt kinship with one another, but others were intensely jealous. Reports indicate that Smith's original wife, Emma, struggled greatly, once telling him to break off a relationship after she had discovered its existence. In 1843 Smith had a revelation he kept secret for years, in which God sanctioned polygamy and told Emma

to accept it or be destroyed. In 1876 this revelation replaced an earlier revelation forbidding polygamy, which had been included in the authoritative collection of Joseph Smith's prophesies known as *The Doctrine and Covenants.*

Polygamy Becomes Open Practice. In 1852 polygamy became open within the Mormon Church, and the practice spread. Modern estimates indicate that between 8 and 20 percent of the Mormons in Utah and as many as 40 percent of married Mormon men were engaged in polygamy. Although a minority of the Mormon population, polygamists were favored for high church positions. In 1884 the church president urged monogamists to resign their church offices. Modern studies have refuted earlier notions that polygamy was necessary because Mormon women outnumbered men. Census figures show that men in fact outnumbered women and that polygamy created further competition for wives. Consequently, one bill introduced into Utah's territorial legislature allowed men to marry girls as young as twelve. Moreover, there was competition for wives among leaders and other members and competition for immigrant converts.

Some polygamist husbands divided their time among their wives, whom they often housed separately. While this worked well for some, tensions arose when men spent more time with the most recent or the youngest wives. Sarah Pratt told her husband Orson that if he was going to spend a week with each of his five other wives and the sixth with her, he may as well skip the week with her. She ended their relationship.

Whereas defenders of polygamy said it reduced infidelity and prostitution, others regarded it as a form of exploitation. An in-law of Brigham Young went so far as to say that if a roof were to be built over Salt Lake City, the city would be the biggest "whorehouse" in the world.

Modern Prohibition Against Polygamy. When polygamy was taught to the entire church, those who practiced it still had to conceal it from government authorities. Some hid constantly, setting up an elaborate warning system. More than one thousand Mormons were jailed. After slavery was abolished in 1865, national attention focused on eliminating polygamy as the second most abusive practice in the United States. Various bills were proposed in Congress to accomplish this. In 1879 the Supreme Court ruled in *Reynolds v. United States* that while government cannot interfere with religious belief, it can interfere with religious practices that violate the law. The Court called polygamy a "heathen" threat. In 1882 the Edmunds Law disqualified polygamists from holding public office. The Edmunds-Tucker Act of 1887 provided for confiscating the Mormon Church's assets and effectively reduced the Mormon vote by almost three-quarters. Leaders realized that the church's temporal power was quickly eroding.

Mormon leaders' initial reaction to governmental pressure was to endorse polygamy as essential to the faith, but this stance later softened. A movement within the church saw Utah statehood as the way to ensure church independence and self-determination. Some were willing to make polygamy a misdemeanor. In an 1890 manifesto, church president Wilford Woodruff suddenly announced that God had directed the church to give up polygamy. He quietly explained to church leaders that it applied only to future marriages. Furthermore, the church surreptitiously authorized new plural marriages; in Mexico one person was authorized to perform 250 plural marriages. Those who took the manifesto at face value were shocked, especially because Mormons had sacrificed so much in following the church's earlier precepts to engage in polygamy. Many others, however, were glad to be rid of the practice.

Following additional damaging publicity, the church issued a second manifesto against polygamy in 1904 and began excommunicating those who took new wives. In 1931 the church announced it would cooperate with criminal prosecutions of polygamists. Committed polygamists reacted by forming separate sects. Three decades later the Utah attorney general's office estimated the number of polygamists in the state at 20,000. In later years the number of Mormon polygamists nationally may have risen to several times that number.

In contrast to the Utah-based Church of Jesus Christ of Latter-day Saints, whose membership in the

---

Mark Twain on Mormon Polygamy

In 1861 Samuel L. Clemens passed through Utah on his way to Nevada, where he was soon to become famous as Mark Twain. His description of his brief stay in Utah reflects the national fascination with Mormon polygamy of that time.

> Our stay in Salt Lake City amounted to only two days, and therefore we had no time to make the customary inquisition into the workings of polygamy and get up the usual statistics and deductions preparatory to calling the attention of the nation at large once more to the matter. I had the will to do it. With the gushing self-sufficiency of youth I was feverish to plunge in headlong and achieve a great reform here . . .

Source: Mark Twain, *Roughing It* (1872), chapter 14.

According to Mark Twain's Roughing It, *Brigham Young's attempt to save money by having a single bed built for himself and all his wives failed when all the wives snored at once.* (True Williams illustrator, *Roughing It,* 1872)

late twentieth century reached nearly ten million, the Reorganized Church of Jesus Christ of Latter-day Saints, whose membership numbers about a half million, has never recognized polygamy as a teaching of Joseph Smith. Formed with the help of Smith's widow, Emma, who always publicly denied her husband's acceptance of polygamy, the reorganized church attributes polygamy to the schemes of those who led the majority of Smith's followers to Utah.

—*Brian K. Morley*

BIBLIOGRAPHY

Brodie, Fawn. *No Man Knows My History: The Life of Joseph Smith.* 2d ed. New York: Alfred A. Knopf, 1971.

Compton, Todd. *In Sacred Loneliness: The Plural Wives of Joseph Smith.* Salt Lake City: Signature Books, 1997.

Hardy, B. Carmody. *Solemn Covenant: The Mormon Polygamous Passage.* Urbana: University of Illinois Press, 1992.

Quinn, D. Michael. *The Mormon Hierarchy: Extensions of Power.* Salt Lake City: Signature Books, 1997.

Tanner, Jerald, and Sandra Tanner. *Joseph Smith and Polygamy.* Salt Lake City: Utah Lighthouse Ministry, 1980.

Van Wagoner, Richard S. *Mormon Polygamy: A History.* Salt Lake City: Signature Books, 1992.

See also Bigamy; Communal living; Family: concept and history; Monogamy; Mormons; Muslims; Polyandry; Polygyny.

Mormons

RELEVANT ISSUES: Marriage and dating; Parenting and family relationships; Religious beliefs and practices

SIGNIFICANCE: Although beliefs and practices about marriage and family life by members of the Church of Jesus Christ of Latter-day Saints, or Mormons, are similar to those of other Americans in many ways, they also uniquely differ from those of other Christian denominations

The Church of Jesus Christ of Latter-day Saints is the fifth largest religious denomination in the United States. It is often called the Mormon Church, because it teaches that the Book of Mormon—a history of the ancient inhabitants of the American continent—is scripture equal to the Bible. From its beginnings in upstate New York in 1830, it has grown to a membership of nearly five million in the United States and had a worldwide membership of nearly 10 million by 1997. One of the features that makes the Mormons (who prefer to be called LDS or Latter-day Saints) unique among Christian churches is their belief about marriage and family life. Indeed, many people know little more about the Latter-day Saints than that they practiced plural marriage, or polygamy, in the late nineteenth century.

LDS Doctrine About Marriage and Family Life. The LDS Church teaches that all human beings were created in God's image, as taught in the Bible. However, its teachings go beyond this common Christian belief. LDS doctrine teaches that each person is literally a beloved son or daughter of heavenly parents and that as such each has a divine nature and destiny. All individuals existed as spirit children in what is called the preexistence, where they lived with God and learned much of him and his divine plan for them as his offspring. Gender, being male and female, has been a part of human nature and human identity from the beginning. In the premortal state, humans came to understand and accept that to become like their heavenly parents they needed to have mortal bodies and come to a mortal sphere to gain earthly experiences to progress toward perfection and ultimately realize their divine destiny as heirs of eternal life. This plan, called the plan of salvation or the plan of happiness, enables family relations to continue beyond earthly life into the eternities. By participating in holy ordinances in special buildings called temples, which differ from the church buildings to which members go for Sunday services and other activities, husbands and wives and their children are "sealed" together for "time and all eternity."

For the family unit to be united in heaven, the family members must keep themselves morally clean, abstaining from sexual relations and related behaviors except in marriage, and treat each other with love and kindness. The first commandment given to Adam and Eve in the Garden of Eden was about their potential for parenthood as husband and wife. Latter-day Saint doctrine teaches that the command to "be fruitful and multiply" re-

Mormon doctrines calling for the faithful to "be fruitful and multiply and replenish the earth" have contributed to Mormon birthrates much higher than the national average, as evidenced by this early twentieth century Mormon man pictured with seven children. (Arkent Archive)

mains in force. Indeed, marriage and family life are not only ordained by God, but are essential to God's plan for his children and their ability to live with him in the eternities. Sexual relations are not seen as degrading or demeaning; sexuality is divinely appointed for bringing children into mortal existence and for strengthening the marital relationship. However, because of the importance of marriage and parenthood, sexual relations are seen as appropriate only between lawfully wedded husbands and wives. Therefore, Latter-day Saints are taught that premarital sex, extramarital sex, and homosexual relationships are inappropriate and detrimental to men's and women's happiness on this earth or hereafter.

Parents are taught that they have a solemn responsibility to love and care for each other and their children. Parents are to rear children in love, provide for their physical and spiritual needs, teach them to love and serve one another, keep God's commandments, and be law-abiding citizens wherever they live. Indeed, parents are told that they will be held accountable before God for how well they fulfill these responsibilities. Church leaders warn that the disintegration of families will bring calamities upon individuals, communities, and nations. The church teaches that happiness in family life is most likely to come about by family members living the teachings of Jesus Christ as taught by the holy scriptures, prophets, and apostles. Success in marriage and family life is "established and maintained on principles of faith, prayer, repentance, forgiveness, respect, love, compassion, work, and wholesome recreational activities," according to "The Family: A Proclamation to the World," issued by the church's governing bodies, the First Presidency and the Quorum of the Twelve Apostles.

This proclamation states that men and women have different, but equally important responsibilities in families. Husbands and fathers have the primary responsibility for providing the necessities of life and protecting their families. Wives and mothers are primarily responsible for nurturing their children. While each has distinct responsibilities, husbands and wives are to help each other in these responsibilities as equal partners. Extended family members are to help when needed but are not to interfere in matters that are primarily the responsibility of husbands and wives. Mem-

bers of the church are not only to fulfill these duties in their own families but are also to be actively engaged in promoting measures in their communities and nations that will strengthen the family as the basic unit of society. Research on LDS marriage and family life has shown that in many ways Latter-day Saints are similar to other Americans but that highly committed members are unique in ways that show the effects of distinct LDS doctrines about marriage and family.

Dating and Premarital Sex. Children in highly committed LDS families are taught from their youth that marriage to another member of the LDS Church in a temple is essential for their eternal happiness. Young people are taught that they should not date until they are at least sixteen years old and that even then they should date in groups rather than pairs. They are further counseled not to participate in any form of sexual behavior prior to marriage, including passionate kissing, sexual foreplay, or sexual intercourse. Parents are encouraged to teach their children about the importance of being "morally clean" and chaste and to establish standards of conduct for their children as they reach the dating age. For this reason, parents are encouraged to find frequent occasions to talk to their children about appropriate male-female relationships.

Young men are encouraged to serve two-year missions when they turn nineteen, and young women may also serve a one-and-a-half year mission after they turn twenty-one. One of the criteria of missionary service is that young people have not participated in serious sexual behavior or, if they have done so, to have thoroughly repented and committed themselves to sexual purity. Therefore, young people should postpone serious dating until after they have served a mission. Young adults, especially after having served a mission, are counseled not to postpone marriage for educational or career reasons once they have found the right person and are mature enough to marry.

Given these teachings, it is not surprising that Latter-day Saints as a group have much more conservative attitudes and values concerning nonmarital sexual behavior than other Americans. Latter-day Saints are less likely to approve of teenagers having sexual relations, of having children out of wedlock, and of cohabitation. Research shows that Latter-day Saints consistently report

Four Mormon missionaries in Denmark take a break from their proselytizing work in 1903. (Arkent Archive)

lower levels of premarital sexual experience, fewer teenage unwed pregnancies, and less premarital cohabitation than other Americans. This is especially true for LDS youths who are active in the church. Religiously inactive LDS youths have attitudes and behaviors that are more similar to those of other American youths. Over the last several decades of the twentieth century religiously active LDS youths seemed to have become less and less like mainstream American youths in premarital sexual attitudes and behaviors.

Courtship and Mate Selection. LDS young adults generally go through the process of selecting spouses much like other Americans. Like other Americans, they view mate selection as a private matter that should be based on attraction and love rather than on having mates chosen by parents. Parents are only peripherally involved in the decision making, although like other American parents they may find ways to encourage or discourage particular matches. However, they do not have the right to tell their children whom they may or may not marry. Parental approval is sought, but it is not required for marriages to take place.

LDS courtships differ from average American courtships in a number of ways. For one thing, they tend to be very short. Average courtships from first meetings to weddings last nine to ten months. One reason for this is that the premarital sexual standards of active Latter-day Saints do not allow sexual interaction as part of the courtship process, as is the case with many American couples. Moreover, LDS members are much less likely to cohabit before marriage. Another reason is that active LDS youths have less to work out because of their similar upbringing and shared values. Furthermore, most active LDS youths seek "spiritual confirmation" before deciding to marry. That is, they pray and seek divine confirmation that the

Mormons Throughout the World in 1997

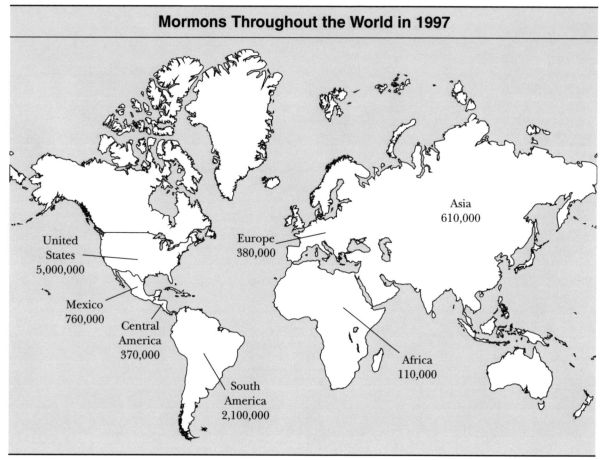

United States
5,000,000

Mexico
760,000

Central America
370,000

South America
2,100,000

Europe
380,000

Asia
610,000

Africa
110,000

Source: Christian Science Monitor.

person they are considering is approved by God. When this spiritual confirmation is received, they feel that there is little reason to delay marriage. Many dating couples terminate their relationships if they do not receive spiritual confirmation. This sense of spiritual confirmation helps them over rough spots and gives them a sense of "we can work it out, because it is right for us to be together," rather than seeing every problem as an occasion to rethink the whole relationship.

LDS Marriage and Divorce. A nationally representative sample of American families has shown that Latter-day Saints are less likely to have never married, more likely to be currently married, and less likely to have ever divorced than other Americans, although the differences are fairly small. Latter-day Saints marry at slightly younger ages than other Americans and are much more likely to say that marriage is better than single life. LDS

couples have reported about the same level of marital satisfaction as non-LDS couples. LDS spouses are no more or less likely than non-LDS couples to have disagreements about marital and family issues or to allow such disagreements to become physical.

Some commentators have suggested that premarital sexual abstinence, such as that taught by the LDS Church, leads couples to experience sexual problems in marriage, such as an inability to adjust to sexual interaction once they are married or the sexually obsessive attitude that they must "make up for lost time." Research has shown that LDS married couples have sexual intercourse at about the same frequency as other American couples and that their sexual behavior in marriage is not extreme in any way.

Latter-day Saints are somewhat less likely to divorce than other Americans. In the late twentieth century about one-third of LDS marriages ended in divorce compared to between 50 and 60 percent of all marriages in the United States. However, Latter-day Saints who marry "for time and all eternity" in an LDS temple are less likely to divorce than Latter-day Saints who do not marry in a temple. For example, Latter-day Saints who do not marry other Latter-day Saints in temples are five times more likely to divorce than Latter-day Saints who do. The remarriage rate for divorced Latter-day Saints is higher than that for the U.S. population as a whole. About three-fourths of divorced Latter-day Saints remarry.

Life in LDS Families. LDS couples both want and have more children than other couples. Most couples say that child care is handled fairly between spouses, and LDS couples are no more inclined to disagreements about family issues, such as children and household tasks, than other families in the United States. LDS parents spend nineteen hours more each week doing routine household chores than other parents. While LDS parents struggle with many of the same issues as other American parents in rearing children, very few of them would like to be free from parental responsibilities. Only 4.2 percent of fathers and 6.5 percent of mothers wished to be free from parenting. LDS families are taught to be self-sufficient and to first attempt to solve their problems with their own personal and family resources before seeking assistance from extended family members. If they exhaust these resources, they are counseled to seek assistance from the LDS Church and finally from government agencies. In general, LDS families are as close to their relatives as are other Americans. They get along well with their own parents, brothers and sisters, and in-laws. They have frequent contact with relatives and are willing to help relatives who are in need.

Family Resources and Assistance. The LDS Church provides numerous resources to strengthen families. The church leadership encourages LDS families to hold weekly "family home evenings" on Monday nights. On these evenings, families come together for instruction and recreational activities. Local church leaders are told not to hold other meetings on Monday nights that might interfere with these family activities. Families are also encouraged to conduct daily family prayer sessions and study scripture together.

Church leaders are provided with handbooks for counseling families with financial, emotional, or spiritual problems. LDS Social Services has social workers and other mental health professionals to assist leaders and families alike with social and emotional problems. The LDS Church's welfare program is designed to help families in financial straits by providing food supplies, work opportunities, clothing, and other essentials until families are better able to provide for themselves.

Because of their belief that families can be together and be sealed across many generations, Latter-day Saints have a great interest in genealogical research and family history. The largest genealogical library in the world is run by the LDS Church and contains millions of genealogical records, so that Latter-day Saints can trace their ancestors.

—*Thomas B. Holman*

BIBLIOGRAPHY

Achieving a Celestial Marriage. Salt Lake City: The Church of Jesus Christ of Latter-day Saints, 1992. Contains fifty-six lessons and study resources for college-age students dealing with the LDS Church's teachings on marriage and family life.

Family Home Evening Resource Book. Salt Lake City: The Church of Jesus Christ of Latter-day Saints, 1983. Contains sample lessons for family home evenings, suggestions for improving home evenings, short ideas for additional lessons on thirty-seven topics, examples and ideas for solving family problems and developing a strong family, and activities and games for family fun and learning.

First Presidency and Council of the Twelve Apostles of the Church of Jesus Christ of Latter-day Saints. *The Family: A Proclamation to the World.* Salt Lake City: The Church of Jesus Christ of Latter-day Saints, 1995. Statement by the leaders of the LDS Church about the necessity and importance of marriage and family that succinctly defines the basic teachings of the church on why marriage and family are important and how members can strengthen marriages.

Holman, Thomas B. "Commitment Making and Mate Selection Processes Among Active Mormon American Couples." In *Mormon Identities in Transition*, edited by Douglas J. Davies. London: Cassell, 1996. Book based on interviews with

LDS couples about their courtship, engagement, and marriage, containing many quotes from couples themselves.

Ludlow, Daniel H., ed. *Encyclopedia of Mormonism.* New York: Macmillan, 1992. Authoritative source for information on various topics related to Mormonism, including families, marriage, and divorce.

See also Family History Library; Family values; Hinduism; Jews; Mormon polygamy; Religion; Roman Catholics.

Mother-daughter relationships

RELEVANT ISSUES: Children and child development; Parenting and family relationships

SIGNIFICANCE: The relationship of mother and daughter is highly complex, enduring, unique, mutually beneficial, and of increasing interest to researchers and families alike

Research has found that the mutually rewarding relationship between mothers and daughters involves their helping and caring for each other. Theories examining this relationship have concentrated on issues of identity formation, affiliation, and separation. Although dysfunctional relationships of dependency exist, the mother-daughter relationship provides an opportunity for optimal social and emotional development. The relationship, however, needs continuous redefinition to maintain a sense of connectedness and an emotional bond.

Children's Identity. It has been hypothesized that because mothers in most cultures are the primary early caregivers, they are the ones from whom young children derive their identity. Basic psychological mechanisms in mother-daughter relationships transcend ethnicity and class. One cross-cultural study found that, generally speaking, there are three cultural conditions that enhance the mother-daughter relationship. In cultures in which the mother teaches her daughter either practical or ritualistic survival skills, the relationship becomes closer. When women are systematically excluded from men's recreational pursuits, they are forced to bond more closely with their daughters. In other cultures in which mothers and daughters live together in family units as opposed to communal groups, there are closer

relationships between them. Factors such as stress, workload, matrilineal descent, industrialization, and education do not affect the mother-daughter attachment across cultures.

In the Western world, as women continue to move into the workforce in increasing numbers, mothers have encouraged earlier autonomy and independence in their daughters. Daughters in turn have been able to identify with mothers whom they may come to view as strong and achieving women.

Bonding and Attachment. It has been said that the umbilical cord between mother and daughter is never completely severed. A daughter's relationship with her mother is her first and possibly most important one. Through her mother, a daughter learns what it means to be a person, to develop her sexual identity, and to understand the cultural expectations for herself as a female. As children develop, males tend to shift their attachment to identify with male role models, whereas females maintain an identity and therefore a relationship with their mothers. At the same time, mothers are thought to form identities with their daughters as a result of their shared gender, a difficulty differentiating from the daughters, and a connection to the daughter as a part of themselves. They want their daughters to have high self-esteem, to be self-confident, and to be capable of supporting themselves economically.

Research has proposed that women base their reality on affiliation, or a sense of connection to others, and that this type of attachment begins with the mother-daughter relationship. Daughters are believed to internalize many of their mothers' behaviors, thoughts, and values. They therefore become like their mothers. Similarities have been found to exist in the areas of sexual behavior, attitudes, employment orientation, and occupational status.

Adolescent Conflict and Identity. Preadolescent girls in late twentieth century America are often faced with contradictory expectations of the more traditional type (domestic roles as wife and mother) and those that encourage freedom from gender roles (being a "tomboy"). Although roles are important at this age and girls are beginning to be more exposed to and affected by the world outside the family, they continue to perceive their mothers as the central figures in their lives.

Mothers and daughters have special, highly complex, and enduring relationships. (James L. Shaffer)

Children derive a large part of their identity from their mothers. (James L. Shaffer)

The naturalness and acceptance of daughter-mother bonds and relationships can work to obscure individual boundaries, causing daughters to engage in an ongoing struggle to separate from their mothers. This need results in periods of conflict and ambivalence over the relationship, as well as issues of identity for the daughter. Conflict or strain often arises over a mother's criticism of her daughter's person (weight, dress, behavior, and so forth). It is the daughter, however, who more often perceives conflict, because it is her task to separate from her mother.

Life-span developmental research points to stages of puberty and the menopause as associated with feelings of self-worth and identity. These stages and feelings also affect the daughter-mother relationship. During adolescence, difficult identity issues arise surrounding emerging sexuality and the social pressure girls feel to be feminine. A girl may form many of her attitudes about sexuality as a result of her mother's responses to questions and her mother's level of comfort with her own sexuality. An example of this is a mother's treatment of the onset of her daughter's menstruation. The daughter's sense of sexual identity becomes either a "curse" or a "blessing." With the onset of the sexual revolution and acceptance of greater sexual freedom, mothers have not abandoned their sense of responsibility for their daughters' health and happiness. To the contrary, they are finding that responsibility to be more complex.

During the early years of adolescence, daughters often turn away from their mothers in their process of separation. Simultaneously, they need a mother in whom they can confide. This situation results in ambivalence as daughters yearn for independence and seek an identity yet remain dependent on mothers. Mothers often go through their own identity crisis at the point that their daughters become teenagers. Mothers in their forties and fifties experience new identity issues that are compounded by the emotional roller coaster of the menopause.

Adult Identity. When daughters move out into the world as adults, their physical separations are opportunities for some amount of emotional separation as well. In the 1980's and 1990's, women faced discontinuities in expectations for careers and families. Many women coped with this issue by delaying marriage and then choosing mates for companionship rather than out of conformity to expectations.

Similarity in education and values between mothers and daughters enhances their level of communication and intimacy. Daughters of well-educated mothers tend to use them as confidantes more than do daughters of less-educated mothers. As daughters choose their career fields, it is hypothesized that their choices are influenced by their mothers' attitudes about employment and their gender-role beliefs and satisfaction. Daughters who perceive their mothers to be satisfied with their role will attempt to pursue a similar role.

Daughters' Own Motherhood. The conflicts reported in adolescence transform into greater closeness, empathy, and mutuality in adulthood. Research has found that a daughter's marriage and first pregnancy increase her desire for closeness and increased interaction with her mother. It has been suggested that only after a woman has a child does she become aware of her similarities to her own mother. Many women feel they have achieved full womanhood when they have a child, and at that time they perceive themselves as peers with their mothers.

Married daughters typically see their mothers more often than do sons. Daughters who live in close proximity to their mothers tend to have less conflict with them (but experience greater conflict with mothers-in-law with decreasing distance from them). Daughters who have themselves become mothers more often ask their own mothers than their mothers-in-law for advice about child rearing.

Stress in the mother-daughter relationship at this developmental stage can result from the mother providing unsolicited advice about child rearing, criticism of the daughter's housekeeping, or criticism of the daughter's spouse. Research, however, supports a much less conflicted relationship and reveals that mutual mothering is the most common pattern for adult mother-daughter relationship. The two individuals involved tend to move back and forth between mothering and being mothered.

—*Robin C. Hasslen*

BIBLIOGRAPHY

Baruch, Grace, and Rosalind C. Barnett. "Adult Daughters' Relationships with Their Mothers." *Journal of Marriage and the Family* 45 (1983).

Chodorow, Nancy. *The Reproduction of Mothering.* Berkeley: University of California Press, 1978.

Eichenbaum, Luise, and Susie Orbach. *Understanding Women.* New York: Basic Books, 1983.

Fischer, Lucy. *Linked Lives.* New York: Harper & Row, 1986.

Gilligan, Carol. *In a Different Voice.* Cambridge, Mass.: Harvard University Press, 1982.

See also Attachment theory; Bonding and attachment; Family life cycle; Father-daughter relationships; Father-son relationships; Freudian psychology; Gender inequality; Incest; Mommy track; Mother-son relationships; Motherhood.

Mother-son relationships

RELEVANT ISSUES: Children and child development; Parenting and family relationships

SIGNIFICANCE: Mothers play major roles in shaping their sons' emotional stability, social adaptability, and sexual identity

The day-to-day care of children has traditionally been shouldered by mothers. While working fathers usually are out of the home for many hours during the day, mothers have had the primary responsibility of nurturing their children's early development. In late twentieth century Western societies, however, increasing numbers of women began pursuing careers outside their homes. While women have taken advantage of the ever-expanding employment opportunities, their role as primary care-givers in the home has not dramatically altered.

While women have been praised for their nurturing skills, they have also traditionally taken part of their own identity from how successfully they mold their children into functional adults. In many societies, sons have historically been more highly valued than daughters. For this reason, bearing and rearing sons was looked upon as a mother's primary focus. While psychiatrists, psychologists, behaviorists, sociologists, and other experts have debated how much "mother love" any son should need, they have concurred in regarding a good rapport between mother and son as essential to healthy male development.

Mothers as Nurturers. Bonds between mothers and sons begin forming at birth. Intimacy between them is reinforced through touching, holding, and breast-feeding. Through a mother's caring and warmth, newborn sons thrive. A mother's touch communicates to a child that he is safe. A child shunned by his mother as an infant may well grow up to feel insecure. In most societies mothers have had the primary responsibility of rearing young sons. While sons may shift their focus to male role models as they advance beyond infancy, it is their mothers who teach them to feel secure in their surrounding world.

Ideas of what constitutes correct "mothering" have fluctuated greatly over time. Even the most famous American baby doctor, Benjamin Spock, altered his prescriptions over the years on such concerns as the need for corporal punishment and how much hugging is too much. Theories changed depending on what a society determined was the correct vision of what it meant to be a male. During the early Middle Ages, for example, many European societies did not encourage mothers to have much contact with their young sons. Life was hard and nurturing children was considered a luxury that most families could not afford.

It was not until the nineteenth century that the value of maternal nurturing was clearly recognized. In the United States, Canada, and Western Europe, many published guides professed to be the last word on rearing sons. Although experts at that time had little concern for what may have been best for the mothers, they confidently put forth many complicated theories on what they thought was best for the children.

Since Western societies value independence and the need for an individual to be able to stand on his own two feet, mothers have been encouraged to wean their sons as early as possible in order for them to establish their own individuality. Once a young son feels safe, the detachment process must begin in order for him to learn to socialize with others around him. Every society has a concept of what it means to be a male. Among infants, boys are generally rewarded for being more aggressive than girls. A society may send mixed signals to mothers. While it praises mothers for their nurturing qualities, it may prod them to "cut the apron strings" as soon as possible.

The Oedipus Complex. In the late nineteenth and early twentieth centuries, Sigmund Freud introduced his theory of the Oedipus complex. According to this theory, sons develop a natural de-

The special bonds between mothers and sons begin at birth and can last through lifetimes. (Hazel Hankin)

While authorities have disagreed about how much motherly love sons need, they concur that good rapport between mothers and sons is essential to healthy male development. (James L. Shaffer)

Freudians have argued that sons who do not push away from their mothers and establish stronger ties with their fathers will become less masculine. (James L. Shaffer)

sire to have sexual relations with their mothers and feel a sense of rivalry with their fathers for their mothers' affection. According to Freud, the Oedipus complex affects sons aged, roughly, between three and five. The term comes from Greek myth, in which the Theban hero Oedipus unknowingly killed his own father and married his mother. As Freud saw it, the Oedipus complex normally ends when a boy can repress the sexual instincts

brought to the surface and begin to identify with his father.

In the late twentieth century, Freud's theory came under attack from psychologists and other researchers. Experts who see social behavior as primarily an outgrowth of evolution through natural selection, look upon Freud's theory as misguided. There is no doubt that conflicts do exist between parents and children, but more research must be done before a comprehensive explanation of all the nuances of these conflicts can be advanced with any authority.

Adolescence and Identity. Freud theorized that sons who do not push away from their mothers and establish strong ties with their fathers will be less masculine than they should be. The derogatory term "mama's boy" is only one manifestation of Western society's reservations about sons who maintain overly close ties with their mothers. As the theory goes, the more time a son spends with his mother the more likely he is to be "feminized." Popular acceptance of this idea contributes to mothers feeling pressure to distance themselves from their sons when they reach school age. In Western patriarchal societies, it has been incumbent on mothers to push their sons toward independence.

Adolescent sons are usually granted greater freedom than daughters. During this maturation process, boys may become confused about how to deal emotionally with interpersonal relationships. Since they may feel cut off from their formerly close ties with their mothers, adolescent males may flounder and try to repress emotions that society discourages them from expressing. Single or divorced mothers find it doubly hard to detach themselves from their sons and steer their sons toward society's view of what it means to be a man. Experts who insist that these boys should find male role models when no fathers are around overlook how strong and self-reliant mothers might also provide appropriate role models for adolescent sons.

Becoming Adults. As sons ready themselves to enter the adult world, they learn from their mothers what it means to be a woman. The women to whom they may be attracted can be traced back almost directly to the relationships they have had with their mothers. Psychologists have stated that men's ways of relating to women and the kinds of husbands they are to likely to become are shaped by their emotional connections with their mothers. Their potential mates would thus do well to understand their prospective husbands' mothers in order to know how the men will respond in marital situations.

Some of the various classic types of mother-son relationships include the "critical mom," the "mother's helper," and the "invisible mother."

While the critical mom is never satisfied with what her son does, the mother's helper relationship finds the son seemingly almost always finding ways to please his mother. No matter what dysfunctional patterns are exhibited by the invisible mother, the important point is that she has found it impossible to nurture her son.

Adult males and their future mates may have numerous "mom issues" to resolve before they can embark on a healthy relationship with each other. No generalizations tell the whole story, but certain clues predict how a man will respond to any adult relationship that can be found in his own mother-son relationship. Since Western society at the dawn of the twenty-first century does not need—for the most part—sons to grow up to be warriors or pioneers, the idea of what is really "masculine," and not feminine, may become more blurred. With more women entering the workplace, more men may eventually fill so-called domestic roles.

—*Jeffry Jensen*

BIBLIOGRAPHY

Arcana, Judith. *Every Mother's Son: The Role of Mothers in the Making of Men.* Garden City, N.Y.: Doubleday, 1983.

Bassoff, Evelyn. *Between Mothers and Sons: The Making of Vital and Loving Men.* New York: Dutton, 1994.

Forcey, Linda Rennie. *Mothers of Sons: Toward an Understanding of Responsibility.* New York: Praeger, 1987.

Gurian, Michael. *Mothers, Sons, and Lovers: How a Man's Relationship with His Mother Affects the Rest of His Life.* Boston: Shambhala, 1994.

Klein, Carol. *Mothers and Sons.* Boston: G. K. Hall, 1985.

Miles, Rosalind. *Love, Sex, Death, and the Making of the Male.* New York: Summit Books, 1991.

Smith, Babette. *Mothers and Sons: The Truth About Mother-Son Relationships.* St. Leonards, Australia: Allen & Unwin, 1995.

See also Attachment theory; Bonding and attachment; Child rearing; Electra and Oedipus complexes; Father-daughter relationships; Father-son relationships; Freudian psychology; Incest; Mother-daughter relationships; Motherhood; Parenting; Son preference; Women's roles.

Motherhood

RELEVANT ISSUES: Children and child development; Parenting and family relationships

SIGNIFICANCE: The concept of motherhood and the definitions of the roles and functions of mothering and parenting change and evolve according to societies' changing needs, values, and structures

The concept of motherhood, and the status, roles, functions, and expectations associated with it, has been a changing one throughout history. Mothers have, at various times, been ignored, idealized, romanticized, and demonized. They have been blamed for social ills and for the psychological and emotional problems of their children, or enormous responsibility and awesome power have been ascribed to them in bringing up the next generation, as demonstrated by the saying: "The hand that rocks the cradle rules the world."

Early Concepts of Motherhood. Archaeological findings of Paleolithic and Neolithic remains reveal that motherhood, especially the mother-child relationship, was held in great reverence and awe. In Siberia, France, and at several other European sites statues of pregnant females have been discovered. Some New Stone Age figurines depicting mothers holding children have also been found. These statues are believed to be representations of the Great Mother, worshiped and revered for her life-giving capabilities.

Throughout human history women have generally been esteemed most for their ability to bear children. (Dick Hemingway)

In time, the awe inspired by women's reproductive powers declined, although women's chief role in early societies remained that of bearing and rearing children. Children were valuable to the Hebrews, and a woman's worth was judged by her ability to produce offspring. In the Old Testament, Sarah, Rachel, and Hannah prayed desperately for children. As mothers, Hebrew women were acknowledged and honored, although power and authority rested with fathers as heads of the household. In Greece and Rome fathers were similarly accorded a higher status than mothers. The Greek dramatist Aeschylus stated that mothers were not true parents. They were merely nurses of the seed planted by fathers, who were the real parents. Fathers were all powerful and could make life-and-death decisions concerning their children. Despite their lesser status, upper class Roman mothers were expected to be teachers of their children, especially teachers of reading. Roman and Spartan mothers taught their daughters duties and roles associated with household responsibilities, and Spartan mothers instilled values of patriotism and courage in their sons.

Motherhood in Medieval Times. The world in which the medieval family lived was, by modern standards, a harsh and stark one. European children during the Middle Ages had few rights, and since childhood and adulthood were not seen as different developmental stages of life, children were treated as miniature adults. Infanticide existed, as it had in earlier times, and many babies were abandoned by parents who could not support them or did not want them. Family life was a public affair, with little space or time for private or extended nurturing of children. In well-to-do families, mothers were not expected to have much contact with their young children. Babies were often sent away to be nourished by wet nurses, who in turn were expected to give up nursing their own children, as feeding two babies was not considered to be a healthy practice. After the age of seven, children of the upper classes were sent away from home to be educated, while poor children were required to join the workforce at an even earlier age. Women, including mothers, were considered by church and society to be corrupting influences. Marriage and procreation were necessary evils that would no longer be required when the world ended, as it was expected to do on December 31, 999.

Paradoxically, it was in the later Middle Ages that the ideal of Mary, or the Madonna, emerged as the divine, compassionate mother who interceded with God on behalf of her erring children. In art, literature, and religion Mary became a symbol of purity and maternal love, free from the sins and weaknesses of mortal mothers.

Motherhood from the Reformation to Modern Times. During the Reformation the concept of family and parents' roles further evolved. The authority of fathers was absolute. Fathers still made all the important decisions concerning their children's lives, including interviewing and hiring wet nurses for infants. Women's role was still chiefly to bear and rear children—Martin Luther stated that women's bodies were obviously created for this purpose. However, as wives and mothers, the prestige of women increased, and they were no longer considered to be physically and morally corrupt.

In the eighteenth century recognition of mothers' importance in nurturing young children and stimulating their development found its way into the works of several philosophers and educators who were to have a strong impact on European and American thinking. The French enlightenment philosopher Jean-Jacques Rousseau (1712-1778) urged mothers to nurture and "cultivate" their children, who were like "young plants." Johann Heinrich Pestalozzi (1746-1827), a Swiss educator, wrote the first parent education book, *How Gertrude Teaches Her Children,* in which he emphasized the need for mothers to nourish children's bodies and minds. To do this, Pestalozzi believed that mothers must continue their own education as well. The ideas of Rousseau and Pestalozzi influenced Friedrich Wilhelm Froebel (1782-1852), who came to be known as the "father of the kindergarten." Froebel stressed the role of mothers in children's development and developed a curriculum that provided mothers with practical information on using songs, nursery rhymes, finger plays, pictures, and educational toys that would stimulate children's learning.

As the concept of family life and the home as a domestic haven evolved, the perception of mothers changed and became romanticized. In art and literature, the mother-child relationship was enthusiastically celebrated. Mothers were now the personification of love and self-sacrifice and mod-

In the late twentieth century mothers were expected to be loving and empathetic and to nourish children's sense of self. (R. Kent Rasmussen)

els of virtue and morality. In the nineteenth century the mother was a domestic angel—the "angel of the house," who nurtured tenderly and lovingly, or the stern angel, who "conquered" her children's willfulness by being a severe disciplinarian, as was the mother of John Wesley, founder of the Methodist movement.

The increasing recognition of maternal responsibility in child rearing during the nineteenth century was reflected in the proliferation of books, journals, and articles devoted to children's upbringing. As early as 1820 a guidebook entitled *Advice to Mothers on the Management of Infants and Young Children* was published in America by W. M. Ireland. There was a *Mother's Magazine* and a *Parents' Magazine*. Information was provided on breast-feeding, clothing, hygiene, moral training, discipline, and other mothering concerns. Mothers' study groups or "maternal associations" were formed in the early 1800's in Portland, Maine, and other parts of the United States. Later in the century child-rearing advice appeared in journals such as *Good Housekeeping* and *Ladies' Home Journal*.

Late nineteenth century society increasingly stressed the impact of mothering on the health, personality, and moral fiber of children. Scientific advances, the emerging fields of child study and psychology, and new discoveries in the areas of health and medicine revolutionized perceptions of motherhood and child rearing. The ideas of the behavioral scientist John Watson and of psychologists like Sigmund Freud and G. Stanley Hall changed the way people looked at children, their experiences, and their behavior. Mothering now became a complex and delicate process: Too little mothering, or "maternal deprivation," could cause enduring psychological problems and neuroses; too much involvement or protectiveness could interfere with children's growth toward self-discovery and autonomy. These ideas continued well into the twentieth century, with shifts from stricter views on upbringing to more relaxed attitudes such as those reflected in Benjamin Spock's *The Common Sense Book of Baby and Child Care* (1946), which was later revised and adapted to keep in step with continuing social change in the late twentieth century.

During the second half of the twentieth century American mothers were expected to be loving and empathetic, nourishing children's budding sense of self. In 1948 *Parents' Magazine* advised mothers to raise children with love and friendliness. In this way, future wars could perhaps be averted. The 1950's came to be known nostalgically as the "golden age" of family life and values, projecting a charming image of calm, neat, self-sacrificing but fulfilled stay-at-home mothers—mothers like those in popular television programs such as *Leave It to Beaver* and *The Donna Reed Show*. Fathers were the breadwinners, mothers were the homemakers. Whether such harmony and symmetry were in reality typical of family life in the 1950's has been the subject of much debate and controversy.

A period of social upheaval followed this decade of idealized family life. The 1960's were the years of the antiwar and Civil Rights movements, the sexual revolution, and feminist protest. The iconoclastic atmosphere affected the concept of motherhood. Mothers were now trivialized and demonized in art and literature, even by feminists, many of whom saw motherhood as enslavement and exploitation by a male-dominated society. Throughout the succeeding decades, however, research has continued to reveal the importance of mothers in their children's lives, development, and education.

Changing Role of Fathers. As the concept of motherhood changed, so did that of fatherhood. Fathers' parenting role came to be increasingly recognized and revised. In the past in most cultures, fathers were considered to be authority figures in families, and they made critical decisions about their children's lives and education. They were, of course, the chief providers for their families. However, fathers did not generally participate in actual child care or housework. As more and more women joined the workforce in the second half of the twentieth century, changes in family management and roles became necessary. American fathers were now advised to share in the pleasures of nurturing, feeding, diapering, and interacting with their children. It was thought that some might even prefer to become the primary caregivers in their families.

The rate of change has been slow. It has been found that men are unlikely to become full-time caregivers and homemakers by choice. While earlier in the century John Bowlby had stressed the importance of attachment and a close mother-child relationship during the first years of children's lives, the father-child bond was discussed in the late twentieth century by child specialists such as T. Berry Brazelton, who also discussed the bond and interactions between mothers and children. Cultural and social change thus enhanced American fathers' role during the latter part of the twentieth century. Parenting was now expected to be a shared responsibility of both mothers and fathers.

Working Mothers. Many mothers throughout history and in all societies have had to work for a variety of reasons. In the 1970's, 1980's, and 1990's an increasing number of mothers joined the American workforce—some out of necessity, others for personal fulfillment. In the early 1990's, 70 percent of mothers with children younger than five years of age held full-time jobs. Women with careers and children attempted to manage their homes, raise their children, and fulfill nontraditional duties. In the 1980's mothers who performed this balancing act came to be known as "superwomen," "supermoms," or "mother managers." Balancing family life and careers caused extreme stress in many women.

Research findings have revealed that work overload is still a problem with which employed wives and mothers have to deal. Numerous studies have been conducted on the effects of mothers' work on family relationships and children. Early results were mixed, but many rewards and gains for mothers and children, especially daughters, have been identified by later research and through interviews with working mothers. Children of mothers with high-status careers have been found to perform better at school and have been more likely to go on to higher education than children of mothers who are not in high-status careers. Such children often have higher self-esteem and learn to be independent and self-directing.

Society gradually focused on the need for alternative, quality child care for dual-career families, single parents, and employed mothers. The

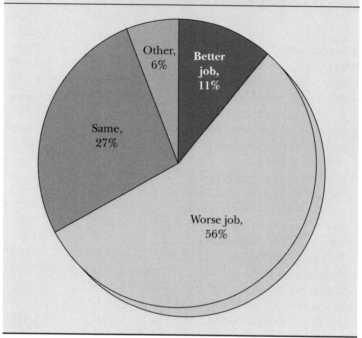

How Mothers of 1997 Compare to Their Own Mothers

Other, 6%

Better job, 11%

Same, 27%

Worse job, 56%

Source: The Pew Research Center (1997)

Note: In a nationwide survey, more than 1,100 American mothers were asked to compare the job today's women are doing as mothers with how their own mothers did. This chart summarizes the responses.

slowness of American society to recognize and meet this need arose out of an ambivalent attitude toward child care outside the home and a failure to relate mothering and child care to authentic early childhood education. Yet, mothers of the 1990's not only worked outside the home; many went off to war in the Persian Gulf, requiring extended quality child care for their children.

Continuing Social, Cultural, and Technological Change. New reproductive technologies have challenged many cultural underpinnings of the concept of motherhood and parenthood. In vitro fertilization, embryo transfers, and surrogacy have caused society to question long-held beliefs about maternal instincts, biological relationships, and traditional family models. Many ethical and legal problems concerning these issues must be resolved. As family structures, lifestyles, and patterns of behavior continue to change, as gender roles blur and social organization is transformed, the roles and functions of mothers and fathers, as well as the responsibility of society toward families, continue to be scrutinized and revised.

—*Nillofur Zobairi*

BIBLIOGRAPHY

Berger, Eugenia Hepworth. *Parents as Partners in Education: Families and Schools Working Together.* 4th ed. Englewood Cliffs, N.J.: Merrill, 1995. Extended examination of parent-school partnerships, historical concepts of child rearing and parenting, and issues relating to parent involvement in children's education.

Brazelton, T. Berry. *Infants and Mothers.* New York: Dell, 1983. Easy-to-read description of the interactions of parents and infants with different types of temperaments.

Clinton, Hillary Rodham. *It Takes a Village: And Other Lessons Children Teach Us.* New York: Simon & Schuster, 1996. Discusses the need to build caring communities and collaborative networks to improve the condition of children and families in the modern world.

Coontz, Stephanie. *The Way We Never Were: American Families and the Nostalgia Trap.* New York: Basic Books, 1992. Examines the nostalgia and myths surrounding "traditional" family life and values and discusses the impracticality of attempting to return to outdated lifestyles that would be irrelevant in the twenty-first century.

Hoffman, Lois W., and F. Ivan Nye. *Working Mothers.* San Francisco, Calif.: Jossey-Bass, 1975. Collection of research findings on issues surrounding working mothers, including child care, effects on children, impact on marital relations, and impact on women's fertility.

Lerner, Jacqueline, and Nancy Galambos. *Employed Mothers and Their Children.* New York: Garland, 1991. Discusses issues and controversies related to families in which mothers or both parents work and makes suggestions on balancing family needs and work.

Moen, Phyllis. *Women's Two Roles: A Contemporary Dilemma.* New York: Auburn House, 1992. Considers the interaction and balancing of family responsibility with work as it affects individuals as well as society.

Ribbens, Jane. *Mothers and Their Children: A Feminist Sociology of Childrearing.* Thousand Oaks, Calif.: Sage Publications, 1995. Investigates the impact of social restrictions and concepts on the way women rear their children.

Rubin, Nancy. *The Mother Mirror.* New York: G. P. Putnam's Sons, 1983. Describes past and modern myths of motherhood and examines the ways in which mothers cope with the demands and problems of mothering in modern America.

Thurer, Shari L. *The Myths of Motherhood: How Culture Reinvents the Good Mother.* Boston: Houghton Mifflin, 1994. Critical analysis of the myths and images associated with motherhood at different periods in history and a discussion of social and cultural conditions which gave birth to these myths.

See also Bonding and attachment; Brazelton, T. Berry; Childhood history; Childlessness; Cult of True Womanhood; Family: concept and history; Fatherhood; Kohlberg, Lawrence; Matriarchs; Mommy track; Parenting; Pregnancy; Women's roles.

Mothers Against Drunk Driving (MADD)

DATE: Founded in 1980

RELEVANT ISSUES: Law; Sociology

SIGNIFICANCE: This citizens' activist organization was founded to fight drunk driving through advocacy of stricter legislation and increased public awareness

Mothers Against Drunk Driving (MADD) is one of two umbrella organizations that began in the late 1970's as an outgrowth of a citizens' movement to fight drunk driving. The first of these umbrella organizations, Remove Intoxicated Drivers (RID), was founded in 1978 by Doris Aiken. The first chapter of MADD, the better-known of the two umbrella organizations, was founded in 1980 by Candy Lightner after her thirteen-year-old daughter Cari was killed by a drunk driver. The driver of the hit-and-run automobile, who had had multiple convictions for drunk driving, received a two-year prison sentence for vehicular manslaughter in the death of Cari Lightner. He served his time in a work camp and a halfway house.

Candy Lightner's dissatisfaction with the response of the legal system to her daughter's death prompted her to form Mothers Against Drunk

Drivers, which was later renamed Mothers Against Drunk Driving. The original chapter of this non-profit organization was founded in Sacramento, California. It was established on the premise that drunk driving is a crime and that injuries and fatalities caused by drunk driving are not inevitable accidents. The mission of the organization was to advocate tougher drunk driving laws, contribute to public policy in an effort to reduce the number of traffic fatalities involving alcohol, provide victim advocates, and spark public awareness about drunk driving. One means to spark public awareness about MADD involved the media. The story of Candy Lightner and her daughter Cari

was made into a movie for national television. Awareness also increased as MADD chapters expanded across the nation and as schools began to sponsor Students Against Drunk Driving (SADD). MADD advocates inform the public about criminal justice procedures, accompany persons to court proceedings, and refer persons to counselors, clergy, and attorneys.

More than two thousand laws concerning drunk driving have been passed in the United States since 1980. These laws provide for sobriety checkpoints, increases in fines, and longer jail sentences. The number of accidents involving fatally injured drivers declined during the 1980's.

Members of MADD silently demonstrating outside a Minnesota state senate judiciary by holding pictures of children killed by drunk drivers. (AP/Wide World Photos)

966 • MULTIPLE BIRTHS

While this success is partly due to traffic-safety and law-enforcement personnel, MADD's campaign against drunk driving has been considered a driving force. —*Kimberly A. Wallet*

See also Al-Anon; Alateen; Alcoholism and drug abuse; Child safety.

Multiple births

RELEVANT ISSUES: Children and child development; Health and medicine

SIGNIFICANCE: Since 1960 there has been a significant increase in the number of multiple births—that is, two or more infants born from a single pregnancy

Two types of multiple births occur—fraternal and identical. Fraternal twins or multiples occur when two or more fertilized eggs are implanted in the mother's uterus, either naturally or through in vitro fertilization (IVF). Identical twins or multiples have the same genes and occur when a fertilized egg divides into two or more embryos. When twins are of the same gender, genetic testing may be necessary to determine whether they are identical or fraternal. In rare instances, the fertilized egg does not split completely, resulting in conjoined (or Siamese) twins. Conjoined twins can be connected at any point, but it will always be the same point on both twins.

Multiples range from as few as two (twins) to as many as seven (septuplets). The term "supertwin" is often used to define triplets and any other higher-order births.

A famous instance of multiple births was the Dionne quintuplets, five girls born to a French-Canadian couple in 1934. The babies, Marie, Emilie, Yvonne, Cecile, and Annette, weighed a total of eleven pounds, one ounce and, in the absence of genetic testing, were assumed to be identical.

In November, 1997, modern technology permitted all the McCaughey septuplets (seven infants) to survive. This was the first time such an event has occurred. (The chances of naturally conceiving septuplets are one in eight to ten million conceptions.)

Unknown Causes of Multiple Births. Except in pregnancies which occur as a result of IVF, the causes of multiple births are generally unknown. Women of African descent have the highest rates

of twinning, while Asians have the lowest. Whites fall somewhere in between. Age is also important—even without fertility drugs, the chance that women will deliver multiples increases until their late thirties. The more children they have, the more likely they will be to have multiples.

According to the National Center for Health Statistics, the number of births involving triplets, quadruplets, and quintuplets rose from 1,005 in 1964 to 4,594 in 1994. Of the 4,594 multiple births, 4,233 were triplets, 315 were quadruplets, and 46 were five or more babies. These numbers reflect actual infants born—the number of twins and multiples conceived is actually much higher. The increased use of ultrasound during prenatal care has revealed that many pregnancies begin as twins, but one of the embryos usually dies before the twelfth week and is reabsorbed into the placenta. This is known as the "vanishing twin syndrome." Smaller numbers of deaths occur between the twelfth and twenty-eighth weeks, whereby the second fetus ceases to grow but is not reabsorbed. The embryo shrivels and comes out at birth with the placenta as a "fetus papyraceus"—a paper fetus.

Before the regular use of ultrasound, it was not uncommon for the second or even third baby to be discovered only after the birth of the first. By the late twentieth century, misdiagnoses occur only when babies are hidden behind a larger sibling. Symptoms of multiple pregnancy include higher than normal maternal weight at given stages of gestation, a higher instance of morning sickness, and a higher level of alphafetoprotein in the mother's blood system. It is also important not to discount mothers' instinct: Some women have found that multiple pregnancies are "different" from other pregnancies and that they just "know" that they are carrying multiple fetuses.

In Vitro Fertilization. Most of the increase in multiple births occurred after 1980 and can be traced to two trends: the growing numbers of births to women over thirty-five (who are more likely to produce two or more eggs at one time) and the increased use of IVF and ovulation-enhancing drugs. With IVF, fertility drugs increase the number of eggs, which are removed from the ovaries and fertilized with sperm. Some or all of the resulting embryos are then transferred to the uterus, although it is rare for more than three babies to be born. Approximately 75 percent of

Medical costs associated with having triplets are about eleven times greater than those for having a single child. (James L. Shaffer)

women undergoing in vitro fertilization do not become pregnant in one attempt. Of the 25 percent who do, approximately one-third have two or more babies.

Specific treatments boost the occurrence of multiples. Pergonal stimulates the ovaries to release more than the single egg typically produced during ovulation. The more eggs produced and

the more embryos transferred, the greater the chance of pregnancy. The chances of pregnancy increase with each embryo transferred—from just over 8 percent with one healthy embryo to 45 percent with six. Unused embryos are sometimes frozen.

Dangers of Multiple Births. For infertility specialists, treatment ends when women become

Thanks largely to modern fertility drugs, the number of "supertwin" births (those producing three or more children) increased five-fold between 1964 and 1994. (James L. Shaffer)

pregnant. Yet, what initially appears as a success often leads to tragedy as the pregnancies progress. In some instances, women who have struggled for years to become pregnant are faced with two grim options: selective abortion to reduce the number of embryos or a risky pregnancy with more embryos than can be safely carried to term.

Women who carry and give birth to multiples risk high blood pressure, uterine bleeding, pre-eclamptic toxemia, and complications from cesarean sections, which are routinely performed in cases of multiple births. Babies may be born prematurely and suffer from inherent complications such as blindness, brain damage, underdeveloped organs, and learning disorders. Multiple babies

are six times as likely as single ones to have cerebral palsy and are twice as likely to have birth defects.

Fetal mortality in twin pregnancies is four times higher than in single births, and the major cause of death is premature birth. According to the Centers for Disease Control (CDC), premature births are defined as those in which gestation lasts less than thirty-seven weeks and babies have a birth weight of less than five and a half pounds. The length of the gestation period and birth weight are important factors in the survivability and health of infants. Among triplets, the gestation period averages seven weeks shorter than that for single babies while the average birth weight is only half that of single babies. While approximately 15 percent of single-baby deliveries require intensive care and approximately 2 percent die before discharge from the hospital, 78 percent of babies born in higher-order multiple births require intensive care and approximately 13 percent die.

Medical Advances and Health Care Costs. The news is not all grim. Medical science has dramatically improved the odds of survival for multiple infants. Between 1983 and 1991 the mortality rate among triplets dropped by 40 percent—from 156.1 deaths per 1,000 live births to 93.7. After twenty-four weeks' gestation, infants' chance of survival in a neonatal intensive care unit (NICU) is about 80 percent. New treatments range from medical to psychological. The Newborn Individualized Developmental Care and Assessment Program (NIDCAP) adjusts the environment of neonatal intensive care units to meet premature infants' developmental needs. Dim lighting, soft sounds, and more infant contact with parents all contribute to a more positive recovery and growth environment. According to experts, NIDCAP calms premature infants' volatile nervous systems, allowing them to gain weight more quickly and graduate from the respirator sooner.

These advances, however, do not come without a cost. In a study of 13,206 expectant mothers from 1986 through 1991, the average total charges for a single-baby delivery were $9,845, compared to $37,947 for twins and $109,765 for triplets. The cost of four weeks of care in a neonatal intensive care unit runs as high as $100,000 per infant. The chance of neurological problems is much greater in twins and triplets than in single babies, leading to extremely high lifetime health care costs.

Health companies are reluctant to cover expensive, repeated fertility treatments and then pay the high medical costs associated with multiple births. Many believe that technologies promoting higher-order multiple pregnancy is counter to nature's intent. In 1996, the American Society of Reproductive Medicine began considering guidelines to limit the number of embryos transferred during in vitro fertilization to four for women age thirty-four and younger. Similar guidelines are already in effect in Japan and throughout much of Europe.

Some ethicists say that such limits violate couples' reproductive freedom. Infertility specialists counter that limits would dramatically lower the chances that women would get pregnant with even one baby and would increase the number of in vitro fertilization cycles required to produce a pregnancy. Because many health insurance companies limit the number of in vitro fertilization attempts that women are permitted to undergo, any limit to the number of eggs transferred would in turn limit the chances of becoming pregnant.

—*P. S. Ramsey*

BIBLIOGRAPHY

Bryan, Elizabeth. *Twins, Triplets, and More: From Pre-Birth Through High School—What Every Parent Needs to Know When Raising Two or More.* New York: St. Martin's Press, 1992.

Cassill, Kay. *Twins: Nature's Amazing Mystery.* New York: Atheneum, 1984.

Clegg, Averil, and Anne Woolett. *Twins: From Conception to Five Years.* New York: Ballantine, 1988.

Noble, Elizabeth. *Having Twins: A Parent's Guide to Pregnancy, Birth, and Early Childhood.* Boston: Houghton Mifflin, 1980.

See also Birth control; Birth defects; Childbirth; Family size; Fertility and infertility; Reproductive technologies; Siblings; Test-tube babies; Twins.

Murphy, Gardner

BORN: July 8, 1895, Chillicothe, Ohio
DIED: March 19, 1979, Washington, D.C.

Murphy, Lois

BORN: March 23, 1902, Lisbon, Iowa

AREAS OF ACHIEVEMENT: Children and child development; Education

SIGNIFICANCE: The Murphys were authors of many books and articles on a wide range of topics related to psychology, including world peace, parapsychology, and children's vulnerability and coping strategies

The Murphys published together and separately on many topics and received many awards for their work. The title of Lois's biography of her husband, *Gardner Murphy: Integrating, Expanding, and Humanizing Psychology* (1990), captures the essence of his contributions. In 1947 Gardner Murphy published *Personality: A Behavioral Approach to Origins and Structure*, which was one of the first attempts to include the full range of issues necessary for a comprehensive theory of personality. He had a long-standing interest in psychic research and was a proponent of research on extrasensory perception. The Murphys were also committed to world peace and social justice.

Lois Murphy met and married Gardner while she was a student at Union Theological Seminary and he a young professor at Columbia University. She later completed a Ph.D. in psychology. In 1962 they moved to the Menninger Clinic in Kansas. In addition to the books they coauthored on social psychology, personality psychology, and Asian and Western psychology, Lois wrote extensively about children. She was one of the first to examine sympathy and coping strategies in children. As a child psychoanalyst, she treated, studied, and wrote about vulnerability and invulnerability in children and adolescents. She also wrote many booklets about child care and participated in planning the federally funded Head Start program.

—*George A. Morgan*

See also Child care; Head Start; Welfare.

Muslims

RELEVANT ISSUES: Parenting and family relationships; Race and ethnicity; Religious beliefs and practices

SIGNIFICANCE: Although changes are apparent in Islam and there are regional and sectarian variations, preindustrial norms and Qur'anic teachings continue to influence the structure and organization of Muslim families throughout the world

Muslim family values and tradition sharply contrast to the secular and cultural values and traditions of the United States and other Western countries. The Qur'an and the Sharia law, interpreted differently by different schools and sects, are the foundations of the Islamic practices that govern marriage, marital roles, divorce, child custody, and inheritance.

Pre-Islamic Background. Much of what the Qur'an teaches about the family is to be understood in the context of pre-Islamic Middle Eastern traditions. Available evidence concerning the cultural practices of the region prior to the seventh century does not give a clear indication as to whether the prevailing family system of the time

was matriarchal and matrilineal or patriarchal and patrilineal. If one were to accept the theory that ancient family systems were generally matriarchal and matrilineal and that only with the rise of an agrarian civilization did they became patriarchal and patrilineal, one could interpret the advent of Islam as the period in Mecca when patriarchy gained the upper hand. The fact that Khadijah, Muhammad's first wife, was a wealthy businesswoman and that Muhammad had been in her employ before she proposed to marry him, is often cited as an example of the high status that women enjoyed in pre-Islamic Arabia. Although this example points to the existence of a culture that allowed some women to rise to leadership positions, it does not necessarily imply that most women during Muhammad's time occupied positions of power. Mecca and Medina were highly stratified, tribal societies. Marriage and family customs and the social position of women in these tribal societies varied a great deal, making any generalization extremely difficult. Islam incorporated some of the existing customs while transforming others. Through its teachings and practices it certainly contributed to the consolidation of a culture centered on patriarchy.

Courtship, Engagement, and Wedding. Courtship and engagement practices in Islamic societies follow the pattern generally found in preindustrial, agrarian societies, according to which it is the responsibility of the father (or male figure who acts in place of the father) to find a bride for his son. The search for a bride is normally conducted through relatives or other intermediaries, who investigate and facilitate contacts between the groom's and the bride's family. Marriage is primarily understood as an alliance between two families rather than a contract between two isolated individuals. The family's social class, descent, reputation, occupation, income level, and social networks are crucial in selecting the future mate. The bride's parents and relatives learn about the groom's character, moral virtues, education, and adherence to religious observances to assess his suitability for the marriage alliance. The Western notion of romantic love as a basis of marriage is foreign to Islam. A young woman who expresses a desire to marry a young man because she "loves" him is looked down upon because of the implication that she may have had clandestine sexual contacts with him. Cohabitation or open sexual relations prior to marriage are unacceptable.

Endogamy, defined as marrying within the same clan, group, or social class, is one way of ensuring family compatibility. Though many forms of blood and guardianship relations are taboo, marrying parallel cousins, such as the daughter of one's father's brother, is not prohibited by the Qur'an. Traditionally, marrying one's cousin on the father's side is considered very desirable. This prac-

Muslims of various ethnic backgrounds on their way to a mosque in Toronto. (Dick Hemingway)

tice dates back to pre-Islamic times and might have originated as a means of strengthening clan networks as well as of ensuring social compatibility. Interestingly, Muhammad married women from outside his clan as a strategy for forming political alliances among diverse clans and consolidating his power.

Once the suitability of the family background has been established, the prospective bride and groom are usually consulted about the choice of their future mate. In most cases, however, the final decision rests with the parents (or those who take the place of the parents) of the concerned parties. By strict law, which is rarely applied in the late twentieth century, fathers or other guardians have the right to arrange the marriage of their daughters without their consent or knowledge. The only exception is in the case of previously married women.

The Muslim wedding ceremony essentially consists of a man and woman signing a contract in the presence of at least two witnesses. While the signing may be accompanied by religious rituals and readings of selected verses from the Qur'an, no religious ceremony as such is required in order for a marriage to be valid.

Consistent with the practice found in agrarian societies, the age at which marriage occurs is relatively early. During Muhammad's time and in later centuries, child marriage was widely practiced. Child marriage is no longer common in modern Islamic societies. Many countries have laws prohibiting child marriage.

Dowry. Parents of both parties must agree on the amount of the dowry (*mahr*), or bride-price, prior to formal engagement. Unlike the East Asian and African practice, where dowries represent the money brides' parents give to grooms, in the Islamic countries dowries are the money wives receive from grooms as gifts. The actual payment is often made by grooms' fathers rather than by the grooms themselves.

In modern Muslim societies there is considerable discussion concerning the implications and appropriateness of the dowry system. While progressives and their Western sympathizers interpret the dowry system as a remnant of the patriarchal culture and an indication of the chattel status of women, traditional Muslims consider it a symbol of generosity on the part of grooms and their families. During Muhammad's time, dowries were often appropriated by the brides' families. Muhammad reformed the dowry system to benefit brides rather than the brides' families by specifying that the money be paid directly to the brides. Although abuses still occur, dowries in the late twentieth century serve as an economic safeguard for wives in the event of divorce or the death of their husbands.

Extended Family. The American and European nuclear family is not the ideal Muslim family. Although modern employment patterns, urban conditions, and geographical mobility often require that new couples be separated from their parents and siblings, the traditional ideal is for young people to live with the extended family. The extended family is the basic social and economic unit of Muslim society. Individuals define themselves in terms of their extended family, a network of close relationships among parents, children, their spouses, aunts, uncles, and cousins. Young couples, particularly in rural areas, stay in the households of husbands' parents for a period before establishing their own households. When they leave, couples usually establish their own households in the same village or city as that of husbands' fathers. Close and frequent interactions are maintained between the new household and the extended family. Such interactions serve as sources of continued emotional support and assistance for everyone within the extended family, particularly in times of crisis, ill health, financial difficulties, new business start-ups, new employment, relocation to another city, or any other major event affecting family members.

Because the traditional method of spousal selection provides brides and grooms very little opportunity to be acquainted with each other before the wedding, one might suspect that there would be a high rate of divorce. Among Muslims, however, this is not the case. The divorce rate is relatively low in traditional Muslim societies. The low divorce rate is attributed to such factors as continued support from extended family, strong social pressures to suppress potential marital conflicts, and acceptance of traditional gender roles within marriage. Divorces, when they do occur, are caused by such common factors as sexual incompatibility, in-law problems, extramarital affairs, and financial difficulties.

Thanks primarily to immigration, the Muslim population of North America was expected to exceed the Jewish population by the year 2000. (Dick Hemingway)

Patriarchy. In an ethical and spiritual sense, Islam views men and women in equal terms. In legal and organizational terms, however, traditional Muslim families are patriarchal and patrilineal. Women and children owe the head of the household respect and obedience. Women marry into the families of their husbands and assume husbands' family name. Children also inherit the family name of their fathers. Major decisions in such matters as children's education, marriage, relocation, and purchase of property are made by fathers.

In case of divorce or separation mothers acquire custody of young children. According to Islamic law, fathers have the right of custody of boys two years or older and of girls seven years or older. Fathers are required to support their legitimate children. Children born out of wedlock have no legal relationship to their father and are not entitled to support.

Perhaps no other facet of Islam so well typifies the expression of patriarchy as laws concerning divorce. Wives cannot divorce their husbands without their consent or a judicial decree, while husbands can unilaterally and extrajudicially divorce their wives without being obligated to offer any justification. Attempts to change the practice of divorcing women without sufficient grounds have been resisted by traditional Islamic countries. In 1967, for example, Iran's Mohammad Reza Shah Pahlavi passed the Marriage Protection Act that prohibited unilateral divorce without sufficient grounds. After the 1979 Islamic Revolution, the Marriage Protection Act was fundamentally modified to bring it in line with the old tradition. Although judges are required to advise couples to reconsider their decision to divorce and to seek reconciliation, divorce with mutual consent is still legal. In practice, however, women's consent to divorce is irrelevant when their husbands intend to divorce them. Some argue that such patriarchal cultural attitudes stem from a fundamental devaluation of women and engender a system of double standards, one applicable to men and another to women. Another example of the devaluation of women in Muslim societies, many argue, is reflected in the law found in several countries that men's testimony in court is equal to that of two women.

The Qur'an permits divorced men and women to remarry, with the difference that while men can marry immediately after they divorce, women must wait at least three menstrual periods to make sure that they are not pregnant. If they are pregnant, they must wait until the child is born and weaned. In contrast to other preindustrial societies, no stigma is attached to divorced women seeking remarriage.

Women's Position and Polygyny. Western feminist scholars are critical of women's position in traditional Muslim families. They note that women are secluded and segregated from public life. Their roles in life are confined to the domestic sphere. Although increasing numbers of women benefit from education, gain entry into public life, and become successful in professional careers, their numbers are still relatively small.

Muslim scholars and leaders who defend the subordinate position of women in society appeal to passages in the Qur'an suggesting that women are emotionally labile and intellectually inferior to men. Like conservative scholars in other religions, they also argue that God created women as natural nurturers and caregivers to the rest of the family.

Gender equality is not a concept understood by the religious and political leaders in traditional Muslim societies. Reform-minded social activists and writers who question the traditional strategy of segregating and secluding women are often silenced or denigrated.

The practice of polygyny that exists in Muslim countries is part of the heritage of the pre-Islamic tradition. The Qur'an accepted this tradition and reformed it by limiting to four the number of wives men are allowed to marry. It also dictated that those who marry more than one woman should deal with them fairly and justly. The initial intent of the Qur'anic acceptance of polygyny was to help provide for widows whose husbands had died in wars and for single women who had no other source of support. Although Islam permits polygyny, the percentage of men who exercise this right is actually small. In modern times, polygyny has become a luxury enjoyed by wealthy men who can afford to pay dowries and who are inclined to display their affluence and social status by having several wives. Among the more secularized, urban professionals the incidence of polygyny is virtually nonexistent. Researchers generally note a trend away from polygyny in all Islamic countries. Yet, to the extent that polygyny exists while polyandry (one woman having several husbands) does not, polygyny is viewed as another indication of the culture of patriarchy. Polygyny is not without its problems, however. It generates constant conflicts among wives on one hand, and among in-laws on the other.

Consistent with what is common in many agrarian cultures, Muslim societies generally have relatively large families. Male children are preferred to females, however, probably because of their economic value in an agrarian society. It appears that female infanticide was a common practice in pre-Islamic times, a practice explicitly condemned in the Qur'an. Infertility is viewed negatively by Muslims. Wives who fail to bear children are sometimes subjected to divorce or even abuse, whereas wives who are fruitful are held in high regard. For practical reasons, however, the tradition of having large families is increasingly being abandoned by educated, urban professionals.

Modesty Codes and Reform Efforts. In addition to being submissive to their fathers and, after marriage, to their husbands, women are bound by strict codes of modesty. The norm that requires women to practice modesty in clothing was already in existence in pre-Islamic Arabia. This modesty code is necessary, it is claimed, to avoid tempting men sexually. The veil (*pardah*) is often cited as the supreme symbol of the code of modesty. Not all modern Islamic countries require women to wear a veil, and the Qur'anic injunction about the veil is understood differently in different countries and regions. While Western scholars interpret modesty codes as a means of controlling women's sexuality, Muslims believe that they are necessary to preserve the stability and sanctity of family life.

Not all Muslim scholars defend Islamic family values. Anxious to lend Islam a modern social image, they interpret the controversial Qur'anic passages relating to women and their place in the family structure as having their origin in the particular social and historical settings of the time period when Islam was founded rather than as constituting the spirit of the Prophet's teachings. They argue, with some justification, that the Prophet defended and protected women's rights against many abuses that were prevalent at the time and required that women be treated with justice and fairness. In their view, social equality is compatible with the spirit of Islam.

—*Mathew J. Kanjirathinkal*

BIBLIOGRAPHY

Abu-Lughod, Lila. *Writing Women's Worlds: Bedouin Stories.* Berkeley: University of California Press, 1993. Brings to life through the stories told by Bedouin women the concepts of patrilineality, polygyny, patriarchy, parallel cousin marriage, and other central concepts.

Ahmed, Leila. *Women and Gender in Islam: Historical Roots of a Modern Debate.* New Haven, Conn.: Yale University Press, 1992. Thoughtful study that examines the concept of gender by placing it in a social and historical context.

Fernea, Elizabeth E., ed. *Women and Family in the Middle East: New Voices of Change.* Austin: University of Texas Press, 1985. Collection of studies that sheds light on the social transformation that impacts the Arab family.

Prothro, Edwin T., and Lutfy Najib Diab. *Changing Family Patterns in the Arab East.* Beirut: American University of Beirut, 1974. Summarizes the major concepts underlying an understanding of the Arab family and documents the changes that impacted family life in a specific region of the Middle East.

Soffan, Linda U. *The Women of the United Arab Emirates.* Totowa, N.J.: Barnes & Noble Books, 1980. Examines the practice of family law in the United Arab Emirates and argues that the low status assigned to women in the Gulf region results from a misinterpretation of the Qur'an.

Tucker, Judith E., ed. *Arab Women: Old Boundaries, New Frontiers.* Bloomington: Indiana University Press, 1993. Collection of studies that critically assess the condition of women in several Arab countries, including Egypt, Palestine, Sudan, and Morocco.

See also Amerasian children; Ancestor worship; Arranged marriages; Cultural influences; Dowry; East Indians and Pakistanis; Extended families; Gender inequality; Matchmaking; Middle Easterners; Patriarchs; Polygyny; Son preference; War brides.

Myths and storytelling

RELEVANT ISSUES: Children and child development; Kinship and genealogy; Parenting and family relationships; Race and ethnicity

SIGNIFICANCE: Family myths and storytelling develop a sense of family identity, encourage bonding among family members, heighten communications skills, and perpetuate the culture of the family

For the modern family, storytelling is a means of coping. Storytelling deals with the primeval needs and fears that children experience and that emerge in dreams or the unconscious. Within the security of the family setting, storytelling also deals with the realities of society and existence.

Family Myths and Storytelling Defined. Stories told within the family setting can include those handed down by society, such as fairy tales and folktales, those invented for specific occasions, such as some bedtime stories, and those specifically about the family, including immediate members, relatives, and ancestors. The first two types of stories are almost totally fictional, while the third usually purports to be true or to be based on the truth. In actuality, some family stories can be totally fictional or contain fictional elements. Whether the stories are true or not becomes irrelevant if families accept and believe them, at which point they become family myths. Family myths are important beliefs that families have about themselves or individual members (frequently ancestors). Typical myths told by families, for example, are that they are descended from royalty (or, conversely, Blackbeard the Pirate), that they produce only beautiful women, that they freed their slaves voluntarily, or that they have some Native American blood. Other myths may be that "Uncle Joe" was a legendary wastrel, boozer, or womanizer while "Aunt Emma" was an angel in disguise.

Influences on Family Myths and Storytelling. Family myths and stories have been promoted by the interest in family history and genealogy. A landmark of family history and genealogy in the United States was the publication of Alex Haley's *Roots* (1976) and the subsequent television miniseries based on the work. *Roots* is a generational saga that traces the author's ancestry from Africa to slavery and segregation in the American South. African Americans as well as members of other ethnic groups were especially inspired by *Roots* to delve into their own family histories. Another landmark was the series of *Foxfire* books from Appalachia, beginning in the 1960's, that was based on collecting oral histories, including family histories. Some families have used the *Foxfire* method to compile their rough-hewn, privately circulated versions of *Roots*. If this method was considered too much trouble, there were agencies that provided ready-made genealogies for a fee, including family coats of arms (sometimes with a disclaimer in fine print).

Family myths and stories have also been promoted by the interest in ethnic heritage awakened by the 1960's Civil Rights movement, first among African Americans and then among other ethnic groups. Earlier, some members of racial minorities and new immigrant groups took an interest in assimilating into the majority society or at least emulating it. Sometimes the desire to assimilate involved turning one's back on one's ancestry, family, or family name. During and after the Civil Rights movement, the urge to assimilate was supplemented by pride in one's ethnic heritage. Since the most intimate embodiment of the heritage was one's ancestry and family, family myths and stories became part and parcel of the interest in ethnicity.

Finally, family storytelling is part of an overall revival in the art of oral storytelling throughout North America. The revival spread from places where storytelling never quite died out, such as Newfoundland and Nova Scotia. The center of the revival is the Appalachian hamlet of Jonesborough, Tennessee, headquarters of the National Storytelling Association and site of an annual storytelling festival. For the twenty-fifth anniversary festival in October, 1997, more than ten thousand people descended on Jonesborough. The festival, a showcase for Appalachian and African American storytellers, also included Native American, Asian American, and Hawaiian storytellers and storytellers from as far away as Ireland and New Zealand. Significantly, many of the stories centered around the family. Similar festivals have sprung up across the continent, leading to a plethora of publications and even college degrees in storytelling.

Family Storytelling as Entertainment. Family storytelling has many uses, but its most important use is as entertainment. The entertainment value of storytelling undergirds all its other uses. Some people want to emphasize the moral of a story, but a moral that does not flow out of a good story is dull and meaningless. The emphasis must first be on telling a good story that engages the attention, imagination, and emotions of the listener. Telling good stories takes skill and practice, but it does not have to be hard work if storytellers enjoy their art.

The ideal setting is a relaxed gathering of two or more people—after a family meal, while entertaining visitors, or while putting a child to bed. Some Appalachian families, for example, entertain informally. People gather at homes in the evening to play music, joke, and tell stories. Families may engage in group singing or their members, including the children—who may have learned to play musical instruments—take turns singing a song or telling a story. Storytelling emerges naturally from the setting, as it did from small gatherings of men, who would sit around, whittle, and swap stories. From bonding at these gatherings, family members even learn when to pause in a story and when to spit. Grandparents may take children on their knees and reel off one story after another. Preachers often use storytelling to spice up their sermons.

Similar examples of storytelling occur in other ethnic groups, often with families or neighborhoods as nuclei. Hispanic families may serve up stories with homemade salsa. Storytelling in Jewish families may be accompanied by feasting and may last late into the night. In an African American neighborhood in Savannah, Georgia, there is a storytelling tree—a live oak draped with Spanish moss—under which neighbors gather to lounge in the shade and swap stories. The tree is reminiscent of a storytelling tree featured in R. K. Narayan's short story collection *Under the Banyan Tree* (1985), in which an Indian village gathers each evening to hear an old storyteller. In Amy Tan's novel *The Joy Luck Club* (1989) four Chinese-American women meet regularly to eat, play mah-jongg, and tell stories, mostly about their families. These examples, like storytelling among Native Americans,

illustrate how storytelling occurs naturally in cultures that have a strong oral tradition.

The Art of Storytelling. Cultures with strong oral traditions, in which storytelling is a natural activity and in which storytellers can emulate each other, tend to produce persons who are good at the verbal art of storytelling. However, one does not have to be good at the art of storytelling in order to practice and enjoy it. It is possible to jump in and learn by doing, through trial and error. The best test of successful storytelling is always the reactions of the audience. Because it helps to know the audience, the family setting is an ideal place to begin. Storytelling involves principles of rhetoric and poetics that hark back to the ancient Greek

Storytelling is a powerful means of holding the attention of young children. (James L. Shaffer)

philosopher Aristotle. Stories have a beginning, middle, and end. They have the same elements as literary art: characters, settings, plots with complications, suspense, twists, surprises, tone or mood, and verbal style. To tell a story requires a good memory, imagination, and a way with words.

Storytelling also draws on the skills of acting. The speech must be delivered trippingly on the tongue, as Shakespeare's Hamlet says, utilizing volume, pitch, tone, pace, and pauses. An accent does not hurt, but is not necessary; on the other hand, a clear voice is. Besides voice, the storyteller makes use of presence and personality—facial expressions, eye contact, gestures, stance, and movements. Some professional storytellers also utilize makeup, costumes, musical instruments, or other props. They may cultivate a symbolic storytelling presence. Family storytellers, such as parents or children, can create similar expectations by donning hats, mantles, or other types of costumes associated with the storytelling persona. Storytellers can also change costumes or props to suit the mood of the story. For example, they may twirl a rose to go along with a romantic story or wear a witch's hat for a Halloween story.

Storytelling and Child Development. Since storytelling is a verbal art, the practice of it is useful for developing communication skills. Children in

As children grow older they place greater demands on the skills of storytellers. (James L. Shaffer)

particular should be encouraged to tell stories, although most need little encouragement. They just need a patient listener. Telling stories exercises their memories, imaginations, organizing faculties, vocabulary, and pronunciation. Eventually children also learn to use their voice and presence, usually by first imitating the mannerisms of adults. Telling stories to a group helps them overcome shyness and contributes to socialization. The same is true for adults, who may find that adopting the storytelling persona helps them overcome inhibitions.

If children imitate the styles of adult storytellers, they also model themselves after the contents of the stories they hear. Using stories to teach is a familiar and age-old practice. Exemplary stories have long been used to mold the moral development of children. Typical kinds of stories that openly teach are animal fables and religious parables, but fairy tales also subtly teach by implying their lessons.

In some preliterate societies, storytelling is the main means of passing on family and tribal traditions. Chinua Achebe's novel *Things Fall Apart* (1959), set in what became Nigeria, depicts a polygynous family in which the father and mothers educate their children by storytelling. Role modeling also takes place through storytelling, with mothers instructing their daughters and the father his sons and adoptive sons. In modern literate societies, storytelling can still be used to pass on family and ethnic traditions.

It is feared that many children in modern societies no longer learn the storehouse of cultural lore embodied in animal fables, religious parables, and fairy tales. This is due to television and other electronic media. Some parents fear that these media have claimed the minds of their children. If the media are raising children, it is feared by many that they will become banal. Thus, another use of family storytelling is to combat the influence of the electronic media.

Family Myths and Storytelling as Therapy. If family storytelling can save children, it can also have other therapeutic uses. Storytelling can have the same effect as Sigmund Freud's "talking cure," which he used in psychoanalysis. Talking out problems vents emotions or at least allows persons to gain control over them. Just as persons in support groups utilize this principle by sharing their sto-

ries, so can family members. Storytelling can also help families to deal with loss or death. In one type of memorial service family members and friends tell stories about the deceased. Telling such stories not only memorializes and recalls dead persons in life but also promotes healing among speakers and listeners.

Family myths can similarly provide support in difficult moments. In times of trouble relatives may aid family members by telling them family myths to help sustain them. These myths may play up relatives admired for their achievements or feature dubious characters. Good or bad, such mythic figures leave a legacy with which later family members can identify. In Frank Chin's novel *Donald Duk* (1991), such a legacy of mythic ancestors enables a young Chinatown hero to experience pride despite his unfortunate name, bullying by street gangs, and the prejudices of American society.
—*Harold Branam*

BIBLIOGRAPHY

Collins, Chase. *Tell Me a Story: Creating Bedtime Tales Your Children Will Dream On.* New York: Houghton Mifflin, 1992. Focuses on the parenting skill of telling stories to one's children that stir their imaginations and form their values.

Davis, Donald. *Telling Your Own Stories: For Family and Classroom Storytelling, Public Speaking, and Personal Journaling.* Little Rock, Ark.: August House, 1993. This little handbook by a master storyteller offers several series of prompts that help one recall stories.

Kindig, Eileen Silva. *Remember the Time . . . ? The Power and Promise of Family Storytelling.* Downers Grove, Ill.: InterVarsity Press, 1997. Christian perspective on how family storytelling can build moral values, promote healing, and bring together the generations.

MacDonald, Margaret Read. *The Parent's Guide to Storytelling: How to Make Up New Stories and Retell Old Favorites.* New York: HarperCollins, 1995. Beginner's simplified handbook on telling children stories, with a sampling of various kinds of stories.

Moore, Robin. *Awakening the Hidden Storyteller: How to Build a Storytelling Tradition in Your Family.* Boston: Shambhala, 1991. Detailed guide to creating and telling family stories, with exercises, references, and a list of resources.

Stone, Elizabeth. *Black Sheep and Kissing Cousins: How Our Family Stories Shape Us.* New York: Penguin, 1989. Using numerous illustrative stories, some from ethnic traditions, the author shows how family myths and stories mold the identity of a family and its members.

Zeitlin, Steven J., Amy J. Kotkin, and Holly Cutting Baker, eds. *A Celebration of American Family Folklore: Tales and Traditions from the Smithsonian Collection.* Cambridge, Mass.: Yellow Moon Press, 1982. Multicultural collection of family stories categorized by themes, with photographs, instructions, and other lore.

See also Bedtime reading; Enculturation; Entertainment; Family life education; Family values; Genealogy; Generational relationships; Haley, Alex; Literature and families; Moral education.

Names

RELEVANT ISSUES: Kinship and genealogy; Parenting and family relationships

SIGNIFICANCE: Personal names reveal the traditional hierarchy and history of a family and may reflect modern social trends as well

Personal names not only distinguish people from other members of a community but also may preserve information about the history, nationality, social class, tastes, or character of a person's family. As one of the first and most influential social functions that a family performs for its offspring, naming bonds the family as well as identifies the named person.

Origin and Types of Names. Personal names existed before recorded history and may well predate the full development of language. The earliest literature places great importance on names and naming, as illustrated by the story of Adam and Eve in the Book of Genesis. Names placed people within society and so contributed to social status.

Like biblical names, personal names in later times typically were single words. In early English society, when two people had the same name in a small community, a descriptive word was added to distinguish the two. This nickname (from Middle English *an eke name*, "an also name"), or byname, commonly referred to the appearance, temperament, occupation, parents, residence, or birth time of the person. Thus, one John, a cobbler, might become John Shoemaker; another John, small in stature, might become John Little. Originally, these descriptors were specific to the persons named and died with them, but during the Middle Ages, such names often became hereditary, surviving as modern surnames, also known as last names or family names.

Multiple-word names existed well before the Middle Ages, however, and revealed crucial links in complex family organizations. For example, the ancient Romans gave each member of a *gens* (clan) a first name, or praenomen; a *gens* name, or nomen; a family name, or cognomen; and sometimes a nickname, or agnomen, in honor of some achievement. Family names were also hereditary from ancient times in China, where the family name comes before the given name.

The sources of modern surnames are quite varied, but most are hereditary. In addition to nicknames that took hold as family names, surnames frequently employ a parent's first name. Some naming systems indicate the father with a prefix that means "son of." Examples include the Norman Fitz-, as in Fitzsimmons; the Scottish-Irish Mac- (or Mc-), as in McDonald (Irish also use O'- to indicate a grandson, as in O'Neal); and the Welsh Ap- or P-, as in Perry (shortened form of Ap-Henry). Other systems use suffixes, such as the Scandinavian-English -son (Johnson) and the English -s (Peters).

Scholars believe that the origin of these affixes, or patronymics, lies in a change from a matriarchal society to a patriarchal society. Parallel forms based on the mother's name have survived, as in Tilson, "son of Matilda."

Surnames also derive from places, such as Woods or Dechamps, seasons (Winters, Summers), colors (White, Brown), and other natural or cultural features.

Naming Customs. In modern Western countries, the basic pattern comprises a first name (Christian or given name), one or more middle names, and a surname. Because it is inherited and thus a basis of family tradition, the surname shows the least amount of variation for social or personal reasons. Some individuals change their last names to escape an unsavory past; others want to enhance the sound of a name for professional reasons, as actors frequently do. Many African Americans have adopted new last names to rid themselves of "slave names" inherited from white masters in the pre-Civil War South.

In the United States, the most common last-name alteration in the second half of the twentieth century sprang from the social movement for women's equality. Traditionally, upon marrying a

The interest people have in personal names is never greater than during the weeks leading up to the birth of their first child. (Hazel Hankin)

woman abandons the name of her birth family, or maiden name, and adopts her husband's name. In accord with the women's rights movement, however, a woman might not alter her name or might combine her family name with that of her husband, connecting the two with a hyphen, as in Wilborn-Smith for a woman named Wilborn who marries a man named Smith.

There is greater freedom in the choice of first and middle names. The parents' preference expresses their character and status and their plans for family life. Middle names may preserve the mother's maiden name, the father's first name, the name of another relative or of a godparent, or a celebrity's name. In some European countries, children do not receive a middle name until baptism or confirmation, when they typically receive a biblical or saint's name. In Russia, the middle name is a patronymic, ending in -vich for sons (Mikhailovich, son of Mikhail) and -ovna for daughters (Mikhailovna). Russians use the first name and patronymic together in familiar address.

First Names. Parental concerns are most clearly revealed in the first names they give their children. Occasionally, parents choose names for their etymological meaning in hopes that something of that meaning will enter the character of their child. For example, parents who hope to raise a son for a military career might name him Walter, from Old High German words meaning "army leader." More often, however, etymological meaning is overlooked; instead, an association lies behind a name choice. Thus, Christian or Jewish parents may choose a biblical name to honor their faith. Likewise, parents may name a child for a famous writer, businessperson, political figure, or athlete; in each case, the namesake is someone whom the parents admire and wish their child to emulate.

A peculiarity of the Anglo-American system involves passing on the father's name to the son and distinguishing between them by adding "Junior" to the son's name, or the Roman numeral "II" if a grandson receives his grandfather's name, but not his own father's, or "III" if the name belonged both to the father and grandfather. No such convention exists when the mother's name is given to her daughter. The male convention derives from concerns for inheritance and legal recognition of male heirs.

As often as not, parents simply like the sound of a name and select it for no other reason. These subjective preferences follow name fads, which arise for many reasons and may fade rapidly. Some names, such as John and Mary, have enduring popularity, but many others identify the name bearer's generation. Mildred, for example, was a common girl's name early in the twentieth century but was relatively rare by its end.

Choosing Distinctive Names. Parental preference, although subjective, can have a practical intention. Families with such ubiquitous last names as Smith and Jones may worry that their children will be lost in the crowd unless given an uncommon first name or a rare variation of a common name—Maren instead of Marion, for instance. In the United States, this practice arises from the national obsession with individuality. Extraordinarily unusual names may record the counterculture wit of the parents or take whim and the desire for novelty as goods in themselves. The names of rock musician Frank Zappa's children are famous examples—Dweezil, Moon Unit, Ahmet, and Diva Muffin—and author John Train reports such remarkable monikers as Verbal Funderbunk and Strangeways Pig Strangeways.

Families may have a special name for use only in family circles. The practice belongs to many cultures, and it can have varying spiritual or social import. In some societies, people have secret names that capture their essence and are not to be spoken in public. In Western countries, pet names indicate affection and intimacy, as do shortened, or hypocoristic, forms of names, as in Bill for William and Cory for Corinna, and diminutives, such as Juanito for Juan. On the other hand, a parent's use of complete first and middle name in sequence may signal pique with and authority over the child: "Jonathan Michael, stop that!"

Cultural Variations. Researchers have found that African American parents coin unique first names more often than other ethnic groups in the United States, although many simply conform to general American practice. The majority of African American first names come from the Bible or, in the case of disciples of the Nation of Islam, the Qur'an. Still others adopt African naming practices to emphasize their non-European heritage.

In giving first names to their children, American Indians follow the majority pattern most of the time. Their last names, however, often preserve old customs under which a name was taken from special circumstances of the birth or family history. In the case of Cherokee chief Wilma Mankiller, her last name honors a warrior ancestor.

Recent arrivals in the United States tend to preserve the customs of their original countries for a generation. Their descendants, however, usually switch to the majority pattern unless they live in a strong, distinctive ethnic community. Thus, Chinese Americans continue to use Chinese first names in many cases, and Latinos prefer traditional Spanish name forms almost exclusively.

—Roger Smith

BIBLIOGRAPHY

Alfred, Richard D. *Naming and Identity: A Cross-Cultural Study of Personal Naming Practices.* New Haven, Conn.: HRAF Press, 1988.

Ashley, Leonard R. N. *What's in a Name?* Baltimore: Genealogical Publishing, 1989.

Hassall, W. O. *History Through Surnames*. Oxford: Pergamon Press, 1967.

Kaplan, Justin, and Anne Bernays. *The Language of Names*. New York: Simon & Schuster, 1997.

Lassiter, Mary. *Our Names, Our Selves*. London: Heinemann, 1983.

Tournier, Paul. *The Naming of Persons*. New York: Harper & Row, 1975.

See also Cultural influences; Genealogy; Godparents; Lineage.

Nannies

RELEVANT ISSUES: Children and child development; Economics and work; Law; Parenting and family relationships

SIGNIFICANCE: The reappearance of the nanny as an employed caregiver in late twentieth century family life demonstrates a renewed need for quality child care in the era of the full-time career women and also raises emergent issues of the obligations of employers to provide child care for female employees, equity for female domestic workers in the "underground economy," and the possibility that inappropriate bonding will occur

The nanny was an institution of family life for aristocratic and upper-class families of the nineteenth and early twentieth centuries. Her role was that of caregiver to the child or children, watchdog of the nursery, emergency medical nurse, and sometimes cook and governess. She might be the sole domestic helper, although it was not unusual for her to be in a position of authority over other domestic workers. Her function was to mind the children, sometimes tyrannize over them, protect them, console them, mediate between them and their frequently absent parents, and encourage them in making the transition from childhood to adulthood.

History of the Nanny. The nanny as a social phenomenon reached its zenith during the reign of Queen Victoria in England (1837-1901), although she was also a typical member of the family among the nobility and royal family in czarist Russia. She served among European colonists or watched the children at home while the parents went out "to the colonies." She monitored the children of the nascent industrialists of the United States and tended to the scions of the European aristocracy.

Before the age of the automobile and conspicuous consumption, the ability to employ a nanny was one of the points of demarcation between the privileged and the lower classes. It was not unusual for a nanny to be employed for life, and provision often was made for her future once she left service, although many nannies ended their days alone and forgotten. Although the virtues of nannies were largely unsung, such well-known figures as Sir Winston Churchill, Edward Sackville-West, and Vladimir Nabokov were raised by nannies and wrote encomiums to them in their memoirs. It was not unusual for children raised by nannies to have a much closer attachment to the nanny than to the natural parents. The resurgence of the nanny has raised issues regarding how children bond to their parents or instead form familial attachments to paid caregivers.

Modern Developments in Family Life. Although the "golden age" of the nanny has been described as ending around 1939, just prior to the outbreak of World War II, developments during and since the end of the war have brought about a resurgence of a need for the nanny in modern life, although for other reasons than to be shepherdess of the privileged class.

This relatively recent renaissance of the nanny has occasioned a whole set of new associated concerns. No longer is the nanny the favored institution only of the aristocracy or nouveau riche. She, or someone filling at least part of her role, is now closer to a basic necessity for anyone wishing to succeed in the modern world without sacrificing family life. The overwhelming causal factor for this new need for dependable and secure child care has been the entry into the workforce of increasing numbers of women during and after World War II. Women in the workforce now include half of the mothers of toddlers and three-fourths of the mothers of school-age children.

The inadequacy of child-care facilities for working mothers is well documented, particularly in the United States. In the past, the extended family, such as grandparents or aunts and uncles, performed much of the care of children of working mothers. Geographic dispersion, generational mobility, and later retirement age or different expectations of retirement, however, have decreased caregiving by the extended family.

The performance by women of a greater range of occupations, and at a higher level, is one of the positive outcomes of the feminist movement. The basic child care and housekeeping functions formerly performed by women as wives and homemakers, however, still need to be performed. During the nineteenth century, there were many women who, whether because of poverty, lack of education, or lack of better employment options, were willing to be engaged as nannies by the upper classes. In the era of the liberated woman, however, most women do not see domestic service as a route to advancement or fulfillment. This leaves a gap in the workforce that is being filled by the very classes that the women's movement purportedly was designed to help: women of color, women with little educational opportunity, and women who might otherwise find it difficult to obtain employment.

The growing number of mothers in the North American workforce has led to a commensurate growth in the use of paid nannies for child care. (Dick Hemingway)

Political and Public Policy Issues. Among the classes of women seeking jobs in domestic service as nannies, perhaps the most desirable, from the point of view of many working mothers, are the large number of undocumented aliens resident in the United States. These might be women of virtually any national background. Many are willing to work for a modest wage and whatever additional amenities might be provided, such as meals, room accommodations, or educational opportunity. Most important to many of these workers is that they be paid "off the books" and thus not risk deportation. Because they do not have a legal right to be in the United States, they cannot take any employment that requires documentation such as a Social Security card.

In large cities such as New York and Washington, D.C., many women, both undocumented and documented, seek positions as nannies. There are also large numbers of successful career women in these same cities seeking nannies. Whether these nannies are paid at least the minimum wage or not, and whether their employment is recorded for Social Security and tax purposes or not, is agreed upon informally between the nanny and her employer.

Although it is illegal to hire an undocumented worker, many families ignore the law to acquire a nanny's services at an affordable price. The practice is not limited to the middle classes. Early in his presidency, in February of 1993, President Bill Clinton intended to appoint the first female attorney general of the United States. He withdrew the proposed nominations first of Zoë Baird and then of Kimba Wood because of alleged irregularities, particularly in the case of Baird, in their employment of illegal aliens as domestic helpers.

This "Nannygate" scandal, although resolved through the appointment of Janet Reno, a childless woman, as attorney general, did much to focus national attention on the difficulties working women face when trying to find adequate child care. The fact that this furor erupted over a female appointee also gave rise to public rhetoric over a "double standard" in taking a woman to task over an issue that might never have surfaced in the case of a male appointee.

Other issues illuminated were the reluctance of American business to establish programs to help their female employees with child care and the practice of paying illegal aliens under the table, thus depriving them of Social Security benefits later on. This focus on legal issues clarified for many private employers their obligations in regard to paying these benefits. It also made the nannies themselves aware of their legal rights and obligations.

Future Outlook of the Nanny. The nanny has changed. Although nannies are not among the highest-paid workers and are not well regulated in their profession, training opportunities do exist in the form of schools accredited by the American Council of Nanny Schools. Although nannies are described in the *Occupational Outlook Handbook* as just one of a variety of private household workers, they constituted about 35 percent of the total of such workers in the United States in the mid-1990's.

The nanny has evolved from being an intimate member of the family circle of her employer's family and is now more clearly an employee. Formerly, she might never take a day off and might as likely tyrannize her charges as love them. She might have had children of her own that she was forced to give up. Nannies now treat their jobs as jobs rather than as sets of familial obligations, and they are much less likely to sacrifice their own families for the families of their employers.

The modern working mother usually works for a combination of monetary and psychological rewards, but in most cases she wishes to be close to her own children and therefore is reluctant to turn over all responsibility for her children to a nanny. This is true even of the British royal family, in which Diana, Princess of Wales, preferred to play an active role in raising her children rather than completely entrust them to a nanny. The arrangement between a mother and the nanny that she employs is more likely than in the past to be explicit in terms of compensation and expectations. The nanny is an integral fact of family life because she fulfills a continuing human need.

—*Gloria Fulton*

BIBLIOGRAPHY

Gathorne-Hardy, Jonathan. *The Unnatural History of the Nanny.* New York: Dial Press, 1973.

Gregson, Nicky, and Michelle Lowe. *Servicing the Middle Classes: Class, Gender, and Waged Domestic Labour in Contemporary Britain.* London: Routledge, 1994.

Harris, Diane, and Peter Richards, "Life After Nannygate." *Working Woman* 18 (June, 1993).

Miall, Antony, and Peter Miall. *The Victorian Nursery Book*. New York: Pantheon, 1980.

Yeiser, Lin. *Nannies, Au Pairs, Mothers' Helpers—Caregivers: The Complete Guide to Home Child Care*. New York: Vintage Books, 1987.

See also Au pairs; Baby-sitters; Child care; Childhood history; Day care; Mommy track; Substitute caregivers.

National Center for Missing and Exploited Children (NCMEC)

DATE: Founded in 1984

RELEVANT ISSUES: Law; Violence

SIGNIFICANCE: The National Center for Missing and Exploited Children (NCMEC) serves as a nationwide clearinghouse to help locate and recover missing children and to raise public awareness about ways to prevent child abduction, molestation, and sexual exploitation

Prior to the creation of the NCMEC, the United States had no national network to aid in the search for missing children and few laws to protect child victims or target offenders who prey upon children. Police departments had mandatory waiting periods of up to seventy-two hours before accepting a missing child report, and there was rarely a coordinated national effort. No states had procedures in place to flag school records of missing children or to cross-check enrollment records against missing-child reports. Moreover, they had only six sex offender registration laws.

In 1980 a congressional mandate established the NCMEC to address these issues. A private, nonprofit organization based in Arlington, Virginia, the NCMEC works in conjunction with the U.S. Department of Justice's Office of Juvenile Justice and Delinquency Prevention to aid law enforcement agencies and parents in locating missing children and prevent child exploitation.

Between 1984 and 1994 the NCMEC handled more than one million calls through its national hotline, trained 138,000 police and other professionals, and disseminated more than twelve million free publications. In that period it worked with law enforcement on more than 50,000 missing-child cases, resulting in the recovery of 32,000 children. The NCMEC provides information on legislation directed at the protection of children and technical assistance to individuals, parents, groups, agencies, and governments involved in locating and returning children. It also operates the national child pornography tip line in conjunction with the U.S. Customs Service, the U.S. Postal Inspection Service, and the Federal Bureau of Investigation (FBI), producing leads that have resulted in many successful investigations.

The primary motive for child abduction by nonfamily members is sexual. Most victims of sex offenders are children, and many who victimize children are serial offenders. The registration of persons who have been convicted of sex offenses and reentered the community protects children. By 1994 thirty-nine states had sex-offender registration laws, thanks in part to the efforts of the NCMEC.

In the case of nonfamily abduction, time is the enemy. The NCMEC believes that the most important tool to help find missing children is a picture or video. Persons may have seen these children or know of their whereabouts. The challenge is getting such pictures distributed as widely and quickly as possible. Through the NCMEC police departments can distribute photographic images and information to the public and to 17,000 other law-enforcement agencies around the country.

In 1990 the NCMEC merged with the Adam Walsh Child Resource Centers, founded by John and Reve Walsh after the poorly coordinated and slow search for their slain six-year-old. John Walsh quit his job and lobbied full-time for the passage of a 1982 act mandating immediate investigation of missing-child reports, and in 1984 he was instrumental in the bill that established the NCMEC.

—*P. S. Ramsey*

See also Child abduction; Child molestation; Child safety; Missing Children's Assistance Act.

National Council on Family Relations (NCFR)

DATE: Founded in 1938, in Chicago, Illinois

RELEVANT ISSUES: Education; Marriage and Dating; Parenting and family relationships

Significance: This interdisciplinary organization provides a forum for practitioners to discuss family issues, education, and practice

Founded as the National Conference on Family Relations in 1938 by lawyer Paul Sayre, sociologist Ernest Burgess, and Rabbi Sidney Goldstein, this organization became incorporated as a nonprofit organization in 1945 and changed its name to the National Council on Family Relations in 1947. The council "provides a forum for family researchers, educators, and practitioners to share in the development and distribution of knowledge about families and family relationships, establishes professional standards, and works to promote family well-being," according to its 1997 statement of purpose. Its membership is multidisciplinary, composed of individuals from various professions, such as home economics, sociology, law, education, social work, family medicine, and psychology. Different forms of membership and membership rates are available for professionals, students, and organizations.

Headquartered in Minneapolis, Minnesota, the NCFR has grown and developed in close connection with the changing historical context in which it has existed. Conference themes have continually reflected the active concerns and conditions faced by families. The 1944 conference theme was "Problems Facing the Family in the Post War Period" while the 1997 theme was "Fatherhood and Motherhood in a Diverse and Changing World." Committees and sections within the organization have changed over time. Initial committees focused on topics such as marriage, religion, and parenthood. By 1997 ten sections existed: Family Therapy, Family Policy, International, Feminism and Family Studies, Family Science, Education and Enrichment, Research and Theory, Ethnic Minorities, Religion and Families, and Family and Health. Moreover, the nature of the research published in the organization's journals has become more diversified. The first edition of the journal *Living* contained pieces on "A Plan for Successful Marriage," "Predictive Factors in the Success or Failure of Marriage," and on children's stories. In the 1990's the council's two journals, *The Journal of Marriage and the Family* and *Family Relations: Interdisciplinary Journal of Family Studies*, published articles reflecting an increasingly inclusive approach to families such as "Assessing Quality of Care in Kinship or Foster Family Care," "The Families of Lesbians and Gay Men: A New Frontier in Family Research," and "Significant Life Experiences and Depression Among Single and Married Mothers."

In addition to coordinating yearly conferences and publishing two journals, the NCFR has put forward various position papers and statements on issues such as "Family Life and the Vietnam War," "Family Life and Sex Education," and "Families and Family Policy." In 1986 it implemented a Certified Family Life Education (CFLE) program, which recognizes the knowledge and skills professionals require to educate others about family life and ensures that certified professionals' knowledge and skills remain up-to-date. Since 1995 university and college academic programs have received curriculum approval status. The council collaborates with various national and international organizations and publishes many books, games, videotapes, and audiotapes related to family issues. Educational and advisory in nature, the council continues to assist individuals and organizations to work effectively toward improving families' lives.

—*Áine M. Humble*

See also Child care; Family caregiving; Family life education; Gay and lesbian families; Parenting; Sex education; Single-parent families; Vanier Institute of the Family (VIF).

Native Americans

Relevant issues: Kinship and genealogy; Race and ethnicity
Significance: Families were very important in nearly all Native American cultures, often functioning as economic units and as the building blocks of government and society

Native American families in North America were joined across village and band boundaries by systems of clan relations that served to tie together confederate political systems. European immigrants to North America were sometimes confounded by the ways in which Native American family life differed from their own. For one thing, among many Native American peoples women were often influential in family as well as political and economic life. Gender relations that were considered by some Europeans to be deviant, such

Most modern Native Americans wear traditional apparel only for special ceremonial occasions. (James L. Shaffer)

as the cross-gender berdache, or homosexual, were accepted in some native cultures. Many Native Americans formed and broke marital bonds more quickly and easily than most European Americans. Bonds other than marriage were also highly significant for many Native Americans. Clan relationships were often so strong that relatives, known as "cousins" by modern European Americans, were regarded as brothers and sisters by Native Americans. For the most part, practices noted by historical observers are still evident among Native American peoples, although these practices have been compelled to undergo modifications because of Native Americans' association with the mainstream culture.

The Iroquois. The Iroquois Confederacy was fundamentally a kinship state. The Iroquois were bound together by a clan and chieftain system that was supported by a common linguistic base. Through the "hearth," which consisted of a

Modern Native American mother holding her baby in a traditional wicker cradle. (Ben Klaffke)

mother and her children, women played a profound role in Iroquois political life. Each "hearth" was part of a wider group, called an *otiianer*, and two or more *otiianers* constituted a clan. The word *otiianer* refers to the female heirs to the chieftainship titles of the league, the fifty authorized names for the chiefs of the Iroquois that were passed through the female side of the *otiianer*. *Otiianer* women selected one of the males within their group to fill a vacated seat in the league.

Such a matrilineal system was headed by a "clan mother." All the sons and daughters of a particular clan were related through uterine families that lived far apart. In this system, husbands went to live with their wives' families, and their children became members of the mothers' clans by right of birth. Through matrilineal descent, the Iroquois formed cohesive political groups that had little to do with where people lived or from what villages the hearths originated.

Upon the judgment of the clan, the oldest daughter of the head of a clan sometimes succeeded her mother at her death. All authority sprang from the people of the various clans that made up a nation. The women who headed these clans appointed male delegates and deputies who spoke for the clans at tribal meetings. After consultation within the clan, issues and questions were formulated and subsequently debated in council.

Peace among the formerly antagonistic Iroquois nations was procured and maintained through their Great Law of Peace (*Kaianerekowa*), which was passed from generation to generation by the use of wampum, symbols (written communication) that outlined a complex system of checks and balances between nations and sexes. A complete oral recitation of the Great Law took several days. Wampum belts, complex designs of purple (or sometimes black) and white shells, acted to prompt the memory of a speaker.

Under the Iroquois Great Law, blood feuds were outlawed and replaced by condolence ceremonies. Under this law, when a person killed someone, the grieving family could forego the option of exacting clan revenge (the taking of the life of the murderer or a member of the murderer's clan). Instead, the bereaved family could accept twenty strings of wampum from the slayer's family, ten for the dead person and ten for the life of the mur-

derer himself. If a woman was killed, the price was thirty wampum strings.

The Iroquois were linked to each other by their clan system—that is, each person had family in every other nation of the federation. If a Mohawk of the Turtle Clan had to travel, he would be cared for by Turtles in the other nations: the Oneidas, the Onondagas, the Cayugas, and the Senecas.

Iroquois political philosophy was rooted in the concept that all life is unified spiritually with the natural environment and other forces that surround humans. The Iroquois believed that the spiritual power of one person was limited, but when combined with other individuals in a hearth, *otiianer*, or clan spiritual power was enhanced. Whenever persons died either natural deaths or violent deaths such as through murder or war, the "public" power was diminished. To maintain the strength of the group, families often replaced the dead by adopting captives of war. This practice of keeping clans at full strength through natural increase or adoption insured the power and durability of the matrilineal system as well as the kinship state.

Child rearing was an important way to instill political philosophy in Iroquois youth. The ideal Iroquois personality was a person that was loyal to the group, yet independent and autonomous. Iroquois people were trained to enter a society that was egalitarian, with power more equally distributed between males and females, the young and the old than in Euro-American society. Euro-American society emphasized dominance and command structures, while Iroquois society was interested in collaboration.

Many Iroquois were members of the Longhouse Religion, based on the Code of Handsome Lake, which combined European religious influences (especially those practiced by the Quakers) with a traditional Iroquois emphasis on family, community, and the centrality of the land to the maintenance of culture. Handsome Lake's largest following developed after his death in 1815. Many Iroquois accepted Handsome Lake's rejection of alcoholic beverages, as well as his concepts of social relationships that closely resemble Quakerism, which he had studied. Handsome Lake also borrowed heavily from the Iroquois Great Law of Peace, popularizing concepts such as looking into the future for seven generations and showing regard for the earth as mother. Subsequently, these ideas became part of pan-Indian thought across North America and were incorporated into late twentieth century popular environmental symbolism. In Iroquois country the Code of Handsome Lake is still widely followed, as is the Longhouse Religion. By the late twentieth century roughly a third of the thirty thousand Iroquois in New York State attended Longhouse rites.

The Wyandots (Hurons). Native Americans living near the eastern edge of Lake Huron in present-day Ontario called themselves Wyandots. The French called them Hurons, a reference, in French, to the bristles on a boar's head, probably because the first Wyandots they met wore their hair in a style that has become known as a "Mohawk."

As with the Iroquois, the Wyandot clans—Porcupine, Snake, Deer, Beaver, Hawk, Turtle, Bear, and Wolf—created familial affinity across the boundaries of the four confederated Wyandot nations. Members of each clan could trace their ancestry to a common origin through the female line. In each village, clan members elected a civil chief and a war chief. The titles were carried through the female family line but bestowed on men, a practice similar to that among the Iroquois. While the titles were in this sense hereditary, they did not pass from one head of a particular family to another, as is the case among most European monarchies.

As among the Iroquois, economic roles among the Wyandots were determined by gender. Women usually tended gardens, gathered plants from the forests, and managed the home. Men marginally participated in agriculture, mainly by clearing fields for women to work, and contributed to the subsistence of the group by hunting. Men were the main visible participants in trade and diplomacy, but women contributed trade goods and political advice, usually behind the scenes.

The Apaches. Apache society was centered around groups of two to six matrilocal extended families, a unit sometimes called a *gota*. Members of the *gota* lived together, and members of the different households cooperated in the pursuit of game and in raising crops. A *gota* was usually led by a headman who assumed his status over several years by the general consensus of the extended families in the *gota*. The headman in some cases

inherited the title of "true chief." He would not retain the position, however, unless he displayed leadership capacity. If no qualified headman was raised through inheritance, a consensus would form in favor of another leader who would be informally "elected" by members of the *gota*. Headmen were invariably males, but women exercised influence as political advisers, and it was their society and kinship lineages that maintained the Apaches' matrilineal society.

A headman could wield considerable influence, but he could do so only if the people in the extended families he led were willing to follow his advice, which could include detailed lectures on how to hunt, the techniques of agriculture, and who should work with whom. He also coordinated labor for foraging and hunting, advised parties engaged in disputes, and was sought out for advice regarding who should marry whom. At times, the wife of a chief would become, in effect, a subchief. As a chief aged, he was charged not only with maintaining exemplary behavior but also with identifying young men who might become leaders in the future. He was expected to tutor younger men in the responsibilities of leadership. A chief was also charged with aiding the poor, often by coordinating distribution of donations from more affluent members of the *gota*. If two or more *gotas* engaged in conflict, their headmen were charged with resolving the dispute.

Each Apache was a member not only of a *gota* but also of one of sixty-two matrilineal clans that overlapped the individual settlements. Members of one's clan—and, in some cases, others identified as being close to it—helped each other in survival tasks and usually did not intermarry. Such a system resembled that of many peoples in the eastern woodlands, such as the Cherokee, Wyandots, and Iroquois.

The Cree. Before challenges from the outside forced them to convene a central council, the Crees, who live in present-day Quebec, had no centralized political organization, as among the Iroquois and Wyandots (Hurons) to the south. Even the individual bands or hunting parties had little or no organized political structure. Scholars sometimes call such a lack of structure "atomistic." Instead of a formal council, Cree bands, which were groups of families, informally selected a wise elderly man, usually the head of a family, as a

Modern Native American teenagers are barely distinguishable from their non-Native American counterparts. (Ben Klaffke)

source of advice. He exercised informal, limited influence. As with the sachems, or confederation chiefs, of the more organized farming and hunting peoples to the south, these informal leaders usually did not relish the exercise of power, probably because most of the people who sought their advice would have resented them if they attempted to dictate. Too great a display of power was resented and feared by those whom it affected.

Cree life was marked only rarely by multifamily celebrations or rituals. Social life and social control were usually a function of the extended family. Outside the family, a Cree might appear ambivalent or reticent, usually out of respect for others' autonomy. People who transgressed social norms of interpersonal behavior became targets of gossip or a type of sorcery that was used widely across the continent. Although their society was family-based, the Cree recognized no clan or other kinship system between different bands. The Cree thus did not maintain the interconnections between settlements that were maintained by the clans of the Iroquois, Wyandots, and Cherokee.

Northwest Coast Peoples. Native Americans who lived along the Northwest Coast of North America did not have the strong clan systems that characterized many other Native American societies. Instead, they had a very class-conscious social system in which family economic status could mean a great deal.

Northwest Coast peoples from the Alaska panhandle to Northern California generally recognized three social classes—nobility, commoners, and slaves—that seemed as imperishable as the red cedar from which they constructed their lodges. The nobility included chiefs and their closest relatives; the eldest son was the family head. He, his family, and a few associates lived in the rear right-hand corner of the family longhouse, with people of lower status on each side. These people were said to be "under the arm" of the chief. The next highest-ranking chief, usually a younger brother of the head chief, invariably occupied the rear left-hand corner of the house together with his family. He, too, had a number of people "under the arm." The other two corners were occupied by lesser chiefs' families. The totem poles of Northwest Coast peoples were family heralds, which often told the history of the people living within a given longhouse. —*Bruce E. Johansen*

BIBLIOGRAPHY

Colden, Cadwallader. *The History of the Five Nations of Canada.* New York: Amsterdam Book Co., 1902. Written in 1765, this work is a well-known primary source on eighteenth century Iroquois life.

Corkran, David H. *The Cherokee Frontier: Conflict and Survival, 1740-62.* Norman: University of Oklahoma Press, 1962. A good survey of Cherokee life in the eighteenth century.

Fenton, William N., et al., eds. *Symposium on Cherokee and Iroquois Culture.* Smithsonian Institution Bureau of Ethnology Bulletin 180. Washington: U.S. Government Printing Office, 1961. Details kinship systems among the Cherokee and Iroquois peoples.

McKee, Jesse O., and Jon A. Schlenker. *The Choctaws: Cultural Evolution of a Native American Tribe.* Jackson: University Press of Mississippi, 1980. General history of the Choctaw people that details aspects of kinship and family life.

Stannard, David E. *American Holocaust: The Conquest of the New World.* New York: Oxford University Press, 1992. Harrowing account of the destruction of Native American peoples as a result of epidemic diseases.

Trigger, Bruce G. *Children of the Aataentsic: A History of the Huron People.* Montreal: McGill-Queen's University Press, 1976. Traces Wyandot (Huron) history in great detail to about 1700, focusing attention on the evolution of family structures under the influence of European society, especially in respect to the fur trade.

Wallace, Anthony F. C. *The Death and Rebirth of the Seneca.* New York: Vintage, 1972. Describes the decline of the Senecas after the Revolutionary War, followed by the evolution of the Handsome Lake religion, with its emphasis on the family and future generations.

See also Alternative family types; Ancestor worship; Clans; Extended families; Latinos; Literature and families; Matrilineal descent; Parsons, Elsie; Tribes.

News media and families

RELEVANT ISSUES: Divorce; Parenting and family relationships; Sociology

SIGNIFICANCE: Public perception of the "typical" family has, in many ways and at various times in history, been formed by news media treatment of families and family issues

Popular culture—via entertainment on television, radio, and cinema—is notorious for presenting audiences with images that are not real. Most people expect more from the media. They expect to see, hear, and read about factual events and people. Those who have studied the media, either professionally or not, know that news coverage is based on facts. Those facts, however, are aired or printed from the perspective of reporters. Even the images captured by cameras have been edited from individuals' perspectives. Thus, one cannot tune into a broadcast news program or open a newspaper or news magazine and expect to see a story about the real, "typical" family; rather one can only expect to see a story about the type of family that has the attention of popular culture and the media.

Nuclear Family Image. Until the mid-1980's the image created by the media was that of the nuclear family—one father, who was employed outside the home; one mother, who took care of the home and the family; and at least two children. This image, as perpetrated through popular culture and entertainment, seemed to be typical and accurate. Yet, the ideal of a nuclear family has always been a myth complicated by divorces, birth control, child-care arrangements, employment situations, historical events, and political trends. For example, after reading about child-care debates throughout the 1990's, one might think that day care was a late twentieth century phenomenon. This is not the case. Facilities owned by the Young Women's Christian Association (YWCA) and the Young Men's Christian Association (YMCA) offered day care in the mid- to late 1800's. Family planning, too, is an old issue. The public arguments over birth control and abortion have been voiced in the media for a hundred years.

World War II changed many people's perceptions about what composed the typical family. With many husbands and fathers away at war, the U.S. Congress appropriated money for day care, since women were needed in the workforce. The number of women workers increased 30 percent, to 19 million, in 1944. Advertising portrayed women in their new roles; many print ads featured women in military uniforms or professional

clothes. Nevertheless, the media presented the situation as a temporary one, much as Congress perceived it. Toward the end of the war, advertisements again portrayed women in the home, making decisions about cleaning products and diapers. Funds for day care were withdrawn at war's end, and women had few child-care options. After the war the U.S. birth rate soared, and many women stayed home to raise children.

Entertainment or News. Researchers disagree on the relationship between television's entertainment shows and news shows. In the 1980's and 1990's, with shows such as *Hard Copy* and *Entertainment Tonight*, many people had trouble distinguishing between the two genres. Surely one emulates the other, but the question has arisen as to whether entertainment programs are based on news programs or vice versa. In any case, most family situation comedies (sitcoms) prefer to rely on a positive—although sometimes alternative—image of family to entertain the masses.

The 1950's was the first decade in which television was a mass medium enjoyed by large numbers of people. On television, simply because viewers could "see" things, everything looked and seemed real. In the 1950's the nuclear family was the most popular institution, both on television and in real life. Viewers saw this image in shows such as *Father Knows Best, Leave It to Beaver, The Adventures of Ozzie and Harriet*, and *The Donna Reed Show*. On these and other shows, the father was employed outside the home while the mother stayed home to take care of the day-to-day needs of the children and to handle the household chores. This pattern reflected the realities of most real-life families in the 1950's. Only about 34 percent of women age sixteen or older were employed outside the home. The divorce rate was climbing steadily, but it was still relatively low.

Free Love. In 1960 the legal introduction of the birth control pill as a method of preventing and planning pregnancies changed the way couples viewed their decisions to start families. Indeed, this phenomenon changed the way couples viewed their sexuality. The media aired and printed pictures of "free love" exhibitions, where nonmarried couples could be seen kissing passionately and groping openly. The attitude left by these images—so predominant in the media in the mid- to late 1960's—seemed to be that families

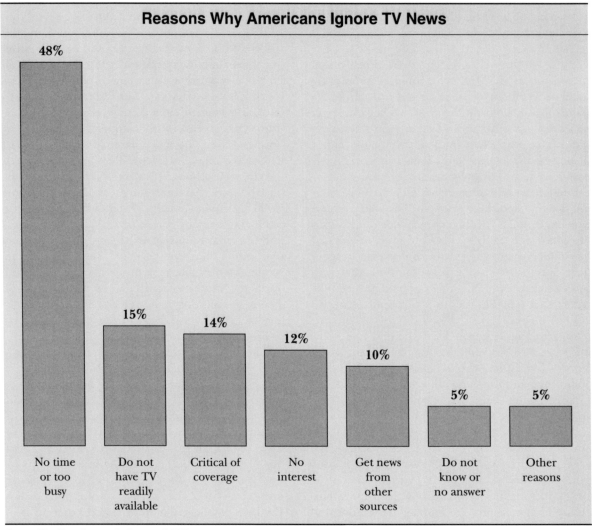

Reasons Why Americans Ignore TV News

Category	Percentage
No time or too busy	48%
Do not have TV readily available	15%
Critical of coverage	14%
No interest	12%
Get news from other sources	10%
Do not know or no answer	5%
Other reasons	5%

Source: The Pew Research Center (1996)

Note: A nationwide survey conducted in 1996 found that fewer Americans were watching television news programs. Among the questions asked in this survey was *why* people were watching less network news programming. This chart summarizes the responses of all adults interviewed. (Figures exceed 100 percent because some interviewees provided more than one response.)

no longer required marriage or monogamy. Some of the television shows of the period still featured the 1950's format of a nuclear family with a structured life, but a few shows added a twist: The women were given new control over their lives and the lives of their families. In *Bewitched*, a housewife and her mother had the magical powers of witches. In *I Dream of Jeannie*, a naïve young woman who washed ashore in a magic bottle used her mystical powers as a genie to attract the attention of the astronaut who rescued her.

The fantasy element that prevailed in entertain-ment shows did not spill over into serious news stories. Instead, reporters covered stories about real-life women seeking to gain power—in politics, the workplace, the family environment. In 1967 the National Organization for Women (NOW) issued a Bill of Rights calling for the establishment of federally regulated child-care facilities. Change was underway for families, as women began to take on long-term careers, instead of temporary employment, outside the home.

In 1973 a major family-related issue was resolved, at least for a period of time, when the

Supreme Court decision in *Roe v. Wade* made abortion legal. By 1975, 46 percent of women age sixteen and older were in the workforce. That figure grew to 50 percent by the end of the decade. Meanwhile, the divorce rate reached an all-time high of 50 percent, a figure that would remain steady for the next twenty years. The media, especially through advertising, began to view the family differently. Women and men were portrayed as professionals, and the typical image of the family included only one or two children.

Women at Work. Some of the more popular television shows in the 1970's portrayed women employed outside the home and offered alternative views of "family." *The Mary Tyler Moore Show, Police Woman, The Bionic Woman, Wonder Woman,* and *Charlie's Angels* all featured women as working professionals with little time for family. Others, such as *The Brady Bunch* and *The Courtship of Eddie's*

Father, showed alternative families resulting from the death of a spouse or divorce. Interestingly, two of the most popular family shows were set in earlier eras. The situation comedy *Happy Days* was set in the 1950's and featured an employed father and a stay-at-home mother. *The Waltons,* a one-hour drama, chronicled the experiences of a large extended family living in rural Virginia during the Great Depression. After the political and social watersheds of the Civil Rights and women's rights movements, the media seemed willing to accept alternative views of family: single parents with one or more children; grandparents raising children; aunts or uncles raising children. More change was evident, however, in the beginning of the next decade.

Conservative Wave. In 1980 Ronald Reagan entered the White House for the first of two consecutive terms as president of the United States. He

Chief Justice Warren Burger (right) administers the presidential oath of office to Ronald Reagan in 1981. (AP/Wide World Photos)

was immensely popular as a person and a president, and a wave of conservatism swept over the country. Admiration for a nostalgic 1950's image of families crept back into politics and casual conversations. The phrase "family values" was debated in the media by journalists, politicians, religious leaders, and those who aligned themselves as political liberals or moderates. The Moral Majority, a conservative religious political organization, took advantage of the popularity of conservative poli-

Former vice president Dan Quayle addressing a "family values" conference sponsored by Youth for Christ and various Alabama organizations in 1995. (AP/Wide World Photos)

tics. In 1980 the group's leader, Jerry Falwell, blasted the proposed Equal Rights Amendment (ERA) for women as an attack on families that would destroy family values in the United States. Throughout the decade and even into the 1990's, the Moral Majority and other conservative groups commanded a lot of air time and print space with their views. On television, viewers could watch *The Wonder Years*, a portrayal of a family living in the 1960's. On cable television, viewers could see reruns of *I Love Lucy* from the 1950's or Happy Days from the 1970's.

In 1988 President George Bush was elected to the White House, keeping the Republicans in power and, along with his more conservative vice president, Dan Quayle, keeping family values in the media. During their re-election campaign in 1992, Quayle criticized the television series *Murphy Brown* for glamorizing unwed motherhood. The show's title character, played by actress Candace Bergen, unintentionally became pregnant by her former husband, a radical activist of the 1960's. In the show, she gave birth to a baby son but did not marry or keep close contact with the baby's father. The vice president and the fictional female character engaged in a kind of debate for several weeks, with the writers of *Murphy Brown* adding to the script lines about family values and the reality of single mothers. This debate drew much media attention and generated much discussion about what constitutes a family and what the phrase "family values" means.

Alternative Family Structures. By the early 1990's it seemed that fewer children were growing up in the traditional nuclear family structure so common in the 1950's. About 57 percent of women over age sixteen were in the workforce. About half of the children in the United States lived with both of their biological or adoptive parents. The divorce rate had remained at 50 percent for three decades. Many women were raising their children alone. Some 75 percent of women with children older than six had jobs.

Two popular yet short-lived family television shows of the late 1980's were about single men raising children. *My Two Dads* featured two men raising a daughter together because they did not know which one of them was her biological father; and *Dads* featured two single fathers living together and raising their children.

Democrat Bill Clinton was elected president in 1992. Although politically liberal or moderate on many issues, Clinton showed he had some conservative values about families. He and his wife Hillary Rodham Clinton spent much time raising issues of children's health, security, and welfare. In 1993 Clinton signed the Family and Medical Leave Act, allowing men and women up to twelve weeks of unpaid leave yearly to care for newborn or newly adopted children or a close family member with a serious illness.

Benjamin Spock, a pediatrician known for his books on child care and his outspoken political views, published a book in 1994 that urged a return to "traditional values." In *A Better World for Our Children: Rebuilding American Family Values*, Spock maintained that materialism, dual-earner families, and single-parent families showed an abandonment of standards that was affecting the welfare of children.

The two most popular radio talk show hosts of the 1990's, Rush Limbaugh and Laura Schlessinger, urged their viewers to stick to issues about family values. Limbaugh, a self-proclaimed ultraconservative who became popular in the late 1980's, blasted feminists for the deterioration of families. Schlessinger also criticized feminists, but in a very different way. A staunch children's advocate, she insisted that the best situation for children under the age of five was to be cared for at home by one parent. Schlessinger did not criticize women or men for having careers but only for spending so much time on their careers that they neglected to make enough time for their families.

In her widely reported 1994 study *The Hite Report on the Family*, researcher Shere Hite noted that the family changes as humans change. She argued that the traditional nuclear family is not necessarily the best one. She found that men raised by single mothers had better relationships with women than those raised in dual-parent families.

Career Shifts. Obvious shifts in careers occurred in the 1990's. Some men began to stay home with their children while their wives were employed outside the home. Many men and women began working part-time, at home, or at jobs with more flexible hours. This idea caught fire with the media. In the 1970's and 1980's magazines, newspapers, and television ran pictures and stories about career women and professional men who worked long hours at the office. Suddenly, articles in newspapers and magazines did not deal with how one could find good day care but about how to arrange flexible working hours or how to work out of the home. In the 1990's many women decided to breast-feed their babies. Even manufacturers of infant formula products announced in their commercials that breast-feeding "is best."

The media's views of the family are connected closely to the social events and political tides of particular periods. The discussion of family issues draws other commentary, other events, more media coverage. When a research study dealing with family issues breaks into the media, other research studies and political commentary follow. An image of family forms in this context. Then those images are distributed through the media and become the subject of popular entertainment—mainly through television and cinema. Media consumers form images in their minds of what constitutes a family, even though those images may not match anything with which they are familiar.

—*Sherri Ward Massey*

BIBLIOGRAPHY

Bernikow, Louise. *The American Women's Almanac.* New York: Berkley Books, 1997. Engaging look at thirty years of the history of women and their struggles at work and in the home.

Biagi, Shirley, and Marilyn Kern-Foxworth. *Facing Difference: Race, Gender, and Mass Media.* Thousand Oaks, Calif.: Pine Forge Press, 1997. Anthology of articles from the scholarly and popular press that addresses race and gender issues as they relate to mass media.

Douglas, Susan J. *Where the Girls Are: Growing Up Female with the Mass Media.* New York: Times Books, 1994. Offers a narrative on the history of the stereotyping of men, women, and families by the media and popular culture.

Faludi, Susan. *Backlash: The Undeclared War Against American Women.* New York: Crown Publishers, 1991. In-depth look at the treatment of women and their families by the media, including a look at entertainment television and Hollywood films.

Lont, Cynthia. *Women and Media.* Belmont, Calif.: Wadsworth, 1995. Includes the experiences of women and their families as news and as news-makers in seven different media: newspapers, advertising, television, women's magazines, television news, film, and music.

Wilson, Stan Le Roy. *Mass Media/Mass Culture: An Introduction.* New York: McGraw-Hill, 1993. Overall look at how the media and popular culture treat individuals and families through advertising, television, public relations, print media, and computers.

See also Advertising; Alternative family types; Child care; Children's magazines; Dual-earner families; Fatherlessness; Mommy track; Second shift; Work.

No-fault divorce

RELEVANT ISSUES: Divorce; Law; Parenting and family relationships

SIGNIFICANCE: Changes in divorce law since 1969 have shifted cultural, social, and economic assumptions about divorce

In 1969, California was the first state to significantly alter its divorce law by instituting the so-called no-fault divorce. Within the next twenty-five years, every state and the District of Columbia had either changed its laws entirely to no-fault divorce or had added no-fault statutes to existing laws. This represented a radical change, making divorce easier to obtain and changing the way the American culture viewed divorce itself.

Background and Definitions. Previously, all divorces were considered "fault" divorces. The law required that to obtain a divorce, one spouse had to prove that the other was guilty of such acts as desertion, cruelty, or adultery. The law recognized that one person was guilty and the other innocent; that is, one person was considered to be at fault for the breakdown of the marriage. Fault divorce laws were designed to protect marriages, making divorce extremely costly, both economically and emotionally, for the "guilty" party.

Under this system, the "innocent" partner had to give permission for the divorce to occur. That is, if one spouse were to have an adulterous affair and want to end the marriage, the other spouse would have to grant permission. In addition, there were large financial stakes involved in proving one spouse guilty. The more blatant the guilt, the larger the financial settlement for the "innocent" spouse. Under this system, nearly all divorce actions were brought by women against men. The law assumed that men would pay alimony and support and that the women would assume custody of any children of the marriage.

Among the many problems with this system, probably the most important was that someone had to take the blame, leading to anger, guilt, and adversarial relationships, all of which tended to damage the children of divorcing couples. In addition, even in cases in which both spouses wanted a divorce on the basis of unhappiness or differences, one spouse would have to be willing to be accused of adultery or cruelty, with all the social stigma attached to such actions. Thus, even when both spouses were innocent of such deeds, the couple would have to lie to obtain the divorce, and the partner choosing to be the "guilty" party would have to assume the financial burden of the judge's decision.

Ramifications of No-Fault Divorce. No-fault divorce was seen as a remedy for the problems of divorce law. Under no-fault divorce, the court recognizes that neither partner is to blame for the dissolution of a marriage, but rather that both partners contribute to such an impasse. In addition, no-fault divorces are not supposed to privilege one gender over another. Settlements are made on the basis of financial considerations as opposed to blame. The spouse who has the larger income and more property may be required to pay alimony and support to the other spouse, regardless of gender. Custody of minor children is no longer granted automatically to the wife. In some cases, joint custody of minor children is granted. Finally, a spouse who wants a divorce does not need to obtain permission from the other spouse but instead can sue for and be granted a divorce on his or her own petition.

Although no-fault divorce laws were enacted to reform a system that had grown increasingly hypocritical and unwieldy, evidence suggests that the reforms produced mixed results. It would seem likely that easing the requirements for obtaining a divorce would lead to a rise in divorce rates, and some researchers credit the shift in divorce law to the precipitous climb in divorce rates in the United States.

Others, however, are not convinced that the rise in divorces is the result of no-fault laws. They see other cultural changes as potential culprits. For example, it is possible that the backlog of unhappy couples forced to stay together under the old divorce laws created a spike in the divorce rates when no-fault laws were enacted. It also is difficult to determine if the cultural and economic changes noted since the institution of no-fault divorce created the need for the change in the law, or if these changes were created by the law itself. In other words, it is not clear what is the cause and what is the effect.

A number of changes can be documented concerning divorces since the change in the laws. First, some researchers have noted an economic decline for women and children after divorce. This is particularly significant in long-established marriages with minor children and wives who do not work outside the home. In addition, there are far more male-initiated divorces under no-fault than under fault laws.

Broader Implications. Other ramifications of no-fault divorce are less clearly established. Some researchers argue that the establishment of no-fault laws led to a breakdown of the American family by placing women with children at an economic disadvantage as the result of divorce. They point to an attitude on the part of the courts that women must go out and get jobs after a divorce rather than relying on their former husbands to support the children. Other researchers argue that even families that stay together are affected by the presence of no-fault divorce. By taking away the protection that fault divorce offered women who chose to stay at home with their children, no-fault laws force women to find jobs outside the home to protect their futures. This is particularly true because their husbands can bring actions for divorce without their consent. Other researchers suggest that it is the growth of better-paying and higher-status jobs available for women that has led to increased employment outside the home, along with women's desire to share the world of work to find fulfillment or simply to expand their social world and escape the monotony of life spent entirely inside the home.

The institution of no-fault divorce also has led to the destigmatization of divorce. Because neither partner needs to assume blame for the breakup of the marriage, neither partner needs to take responsibility. This allows both spouses to escape the guilt and social stigma formerly associated with failed marriages. Some researchers believe that divorce rates have increased because of emulation. Unhappy couples now see other couples divorcing rather than trying to work out their problems, and because less stigma is attached to divorce than in the past, they also choose that option.

Some studies connect the effects of no-fault divorce laws with the welfare of children. In general, they point to two factors that negatively affect children: the sharp, downward economic shift that

Covenant Marriage

During the 1990's a backlash arose against no-fault divorce, with many Americans criticizing the ease with which couples could marry and divorce. One concrete proposal to make marriages endure longer was the notion of "covenant" marriage licenses, which would legally obligate couples planning to marry to go through a number of procedures not normally required of marrying couples. A unique marriage covenant law considered by Louisiana's state legislature in 1997 laid down a series of conditions for marriage and divorce for couples taking out such marriage licenses. Under the proposed law couples signing covenant licenses would obligate themselves to undergo counseling before marrying. Moreover, they would also have to sign affidavits affirming that they understood the conditions of their covenants and promising to seek counseling if their marriages started to fail. Couples signing such covenants would make themselves ineligible for no-fault divorce.

accompanies divorce and the trauma and strife in the family. Studies from the 1990's indicate that in terms of physical and mental abuse, children are much better off if their parents divorce. In terms of other measures of well-being, however, children seem to fare better if their parents stay in the marriage in spite of dissatisfaction with each other. As a result of these and other studies, states are once again looking at reforming divorce laws to take into account the effects on families and children.

Reform Movements. In California, lawmakers are considering systems of mediation that would encourage couples to work out their differences rather than face each other in court with adversarial lawyers arguing the cases. Prior to 1997, Michigan required that couples pay a $20 fee and have a three-day waiting period for a marriage. In a move that focused national attention on the debate, the state changed its laws in 1997. It maintained the $20 fee and three-day period for couples who can demonstrate that they have completed a course of premarital education and counseling, but those who cannot document such education must pay a $100 fee and wait thirty days.

States such as Georgia, Iowa, and Pennsylvania are considering ways to make divorce more difficult. Most states hoping to reform their divorce laws are looking for combinations of premarital counseling, programs that work through social and religious institutions designed to sustain and nurture marriages, and adjustments to no-fault laws leading to mutual consent divorces.

Critics of the reform movement argue that more restrictive divorce statutes will lead to more serious problems than experienced under no-fault, especially in cases of spousal abuse. Reformers, however, argue that the family is at risk in the face of the high divorce rate. Although it is unclear what effect legislative changes will have on the structure of the family, it seems certain that no-fault divorce laws will be modified.

—*Diane Andrews Henningfeld*

BIBLIOGRAPHY

DiFonzo, J. Herbie. *Beneath the Fault Line: The Popular and Legal Culture of Divorce in the Twentieth Century.* Charlottesville: University Press of Virginia, 1997.

Furstenberg, Frank F. *Divided Families: What Happens to Children When Parents Part.* Cambridge, Mass.: Harvard University Press, 1991.

Halem, Lynne Carol. *Divorce Reform: Changing Legal and Social Perspectives.* New York: Free Press, 1980.

Parkman, Allen M. *No-Fault Divorce: What Went Wrong.* Boulder, Colo.: Westview Press, 1992.

Wallerstein, J. S. *Second Chances: Men, Women, and Children a Decade After Divorce.* New York: Ticknor & Fields, 1989.

See also Alimony; Child custody; Cruelty as grounds for divorce; Desertion as grounds for divorce; Divorce; Divorce mediation.

Nuclear family

RELEVANT ISSUES: Demographics; Parenting and family relationships

SIGNIFICANCE: The nuclear family unit, the type of family unit traditionally found in North America, was, and in some cultures still is, considered to be the most basic form of social organization

The nuclear family is a group of people linked together by the ties of marriage, parenthood, and siblinghood. It is composed of a man, a woman, and their socially-recognized children, who may be natural or adopted offspring. The husband and wife hope to share companionship, love, and a sexual relationship. By law, the parents are required to feed, clothe, shelter, and educate their children. In turn, the children give emotional support to their parents and siblings. Nuclear families consist only of primary relatives—husband-fathers, wife-mothers, son-brothers, and daughter-sisters—and include only two generations. Traditionally, husband-fathers are required to support their wives and children, and wife-mothers are expected to run the home and care for the children. In the nuclear family fathers are typically the heads of the family, and they alone make major family decisions. The nuclear family unit is geographically mobile, a characteristic of societies whose mode of subsistence depends on people's moving from place to place, such as hunter-gatherer and modern industrial societies.

Since the 1960's many Americans have turned away from traditional family roles to more egalitarian relationships. Parents share equal family

The traditional nuclear family unit comprises a mother, a father, and one or more children. (Dick Hemingway)

authority and make family decisions together, and children express their desires and opinions and have much freedom within the family. In many families both parents work outside the home. Chores that were traditionally performed by wives have increasingly come to be shared by husbands and children. Furthermore, if couples divorce, they sometimes choose not to remarry, deciding instead to live as single parents. In addition, some persons have interracial families, and many couples choose to cohabit—that is, they live together without being married.

Because there is so much international variability in the form of the traditional nuclear family, it is more appropriate to refer to a nuclear family "complex," in which the roles of husbands, wives, fathers, mothers, daughters, sons, sisters, and

brothers refer to a group of people whose biological relationships do not necessarily conform to the typical American definitions of these individuals. For example, in matrilineal societies children, instead of being the responsibility of biological fathers, may be the responsibility of biological mothers' brothers, who are referred to as "fathers." Consequently, many sociologists and anthropologists prefer a broader definition of the nuclear family to the extended family, in which family or household groups are larger than the nuclear family. For example, conjugal families, consisting of mothers, fathers, their children, and some close relatives, are knit together primarily by marriage ties. Another extended family unit, the consanguinal family, which consists of parents, their children, their grandchildren, and the children's spouses, groups itself around a descent group or lineage, whose members are called blood relatives.

—*Alvin K. Benson*

See also Alternative family types; Conjugal families; Consanguinal families; Extended families; Family: concept and history; Family values; Institutional families; Monogamy.

Nursing and convalescent homes

RELEVANT ISSUES: Aging; Health and medicine

SIGNIFICANCE: Many people with debilitating illnesses and disabilities, especially the elderly, find it necessary to stay in residential institutions designed to provide nursing and custodial services

The nursing home industry continues to grow in modern industrial countries. In 1994 in the United States there were about 19,000 nursing homes, with almost 1.5 million residents. On any given day there are twice as many people in nursing homes as in hospitals. Roughly 20 percent of nursing homes are run by nonprofit organizations, while some 75 percent are operated for profit. In the United States, only 5 percent are operated under governmental auspices, but this percentage is much greater in Canada. Approximately 40 percent of nursing home patients stay less than a year in order to convalesce from illnesses or surgery, but the majority of residents are frail and elderly, typically suffering from two or more chronic illnesses as well as serious mental impairment.

Types of Nursing Homes. Although only 5 percent of Americans older than sixty-five years of age reside in nursing homes at any given time, more than 20 percent of those age eighty-five and older do so. Approximately 30 percent of the elderly will spend at least some time in a facility. The needs of patients differ greatly. Some patients need only minimal care, while 500,000 older patients must be tied to a bed or chair each day. In the United States, federal and state regulations provide broad standards for three types of nursing homes, which differ according to the characteristics of patients and services.

The first type, known as residential care facilities (RCFs), emphasizes nonmedical services such as assistance in daily tasks, sheltered living, and the preparing and serving of meals. Most of the residents of RCFs do not suffer from seriously debilitating illnesses, but they are no longer able to manage their daily chores. For example, they sometimes find it necessary to have help in dressing themselves, or they might not be able to handle their personal finances. Since the residents do not usually require much medical attention, physicians only visit such homes to do routine examinations or when there is an unexpected emergency. RCFs are much less expensive to operate than the other two types of nursing homes.

The second type of nursing home, intermediate care facilities (ICFs), also provides basic and regular nursing services but not twenty-four-hour care. Most of the men and women in ICFs suffer from long-term illnesses, but they generally do not require intensive medication. In ICFs registered nurses direct day-to-day nursing programs, but physicians also make visits on a regular basis. ICFs commonly provide recreational activities, physical therapy, speech therapy, and social-work services. Most facilities are certified for public funding.

The third type of nursing home, skilled nursing facilities (SNFs), provides twenty-four-hour services by registered nurses, licensed practical nurses, and nurses' aides. SNFs provide extensive therapy programs as well as diagnostic, medication, and laboratory services. Such institutions are supervised by a licensed medical director, and physicians visit the homes frequently. Care at SNFs is expensive and is appropriate only for persons who are in need of intensive nursing services. Such facilities normally have transfer arrangements with hospitals, ICFs, and other health care institutions. When patients need more extensive medical services, they are temporarily transferred to hospitals, and if their health improves, they are transferred to ICFs. A few SNFs rely on private funding, but the vast majority must be certified to participate in Medicare and Medicaid, the two main governmental programs for medical treatment

Costs and Financing. Although nursing homes are less expensive than hospitals, the cost of occupying a nursing home bed in 1997 started at a minimum of $25,000 a year, and some skilled nursing facilities charged as much as $75,000 a year. Estimates of nursing home care in the United

States for 1996 reached $70 billion. About 60 percent of these expenses are paid by Medicare and Medicaid. Medicare, the nation's health-insurance system for the elderly, pays for a maximum of one hundred days of nursing care for each benefit period. Medicaid pays for long-term care, but persons must own very little property in order to be eligible. Nursing homes prefer patients on Medicare, which pays considerably more than Medicaid.

A long stay in a nursing home commonly means financial ruin for all but the wealthiest of residents. Only a small percentage of the elderly have private nursing-care insurance, which is extremely expensive. A common strategy is for the elderly to "spend-down" their assets in order to qualify for Medicaid. It is illegal for parents to give assets to their children with the intention of qualifying for Medicaid, but all states allow spouses to keep a minimum of assets, which varies from state to state. Sometimes elderly persons commit suicide rather than allow nursing home costs to impoverish their spouses.

Costs increase faster than inflation for several

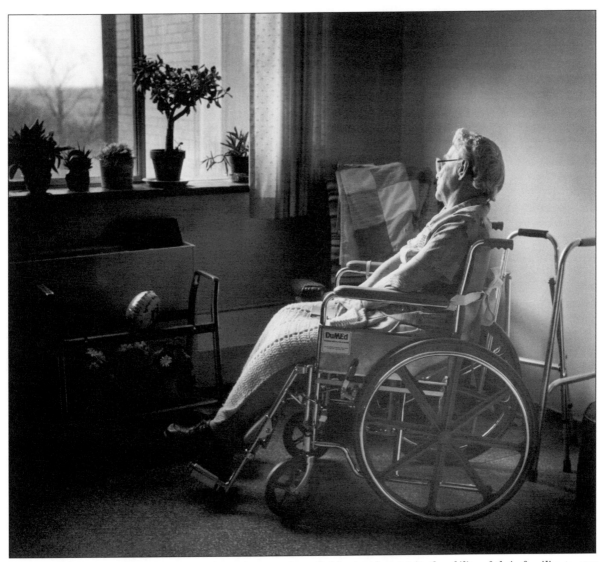

The disabilities and medical problems of growing numbers of older people outstrip the ability of their families to care for them, making it necessary for them to live in nursing homes. (James L. Shaffer)

Nursing and convalescent homes provide more satisfactory environments when residents can give them familiar touches of home. (James L. Shaffer)

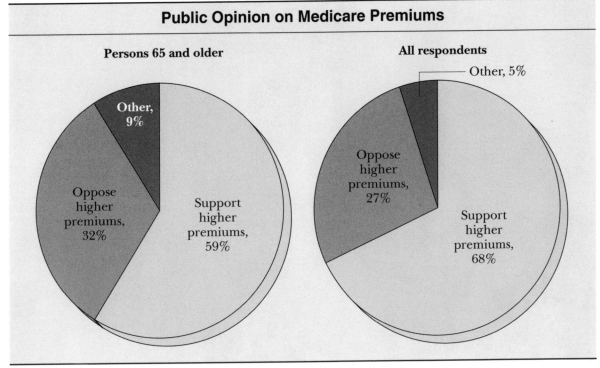

Public Opinion on Medicare Premiums

Persons 65 and older

Other, 9%

Oppose higher premiums, 32%

Support higher premiums, 59%

All respondents

Other, 5%

Oppose higher premiums, 27%

Support higher premiums, 68%

Source: Los Angeles Times (Sept., 1997)
Note: In September, 1997, the *Los Angeles Times* asked more than 1,250 adults nationwide whether they would support raising Medicare premiums for the more affluent as a way to keep Medicare solvent in the future. These charts summarize the responses.

reasons. The very old—those older than eighty-five years of age who have the most health problems—are the fastest growing component of the U.S. population. Federal and state regulations require higher-quality medical care in nursing homes, and fewer families seem to be willing and able to take care of the frail elderly. Moreover, the elderly increasingly promote their interests in political organizations such as the American Association of Retired Persons (AARP).

In Canada, all citizens have the advantage of national health insurance for medically necessary services under the Canada Health Act. This means that nursing care is considered more of an entitlement than is true in the United States, and access is not as dependent on persons' ability to pay. The elderly pay about the same percentage of their income for health care as do other Canadians, but they use the services more frequently. The health care system pays for the medical costs of residents in long-term care facilities, but residents are usually charged a per diem fee for shelter and food.

The programs are administered by the provinces with contributions by Canada's federal government.

Quality of Care. There have long been concerns about the quality of nursing home care. Until the 1960's there were few regulations in the United States, and many frail elders resided in private homes, in which there were widespread allegations of financial abuses, fire hazards, and mistreatment of patients. The Social Security Act of 1965 established federal standards with eligibility requirements for receiving Medicare and Medicaid reimbursements. Nevertheless, a study conducted by the Institute of Medicine (IOM) in 1986 concluded that care in most homes was poor and that regulations were inadequate. The following year Congress accepted most of the IOM recommendations in the landmark Nursing Home Reform Law, which was part of the Omnibus Budget Reconciliation Act (OBRA '87). Because of their complexity and expense, many of the regulations did not go into effect until 1995.

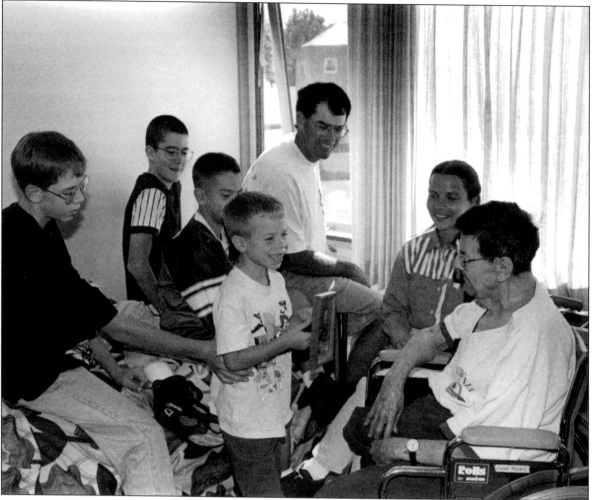

One of the greatest fears of older persons moving into nursing homes is that they will be ignored and forgotten by their families. (James L. Shaffer)

OBRA '87 requires that nursing homes have adequate professional staffing and provide services and activities that attain "the highest practicable physical, mental, and psychosocial well-being." Emphasis is on the rights of patients. When entering nursing homes, residents are to be given a comprehensive assessment of their physical and mental condition. This information is then used to develop a plan of care, which is reviewed four times a year. OBRA '87 attempted to protect residents from abuse and unnecessary physical restraints, and it guaranteed the right of residents or family members to participate in medical decisions.

Although OBRA '87 did much to improve the quality of care, it also added enormously to costs and contributed to a shortage of beds in some areas. Nurses, physicians, and other providers often complained about the great time and effort involved in keeping records for the required documentation. In spite of federal and state regulations, there will always be concerns about the quality of nursing home care, especially for poor patients who must depend on Medicaid.

Family members of impaired elders are often called upon to help in arranging nursing home placement, and they often have difficulty in finding high-quality homes that are affordable. To minimize unpleasant surprises, experienced persons recommend that family members visit facilities before deciding on placement. To obtain information about the nursing homes in particular regions, one may consult the Area Agency on Aging (AAA), a public or private nonprofit agency designated by states to oversee services for older Americans. The regional AAA is usually listed in the telephone directory. —*Thomas T. Lewis*

BIBLIOGRAPHY

Dow, Marion Merrell. *Managed Care Digest: Long-Term Care Edition.* Kansas City, Mo.: Author, 1992.

Gillick, Muriel. *Choosing Medical Care in Old Age.* Cambridge, Mass.: Harvard University Press, 1994.

Harper, Mary, ed. *Management and Care of the Elderly: Psychosocial Perspectives.* London: Sage Publications, 1991.

Horne, Jo. *The Nursing Home Handbook: A Guide for Families.* Washington, D.C.: MRP Books, 1989.

Kane, Robert, and Rosalie Kane. *A Will and a Way: What the United States Can Learn from Canada About Caring for the Elderly.* New York: Columbia University Press, 1985.

Ouslander, J., et al. *Medical Care in the Nursing Home.* New York: McGraw-Hill, 1991.

Pynoos, Jon, and Phoebe Liebig. *Housing Frail Elders: International Policies, Perspectives and Prospects.* Baltimore: The Johns Hopkins University Press, 1995.

See also Aging and elderly care; Earned income tax credit; Elder abuse; Family life cycle; Gender longevity; Health problems; Home sharing; Older Americans Act (OAA); Retirement; Retirement communities; Senior citizen centers; Social Security; Welfare.

Older Americans Act (OAA)

DATE: Enacted on July 14, 1965
RELEVANT ISSUES: Aging; Law
SIGNIFICANCE: As the legal basis for most services for older adults, the Older Americans Act of 1965 continues to evolve in order to meet the needs of this population segment

The Older Americans Act of 1965 was the result of the growing realization that people were living longer and that the number of older Americans was rapidly increasing. Enacted after the 1950 and 1961 National Conferences on Aging, the Older Americans Act called for a broad range of services similar to those being enacted for children and low-income families. Many federal assistance pro-

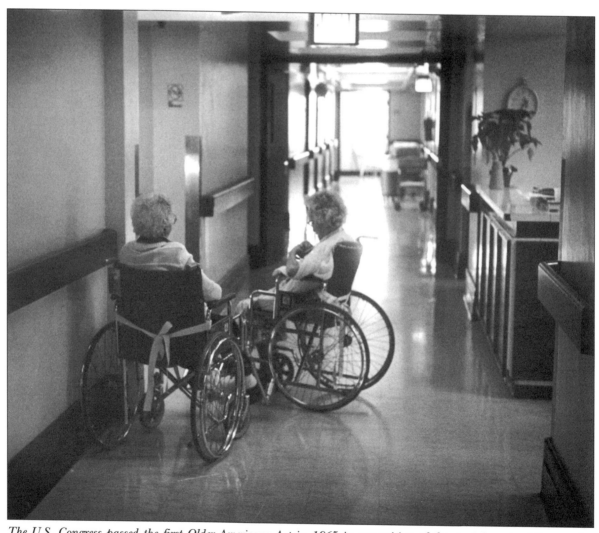

The U.S. Congress passed the first Older Americans Act in 1965 in recognition of the special needs of the growing numbers of older people. (James L. Shaffer)

grams were being initiated. Originally, the 1965 act encompassed ten sweeping objectives that have been modified progressively with amendments. Important results of the act include the establishment of the Administration on Aging; the development of a framework for a range of services, including transportation, crime prevention, nutrition programs, and senior centers; programs for training and research; and community employment opportunities. The intent of the act is to safeguard older adults' independence and ensure that they remain part of mainstream society.

Although most older Americans live alone, their ability to successfully do so declines as their health declines. The Older Americans Act does not replace the family as a supportive entity but rather eases family caregiving responsibility as the need for assistance in self-care increases. While continuing to support the original range of services, the act has changed to meet the needs of elderly persons, focusing on elder rights and on the needs of older women and minority elders.

—*Karen Chapman-Novakofski*

See also Aging and elderly care; Elder abuse; Nursing and convalescent homes; Retirement; Senior citizen centers.

Only children

RELEVANT ISSUES: Children and child development; Parenting and family relationships

SIGNIFICANCE: The prevalence of only children is increasing, and negative stereotypes about only children are diminishing as birthrates fall and the one-child family gains societal approval

The number of one-child families in the United States has varied with changing birthrates. From 1920 to 1940, a period of declining birthrates, the proportion of women having one child rose from 20 to 30 percent. The baby boom following World War II produced a decline in single-child families to only 15 percent of all families.

With changing childbearing attitudes, increased marital instability, greater availability of reliable birth control, and increased employment of women outside the home, the average family size has declined since the 1960's. In the mid-1990's, about 20 percent of families in the developed world had only one child, and population experts predict the proportion to grow through the early twenty-first century to perhaps as high as 30 percent in the United States.

Reality of Families with Only Children. Social, economic, and normative factors influence family size. During most of the twentieth century, families with between two and four children were considered typical, and the single-child family has long been viewed as abnormal. Child development experts and popular opinion believed that children need siblings for proper social and personal development. Only children were labeled "problem children" who were egotistical, selfish, lonely, spoiled, and antisocial.

Negative attitudes about only children persisted through the mid-1970's, when the term "onlyism" emerged to illustrate the prejudice against and negative stereotypes about children without siblings. Even in the 1990's, parents frequently stated that they wanted a second child to avoid having an only child.

Studies on family size and birth order conclude that childhood experiences shape enduring personality characteristics and behavior patterns. Common sense and many social psychological theories suggest that there should be differences between only children and children with siblings. Children without siblings receive more parental attention and financial resources than children with them. The single child must meet all parental expectations that otherwise would be shared among siblings. In addition, only children need to go outside the home to find peer companionship. Empirical research has found that only children and children with siblings differ less than expected. Popular notions of the maladjusted only child are not supported by scientific evidence.

Family Environment. Society has viewed the single-child family as providing an environment that deprives the child of critical learning experiences because of the lack of siblings. This environment also is said to lead to the overindulgence and overprotectiveness of the child.

The environment of an intact single-child family, however, also offers advantages to the child. Only children tend to have older mothers who have delayed childbearing, and these mothers may be more settled and stable, as well as more prepared psychologically for the burdens of motherhood. Parents of only children usually have been married longer and are more financially stable. Only children live disproportionately in the upper-middle and upper classes. Their parents usually are college graduates, and only children often are part of a dual-career family in which both the father and mother work outside the home. Single-child families tend to be egalitarian, with a nontraditional household division of labor.

Only children receive large amounts of parental attention and report more positive parental interactions than children with siblings. Only children are socialized early and rapidly into adult-oriented households that allow the children opportunities to mature and grow. Parents of only children set high standards for their child, and only children primarily have adult models for behavior within the family environment, rather than siblings who might model inappropriate behavior.

Some one-child families are the result of marital disruption or birth out of wedlock. Only children are almost twice as likely as those with siblings to come from a single-parent home. Some only children may be disadvantaged because of lower socioeconomic status, more prevalent in single-parent families.

Personal Development. The most consistent differences between children without siblings and those with them lie in intelligence and achievement. Overall, the smaller the family, the higher the intelligence scores of the children. Only children score higher on tests of intelligence than children with siblings, except for firstborn children from two-child families. This discontinuity in intelligence scores can be explained by the sibling tutoring hypothesis: Older siblings tutor younger ones, and through teaching, they enhance their own intelligence. Because only children lack younger siblings to tutor, they lag behind oldest siblings in a two-child family in intellectual development.

Only children also show high achievement motivation, particularly in comparison to children from larger families. Only children express more interest in white-collar, professional, and scientific occupations. More than children with siblings, only children state occupational plans for careers in the physical or natural sciences, mathematics, and computer science. Only children receive better grades, earn a disproportionate number of advanced degrees, and appear more frequently on

the cover of *Time* magazine and among *Who's Who* entries when compared to children with siblings.

The achievement levels of only children can be attributed in part to their status as only children. Theories suggest that the substantial parental attention and encouragement that a single child receives instills high achievement motivation. Achievement also results from higher socioeconomic status and greater opportunity for education, factors found in smaller families.

Sense of Self and Interpersonal Skills. Societal myths suggest that only children lack interpersonal skills. Specifically, only children are viewed as being lonely, selfish, and lacking social skills. These myths, however, appear unfounded. No relationship exists between loneliness and number of siblings. Single children lack interaction with siblings, but parents make more efforts to provide companionship for them through the use of play dates, summer camp, and other group activities such as athletics and scouting.

Only children, however, do seem more independent and self-reliant. They belong to fewer organizations, report lower numbers of friends, and visit friends and relatives less often than children with siblings. Only children spend more time by themselves and engage in more solitary activities such as reading than do children with siblings, but they report feeling no less popular or happy than their peers with siblings. Only in times of stress do single children report a high need for affiliation with others, possibly because of the intense parental attention they typically receive.

In general, children without siblings are less selfish than those with them. Some child development experts contend that siblings actually inhibit sharing. They suggest that selfishness results from lack of personal possessions. Because only children often possess sufficient material items to call their own, they do not mind temporarily sharing with others. Furthermore, when working on group tasks, only children are more trusting and cooperative than those with siblings.

Lack of siblings has little effect on self-esteem. Only children and children with siblings report no difference in the global appreciation of self. Only children, however, have a strong sense of personal control when compared to children with siblings. They believe they can control their destinies and take individual responsibility for the con-

Once looked upon with suspicion, one-child families have gained more widespread approval as birthrates have fallen and the public has increasingly appreciated the value of limiting population growth. (James L. Shaffer)

sequences of their actions. Because of the adult environment in which they are raised, only children are more cultured, mature, and socially sensitive than those with siblings. Single children possess good social skills and are popular with their peers. Lack of siblings does not restrict the social skills of only children, as once thought.

Only Children as Adults. Most studies of only children have been conducted on children and adolescents, but the limited research on only children as adults suggests that they have slightly more success socially, hold more prestigious jobs, and marry better-educated spouses than children raised with siblings. Only children marry at similar ages as children with siblings, but they want and have fewer children. Women raised without siblings are particularly likely to delay having children so that they can establish a career. Furthermore, consistent with their behavior as children and adolescents, single children as adults report spending less time with friends but experiencing more pleasure in life than those from larger families.

Only children are not disadvantaged in society. A single-child family offers a family environment in which the child does not interact with siblings but receives much parental attention. Most differences between only children and those with siblings are trivial. The one-child family has gradually gained societal approval, and some researchers suggest it will be the family of the future. Having one child allows a couple to experience parenting and still have time for personal growth and development.

—*Barbara E. Johnson*

BIBLIOGRAPHY
Falbo, Toni. *The Single Child Family.* New York: Guilford Press, 1984.
Falbo, Toni, and Denise F. Polit. "Quantitative Review of the Only Child Literature: Research Evidence and Theory Development." *Psychological Bulletin* 100 (1986).
Rosenberg, B. G., and Janet Shibley Hyde. "The Only Child: Is There Only One Kind of Only?" *Journal of Genetic Psychology* 154 (1993).
Sifford, Darrell. *The Only Child: Being One, Loving One, Understanding One, Raising One.* New York: Viking Press, 1990.

See also Alternative family types; Birth order; Child rearing; Childlessness; Family demographics; Family size; Imaginary friends; Nuclear family; Reproductive technologies.

Open marriage

RELEVANT ISSUES: Divorce; Marriage and dating
SIGNIFICANCE: At a time when liberalized divorce laws and a popular desire for self-exploration and personal growth caused the divorce rate to soar, discussion arose about open and free rather than closed and restrictive marriage, a deeply personal and mutual commitment in a relationship that would not bind or restrict growth

The term "open marriage" originated in the 1972 book *Open Marriage: A New Lifestyle for Couples* by the husband-and-wife anthropology team of George and Nena O'Neill. They defined open marriage as an honest and open relationship based on freedom, equality, honest communication, trust, and personal growth. They conceived of a form of marriage in which both partners have some separate interests, activities, and friends, a view that contradicted the postwar concept of "togetherness," in which married couples always appeared together as couples, had friends in common (usually other couples), pooled finances, shared vacations, and shared as many activities as possible. The goal of such marriage was to reinforce bonding.

The O'Neills believed that open marriage could resolve the conflict between relatedness and freedom in marriage and make relationships more interesting and stimulating, so that couples could continually renew their marriages. The O'Neills did not advocate extramarital sexual relations, but rather accepted the possibility of such sexual relations as an option in the context of loving, trusting, nonpossessive relationships in which partners enjoyed freedom, equality, and a strong sense of identity.

—*William L. Reinshagen*

See also Adultery; Bonding and attachment; Gray, John; Group marriage; Marriage; Sexual revolution; Sexuality and sexual taboos.

Orphans

RELEVANT ISSUES: Children and child development; Parenting and family relationships

SIGNIFICANCE: Until public assistance programs and foster care superseded them, orphanages were the most widely used institution for the care of children who were unable to live with their parents

Orphanages were the most widely used form of child care for thousands of children from the 1830's to the Great Depression of the 1930's. Their mission was usually to clothe, house, and educate children within a specific moral and religious code. Orphanages cared for children until they could be apprenticed or indentured to individuals or families or until they could be returned to their own homes. Foster homes and financial aid to families largely superseded asylums after the 1930's. Late in the twentieth century the simultaneous epidemics of drugs, violence, and acquired immunodeficiency syndrome (AIDS) sparked a renewed interest in orphanages.

The raising of children in orphanages has a long and not widely known history. Orphan asylums cared for children who had lost both parents. They also cared for children who had lost one parent through death and children whose parents were unable to care for them because of illness, unemployment, poverty, and desertion. Many managers of orphanages believed it was their duty to help poor families survive harsh times by temporarily caring for their children. Orphanages, in their view, helped break the cycles of poverty, neglect, and abuse for many children. Direct parental placements were the main source of children for orphanages, especially in the nineteenth century. However, courts, government officials, and charities brought their share of children to orphanages. Parents often approached these institutions and asked them to take care of their children. Abused and neglected children were taken away from their parents and placed in orphanages.

Critics, especially from the 1890's on, attacked orphanages as overcrowded, regimented, sparse, impersonal, and dehumanizing institutions. Large asylums offered children little chance of developing strong relationships with parental figures. Opponents also accused orphanages of allowing undeserving parents to shirk their parental duties by having strangers care for their children. Orphanages came in all sizes. In 1880, the median-size

orphanage held 42 children. About one-fourth held fewer than 30 children. In 1923 approximately 18 percent of the residents of orphanages, or 25,350 children, lived in large institutions holding 250 to 1,500 children or more. The New York Catholic Protectory, for example, once housed 2,000 children.

Orphanages returned most children to their parents or placed them in other homes within two years of their admission. Some children, however, remained in orphanages for many years because of the difficulties of finding good foster and adoptive parents. Because most private institutions lacked the right to place children elsewhere without parental permission, most half-orphans—children with one living parent and the majority of children living in asylums—remained there until their parent or parents could afford to reclaim them or until they came of age.

The First U.S. Orphanages. Ursuline nuns established the first orphanage in French New Orleans in 1729. The nuns cared for their first orphan in 1727 but established an orphanage following Indian attacks two years later. Protestant churches and groups managed most of the orphanages built before 1830. Roman Catholic and Protestant churches founded most of the orphanages begun in the 1830's. Nuns founded orphanages to educate poor children, to care for the ill, and to stop Roman Catholic orphans from growing up in Protestant households or institutions. Roman Catholic, Protestant, and Jewish orphanages all accepted mostly children of their own faith, with the express intention of preserving the faith.

Industrialization, urbanization, and immigration spurred the growth of orphanages and alternative forms of child care. In 1853 Charles Loring Brace, who founded the New York Children's Aid Society, advocated placing children in rural homes in the West rather than in institutions. He sent thousands of children on "orphan trains" to live in rural areas, usually with Protestant farmers. Brace and other reformers idealized rural America and feared urban growth. Between 1853 and 1930 approximately 150,000 children were placed with families for foster care and adoption.

Missionary zeal, urban growth, and an increased emphasis on children's environment and development also contributed to the growth of orphan-

Overcrowding and other problems in orphanages caused the social welfare system to look to other systems of care for parentless children after the 1930's. (Library of Congress)

ages. Asylums worked hard to turn children into good, working-class adults with Roman Catholic, Jewish, or Protestant and middle-class values. Asylums were also founded to cope with children who had been orphaned by epidemics of cholera, yellow fever, and other diseases.

After the Civil War ended in 1865, orphanages multiplied because of industrialization and the increased poverty it brought to cities. Citizens consumed by the fear that poor but innocent children would mix with adult paupers and criminals in almshouses founded orphanages. Most asylum residents after the Civil War were half-orphans, but many had two parents. The number of orphanages more than tripled between the Civil War and 1890, when almost half of the nearly 50,000 children in orphanages lived in Roman Catholic asylums. The other orphans lived in public, Protestant, Jewish, and fraternal facilities, including those run by Freemasons.

By the late nineteenth century, children were increasingly viewed as emotional rather than economic assets for families. Reformers condemned orphanages because children who remained there for years often lacked creativity and were unable to live normal family lives. Because orphanages received public money, reformers demanded more state regulation of orphanages. They also believed that the public was responsible for dependent children. Cases of abuse or neglect within orphanages often spurred calls for official oversight.

Replacing the Orphanage. Besides the belief that children should be raised in homes rather than institutions, orphanages declined as professional social workers came to dominate welfare reform by the 1920's. Social workers favored an individual, family-based approach. Foster care and public assistance to help mothers keep their children supplanted orphan asylums as the most common method of caring for dependent children in the 1930's. Many orphanages responded to these developments by transforming themselves into foster care and adoption agencies or homes for troubled children. Social workers and public officials considered carefully selected, loving foster homes to be superior to institutions.

Restrictions on immigration in the 1920's also diminished the need for ethnic and religious orphanages. Advances in medical science meant that fewer parents died during epidemics and that fewer children became orphans.

From the 1930's on the children's welfare system used both foster care and other institutions to maintain children in, or return them to, their own homes. Mothers' pensions allowed many families to survive without charity or public agencies and to keep children in their homes. During the New Deal of the 1930's, the Aid to Dependent Children program replaced mothers' pensions and was the backbone of the effort to keep children at home. Public assistance, Social Security, and the development of welfare programs enabled most orphans to remain at home with either a parent or relatives.

Proposals to revive orphanages surfaced in the 1990's. Proponents argued that orphanages were necessary because of the growing number of children born to teenage mothers, the increasing number of children in foster care, and the ending of support for unwed mothers. The number of licensed foster family homes was declining, while the number of children in the foster care system was rising. Still others contended that keeping children in their biological families no matter what is contrary to the best interests of the children. Some children, they argued, would be better off in institutions.

Debates over dependent children showed that orphanages and foster homes suffered from the same problems—inadequate resources, under-staffing, the great numbers of children in need, and insufficient bonding between adults and children. Critics have claimed that neither foster care nor orphanages attempted to deal with the underlying causes of poverty. They only cared for the children, not the factors that contributed to their being placed in foster care or orphanages. Supporters of orphanages have argued that thousands of children called orphanages a home away from home. For such children, orphanages were a place of refuge. For people concerned about the welfare of children in need, orphanages were a problem-solving tool.

—*Fred Buchstein*

BIBLIOGRAPHY

Bremner, R. H., ed. *Children and Youth in America: A Documentary History. Volume II: 1866-1932* (Parts 1-6). Cambridge, Mass.: Harvard University Press, 1971.

Hiner, N. Ray, and Joseph M. Hawes, eds. *Growing Up in America: Children in Historical Perspective.* Urbana: University of Illinois Press, 1985.

Holt, M. I. *The Orphan Trains: Placing-out in America.* Lincoln: University of Nebraska Press, 1992.

Smith, Eve P., and Lisa A. Merkel-Holguin. *A History of Child Welfare.* New Brunswick, N.J.: Transaction Publishers, 1996.

Zmora, Nurith. *Orphanages Reconsidered—Child Care Institutions in Progressive Era Baltimore.* Philadelphia: Temple University Press, 1994.

See also Adoption issues; Adoption processes; Aid to Families with Dependent Children (AFDC); Child abandonment; Child care; Childhood history; Death; Family: concept and history; Foster homes; *In loco parentis*; Institutional families; Juvenile courts; Social workers; Substitute caregivers.

Pacific Islanders

RELEVANT ISSUES: Demographics; Parenting and family relationships; Race and ethnicity

SIGNIFICANCE: The structure of traditional Pacific Islander families has been considerably altered as a result of the influx of Western influences

The various differences among the Pacific Islanders make it extremely difficult to construct any generalizations about their family life. Precolonial island societies exhibited a preference for an extended kinship group rather than a traditional nuclear family. Operating within a communal system that emphasized the importance of shared responsibilities, including an obligation to care for the elderly, provide financial aid to needy family members, and provide mutual assistance with housing and child-care needs, Pacific Islanders were the beneficiaries of a strong family support system. However, with the advent of Western colonialism, followed by urbanization and modernization in the nineteenth and twentieth centuries, the number of native islanders has dropped significantly and the traditional values system has experienced a transformation that has ultimately led to a breakdown in traditional family life in the Pacific Islands.

Traditional Hawaiian and Polynesian Family Structure. Prior to widespread Western contact in the nineteenth century, Hawaiian family life revealed a hallowed respect for every member of the extended kinship group. Concern for social cooperation and harmony guided household affairs, and Hawaiians displayed a large degree of respect for the elderly. Family tasks were shared, and every member was free to fish, plant, and associate with other households.

Since Hawaiians viewed women as the source of all life, mothers benefited from a distinctive and venerated status position within the family. Marriages were often the result of an informal union between partners, and society permitted polygamy. Child-rearing responsibility was also shared between family members. During the first few years of children's lives, mothers and their relatives cared for children, but as the children reached adolescence a clearly delineated sexual division of labor unfolded. Mothers assumed responsibility for training their daughters while fathers controlled sons' social development. Children were expected to conform to the norms and values of the household, and rebellion was not tolerated. Parents, however, usually did not have to resort to physical punishment. Since discipline resulted in a significant blow to children's self-esteem, fear and verbal threats proved to be quite effective in Hawaiian families.

Although fathers served as the official heads of households, decision making was shared. Fathers called family meetings, offered suggestions, listened to advice from their wives and children, and, in the spirit of harmony, accepted input from all family members. As it was extremely important for Hawaiians to present a united front to the larger community, children enjoyed a level of respect often absent in Western families. Because of the influx of Western influences, formal territorial annexation by the United States in 1898, an overwhelming flood of foreign workers, high rates of intermarriage, and considerable movement of Hawaiians between the islands and the U.S. mainland, the traditional Polynesian family structure has virtually disappeared.

Samoa. In Samoan villages, the size of family households may vary from small nuclear units to larger groups of fifteen to twenty people who are often not even related. These families, however, are beneficiaries of a clearly defined kinship network. Although children have little contact with persons outside their parental households before the age of seven, as they enter adolescence they are free to roam and temporarily reside with various relatives. This opportunity tends to undermine parental authority and family discipline, but if a parent exercises abusive behavior, such as a father's unjustified beating of a daughter, the kinship group provides the child with a safe haven. Since human kindness represents the highest

The great diversity of Pacific Islander cultures renders generalizations about family life difficult to make. (James L. Shaffer)

good for Samoans, such acts of brutality are rare.

Family rank is determined by age, and the youngest child occupies the lowest status. Married couples usually live with either set of parents, but married women are not entitled to any more authority that older single women. Samoan families also adhere to a specific division of labor. Male heads of households, or matais, possess the highest rank and control all the important functions, including all economic pursuits and family feasts. The men are responsible for most of the cooking, and they control the building of canoes and fishnets. Women are required to do all the heavy agricultural work and the daily reef fishing for octopuses, crabs, jellyfish, and other animals. Young girls must draw and carry water back to their households and clean and care for oil and lamps.

There is a strict code of conduct for relatives of the opposite sex. Once children reach adolescence, they are forbidden to touch one another. They are not permitted to eat or sit together, and all sexual references are taboo. They cannot dance with one another, take unsupervised walks together, or participate in any small group activities. This applies to all relatives in the household who are within five years of age of one another. These restrictions are lifted, however, when they reach old age.

Tonga. During the initial stages of contact between the Tongans and persons from traditional Western European societies, family values among the former were considerably different and much more liberal than among the latter. While a gender hierarchy did exist in Tongan society, sexual attitudes and mores were more permissive, and women were allowed to engage in premarital sex without damaging their reputations. They could also exchange sexual favors with foreign traders for certain valuable commodities, such as cloth or building materials. In fact, relatives often arranged liaisons with Pacific travelers in order to obtain goods and services. The Tongans considered it to be an acceptable way of transacting business.

Although most marriages were arranged and influenced by families' desire to consolidate their power and improve their social rank, women retained a considerable amount of economic and personal freedom within the family structure. Marriages were viewed as a monogamous partnership with shared decision-making power, and if either party committed adultery, a divorce could be obtained without any social consequences whatsoever. Incidents of spousal abuse and rape were also rare. A chief's wife, however, was subjected to much more patriarchal control.

Women also received considerable help from their extended kinship network during the early stages of child care. Immediately following birth, mothers were secluded for one month, and other women from both sides of the family attended to their needs. Tongan culture also placed strong emphasis on breast-feeding. In order to prevent another pregnancy while nursing their children, women were required to abstain from sexual intercourse. After Western missionaries attempted to eliminate periods of abstinence during the late nineteenth century, Tongans complained that children should not be weaned until they could digest solid foods. While chiefly women were expected to provide most child care, lower-class women shared responsibilities with their husbands. With the increase of labor migration and urbanization in the twentieth century, however, women have been forced to accept full responsibility for child rearing.

While other Pacific Islander families share responsibility with members of an extended kinship group, Tongans consider it inappropriate for aunts, uncles, and other family members to discipline Tongan children. By the time males reach adolescence, they spend more time away from home and are expected to begin fishing and gardening. Females, on the other hand, remain at home until they are at least sixteen years old or until they marry. Despite the widespread permissive attitudes Tongans exhibit toward their children, incidents of rebelliousness and insubordination are low.

When punishment is required, mothers traditionally exact discipline. Fathers refuse to get involved unless the children display antisocial behavior such as rebelliousness, violent hostility, or open disrespect to others. Most problems remain small in nature, since mothers spend much of their time disciplining children for torn clothes or uncleanliness. Fathers are rarely involved in the daily management of family affairs, and with some exceptions household tasks are managed by mothers.

Tahiti. Tahitian parents desired large families. Pregnancies were considered a blessing, and childbirth was a highly anticipated event. Unlike in

Tonga, there were no postpartum taboos on sexual intercourse, and as soon as women were physically capable of conceiving, they attempted to have another child.

Mothers remained the primary caretakers of their children during the latters' early childhood. To avoid illness, babies were not taken outside until they were two months old. Parents ensured that babies had no contact with water and rubbed them consistently with coconut oil. Once children reached the age of five years old, however, both parents granted them considerable autonomy, beginning with a process of maternal distancing. Since older children and siblings were expected to serve as caretakers and teachers, most of children's learning occurred within their own peer groups. —Robert D. Ubriaco, Jr.

BIBLIOGRAPHY

Dodge, Ernest S. *Islands and Empires: Western Impact on the Pacific and East Asia.* Minneapolis: University of Minnesota Press, 1976.

Firth, Raymond. *We, the Tikopia: A Sociological Study of Kinship in Primitive Polynesia.* Reprint. Boston: Beacon Press, 1965.

Gailey, Christine Ward. *Kinship to Kingship: Gender Hierarchy and State Formation in the Tongan Islands.* Austin: University of Texas Press, 1987.

Levy, Robert I. *Tahitians: Mind and Experience in the Society Islands.* Chicago: University of Chicago Press, 1973.

Mead, Margaret. *Coming of Age in Samoa.* Reprint. New York: Morrow Quill Paperbacks, 1961.

Schmitt, Robert C. *Demographic Statistics of Hawaii: 1778-1965.* Honolulu: University of Hawaii Press, 1968.

See also Chinese Americans; Cultural influences; Extended families; Filipino Americans; Gender inequality; Japanese Americans; Kinship systems; Korean Americans; Mead, Margaret; Men's roles; Polygyny; Southeast Asian Americans; Vietnamese Americans; Women's roles.

Parallel cousins

RELEVANT ISSUES: Kinship and genealogy; Parenting and family relationships

SIGNIFICANCE: A unique kin relationship that accompanies cross-cousin terminology, parallel cousins are found in either patrilineal or matrilineal clans, in which men or women call certain cousins "brothers" or "sisters" and thus cannot normally marry them

Parallel cousins are usually found in societies that also classify cross cousins through bifurcate merging. Persons' parallel cousins are the children of their mother' sisters and their father's brothers. Some societies require that persons marry within their groups (endogamy) in order to maintain political and economic affiliations as well as social rights and obligations. In societies in which the so-called Hawaiian Kinship terminology or generational system exists, persons' cousins are all called either "brother" or "sister." That is, all relatives of the preceding generation are persons' "fathers" or "mothers," and their offspring are called "brothers" or "sisters." Since brothers and sisters are not permitted to marry, persons are forced to marry outside their respective kin groups. This form of exogamy tends to reinforce socioeconomic ties with other kin groups.

Marriage between parallel cousins is found in some patrilineal societies, particularly among the Bedouin and other Middle Eastern and North African tribes. These people not only permit but also often prefer parallel-cousin marriage. The preferred or prescribed form involves marriage between men and their father's brother's daughters. Patrilineal parallel-cousin marriage tends to keep males within the kin group, thereby creating male cadres by maintaining residence groups. —John Alan Ross

See also Clans; Cousins; Cross-cousins; Endogamy; Exogamy; Kinship systems; Lineage; Matrilineal descent; Muslims; Patrilineal descent; Tribes.

Parental divorce

RELEVANT ISSUES: Kinship and genealogy; Parenting and family relationships

SIGNIFICANCE: Whereas the termination of parental rights has historically not been initiated and decided by children, parental divorce presents children with the possibility of seeking such action on behalf of themselves

Parental divorce calls into consideration at least two related issues: children's rights and legal precedents in cases involving minors. The Florida cases of Gregory K. and Kimberly Mays drew national attention to the idea of parental divorce in the early 1990's. At that time, it was feared that the courts would be deluged with children wanting to divorce their parents. It would appear that those fears were unfounded. Information on "parental divorce" between 1993 and 1998 is limited.

Children's Rights. With the ratification of the compulsory education law by the last of the U.S. states in 1918 and the passage of the Fair Labor Standards Act of 1938, children were recognized as needing protection under the law. Since then, children's rights have been the subject of much international debate and policy. Perhaps the most far-reaching of the recent discussions are those that resulted in the United Nations Convention on the Rights of the Child. Beverly C. Edmonds and William R. Fernekes in *Children's Rights: A Reference Handbook* offer a thorough discussion of the Convention on the Rights of the Child, calling it "a watershed of 200 years of effort on their [children's] behalf." The convention uses three broad categories to characterize children's rights: protection, provision, and participation. Children's right to protection speaks to the need for specified safeguards for all children; the right to provision addresses the need to assure that children receive their rights and, when necessary, allocated funds; participation rights include the right of

Regardless of how children may feel about their parents, actions to terminate their relationships with their parents are almost always initiated by adults. (James L. Shaffer)

children to develop and to participate in society. The convention is relevant to the background of the issue of parental divorce, because it specifies that children have a right to express their own views and must be heard in matters affecting them (article 12).

Legal Precedents. Even though children were recognized as needing safeguards to guarantee their safety, legal proceedings had to be initiated on their behalf by someone else. Children were not perceived as having the reasoning ability to bring suits themselves. The termination of parental rights was initiated by agencies, as children were not seen as capable of making such a decision. In custody cases the courts were mandated to act in the best interests of children. However, court decisions were frequently in conflict with what children wanted. Children were not free to act on their own behalf nor were their preferences legally acknowledged. In many ways, rights for adults meant "freedom to" and rights for children meant "protection from."

In recognizing that neither the Fourteenth Amendment of the U.S. Constitution nor the Bill of Rights (the first ten amendments of the U.S. Constitution) were limited to adults, the U.S. Supreme Court in the case *In re Gault* (1967) narrowed how children were viewed. Thus, children were guaranteed the same rights to "equal protection of the law" as adults. With this case the door was opened to considering children as persons entitled to many of the same rights as adults.

Florida Cases. The Florida cases of Gregory K. and Kimberly Mays brought national attention to the issue of children requesting the termination of their biological parents' parental rights. While the media reported on these cases under headlines such as "Child Seeks Divorce from Parents," these children sought a termination of the parental rights of biological parents with whom they had not lived for an extended time.

In the case of twelve-year-old Gregory K. there was a history of abuse by his biological parents. Gregory K. won the right to file a suit on his own behalf to sever his parents' parental rights so that he could be adopted by the foster family with whom he was living. His suit was a last resort after the Florida Department of Health and Rehabilitative Services (HRS) failed to refer his case to the adoptions unit and to seek on his behalf the termi-

nation of parental rights. His parents were divorced, his father relinquished his parental rights, and Gregory had lived with his mother a total of seven months in the eight years prior to the filing of the suit. He had had no communication with her in the eighteen months prior to the filing of his petition with the Florida court system in the spring of 1992. The Circuit Court of Orange County, Florida, terminated his biological parents' parental rights and permitted Gregory K.'s foster family to adopt him. Gregory's biological mother, Rachel K., appealed the decisions.

Kimberly Mays was switched at birth with another infant and was raised by the Mays, the family she thought to be her biological family. In the meantime, the Twigg family raised a daughter they thought to be their biological child. Their daughter became ill and ultimately died at the age of nine. As the result of a blood test during their daughter's illness, the Twiggs learned that she was not their biological child. They sought and found Kimberly (who was by then fourteen years old) and filed suit to gain custody of her. Eventually, the Twiggs dropped their suit in exchange for visitation rights. Kimberly made five visits to the Twigg home. She was dissatisfied with the arrangement, her grades dropped, she was grounded and, after much conflict, the custody suit was revived. As Kimberly was familiar with the case of Gregory K., she contacted his foster father, a trial lawyer, and asked him to represent her in her petition to the court to intervene on her behalf in the Twiggs's custody suit. He did so.

Judgments in both cases were rendered on August 18, 1993. In Rachel K.'s appeal, the District Court of Appeal of Florida, Fifth District, let stand the termination of her parental rights to Gregory K. but reversed his adoption by his foster parents. The adoption was reversed on the grounds that termination and adoption proceedings should not have been tried simultaneously. On the same day, the Sarasota, Florida, County Circuit Court ruled that Kimberly Mays was a natural person under the constitution with standing to address the court. Evidence supported her plea, and the Twiggs' parental rights were terminated. However, Kimberly later chose to live with the Twiggs.

Implications. The cases of Gregory K. and Kimberly Mays are significant in that they raise important issues in the continuing discussions regarding parental and children's rights. While Gregory achieved his goal of having his biological parents' parental rights terminated, he succeeded not because of his own petition, but because concurrent petitions were filed by his natural father, his foster family, and the Florida HRS. In actuality, the court determined that because Gregory was a minor, he did not have the capacity to file on his behalf. The capacity of children to have the legal right to speak and act for themselves undoubtedly will continue to be an issue in discussions about children's legal rights and, thus, parental divorce.

In Kimberly Mays's case, the issue of psychological parents' rights versus natural parents' rights versus children's rights arose. Kimberly had a psychological bond with the Mayses, and at the time of the custody case she wanted to stay with Mr. Mays, the only father she had ever known (Mrs. Mays had died when Kimberly was two years old). The issue of psychological versus natural parents presents a three-pronged dilemma: the rights of persons with whom children have a psychological bond, the rights of persons with whom children have a biological bond, and the rights of children themselves. Discussions of parental divorce must address whose rights are to be served, especially in cases where neglect and abuse are not at issue.

Conclusion. Parental divorce is a relatively new concept in the long history of family relationships. It is intertwined with a number of related issues: the distinction between children and adults, children's capacity (ability) to render decisions regarding their lives, children's rights, parental rights, burden of proof, and adequate representation for children in court. C. J. Harris, one of the judges in Rachel K.'s appeal, stated well the fears of many when he wrote, "While the child has a right not to be abused, . . . there is no right to change parents simply because the child finds substitutes that he or she likes better or who can provide a better standard of living." In an article written by Georgia Sargeant in the October, 1993, issue of *Trial*, Jerri Blair, Gregory K.'s lawyer, expressed concern about children who do not have adults willing to "go to the mat for them." In the same article, Howard Davidson, head of the American Bar Association's Center on Children and the Law in Washington, D.C., was quoted as saying, "Traditionally, cases on care and custody are heard without zealous representation of the

children . . . [thus, it is] important . . . for states to ensure that child advocates are available, well trained and adequately paid." Until other issues are resolved, ensuring competent advocates for children offers a way for children to have a voice in matters related to their custody.

—*Carolyn S. Magnuson*

BIBLIOGRAPHY

Blair, Jerri A. "Gregory K. and Emerging Children's Rights." *Trial* 29 (June, 1993).

Edmonds, Beverly C., and William R. Fernekes. *Children's Rights: A Reference Handbook.* Santa Barbara, Calif.: ABC-Clio, 1996.

Goldstein, Joseph, Anna Freud, and Albert Solnit. *Beyond the Best Interests of the Child.* New York: Free Press, 1973.

Ladd, Rosalind E. *Children's Rights Re-Visioned: Philosophical Readings.* Belmont, Calif.: Wadsworth, 1996.

Purdy, Laura. *In Their Best Interest? The Case Against Equal Rights for Children.* Ithaca, N.Y.: Cornell University Press, 1992.

Sargeant, Georgia. "'Parental Divorce' Cases Highlight Need for Children's Advocates." *Trial* 29 (October, 1993).

See also Child custody; Childhood history; Children's rights; *In re Baby M*; *In re Gault*; United Nations Convention on the Rights of the Child.

Parental Kidnapping Prevention Act (PKPA)

DATE: Enacted on December 28, 1980

RELEVANT ISSUES: Divorce; Law

SIGNIFICANCE: Congress enacted the Parental Kidnapping Prevention Act (PKPA) to discourage drawn-out interstate custody battles and prevent parents from fleeing with their children to states with more sympathetic custody laws than their states of residence

According to the U.S. Department of Justice, approximately 350,000 children are abducted by family members each year in custody disputes. Revenge is often the motive, and nearly half of these cases involve concealment of the children, transportation of the children out of state, or the intention of keeping the children permanently.

Before 1968 noncustodial parents were able to take children out of state and get a new custody order, even if the children were wrongfully kept after visitation. Courts viewed custody orders as subject to modification, and the presence of the children in a different state, even if briefly, gave new courts jurisdiction. The Uniform Child Custody Jurisdiction Act (UCCJA) was drafted in 1968 to remedy the problem of conflicting state custody laws.

By 1980 only forty-three states had enacted the UCCJA, prompting Congress to institute a federal law. The PKPA applies to all interstate child-custody cases, requires all states to honor and enforce other states' custody and visitation decrees, and prevents other states from modifying already existing custody and visitation orders except under very limited circumstances. —*P. S. Ramsey*

See also Child abduction; Child custody; Family courts; Family law; Missing Children's Assistance Act; Uniform Child Custody Jurisdiction Act (UCCJA).

Parenting

RELEVANT ISSUES: Children and child development; Parenting and family relationships

SIGNIFICANCE: Successful parenting, a challenging but rewarding task, involves providing a safe and rich environment for children to gain experience and learn through emotional support and encouragement

Three methods of parenting have developed in Western culture: authoritarianism, permissiveness, and the authoritative approach. Authoritarianism combines high expectations and harsh punishment. In contrast, permissiveness, first advocated in modern times by the French enlightenment philosopher Jean-Jacques Rousseau in the eighteenth century, assumes that children are essentially good, complete, and natural. It is the harsh treatment and the contradictory rules of civilization that cause children to do evil. The remedy for this situation is to indulge children's desires and whims, thereby allowing infallible nature to guide them from within. One modern advocate of permissive parenting was the psychologist Carl Rogers, who advised parents to give their children unconditional positive regard, regardless of their behavior. This belief was popularized in the 1960's by practices such as hugging children after they hit someone or refraining from ever saying no.

Authoritative parenting emphasizes parents' role as teachers, mentors, and protectors of children. Authoritative parents typically reason with their children, encourage them to make choices and set their own goals, and emphasize affection and encouragement over punishment and obedience. Authoritative parenting is favored by most developmental psychologists and educators, in part because research has shown that child behavioral problems, school problems, and other poor life outcomes are highest for children whose parents have very high and rigid expectations and use frequent or harsh physical punishments and anger to discipline them. Parents who have reasonable expectations based on accurate knowledge of child development and who are affectionate, calm, and assertive have children with the fewest behavioral problems and the best life outcomes.

Special Parenting Needs of Infants and Toddlers. The physical needs of infants are daunting. Newborn infants must be fed, cleaned, and cuddled; they require interaction around the clock. Most newborns sleep nine to fourteen hours and cry one to three hours per day, and most awaken two or more times at night. Toward the middle of their first year, infants learn to scoot, roll, and crawl around. Once infants are mobile, parents must continually supervise them, because they can easily be injured by falling, choking on small objects, or encountering other hazards.

Parents must also meet the psychological needs of their infants. Although infants are probably born with different temperaments, parental sensitivity and responsiveness appear to have the greatest influence on children's long-term development. Parents can be sensitive and responsive by imitating their children's facial expressions, expanding on their vocalizations, responding quickly to their physical needs, engaging in vigorous play when they smile, and shifting to quieter activities when they look away or seem overwhelmed. Such responsiveness has a positive effect on intelligence and helps infants to learn language. Infants also learn how to influence the emotions and behavior of other people by communicating their emotions and needs.

Toddlers, children between the ages of twelve

and thirty-six months, learn to walk, speak, eat adult food, and use the toilet. The need for constant parental supervision increases during this time, as children become increasingly mobile but lack the life experience to act safely. The greatest number of injurious and fatal accidents during childhood occurs during the toddler stage. The skills that toddlers learn may seem basic, but in

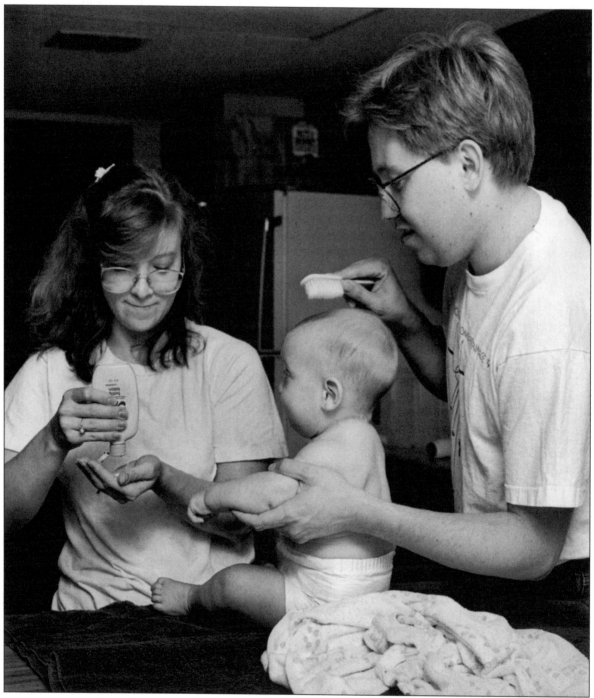

The physical needs of infants are daunting. (James L. Shaffer)

fact they are quite complex. For example, toddlers go from one-word utterances at twelve months of age to a vocabulary of several hundred words by age three. Learning so much so fast can be frustrating for both toddlers and their parents, and temper tantrums sometimes occur at this stage. Toddlers need constant supervision, safe places to explore, and sensitive parenting.

Secure and Insecure Attachment. The parent-child relationship continues to be most important for toddlers. Signs of attachment are first seen during the toddler years, although the foundation of the attachment relationship is built by parents' sensitivity and responsiveness during infancy. Most children have secure attachment relationships in which affection is frequent and conflict low. Most children seek out parents for comfort and reassurance, while parents are usually able to help their children calm down when they feel distress. Insecure attachment relationships, in which children seek out parents but are often angry, anxious, or hard to comfort, are less frequent than secure attachment relationships. Boys and all children in highly stressed families have the highest risk of insecure attachment.

Many instances of parental anger and frustration toward toddlers occur when parents expect children to perform beyond their level of ability or when the arrangement of the home conflicts with children's developmental needs. For example, toddlers develop their cognitive abilities by exploring their environment and by touching and moving objects. Because they do not grow very quickly at this stage, they are very active and fast, expending much physical energy in developing their new motor skills. If there are many fragile or dangerous objects within children's reach in the home, parents will spend much time fighting their childrens' natural and healthy tendency to move around and touch everything. Parents who expect their children to respect property or take care of

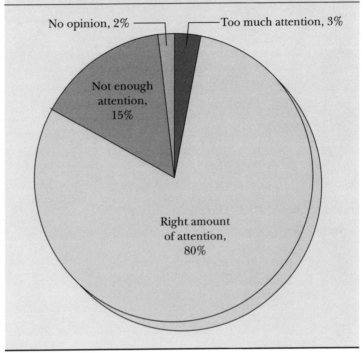

How Americans Feel About the Attention Their Parents Gave Them

No opinion, 2% — Too much attention, 3%

Not enough attention, 15%

Right amount of attention, 80%

Source: CNN/*USA Today*/Gallup Poll
Note: In 1994 a cross-section of Americans were asked how they felt about the amount of attention they received from their parents when they were growing up. This chart summarizes their responses.

valuable objects—concepts that are beyond toddlers' understanding—may be disappointed, even striking them in an attempt at discipline.

If parents arrange their homes so that their children can safely explore almost everything within reach, children will learn about objects and spatial relationships. This experience will eventually help them understand why certain objects can break and how to discriminate between nonfragile objects and those that must be treated with care. Once children are able to talk with their parents about rules—usually after they reach the age of three—they can then learn about respecting property without incurring their parents' anger or having to undergo physical punishment.

Preschoolers. Preschoolers, children between the ages of three and five, continue to need parental supervision and protection. They learn the rules of social interaction, concepts such as space, time, and quantity, and the meaning of abstract

Physical tasks of parenting lessen as children reach school age. (James L. Shaffer)

symbols such as pictures, shapes, numbers, and letters. They need challenges, opportunities to play, and time to interact with parents, other adults, and peers.

Because preschoolers have a better grasp of language than do toddlers, they are more able to remember, understand, and follow general rules. They tend to interpret rules from a more egocentric perspective than that of older children and adults, however. For example, young children may believe that it is "fair" for peers to let them play with peers' toys but "not fair" for them to have to let peers play with their own toys. Similarly, their understanding of the reasons behind rules is limited. When asked why it is forbidden to hit other children, for example, preschoolers are likely to say, "Because it is bad" or "Because it is the rule and you should follow rules."

Because preschoolers have limited understanding of reasons and abstract concepts, parents cannot rely solely on reasoning or explaining to obtain compliance. Parents must show preschoolers how rules operate by reacting positively when rules are followed and setting limits when they are not. Although affection should continue to be an everyday part of the parent-child relationship, children sometimes need extra encouragement when parents attempt to teach difficult lessons. Parents motivate their children by employing several techniques. Feedback, or simply telling children whether their behavior is good or not, can provide not only information but also motivation. If children are very eager to please their parents and the tasks at hand are not difficult, feedback alone may be enough to motivate them. Praising children for trying to do well and applauding their successes are even more motivating as long as the praise is sincere and enthusiastic.

Some parents give small treats or award special privileges to reward their children's good behavior. Because rewards make parents' pleasure clear, they can be especially effective with very young children or those with disabilities that make it hard for them to understand verbal praise and instructions. However, if material rewards are used too frequently at the expense of spending sufficient time showing children genuine affection, they may lose their effect or even exacerbate children's negative behavior. Rewards are most effective when they are small, immediate, personal, and

surprising. The least effective way to use rewards is to promise them in advance of very large and difficult tasks. A good rule of thumb is to remember that large rewards promised in advance are like bribes that will undermine children's desire to learn for the sole sake of emotional satisfaction. Surprise rewards, especially those that have personal meaning and are shared by parents and children alike, strengthen the parent-child relationship and motivate children to learn.

School-Age Children. School-age children are in many ways easier to care for than are toddlers or preschoolers. They spend much of the day outside the home; they are more independent and less demanding. School-age children still need time with parents. Parents are less often needed for help with daily life activities, companionship, and self-regulation, and are more often needed as role models and sources of advice. Although peers become an increasingly important part of children's life at this stage, most children want to spend as much time as possible with their parents and other adults in the family throughout middle childhood.

Modeling, or teaching by example, is one of the most important parenting techniques for this age group. Modeling is effective because children are naturally inclined to imitate adults as long as the parent-child relationship is positive and secure. Another effective technique for school-aged children is to prepare them in advance of situations by discussing expectations and the reasons for good behavior. If children actively participate in these discussions by offering their own ideas and examples, they learn how to make decisions and control their own behavior. The more freedom children have to make choices and develop their own rationales for good behavior, the more likely it is

A Month for Parents

In order to encourage parents to incorporate more purpose in their parenting, Parents Without Pressure sponsors National Purposeful Parenting Month every July. The organization's goal for this annual event is to help parents become effective as parents by helping them increase their awareness of their tasks and by providing them with specific guidance.

Parents can help their children succeed in school by taking an active interest in their progress and rewarding them with their approval. (James L. Shaffer)

that they will follow through when parents are not present to help them. For safety's sake, parents should also set the limits within which children can make choices and select the challenges that children have to face alone.

Parents and Adolescents. Adolescents develop adult characteristics such as sexual maturity and physical strength before they have the life experi-

ence, economic independence, or legal right to use them with the same freedom adults enjoy. As during the toddler years, the challenges posed by new abilities often lead to frustration. Adolescents still see their parents as sources of inspiration and support. Unlike younger children, however, they also evaluate parental choices according to their own standards. This evaluation is an important part of adolescents' search for a future adult identity, but it can cause family stress and conflict.

Adolescents' moral reasoning and judgments about other people tend to be more extreme and clear-cut than those of adults. Such all-or-none thinking often leads to intense conflicts with parents, but it is both necessary and understandable. All-or-none thinking is necessary because it helps adolescents to deal with the many new situations they confront every day. If they can follow a clear set of abstract principles such as "I support my friends no matter what the consequences," adolescents find it much easier to decide with whom to associate, when to become sexually active, and whether to imitate parents or peers. Adolescents are capable of understanding these abstract principles, but they lack the life experience that makes their parents more accepting of exceptions to rules, negotiation, compromise, contradictory ideas, and personal shortcomings.

In the film Parenthood *(1989) actor Jason Robards, playing Steve Martin's father, makes the painful discovery that parental responsibility does not end when one's children become adults.* (Museum of Modern Art, Film Stills Archive)

Adolescents require less supervision than other age groups, but they still need time with adults. This age group has the second highest accident rate during childhood and the highest murder and suicide rate. Adolescents need safe places to socialize with peers and opportunities to participate in major decisions that affect them.

Special Parenting Problems. Sometimes parents' ability to care for children is compromised, which may lead to abuse, neglect, family violence, or harsh parenting. These problems place children at risk of long-term developmental and mental-health problems, although some children are resilient and go on to thrive in spite of negative experiences. Neglect, abuse, and harsh parenting all have pervasive effects on children's well-being. Harsh parenting includes rigid and unrealistic expectations, a belief that children's misbehavior is intentional, a high level of parental anger, and frequent verbal and physical punishment. Physical abuse is more common in families who also practice harsh parenting. Abuse, neglect, and harsh parenting are more likely in families suffering chronic stress from mental illness, substance abuse, or economic hardship.

Two factors contribute to children's resilience in the face of a harsh or abusive childhood. The first is intelligence, which can be promoted by early education and positive social interaction with adults. The second is consistent help and support from adults other than parents for most of childhood. Extended families and the community may play important roles. Parenting is difficult in the best of circumstances. When parents do not provide for their children's needs because of their own mental illness, inability to cope with stressful circumstances, poor health, or overwhelming economic and family problems, children can develop positively if they and their parents receive help.

—*Kathleen M. Zanolli*

BIBLIOGRAPHY

Brazelton, T. Berry. *To Listen to a Child: Understanding the Normal Problems of Growing Up.* Reading, Mass.: Addison-Wesley, 1984. Easy-to-understand, parent-friendly book providing many examples and anecdotes that discusses how parents and professionals can talk to children about social and emotional challenges and problems.

Curry, Nancy E. *Beyond Self-Esteem: Developing a Genuine Sense of Human Value.* Washington, D.C.: National Association for the Education of Young Children, 1990. Discusses relationships among self-esteem, positive child rearing, and children's later moral reasoning, relationships, and sense of justice.

Golant, Mitch, and Susan Golant. *Finding Time for Fathering.* New York: Columbine, 1992. Describes ways that fathers can spend more time with their children, including helping with household chores, involving children in work, and playing with them.

Gootman, Marilyn E. *The Loving Parents' Guide to Discipline.* New York: Berkeley, 1995. Emphasizes parent-child relationships based on mutual respect and understanding and encourages parents to plan for their children's discipline and to evaluate what works for them.

Hardyment, Christina. *Dream Babies: Three Centuries of Good Advice on Child Rearing.* New York: Harper and Row, 1988. Offers child-care advice from philosophers, clergy, doctors, nurses, mothers, social reformers, and psychologists from 1700 to the 1980's and examines the recurrent issues of harsh discipline versus permissiveness and natural versus scientific child rearing.

See also Child rearing; Child safety; Childhood fears and anxieties; Family caregiving; Fatherhood; Full nest; Motherhood; Single-parent families; Spock, Benjamin; Systematic Training for Effective Parenting (STEP); Time-out; Tough love.

Parents Anonymous (PA)

DATE: Founded in 1970

RELEVANT ISSUES: Children and child development; Parenting and family relationships; Violence

SIGNIFICANCE: Parents Anonymous is a nonprofit, national organization with two goals: stopping child abuse and developing parenting skills that strengthen and benefit the entire family

In 1970 Jolly K., an abusing mother undergoing therapy with Leonard Lieber, founded Parents Anonymous after becoming frustrated with existing agencies and organizations that failed to meet her needs. Jolly K. and Lieber enlisted three other abusing mothers who wanted help with their problems. The program grew as local counselors and clinicians heard about the work that parents were doing to help themselves. In 1971 Parents Anonymous formally organized as a nonprofit corporation in California. The organization's goals center on intervention and improvement of family dynamics, especially child discipline. Its goals include identification of abusive patterns, family treatment, and ultimate prevention of child abuse. Offices for Parents Anonymous exist in all states of the United States and in some Canadian provinces.

Membership is open to persons from all levels of society and includes representatives of most professions. All parents qualify for group therapy. Some parents attend as part of court-ordered family therapy. Others are referred by school counselors, social service organizations, ministers, and family therapists. Weekly group meetings usually last less than two hours, and everyone is encouraged to share and participate at some level. Trained volunteer group leaders focus discussions on achieving changes in personal parenting styles of communication and discipline. Group facilitators use a problem-solving format that seeks everyone's input during group sessions. Membership and the content of all meetings are confidential. The nonjudgmental attitudes of the group encourage parents to attend who might not otherwise seek help.

Free child care is provided for children in separate meetings while parents are involved in their own sessions. Children's group leaders use a structured program focusing on development of self-esteem and self-confidence. Children usually receive a snack and enjoy a program using books, puppets, stories, and toys that provide play therapy while parents learn positive parenting and leadership skills.

Parents Anonymous is funded through private and public sources that include individuals, corporations, state social-service agencies, and various state departments dedicated to the needs of families. Its services are free of cost to parents who attend meetings. Individual Parents Anonymous groups offer twenty-four-hour hotlines, and many organizations have crisis counselors available at all times.

Parents Anonymous groups first deal with present neglect and psychological, physical, verbal,

and sexual abuse of children. However, group leaders also address parents' past abuse of themselves. The goal is positive change by teaching parents how to break negative patterns of abusive behavior, choosing instead positive communication and discipline techniques that allow children and parents to maintain their dignity. Many parents use abusive styles of discipline learned from their parents. Under pressure, uninformed parents react by hitting, yelling, and nagging. Parents Anonymous provides parents with effective alternatives.   —*Thomas K. McKnight*

See also Child abuse; Child Abuse Prevention and Treatment Act (CAPTA); Community programs for children; Elder abuse; Family therapy; Family Violence Prevention and Services Act; Parenting; Support groups.

Parents Without Partners (PWP)

DATE: Founded in 1957

RELEVANT ISSUES: Divorce; Marriage and dating; Parenting and family relationships

SIGNIFICANCE: A nonprofit, educational support group, Parents Without Partners is dedicated to the welfare and interests of single parents and their children

Parents Without Partners (PWP) was founded in 1957 in New York City by two single parents: Jim Egleson, a noncustodial parent, and Jacqueline Bernard, a custodial parent. Although they were concerned and involved parents, they felt isolated from society because of their marital status. As a result, they decided to form a mutual support organization to address their unique needs. They placed notices in local newspapers directed at "parents without partners," which resulted in the attendance of twenty-five single parents at their first meeting in a Greenwich Village church basement. Some years later, attention from the national media brought inquiries from all over the country. In the 1990's PWP was an international, nonprofit membership organization headquartered in Chicago with more than five hundred chapters in the United States and Canada.

Parents Without Partners serves to provide single parents and their children with an opportunity to enhance personal growth, self-confidence, and sensitivity toward others by offering an environment for support and friendship and a forum for the exchange of parenting techniques. Although the majority of members are divorced or separated, the support group is open to single parents of all types, including custodial, noncustodial, widowed, and never-married parents. About 65 percent of the membership is female and 35 percent male, which may reflect either the greater ease with which women share personal problems or the reality that more women have primary custody than men and thus have the preponderance of day-to-day concerns regarding child rearing. Members range in age from eighteen to eighty years old.

Parents Without Partners focuses on helping parents who are in a process of transition and need strength and community to face the changes in their lives. In an already fragmented society, when loneliness and isolation are prevalent, single parents are particularly anxious about their ability to enter into relationships anew and conflicted about whether they should raise their children alone or jointly. PWP provides a community in which to share these concerns and encourages a positive outlook. The membership is composed of typical middle-class parents from all occupations, educational and political backgrounds, and religions who have a variety of interests and incomes. The group is open to parents with children of all ages, although most members' children are teenagers. Newcomers to a region often join a PWP support group. The average length of membership is four years.

Perhaps because PWP began primarily as a support group for divorced parents, never-married parents are underrepresented in PWP in proportion to their numbers in the United States and Canada. On the other hand, widowed parents' membership proportionally reflects their numbers in the population.   —*Lee Williams*

See also Divorce; Parental divorce; Single-parent families; Support groups; Widowhood.

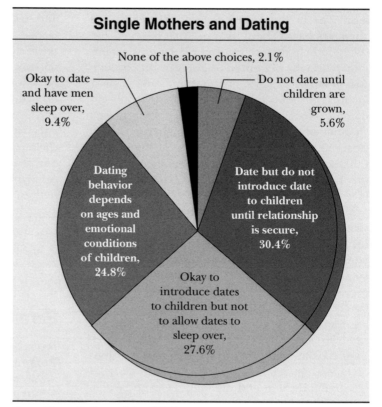

Single Mothers and Dating

None of the above choices, 2.1%

Okay to date and have men sleep over, 9.4%

Do not date until children are grown, 5.6%

Dating behavior depends on ages and emotional conditions of children, 24.8%

Date but do not introduce date to children until relationship is secure, 30.4%

Okay to introduce dates to children but not to allow dates to sleep over, 27.6%

Source: Moms Online website (1998)

Note: In early 1998 Moms Online conducted an informal poll among visitors to its website. This chart summarizes respondents' views on single mothers dating. Percentages are rounded to the nearest 0.1%.

Parsons, Elsie

BORN: November 27, 1874, New York, N.Y.
DIED: December 19, 1941, New York, N.Y.
AREAS OF ACHIEVEMENT: Parenting and family relationships; Race and ethnicity; Sociology
SIGNIFICANCE: Parsons emphasized female independence in marriage and also investigated and described Navajo and other American tribal customs and cultures

Elsie Parsons completed her Ph.D. in sociology at Columbia University in 1899. After teaching sociology at Barnard College from 1899 to 1905, she became a lifelong independent scholar. Her early writings centered on conflicts between personal free expression and conventional constraints. Between 1906 and 1915 she published six books arguing against outmoded conventional constraints on personal life. *The Family* (1906) included an argument favoring trial marriage and provoked public controversy.

Beginning in 1915 Parsons began to conduct anthropological and ethnological research in support of her ideas. *Mitla: Town of the Souls* (1936), a study of a community in Oaxaca, Mexico, and *Pueblo Indian Religion* (1939) are generally considered her best works on Native American culture. Parsons' detailed anthropological observations gave her work permanent value, but her historical speculations and theories of social change were contested from the beginning.

Parsons was an early and prolific publisher of African American and Native American folktales. She was president of the American Folklore Society from 1919 to 1920 and was elected as the first woman president of the American Anthropological Society in 1935. She also helped found the New School for Social Research in 1919.

—*Ralph L. Langenheim, Jr.*

See also African Americans; Feminist sociology; Myths and storytelling; Native Americans.

Paternity suits

RELEVANT ISSUES: Children and child development; Divorce; Law; Parenting and family relationships

SIGNIFICANCE: Paternity suits are legal actions to establish the identity of illegitimate children's fathers and to compel such fathers to provide financial support for their children

Historically, the fathers of illegitimate children had no legal duty to support these children. Illegitimate children were considered "nullius filius"—the child of no one—and their nonfathers owed them no obligations. The social result of this legal immunity from support was that illegitimate children were generally supported by their mothers, often in situations of poverty, or they became the objects of government welfare programs. In more recent times, however, most jurisdictions have reevaluated the duties owed by fathers to illegitimate children and have concluded that fathers' duty to provide financial support to their children—including their illegitimate children—does in fact exist.

In many cases, this reorientation of the law has occurred through statutes, such as those modeled on the Uniform Parentage Act or the Uniform Act on Paternity, which specifically allow illegitimate children to bring suit to establish paternity and obtain support. Some courts, moreover, have allowed paternity actions even in the absence of specific statutes. In addition, federal law now requires that mothers seeking certain federal welfare benefits must cooperate with authorities in establishing the paternity of their children whose paternity is not otherwise determined. States that receive federal funds for distribution as welfare benefits are required to establish procedures for determining the paternity of illegitimate children.

To enforce fathers' support obligations, most jurisdictions provide some mechanism for determining the paternity of illegitimate children. Paternity proceedings, also known as filiation proceedings, are intended to serve the important social purposes of reducing child poverty and of seeking sources of support for illegitimate children as an alternative or a supplement to government welfare programs. Most jurisdictions authorize the mothers of illegitimate children to inaugurate these proceedings, although several states also allow illegitimate children themselves to initiate paternity suits on their own behalf. A few jurisdictions allow paternity suits to be brought by natural fathers who wish to establish the paternity of their children and thus secure their parental rights.

Blood and tissue testing has played an increasingly important role in paternity determinations. Blood tests are used most effectively to disprove rather than establish a claim of paternity. Courts are generally less willing to admit the results of blood tests to prove that particular individuals are children's fathers than to disprove fatherhood. More recently, the growing acceptance of deoxyribonucleic acid (DNA) matching has provided a means for proving that particular individuals are, based upon statistical probabilities, children's likely fathers. Because DNA tests rely on genetic material that can survive individuals' death, paternity can be established to a reasonable certainty using DNA tests even after putative fathers have died.

—*Timothy L. Hall*

See also Child abandonment; Child support; Child Support Enforcement Amendments; Children born out of wedlock; Children's rights; Fatherlessness; Unwed fathers.

Susan Faludi, author of Backlash: The Undeclared War Against Women. (AP/Wide World Photos)

Patriarchs

RELEVANT ISSUES: Kinship and genealogy; Parenting and family relationships; Sociology

SIGNIFICANCE: The term patriarch may signify any strong paternal figure, but in cultural history it means rule by the father

The term patriarch derives from the Latin word *pater*, meaning father, and from the Latin suffix *arch*, meaning chief or ruler. Related terms in social science disciplines include patriarchy and patriarchate, both of which indicate social systems in which men are the dominant authority figures and in which genealogy and relationships are traced through the father's bloodline rather than the mother's. Religious uses of the term patriarch may also denote significant Old Testament biblical ancestral figures, such as Abraham and Jacob, or high-ranking figures in church establishments such as in the Eastern Orthodox branch of Christianity.

In the early literature of the social sciences, social organizations in which patriarchs or males in general are dominant are called patriarchal. In the nineteenth century the application of classical evolutionary theory to the development of social systems led to a debate between anthropologists over which came first—rule by matriarchs or rule by patriarchs. The patriarchalists, including Henry Maine and Edward Westermarck, argued that society from its first formations was ruled by strong male authority figures.

Patriarchal civilizations favored strong hierarchical groupings, powerful military and priestly elites, and a general undervaluing of females. Such societies were also patrilineal—that is, family names and the inheritance of property and titles descended through the paternal side of the family. In its most extreme form in Roman law, *patria potestad*, fathers theoretically had life and death powers over wives and children. The weight of the evidence in the historical record gives significant but not conclusive support to the patriarchal position, but the issue remains speculative.

The term patriarch is no longer common in modern empirical social science. When mainstream social scientists discuss male roles in the family, they use the term "father" instead of "patriarch," and issues discussed are economic and social in nature, such as divorce and child-support laws, fathers' role in child rearing in dual-earner families, and the numerical decline and fragmenting of the traditional nuclear family.

Patriarchs are not forgotten in literary and cultural criticism and theory, in which the term and concept live on. Literary figures such as William Shakespeare's King Lear and Tennessee Williams's Big Daddy are still studied and performed. A major impetus for keeping the figure of the patriarch and the concept of patriarchy alive has been feminist cultural theory. From Kate Millett's *Sexual Politics* (1971) to Susan Faludi's *Backlash* (1991), patriarchy has become synonymous with male dominance and the oppression of women.

Responses to the feminist critique have been varied. In academic circles, fledgling men's studies programs have taken up the task of reexamining the male role in culture from a less oppositional point of view. In popular culture, men's movements, such as that led by poet Robert Bly, seek to refurbish the figure of the patriarch by returning to myth and ritual. At a more pragmatic level, the feminist critique has made society more sensitive to such issues as domestic violence, sexual harassment, and salary and hiring inequities.

—*Roger James Stilling*

See also Communities; Father figures; Father-son relationships; Fatherhood; Feminist sociology; Freudian psychology; Matriarchs; Muslims; Patrilineal descent; Primogeniture.

Patrilineal descent

RELEVANT ISSUES: Kinship and genealogy; Parenting and family relationships

SIGNIFICANCE: Patrilineal descent, the most common of all lineage systems, determines family membership through the male line

In patrilineal descent systems, descent is traced exclusively through the male line and predominance is given to family ties running from sons to fathers to grandfathers to great-grandfathers and so on. In such systems mothers' side of the family and paternal grandmothers' branch are essentially ignored when tracing lineage or determining inheritance.

In the eleventh century the surname, or last

name, appeared for the first time in European history. It was passed down through fathers, so that children took their fathers' last names. Some common surnames, such as Johnson, or "son of John," reflect patrilineality. Forty-two percent of the world's cultures practice patrilineal descent. This system is common in societies in which men are dominant and sons tend to inherit their livelihood from their fathers and live near their fathers after they marry.

U.S. society is primarily patrilineal, as children usually take the last names of their fathers. Even when mothers keep their original last names, their names are generally inherited from their fathers. However, in some respects family descent in modern America is bilateral—that is, it is determined through both fathers and mothers. For example, family membership determines the inheritance of property, and children may inherit property from both fathers and mothers.   —*Glenn Canyon*

See also Bilateral descent; Clans; Genealogy; Kinship systems; Lineage; Matrilineal descent; Patriarchs; Patrilocality, matrilocality, and neolocality.

Patrilocality, matrilocality, and neolocality

Relevant issues: Kinship and genealogy; Parenting and family relationships

Significance: Terms distinguishing residence patterns for new couples, patrilocality denotes couples' living with or near husbands' families, matrilocality couples' living with or near brides' families, and neolocality couples' establishing new residences

Where couples live can have a profound impact on them. The relatives they live near may figure prominently in their futures and influence the relative status of husbands and wives. Sometimes location even determines the occupations in which husbands and wives engage. In neolocal contexts, the influence of families is partly replaced by friends, neighbors, or business associates.

Among the more than five hundred identifiable world cultures, the dominant residence pattern continues to be patrilocal (also called virilocal), which accounts for an estimated 67 percent

of all societies. Matrilocal (or uxorilocal) societies account for 15 percent of all societies. Other patterns include bilocality, in which couples may reside with or near either family (7 percent); neolocality (5 percent); avunculocality (or viriavunculocality), in which sons and their wives live with or near their mothers' brothers' families (4 percent); and duolocality, in which spouses live apart from each other (very few cases).

The relative scarcity of neolocal societies is partly a function of societies' economies. In traditional societies, in which land, crops, and animals constitute real wealth, families can enforce locality by withholding help from couples that break the approved pattern. Typically, in such societies families needing husbands or wives might accept prospective spouses, but they are less likely to take in whole families. In a money economy, however, people may be able to sell their labor or products for money, with which they can buy what they need. Because they can also save money for much longer periods of time than they can store perishable items, they may be able to weather periods of unemployment or loan excess money to others. While a money economy may be necessary to support neolocal families, it does not always lead to neolocality.

In the United States the dominant pattern is neolocality. When young Americans marry, if not before, they rent their first apartments or, in a few cases, buy their first houses. Entering military service or attending colleges or universities is a preliminary step. Among wealthy families, adolescents may be sent to boarding schools and thus begin to learn new residence patterns even earlier than do adolescents from nonwealthy families. There are, however, exceptions to neolocality in the United States. Among traditional groups, for example Native Americans, other residence patterns may be found. Moreover, among poorer Americans economic necessity may force young couples to reside with one or another set of parents (or even with both at different times). Finally, if families own farms, their married children may reside on or near the farms, especially if they expect to inherit them or buy out other heirs.

—*Paul L. Redditt*

See also Endogamy; Exogamy; Matriarchs; Matrilineal descent; Patrilineal descent.

Pediatric AIDS

RELEVANT ISSUES: Children and child development; Health and medicine; Parenting and family relationships

SIGNIFICANCE: As a segment of the growing AIDS epidemic, pediatric cases offer a unique set of issues pertaining to the transmission, physical health, and psychological care of children and their families

Awareness and detection of the disease known as acquired immunodeficiency syndrome, or AIDS, began in the 1980's, and the first cases of children with AIDS appeared in 1982. AIDS was diagnosed only after the struggle to determine the reason behind immunodeficiency and opportunistic infections that began to occur in children under the age of two. Such baffling cases had appeared in the late 1970's but were not yet linked with the AIDS disorder.

Incidence and Spread. The number of pediatric cases of AIDS reached 189 by the end of 1981. The number of cases increased during that decade, and by the middle of 1992 more than 4,000 cases of Pediatric AIDS in the United States had been reported to the Centers for Disease Control (CDC). In comparison to the number of AIDS cases reported for individuals age thirteen and older, pediatric cases represented only 2 percent of all diagnoses. At the same time, however, AIDS continued to climb as one of the leading causes of death among children.

Cases of pediatric AIDS are distributed throughout the United States. The metropolitan areas and larger cities, such as New York, Miami, and Washington, D.C., have a greater proportion of pediatric AIDS cases. In addition, a greater number of pediatric AIDS cases are found among African American children. There are slightly more cases of AIDS among male children than among female children, a difference attributed to transfusions of tainted blood to male hemophilia patients.

Transmission of the Virus. Most children acquire AIDS through the transmission of human immunodeficiency virus (HIV) by their mothers. Known as "vertical transmission," this can occur during pregnancy through the placental tissue or amniotic fluid, during labor and delivery via blood or vaginal secretions, or postnatally through mothers' breast milk. Nevertheless, not all infants born to HIV-positive women acquire HIV. About half of all infected infants test positive for HIV soon after birth, indicating that the virus was transmitted during pregnancy. Some cases of HIV in fetuses have been detected as early as the first and second trimesters by testing fetal tissue. Evidence of infection, however, may not be evident until a few days, months, or even years following birth.

HIV-infected children are thus often the result of HIV-infected mothers. Many such mothers are intravenous drug users. Most other women infected with HIV are believed to have acquired the virus by heterosexual contact with male intravenous drug users. Some of these women may also have exchanged sex for drugs, engaged in unprotected sex, and had sex with multiple partners.

Cases of pediatric AIDS can also be transmitted through the receipt of blood and blood products. The number of cases of HIV transmission linked to blood transfusions has drastically decreased since 1985 because of more stringent procedures for screening blood by medical personnel. While not generally acknowledged, it is also possible for children to acquire HIV through sexual abuse, child prostitution, or children's use of intravenous drugs.

Physical Health Experiences. HIV affects the immune system, thus rendering infected children vulnerable to common infections and opportunistic infections. Children are more susceptible to infections than adults, because, unlike adults, they have not had the ability to develop a healthy immune system prior to becoming infected. Symptoms of the disease vary in number, duration, and severity from child to child. Children infected with HIV alternate between ill and healthy periods and are often asymptomatic in their early lives. The earlier children show symptoms of HIV, the more rapid the advancement of the disease and the progression toward death.

In 1987 the CDC designed a classification system specifically for children. This classification system lists many diagnoses as AIDS indicators and is arranged in such a way so that practitioners can track the progress of the disease. Although this system is very similar to that used for adults, two conditions are listed for children only: a chronic lung condition called lymphoid interstitial pneumonitis and recurrent serious bacterial infections.

Some of the more common symptoms in HIV-infected children include recurrent diarrhea, thrush, fever, malnutrition, and failure to thrive. Failure to thrive can include a lack of height and weight gain and a lack of growth of head circumference. HIV-infected children may also experience bacterial infections, such as sinusitis, meningitis, pneumonia, urinary tract infection, and anemia—an extremely common symptom.

The opportunistic infection pneumocystis carinii pneumonia (PCP), considered to be the most common opportunistic infection for infants and children, affects about half of all children with AIDS. The signs of PCP include shortness of breath, fever, cough, and rapid breathing. Often the disease indicating the presence of HIV, it is most often diagnosed in the early months of life and is associated with a high rate of mortality.

Neurologic disease, another potential diagnosis, can cause developmental delay, loss of previously achieved milestones, and attention deficits. Children with neurologic disease may experience seizures, weakness, or even blindness. In the advanced stages of HIV infection, the virus can cause damage to the central nervous system, the heart, lungs, and kidneys.

Effects on Families. Children and other family members can be affected by pediatric AIDS in numerous ways. If children require hospitalization, they may be separated from their families for extended periods, thus necessitating their segregation from the family environment. In other circumstances, infants may be abandoned or relocated to other family members' homes, because caregivers are unable to care for their children's needs, as in the case of drug-addicted mothers. In addition, caregivers may also be infected with HIV, thus intensifying the impact of all aspects of the disease.

Families with HIV-infected children may also suffer financially. Physical care equipment, visits by doctors and specialists, and the costs of hospitalization and medication are just some of the expenses that families with seriously ill members face. If families' resources are limited, provisions for basic needs may be inadequate. Proper nutrition, vital to attempting to maintain children's health, may have to be sacrificed in order to pay health costs. Caregivers' health may also be at risk, as they ignore their own needs while trying to meet those of their sick children.

Family members may find that they must take on new roles, as they become nurses or income providers. Siblings may report feeling neglected or may feel burdened by the added responsibilities placed on them. Grandparents or other extended family members may assume greater primary caregiving responsibilities. Married couples may experience stress because their time and energy often become focused on their ailing children. Such experiences can emotionally drain family members, especially those who do not have adequate coping skills. Taking time for other family members and expressing appreciation for their contributions can help to reduce the intensity of these difficulties.

Anticipatory grief, guilt, anxiety, and depression are some of the commonly faced emotional problems. These emotions can be triggered or heightened by social stigmatization, lack of social support, a reduction in the amount of time for socializing or being alone, and a sense of being overwhelmed by the physical and emotional burden of caring for terminally ill loved ones.

Other children may be discouraged from spending time with children who have pediatric AIDS because of the fear of transmission. However, this fear is often based on a lack of knowledge about the disease. On the other hand, in order to ease some of the burden on families with ill children, the community may provide them with support, such as child care while parents run errands or require time to themselves. The medical community can potentially offer support and understanding, providing parents with referrals to community programs and personnel that may be of assistance. The reaction and assistance of family members and the community are key to the impact upon the family system.

—*Kimberly A. Wallet*

BIBLIOGRAPHY

Anderson, Gary R., ed. *Courage to Care: Responding to the Crisis of Children with AIDS.* Washington, D.C.: Child Welfare League of America, 1990.

Barth, Richard P., Jeanne Pietrzak, and Malia Ramler, eds. *Families Living with Drugs and HIV: Inter-*

Young Canadian couple with a baby participating in a march in support of greater funding for AIDS research.
(Dick Hemingway)

vention and Treatment Strategies. New York: Guilford Press, 1993.

Cohen, Felissa L., and Jerry D. Durham, eds. Women, Children, and HIV/AIDS. New York: Springer, 1993.

Henggeler, Scott W., Gary B. Melton, and James R. Rodrigue. Pediatric and Adolescent AIDS: Research Findings from the Social Sciences. Newbury Park, Calif.: Sage Publications, 1992.

Kelly, Patricia, Susan Holman, Rosalie Rothenberg, and Stephen Paul Holzemer, eds. Primary Care of Women and Children with HIV Infection: A Multidisciplinary Approach. Boston: Jones and Bartlett, 1995.

Pizzo, Philip A., and Catherine M. Wilfert, eds. Pediatric AIDS: The Challenge of HIV Infection in Infants, Children, and Adolescents. Baltimore: Williams & Wilkins, 1991.

See also Acquired immunodeficiency syndrome (AIDS); Birth defects; Health of children; Health problems.

Personal Responsibility and Work Opportunity Reconciliation Act

Date: Enacted on August 22, 1996
Relevant issues: Economics and work; Law
Significance: Signed into law by President Bill Clinton, this act represented the most significant change in public welfare policies since the inception of Aid to Families with Dependent Children (AFDC) in 1935

The Personal Responsibility and Work Opportunity Reconciliation Act of 1996 dramatically changed the impact of the welfare system on recipient families. The new welfare system demanded work in return for time-limited aid. Under this act, states were given broad discretion to design their own welfare policies, as long as most recipients were required to go to work and aid ended after two years. A maximum of five years of aid was to be granted over persons' lifetimes, and state spending on welfare was to be maintained at no less than 80 percent of what was spent in 1994. Some $14 billion was allocated for child care. Recipients' skills and needs were to be assessed formally, and Medicaid coverage was provided for at least one year after recipi-

ents began employment. There were also provisions for stringent child-support enforcement and possible job subsidies.

These provisions set out to make welfare a transitional program, to move recipients toward work and family independence. Proponents believed that long-term poverty would be reduced, improving the lives of millions of families. Opponents argued that public assistance would decline significantly without any guarantee of jobs, driving families deeper into poverty. The intensity of the debate highlighted the dramatic nature and significance of the act. —David Carleton

See also Aid to Families with Dependent Children (AFDC); Family Support Act; Poverty; Social Security; Welfare.

Persons of opposite sex sharing living quarters (POSSLQ)

Relevant issues: Demographics; Marriage and dating
Significance: This term was used by demographers to describe the increasing number of American families made up of a woman and a man choosing to live together without marriage

The phrase "Persons of Opposite Sex Sharing Living Quarters" (also known as "Partners of Opposite Sex Sharing Living Quarters") was first used by the U.S. Census Bureau for the national census of 1980. This phrase, often abbreviated POSSLQs, was used to refer to a person cohabiting with a person of the opposite sex. This term described the status of many people more accurately than the terms "single" or "married."

This term reflected the fact that an increasing number of families consisted of an unmarried heterosexual couple with or without children. During the late 1960's about 10 percent of adult Americans had cohabited with a partner of the opposite sex prior to a first marriage. By the early 1980's this number had increased to approximately 45 percent. The number of Americans categorized as POSSLQs continued to increase during the 1980's, reaching a total of 2.9 million by the time of the 1990 census. Of this number, about two-thirds had never been married and about one-

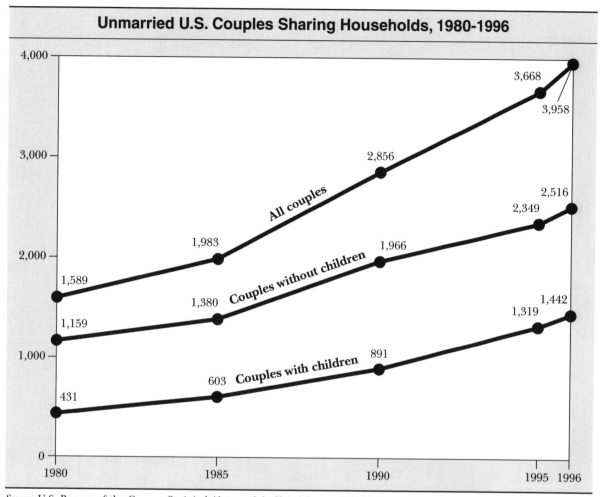

Unmarried U.S. Couples Sharing Households, 1980-1996

All couples: 1,589 (1980); 1,983 (1985); 2,856 (1990); 3,668 (1995); 3,958 (1996)

Couples without children: 1,159 (1980); 1,380 (1985); 1,966 (1990); 2,349 (1995); 2,516 (1996)

Couples with children: 431 (1980); 603 (1985); 891 (1990); 1,319 (1995); 1,442 (1996)

Source: U.S. Bureau of the Census, *Statistical Abstract of the United States: 1997.* Washington, D.C.: GPO, 1997.

third were divorced. The number of American families composed of POSSLQs was expected to be even higher by the time of the census in the year 2000.
                                                                    —*Rose Secrest*

See also Cohabitation; Couples; Domestic partners.

Pets

RELEVANT ISSUES: Aging; Health and medicine; Parenting and family relationships

SIGNIFICANCE: Companionship is the most common reason for pet ownership among residents of North America

Pet ownership differs from other forms of ownership in that its primary aim is the development of a complex and intimate relationship. While most domesticated animals provide some economic or practical benefits, rewards from companion animals are derived from the relationship bond itself. Pets are exceptional because they alone share intimacy as well as proximity with their human keepers. The reasons people develop relationships with pets vary greatly, but they usually reflect individuals' or families' personalities and attitudes.

Pets and Other Domesticated Animals. The value of most domesticated animals is almost exclusively determined by their material utility, and such animals do not commonly provide or benefit from nurturing or affectionate interchanges with humans. Although pets, almost by definition, have no material utility, they are kept as vehicles for displays of affection, nurturance, and dominance.

However successful people are in their relationships with other human beings, they can usually rely on their pets to return their affection. (Mary LaSalle)

The relationship that develops between pets and family members is comparable to relationships that develop between human companions and family members. Such relationships can form in similar ways and vary greatly in intensity, respect, responsibility, commitment, and communication. It was previously thought that the sole benefits of pet ownership were confined to the fulfillment of emotional or social needs, but research beginning in the 1970's has suggested that humans as well as pets form positive human-pet relationships that include improvements in psychological and physiological health.

Pets as Companions. Many values and needs are associated with pet ownership. Pets provide companionship for lonely people who feel alienated from or dehumanized by society. Pets offer a sense of family and community to many older people and to childless couples, since pets act as significant nonhuman companions or child substitutes. Pets tend to be accepting of others and are givers of unconditional love. As a result, pets have proven to be beneficial for persons' emotional well-being. Retirement home residents who have pets display a significantly lower rate of depression than do residents without pets; they also have lower blood pressure, maintain higher levels of activity, are in better overall health, and have an increased life expectancy. Humans have a need to share loving relationships, and pets can fulfill this

Pets often provide links through which people connect with each other. (Dick Hemingway)

Companionship—the primary reason most people own pets—is especially important among older persons. (AP/Wide World Photos)

need. Pets' loyalty and devotion can help insecure children and adults maintain a sense of belonging and can be a nonthreatening presence that offers a sense of unconditional acceptance.

Pets provide a source of satisfaction for various human needs and dependencies. Pets can serve as companions, confidants, and sibling partners. They are also givers of unconditional emotional support, and serve as links with natural, uninhibited, and honest emotions and responses. In such relationships, pets become more important in proportion to the depth of persons' emotional needs.

Pets act as psychotherapeutic supports, guardians, or allies. They can also serve as significant social catalysts and emotional bridges in the home, facilitating interactions between family members. In its most mature state, pet ownership becomes an actualizing relationship in which pets are appreciated and respected for their own attributes instead of for reasons of status, utility, or emotional support.

Pets as Family Members. Most families who own pets refer to them as "members" of the family. Those who designate pets as family members have a greater tendency to talk to and confide in them, display photographs of them, celebrate their birthdays, and allow them to sleep in family members' beds. They commonly purchase special food, toys, furniture, and other accessories for their pets. Such persons often engage in the same social acts with their pets as they do with fellow humans with whom they have close, friendly relationships. The majority of pet-owning families claim that they experience increased closeness expressed around the care of pets and spend more time together playing with them. At the same time, many families report that children with pets spend less time interacting with their parents. Some spouses also experience jealousy when their partners spend more time with their pets than with them.

The educational function of pets in families is also important. In learning to play with and care for pets, children develop empathy and compassion for others, learn responsibility, and learn about important life events such as birth and death. Many adults learn valuable nurturing skills from pet care. Pets often provide adults with a sense of constancy and contentment. Adults do not demand that their pets progress and expect less of them than of their children, who are expected to grow physically, intellectually, and morally.

Sociologists report that the overwhelming majority of pet owners admit that they find it easier to focus attention and affection on their pets than on other family members. Animal behaviorists have also noted that family pets often serve as barometers of anxiety in a family. Changes in pet behavior and physiology often indicate and reflect family tensions and conflicts. Many psychologists believe that pets play a valuable role in family emotional systems. In many cases, when tension within a two-person emotional system exceeds a certain level, intense feelings are often transferred to third parties—pets. Displays of affection, anger, or distance are commonly transferred to pets rather than to family members. Research has identified pets who fight with one another when family members are upset and who interfere when family members show affection or fight with one another.

The Responsibility of Pet Ownership. When family members accept pets into their households, they accept responsibility for providing them with everything they need, from social partners to suffi-

cient space, sanitation, food, and water. In the late twentieth century, as fewer people chose to have children and parents decided to have fewer children, pets came to play an important surrogate role. Modern family photographs including pets usually show humans in close physical contact with the heads or faces of their pets—a common pose for parents and children. When photographed alone, family pets are often shown posing like children. This contrasts with old, historical portraits of persons and their pets, in which pets were usually shown at their owners' feet.

Perhaps the greatest challenge facing families is remembering that their pets are animals, not human beings. The most common attitude of pet-owning families toward their pets is a humanistic one emphasizing affection and strong attachment. Pets become the recipients of feeling and emotional projections somewhat analogous to those expressed toward other family members, especially children. Because of selective breeding, overindulgence, and permissive rearing, pets may become neurotically overattached to their owners. Many behavioral disorders in such pets can be directly linked to their owners' need to indulge them as child substitutes.

Such humanistic attitudes value pets primarily as a basic source of affection and companionship. Because considerable empathy for animal emotions and thought accompanies this perspective, many people have an idealized view of their pets, anthropomorphically endowing them with human characteristics and capacities. Such individuals often develop a romanticized notion of pets' innocence and virtue. Yet, no amount of affection for pets can compensate for intrinsic biological differences. Family pets often develop serious behavioral problems and become the target of human anger and frustration when they fail to live up to anthropomorphic expectations. Families have better relationships with their pets if they adopt a more balanced attitude, accepting pets for their strengths and weaknesses instead of indulging or exacting severe punishment for animal misbehavior.
—*Randall L. Milstein*

BIBLIOGRAPHY

Fogle, Bruce. *Interrelations Between People and Pets.* Springfield, Ill.: Charles C Thomas, 1981.

Hoage, Robert J., ed. *Perceptions of Animals in Ameri-*

can Culture. Washington, D.C.: Smithsonian Institution Press, 1989.

Katcher, Aaron H., and Alan M. Beck, eds. *New Perspectives on Our Lives with Companion Animals.* Philadelphia: University of Pennsylvania Press, 1983.

Robinson, Ian, ed. *The Waltham Book of Human-Animal Interaction: Benefits and Responsibilities of Pet Ownership.* New York: Pergamon, 1995.

Robinson, Michael H., and Lionel Tiger, eds. *Man and Beast Revisited.* Washington, D.C.: Smithsonian Institution Press, 1991.

See also Child safety; Emotional expression; Single life.

Planned Parenthood Federation of America (PPFA)

DATE: Founded in 1916 in Brooklyn, New York
RELEVANT ISSUES: Health and medicine; Parenting and family relationships
SIGNIFICANCE: Planned Parenthood is the world's oldest and largest voluntary reproductive health care organization

The Planned Parenthood Federation of America, Inc. (PPFA) is dedicated to the principle that every individual has a fundamental right to choose when and whether to have children. Planned Parenthood not only provides medical, educational,

The support that the Planned Parenthood Federation has given to abortion rights has caused the organization to be targeted by militant antiabortion groups. (AP/Wide World Photos)

and counseling services to individuals but also sponsors research on contraceptives and contraceptive behavior, advocating reproductive freedom through lobbying, legal action, and voter education.

Although the organization adopted the name "Planned Parenthood Federation of America, Inc." in 1942, it dates its founding to 1916, when Margaret Sanger established a birth control clinic in Brooklyn, New York. Five years later, she and others started the American Birth Control League and, in 1925, the Birth Control Clinical Research Bureau. These two institutions merged in 1939 to form the Birth Control Federation of America, later to become the PPFA. The first woman to head the organization since Sanger, Faye Wattleton, served as president of PPFA from 1978 to 1992 and focused her energies on advocacy for reproductive rights. Gloria Feldt became the third woman president in June, 1996. In the late 1990's Planned Parenthood maintained a national office in New York City, a legislative and public affairs office in Washington, DC, 152 affiliates, and more than nine hundred clinic sites in forty-eight states and the District of Columbia. PPFA has an international service arm known as Family Planning International Assistance. Supported by PPFA, the Alan Guttmacher Institute is an independent, nonprofit corporation for reproductive health research, policy analysis, and public education.

Planned Parenthood's services to individuals vary according to the individual affiliates but may include education, counseling, and services in the following areas: well-woman care, pregnancy testing, contraception, infertility, therapeutic abortion, sexually transmitted diseases, HIV testing, and hormone replacement. PPFA's early research efforts included grants for the development of the birth control pill. Ongoing research is conducted by the Alan Guttmacher Institute. PPFA and others in the birth control movement have been involved in legal challenges, public policy advocacy, and in mobilizing public opinion to establish the rights of individuals to reproductive freedom. PPFA also influenced the establishment of publicly funded contraceptive services for poor women. Most recently PPFA has been involved in maintaining therapeutic abortion as safe and legal.

PPFA's efforts have contributed to a dramatic decrease in maternal and infant deaths since 1916.

Families can decide how many children they want to have. Contraception is now affordable and accessible to most Americans.

Planned Parenthood has been controversial since its inception. Sanger was jailed and fined for violating the 1870's Comstock Law, which defined contraceptives as "obscene." The Roman Catholic Church opposed both PPFA's early contraception efforts and, in the last third of the twentieth century, abortion. Political and religious conservatives have joined the Church in opposition to Planned Parenthood and other family-planning organizations' activities, describing them as "anti-family."

—*Rebecca Lovell Scott*

See also Abortion; Birth control; Family size; Reproductive technologies; Sanger, Margaret; Sex education; Wattleton, Faye; Zero Population Growth movement.

Political families

RELEVANT ISSUES: Parenting and family relationships; Sociology

SIGNIFICANCE: The notion of "political culture" offers one way to understand the phenomenon of prominent families that play major roles in American politics

Since the nation's founding, prominent families have played major roles in American politics. In the twentieth century the involvement of notable families in politics, often led by strong personalities such as Albert Gore, Sr., and Joseph P. Kennedy, has had a major influence on American government. Although there have been significant changes since the 1970's, certain families continue to occupy key positions in federal, state, and local governments. In the years following the Watergate scandal of the early 1970's, public confidence in American institutions declined. In conjunction with this, public attitudes toward career politicians declined. Yet, prominent families continue to be important actors in American politics. Understanding the dynamics of how the public can express cynical attitudes toward politicians while returning members of famous families to office is one of the great mysteries of American politics.

Yankees in Massachusetts. The Adamses, one of the most notable examples of a political family, produced two presidents. The nation's second president, John Adams, an active leader of the drive for American independence, also served as vice president under George Washington. Adams's son, John Quincy Adams, served as secretary of state under President James Monroe and became president in 1825.

The Adamses came from Massachusetts, a state that helps to explain the dynamics of family relationships in politics. In the early nineteenth century Massachusetts was dominated by a political culture that permitted families, such as the Adamses, to remain politically influential. The political culture of early Massachusetts, called "moralistic" by political scientist Daniel J. Elazar, justified "interven[tion] into the sphere of private activities when . . . necessary . . . for the public good." The Adamses belonged to this culture, and because the state shared this viewpoint, they were very influential in Massachusetts state politics. However, immigration to Massachusetts, beginning in the mid-nineteenth century, changed the state's political culture. The newcomers, primarily Irish Catholics, belonged to a different church and rejected the state's dominant moralistic culture. As the number of Irish Catholics increased, the tension between the old-time residents (Yankees) of the state and the immigrants intensified.

Conflict Between Yankees and Irish Immigrants. The intensity of the conflict was magnified by the disparity in wealth between the Yankees and Irish. Without the personal wealth or social standing of the Yankees, the many Irish families turned to politics, serving in the Boston city government as well as in the Massachusetts state government. The Irish, in contrast to the Yankees, adhered to an "individualistic" political culture, which placed primary emphasis on personal success. At times, this resulted in corruption in city and state government that evoked outrage among members of the Yankee establishment and a more mild reaction within the immigrant community.

The Kennedy family, as one of the leading Irish families in the city, became politically active in Boston politics. Joseph P. Kennedy used his father's political success to build a business career. By the 1920's Joseph Kennedy was one of the nation's wealthiest men. Having secured a personal fortune, he entered politics in the 1930's, serving in a number of capacities under President Franklin D. Roosevelt. While Joseph Kennedy had presidential ambitions, the controversial nature of some of his ideas precluded him from running for president.

One of his sons, John F. Kennedy, entered politics shortly after World War II. In the meantime, the old conflict between the Irish and Yankees had not disappeared. Well-established Yankee families continued to play significant roles in Massachusetts politics. In 1952 John F. Kennedy decided to challenge Senator Henry Cabot Lodge, a Republican who was a member of a very prominent Yankee family.

Political Culture in the South. Massachusetts provides one example of how states' political culture shapes the ability of prominent families to be politically successful. The American South's political culture, a traditionalistic political culture, expects "those at the top of the social structure to take a special and dominant role in government," according to Elazar. Thus, certain families, because of social standing and wealth, have held positions in local and state governments. In those states where the traditionalistic political culture dominates, political participation levels have been lower than in the rest of the United States. In 1949 political scientist V. O. Key published a leading study on the South's political history, *Southern Politics in State and Nation*, in which he described a region whose political arrangements favored the social "haves" over the "have nots." Southern political leaders resisted changes that threatened the established order. This attitude meant maintaining a system of racial discrimination, which excluded millions of African American citizens from participation in public life. Although the old system of racial segregation has ended, the South's traditionalistic culture continues to be in evidence. Voter turnout levels in the South are lower than anywhere else in the United States.

Civil Rights and Changing Political Culture. The reform of the nation's civil rights laws that took place in the 1960's altered the political positions of the Republicans and the Democratic Party. Presidents John F. Kennedy and Lyndon B. Johnson, both Democrats, supported major changes in civil rights. Many Southerners, who had traditionally voted Democratic, reacted by turning to the Republican Party. As more Southerners identified with the Republicans, the Republican Party became more conservative. This, in

Joseph P. Kennedy (top) and his son, future president John F. Kennedy, in the late 1930's. (Reuters/Archive Photos)

turn, had ramifications for one of the nation's most noted political families: the Landons.

Alfred M. Landon was the Republican Party presidential nominee for 1936, and his daughter, Nancy Kassebaum, became a U.S. senator from Kansas. Kassebaum, a popular moderate Republican, was often mentioned as a possible vice presidential candidate. Because of opposition from Republican conservatives, however, Kassebaum was never selected. Many of these conservatives were from the South. Similarly, Sam Nunn of Georgia, a popular Democratic senator, was frequently mentioned as a Democratic candidate for president. Although Nunn's family had a long history of involvement in Democratic Party politics, the movement of many of his fellow Southerners to the Republican Party weakened his chances of receiving the Democratic nomination.

U.S. states often contain a mixture of political cultures, generating conflict between notable families. Illinois, a midwestern state, contains elements of the moralistic, individualistic, and traditionalistic cultures. Members of the Stevenson family have been active in Democratic Party politics since the nineteenth century. Adlai Stevenson served as vice president under Grover Cleveland, who was U.S. president from 1885 to 1889 and from 1893 to 1897. Stevenson's grandson, Adlai Stevenson II, became Governor of Illinois and served as the Democratic Party's presidential nominee in 1952 and 1956. Adlai Stevenson III served as a U.S. senator and ran, unsuccessfully, for governor of Illinois. Although the Stevensons have had successful political careers in Illinois politics, they come from a section of the state with moralistic influence. Since the moralistic culture is in the minority in Illinois, the family's political viewpoints have often been at odds with other members of the state's political establishment.

Conclusion. The concept of "political culture" is one way of viewing the role of prominent families in politics and useful for interpreting American politics. Clearly, the United States is a culturally diverse nation-state, lending itself to regional variations. In Massachusetts and in other states, where Irish immigrants came into contact with established elements, tensions resulted. Often, as in Massachusetts, the conflict was class-based, as the more affluent Yankees resented the newcomers. The old tensions between the Yankees and Irish account for the rise of the Kennedy family to political prominence. The Kennedy family, of Irish heritage, was not socially-prominent until the latter half of the twentieth century. As late as the 1952 senatorial campaign between Henry Cabot Lodge and John F. Kennedy, the old divisions were evident between Irish and Yankees.

The three political cultures of moralism, individualism, and traditionalism remain viable. The movement of the South's political culture to the Republicans has influenced the careers of Republican moderates. Indeed, political culture demonstrates that the ability to develop a "following" seems to be a prerequisite for families to achieve long-term political success. —*Michael E. Meagher*

BIBLIOGRAPHY

Barber, James David. *The Presidential Character: Predicting Performance in the White House.* 3d ed. Englewood Cliffs, N.J.: Prentice-Hall, 1985.

Black, Earl, and Merle Black. *Politics and Society in the South.* Cambridge, Mass.: Harvard University Press, 1987.

Cochran, Bert. *Adlai Stevenson: Patrician Among the Politicians.* New York: Funk & Wagnalls, 1969.

Collier, Peter, and David Horowitz. *The Kennedys: An American Drama.* New York: Summit Books, 1984.

Elazar, Daniel J. *American Federalism: A View from the States.* New York: Harper & Row, 1984.

Key, V. O. *Southern Politics in State and Nation.* New York: Alfred A. Knopf, 1949.

Miroff, Bruce. *Icons of Democracy: American Leaders as Heroes, Aristocrats, Dissenters, and Democrats.* New York: Basic Books, 1993.

See also Communities; Cultural influences; Wealth.

Polyandry

RELEVANT ISSUES: Kinship and genealogy; Marriage and dating; Parenting and family relationships

SIGNIFICANCE: A form of plural marriage, or polygamy, polyandry permits women to have more than one husband at a time

"Polyandry" is a term adopted by anthropologists to describe the rare form of plural marriage in which women have multiple husbands at one time.

The more common variant is "polygyny," in which men have more than one wife at a time. In the United States and Canada marriage is so closely tied to sexual and emotional exclusivity that it is difficult for most Americans to understand that sexual jealousy is seldom a problem in societies that do not idealize romantic love and exclusive sexual rights in marriage. In such societies the economic and social functions of the family are of primary importance.

Most of the world's polyandrous peoples live in the South Asian countries of Tibet, Nepal, India, and Sri Lanka. A common explanation for the existence of polyandry is a shortage of females, perhaps due to the relative neglect of baby girls in these patrilineal societies. Arable land is scarce, and small, subsistence farms are passed on to the next generation through the male line. If families have several sons, the only way the family farm can be passed to all sons as a unit is through fraternal polyandry, the most common form of polyandry, by which all the sons share one wife. Formal rights of sexual access generally prevent frictions or jealousy.

—Robert D. Bryant

See also Bigamy; Family: concept and history; Marriage; Monogamy; Patrilineal descent; Polygyny; Sexuality and sexual taboos.

Polygyny

RELEVANT ISSUES: Kinship and genealogy; Parenting and family relationships; Religious beliefs and practices

SIGNIFICANCE: Polygyny is a marriage system in which men have two or more wives

Polygamy is a marriage system in which persons may have more than one spouse at the same time. Polygyny exists when men have more than one wife and polyandry exists when women have more than one husband. Polygyny was historically the most common marriage system across human cultures. By the late twentieth century polygyny was still widely practiced, although monogamy (or, more accurately, serial monogamy) had become the dominant system.

In cultures that practice polygyny, it is not the case that most men have multiple wives. Because the adult ratio of men to women is approximately one to one, for each man who has two wives there

is a man who has no wife, and for each man who has three wives, there are two men who have no wife. Most men in polygynous cultures have only one wife, because only older men with high social status and power can afford to support more than one family. Depending on the culture and on the wishes of specific persons, polygynous cowives and their children may live together in the same household or may live separately in different households. Spousal jealousy often contributes to marital and family stress, but conflicts tend to center on family economics, job and school choices, vacation plans, and other day-to-day decisions common to all families.

The practice of polygyny is illegal in the United States and Canada, but it is practiced informally by members of some religions. In the United States polygyny was at one time promoted by the Church of Jesus Christ of Latter-day Saints, or Mormons. When Utah applied for statehood, however, Mormons came under intense pressure to abandon polygyny. The church reversed its policy on plural marriage in 1890. At that time many polygynous Mormon families moved to other territories in the western United States, Mexico, and Canada. In the 1990's remnant religious splinter groups, including descendants of original polygynous families, continued to practice polygyny. While families and local religious communities may recognize and support such marriages, only monogamy is recognized by law.

Other religious groups in the United States and Canada, particularly Muslims, practice polygyny. Even with the freedom of religion that U.S. and Canadian citizens and immigrant residents enjoy, such marriages are not officially recognized. As with other religious practices that are deemed illegal, the courts have determined that outlawing behavior is not the same as outlawing beliefs. Despite its illegal status, polygyny in the United States and Canada is rarely prosecuted, because it is believed that the harm to involved children and communities would likely outweigh any possible benefits. Furthermore, as with many other so-called victimless crimes, it is unlikely that the prosecution of polygyny would deter persons from continuing to practice it.

—Linda Mealey

See also Alternative family types; Bigamy; Communal living; Extended families; Group marriage;

Kinship systems; Monogamy; Mormon polygamy; Muslims; Polyandry; Religion.

Pornography

RELEVANT ISSUES: Art and the media; Law; Violence

SIGNIFICANCE: Considerable public controversy has arisen in the United States over the possible harmful effects of sexually oriented materials on families in general and children in particular

The term "pornography" (from Greek words meaning "writings about prostitutes") refers to a large variety of written, recorded, or pictorial materials that deal with sexuality in ways considered by some to be obscene, indecent, or offensive. Although the terms "pornography" and "obscenity" are often used interchangeably, the latter term is sometimes used to describe materials depicting cruelty and violence. Usually soft-core pornography has the connotation of art or literature that promotes erotic stimulation in more subtle ways, while hard-core pornography connotes explicitly obscene materials that appeal almost exclusively to prurient interests. The distinction between the two, of course, is not always clear, and either form can also contain depictions of violence.

The effects of various pornographic materials and whether they should be legally proscribed have been issues of major controversy for the last two hundred years. One of the more difficult questions has been the definition of pornography for the purpose of legal prohibition. Materials that are considered highly objectionable to some people are considered acceptable or harmless to others. People with conservative moral beliefs often think that government should prohibit any materials that corrupt the sexual morality of the population. Likewise, many modern feminists want to ban some forms of pornography, concentrating their opposition on those forms that dehumanize and exploit women by treating them as sex objects. Libertarians, on the other hand, argue that any antiobscenity laws violate the freedom of expression that is guaranteed by the First Amendment of the U.S. Constitution.

The Censorship Debate. During the 1960's laws in the United States were liberalized so as to remove many traditional restraints on the contents of publications and cinema. As public debate intensified, the U.S. Congress authorized a Federal Commission on Pornography and Obscenity to investigate the issue, the result of which was a 1970 report that found no reliable evidence that pornography caused crime by adults or delinquency among young people. The commission recommended the repeal of all laws prohibiting the sale of pornographic materials to consenting adults. Several members of the commission, however, did not agree with the majority's conclusion, and they advocated stricter enforcement of antiobscenity laws.

Disagreeing with the majority report, President Ronald Reagan appointed a new commission to be headed by Attorney General Edwin Meese. In 1987 the Meese Commission's report found that there was a cause-and-effect relationship between pornography and sexual violence. Although the commission referred to numerous empirical studies, critics argued that the data of such studies was badly flawed. Critics also charged that the Meese Commission did not give adequate attention to the arguments and investigations of anticensorship groups.

As the debates about the two commission reports indicate, social scientists disagree about whether or not pornography is a cause of violence. Sex offenders are often consumers of pornographic materials, and some offenders such as Ted Bundy have even claimed that such materials had a harmful influence on their development. Although some assert that the evidence indicates that vulnerable individuals sometimes are motivated to commit acts of violence by viewing violent pornography, the causes of human behavior are so complex that it is impossible to be certain about the relative significance of various causative influences. Also, even if much hard-core pornography contains explicit depictions of sadism and masochism, it often contains less violence than materials with little or no sexual content. Moreover, although tens of millions of pornographic videos and printed materials are purchased and rented in the United States each year, most persons who enjoy pornography do not commit violent crimes.

Some moderate proponents of limited censorship emphasize the difference between violent pornography and nonviolent erotica, and they advocate legal restrictions on the former but not on the latter. For people who take this viewpoint, it is important that they clearly define violence as depictions in which participants are either physically harmed or forced to engage in activities contrary to their will. Much evidence suggests that young people developing their sexual identity can learn to associate physical pain with sexual gratification, suggesting that particular kinds of violent pornography might have very harmful effects in the formative stages of personality development. Actual life experiences, of course, have greater impact on development than stimulation through publications, cinema, or recordings.

The First Amendment and Censorship. The First Amendment of the U.S. Constitution prohibits Congress from "abridging" the freedom of speech or the press. Designed to ensure a robust debate about political and intellectual ideas, the amendment was not meant to protect all forms of expression, such as libel, slander, perjury, or criminal conspiracy. At the time the amendment was adopted, there was not a great deal of concern about the question of pornographic materials, and apparently such materials were not very common in North America. Regulations were left up to state and local governments, which were not required to follow the First Amendment. As pornography became common in the 1820's, most states tried to restrict it with either legislation or the common law. Few people in the nineteenth century suggested that these restrictions violated a constitutional freedom of expression.

Congress first began to regulate pornography in a customs law of 1842, prohibiting the importing of sexually suggestive art. In 1865 Congress made it illegal to send indecent materials through the mails, and an amendment to the law in 1873, known as the Comstock Law, established strict criminal sanctions. Even classic works by such Italian Renaissance writers as Giovanni Boccaccio were sometimes proscribed. During this period, American courts often decided on the legality of materials by making use of Britain's Hicklin Rule, which allowed the government to ban any publication containing isolated passages that might exert "immoral influences on susceptible persons."

Although upholding the constitutionality of the Comstock Law, American courts in the twentieth century gradually rejected the extreme restrictions of the Hicklin Rule. Many judges began to insist that a literary work must be evaluated on the basis of "its dominant effect" rather than on isolated passages, and they also demanded that for a work to be proscribed it must be offensive to average adults in the community. In the mid-1930's federal appellate courts ruled that James Joyce's novel *Ulysses* (1922) and similar works could not be proscribed. About this time the U.S. Supreme Court ruled that the First Amendment's right to free expression was binding on state and local governments, and this meant that the constitutionality of all censorship would ultimately be decided in federal courts. In *Burstyn v. Wilson* (1953) the Supreme Court overturned an earlier precedent, ruling that films were a form of expression protected by the First Amendment.

Liberal Approach. The Supreme Court really began to take a liberal approach toward pornography in the watershed case of *Roth v. United States* (1957). Ruling that the Hicklin Rule was unconstitutional, the Court declared that government could only prohibit "obscene" materials in which the dominant theme appealed to "prurient interests" according to the standards of average adults. The meaning of the decision in *Roth v. United States* was that merely "indecent" materials could not be prohibited. As a result, erotic literature by writers such as D. H. Lawrence suddenly became widely available for the first time. During the early 1960's the decisions of the Court made it increasingly difficult for governments to prosecute the distribution of pornography. In 1966 the Court ruled that John Cleland's 1749 novel *Fanny Hill* was not legally obscene.

After much debate, the majority of the Supreme Court finally agreed on a compromise for judging obscenity in the case of *Miller v. California* (1973). The so-called Miller test included three components: that laws might proscribe materials appealing to prurient interests judged by the "average person" using "contemporary community standards"; that any laws must clearly define the "patently offensive" sexual depiction that is illegal; and that the material must lack "serious literary, artistic, political, or scientific values." Although strict libertarians argued that the Miller test was overly restrictive, the three criteria actually prohibited government from prosecuting the sale or production of soft-core pornography, forcing government to prove that materials were legally obscene.

Rita Moreno played a prostitute servicing Jack Nicholson in Carnal Knowledge. (Museum of Modern Art, Film Stills Archive)

Applying the test in 1974, the Court ruled that the R-rated film *Carnal Knowledge* (1971) was not obscene. In contrast, courts usually allowed communities to prohibit X-rated films such as *Deep Throat* (1972).

The Court was generally sympathetic to zoning ordinances that regulated the locations for "adults only" bookstores, theaters, and bars. In 1976 the Court upheld Detroit's ordinances that prohibited such facilities within 1,000 feet of each other or within 500 feet of a residential area. Such regulations were justified as a reasonable means to prevent "skid-row" regions and to preserve orderly neighborhoods. Zoning laws were not primarily aimed at preventing adults from obtaining pornographic materials but were designed to control the secondary effects of such materials on communities.

Feminist Opposition. The First Amendment places limits on governmental restrictions of free expression, but it does not limit the efforts of individual citizens to criticize any and all expressions. Thus, individual citizens and groups of citizens have the right to present petitions or picket the distribution of materials they dislike. Private groups have sometimes been very successful in convincing commercial stores not to sell materials judged to be pornographic, and they have also convinced commercial businesses not to advertise or promote such materials.

In the 1980's feminist groups tried to enact city ordinances prohibiting those kinds of pornography that portrayed women as "sexual objects" by men, while allowing materials that accepted gender equality. Feminist lawyer Catherine MacKinnon drafted civil ordinances of this kind for the city councils of Minneapolis and Indianapolis. The courts found that such regulations were unconstitutional because they proscribed some materials that were not judged to be obscene by the Miller test and also because the ordinances proscribed materials on the basis of the ideas they endorsed.

The Canadian courts, using the Canadian Constitution, have been more sympathetic to the feminist perspective. In 1992 the Supreme Court of Canada ruled in *Crown v. Butler* that the government was authorized to prohibit materials that are "degrading" or "harmful" to women because of their graphic depictions of rape or humiliation. Opponents of violent pornography were encour-

aged by this decision, but libertarians charged that it stifled creativity and allowed for the censorship of ideas that were unpopular or "politically incorrect."

Protection of Children. The Supreme Court has always held that the First Amendment does not prohibit government from protecting children against sexual exploitation. Congress in 1977 passed the Protection of Children Against Sexual Exploitation Act, which criminalized the interstate distribution of visual depictions of minors engaging in sexual acts, even if the materials were not obscene according to the Miller test. About half of the states soon passed similar legislation. In the case of *Ferber v. New York* (1982) the Court unanimously upheld the constitutionality of these laws, based on a finding that the distribution of "child pornography" promoted the exploitation of children.

Although the Supreme Court has allowed laws that make it illegal for children to obtain "indecent" materials, it has also tried to protect the right of adults to acquire such materials. Because many minors were telephoning "dial-a-porn" messages, an amendment to the Federal Communications Act of 1988 imposed a general ban on commercial telephone messages that were either "indecent" or "obscene." One commercial company challenged the constitutionality of this law, and the Court in *Sable Communications of California v. Federal Communications Commission* ruled that the "indecent speech" provision of the federal law was unconstitutional. The Court determined that modern technology made it possible to protect minors without the use of a total ban. Although the government had a legitimate interest in protecting children from indecent messages, the 1988 amendment was invalid insofar as it limited adult telephone conversations to content that was suitable for children.

With the widespread usage of the Internet, many parents and educators were disturbed at the extent to which minors were obtaining sexually oriented materials. In 1996 large majorities in both houses of Congress passed the Communications Decency Act (CDA), which prohibited "indecent" or "obscene" communications that might be received by minors under the age of eighteen. The American Civil Liberties Union (ACLU) and other libertarian organizations argued that the

During the 1990's the use of scantily clad teenagers in provocative poses in advertisements brought charges of "kiddie porn" against clothing manufacturers such as Calvin Klein. (AP/Wide World Photos)

CDA was unconstitutional because the definition of "indecent" included sexually oriented materials that were not "obscene" according to the Miller test. The Supreme Court agreed with the critics in *Reno v. American Civil Liberties Union* (1996), ruling that the law was unconstitutional. The Court's official opinion insisted that Congress cannot limit the right of adults to see materials that are only "fit for children."

The Reno decision made it impossible for concerned citizens to depend upon a general law to prevent minors from receiving soft-core pornography over the Internet. This meant that parents and schools would have to spend more time and effort supervising what minors might receive. The decision also stimulated new interest in filtering devices that would allow programmed restrictions on computers when used by children. Although parents clearly have the right to regulate what their children have access to, there were many problems associated with filtering devices. It was unfortunately impossible for such devices to make a distinction between materials promoting prurient interests and those providing serious information about issues of sexuality. Also, children often are able to use the Internet in schools and libraries, and public libraries and universities are required to respect adults' right of access to both relevant information and a variety of views.

Even if it is difficult to prove that pornography is a major cause of violence and the decline of stable families, many reasonable people judge that pornographic materials tend to promote the kinds of values that are not conducive to raising morally healthy children. In general, pornography usually endorses physical gratification and the pursuit of sensual pleasure. Whatever the limits on governmental censorship, parents have both the legal right and the moral obligation to exercise some control over the materials read and observed by their children, especially when children are relatively young.

—*Thomas T. Lewis*

BIBLIOGRAPHY

Attorney General's Commission on Pornography. *Final Report.* Nashville: Rutledge Hill, 1996. One-sided and controversial work that emphasizes the harmful effects of violent pornography and endorses limited censorship.

DeGrazia, Edward. *Girls Lean Back Everywhere: The Law of Obscenity and the Assault on Genius.* New York: Random House, 1992. Comprehensive historical and cultural analysis, defending an extreme libertarian point of view.

Gorman, Carol. *Pornography.* New York: Franklin Watts, 1988. Relatively short discussion that is critical of pornography while opposing most censorship over what adults may read.

Itzen, Catherine. *Pornography: Women, Violence, and Civil Liberties.* New York: Oxford University Press, 1993. Good collection of articles by British and American feminists who believe that pornography contributes to violence against women and to sexual inequality.

MacKinnon, Catharine. *Only Words.* Cambridge: Harvard University Press, 1993. Feminist lawyer's case for regulating pornography on the basis of its discriminatory effects on women.

Schauer, Frederick. *The Law of Obscenity.* Washington, D.C.: Bureau of National Affairs, 1976. Excellent and comprehensive history of censorship in the United States, especially useful for the early period.

Stossen, Nadine. *Defending Pornography.* New York: Schreiber, 1995. Head of the American Civil Liberties Union denies most charges against the effects of pornography and argues that the First Amendment prohibits almost all forms of censorship.

Wekesser, Carol, ed. *Pornography: Opposing Viewpoints.* San Diego: Greenhaven Press, 1997. Useful collection of short and cogent essays that argue for and against censorship.

Wallace, Jonathan, and Mark Manga. *Sex, Laws, and Cyberspace.* New York: Henry Holt & Co., 1997. Useful analysis of the important issue of censorship over the Internet.

See also Child abduction; Child molestation; Family values; Film depictions of families; Moral education; Sex education; Sexuality and sexual taboos.

Postpartum depression

RELEVANT ISSUES: Health and medicine; Parenting and family relationships

SIGNIFICANCE: While many women suffer a few days of "baby blues" following childbirth, 10 to 15 percent develop serious postpartum depression and 0.1 to 0.2 percent become psychotic

Between 26 and 85 percent of women experience "baby blues," also known as "maternity blues" or "new-mother blues." For one to ten days after giving birth, new mothers may cry easily, feel agitated or experience exhaustion. They may also have difficulty sleeping, experience loss of appetite, feel sad, or undergo mood swings. This is considered a normal reaction to the stress of giving birth.

At least one woman in ten develops a more serious and long-lasting depression during the first year after the birth of a baby. Health care providers may not recognize this as postpartum depression, dismissing women's concerns as "the blues" or attributing symptoms to the stresses of being a new parent. Depression may occur when women begin menstruating again or when they stop breast-feeding. Women with postpartum depression may have feelings of despair and inadequacy, be unable to cope with the demands of mothering, or suffer from guilt. Some lose interest in normal activities, feel agitated, or have thoughts of suicide. They may hide their depression for fear of being labeled "bad mothers."

A very small number of women experience psychosis, usually beginning on the second or third day after childbirth. This usually comes on suddenly, with patients showing excessive energy, extreme confusion, hallucinations or delusions, paranoia, and incoherence. Women experiencing postpartum psychosis rarely commit suicide or kill their infants.

Researchers have not been able to determine the cause of either postpartum depression or postpartum psychosis. Theories accounting for postpartum depression include hormonal imbalance, thyroid problems, and stress. No scientific evidence clearly links hormone changes to postpartum depression, although some women respond well to hormone treatment. Some women experiencing symptoms of postpartum depression have slowed or sluggish thyroid glands. Neither of these theories explains the fact that new fathers and adoptive parents may also experience postpartum depression. Women under significant stress are more likely to experience postpartum depression than women who are not under significant stress. Women more at risk of postpartum depression include those who have a history of depression or manic-depression, those who did not want to have a child, those who have experienced a personal loss within the previous two years, those who are divorced or separated, those who were abused or neglected as children, those who lack family support, those who suffer from a traumatic birth experience, or those who have high birth or parental expectations. Some women who experience postpartum psychosis have a family history of manic-depressive illness (bipolar disorder).

Women experiencing "baby blues" usually require no treatment other than rest and support from loved ones. Postpartum depression is treated with antidepressant medications, counseling, supportive care, or hospitalization. Several antidepressant drugs are compatible with continued breast-feeding. If women suffering from postpartum depression must be hospitalized, infants should remain with their mothers if at all possible in order to maintain the mother-infant relationship. Postpartum psychosis requires immediate hospitalization, antipsychotic medications, antidepressants, and possibly electroconvulsive therapy.

—*Rebecca Lovell Scott*

See also Battered child syndrome; Bonding and attachment; Childbirth; Infanticide; Parenting; Pregnancy; Suicide.

Poverty

RELEVANT ISSUES: Children and child development; Economics and work; Health and medicine; Marriage and dating; Parenting and family relationships

SIGNIFICANCE: Poverty, a key social problem, has a crucial effect on families, because it severely limits opportunities and molds outlooks

There is no greater influence on families than poverty. Poverty not only limits families financially but also takes the heart out of people. Constant stress in trying to pay monthly bills and failing to do so is a heavy burden to bear. Year after year of this stress negatively affects families. Breadwinners daily believe that they are failures when it comes to providing for their families. Insufficient food, deteriorating homes, and unsafe neighborhoods are constant reminders of poverty.

The children of poor families are not able to do what other children do, such as eat at nice restaurants, visit zoos, or go on vacations. When teachers ask, "What did you do last summer?" children from poor families are less likely to report that they went to the lake, the ocean, a baseball game—or learned how to use maps as the family traveled from state to state. These children do not have such experiences because of one main reason—poverty.

Poverty: Definition and Description. The federal government defines poverty as three times the amount of money required to provide an adequate diet for a family. The reason for this definition is that in the 1950's, when the government was first struggling to define poverty, it conducted a study on how poor people lived. After interviewing people who lived in the worst housing available and had the lowest paying jobs, the government found that such people spent one-third of their income on food. Hence, the definition of poverty. In the late 1990's the poverty level for a family of four was $15,600. In arriving at the poverty level, the government takes into account families with fewer or greater family members. About 15 percent of all people in the United States, or 40 million people, are poor.

Poverty afflicts families of all races. All poor people have fewer opportunities in life than persons who are not poor, and they worry about how to earn enough money to pay the bills. There are, however, different rates of poverty among families of different races and ethnic groups. For example, while 33 percent of all African American families are poor, only 12 percent of all white families are poor. Social scientists, having posed the question as to why families of one race are more afflicted by poverty than families of other races, have concluded, on the basis of hundreds of studies and years of research, that the main reason for this difference has been prejudice and discrimination against certain racial and ethnic groups, such as African Americans, Native Americans, and Latino Americans. Over hundreds of years whites have constructed a social structure of norms, values, methods of social control, and ideologies that have consisted of legal and illegal prejudice and discrimination.

Once constructed, this social structure has been transmitted via the process of socialization and has persisted from one generation to another. The result has been a castelike social structure for African American, Native American, and Latino American families that has prevented their upward mobility. Consequently, until the 1960's class and caste systems existed side by side in the United States. Whites lived their daily lives in the class system where there was upward mobility. African Americans, Native Americans, and Latino Americans lived their daily lives in a caste system with little or no upward mobility. For example, African American slaves could not get an education,

Based on John Steinbeck's novel about the impact of Dust Bowl conditions on farming families during the Great Depression, The Grapes of Wrath (1940) *is one of the most moving depictions of poverty in American film history.* (Museum of Modern Art, Film Stills Archive)

choose the jobs they wanted, live where they wanted, vote, or hold public office. Moreover, if they expressed disagreement, they were severely sanctioned.

Once this caste and class system had been created and perpetuated by socialization, it continued into the middle of the twentieth century.

Remnants of it have persisted to the degree that persons hold prejudices and discriminate. The overall result of this caste system for families of discriminated races was that their ancestors were less likely to work in occupations that provide decent wages and allow for the accumulation of wealth, such as land, homes, and stocks. Thus, no

Poverty in the United States in 1995

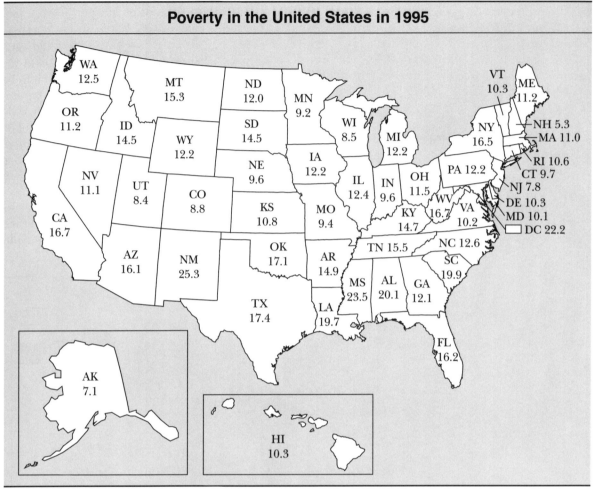

Source: U.S. Bureau of the Census, *Statistical Abstract of the United States: 1997*. Washington, D.C.: GPO, 1997.
Note: Percentages of state populations below the poverty line.

matter how honest, hardworking, and smart they were, they were greatly restricted by the larger social structure of caste.

Jobs and Child Care. The family living in poverty faces a number of daily struggles, some more apparent than others. The most apparent one is the struggle to satisfy basic needs—that is, the struggle to attain enough food and the struggle to keep the electricity and water turned on. Persistent questions are whether heads of households will bring home enough money to pay for the bare essentials and whether they will remain positive, calm, and confident in order to instill these attributes in their children. Many heads of households succumb to pessimism, cynicism, and hopelessness.

Given the immense obstacles that families living in poverty face, there are four issues that directly impinge on them: child care, marriage and family skills, jobs, and health care. Members of local, state, and federal governments struggle with these issues. There is increasing agreement that these four issues must be solved if families in poverty are to live decently.

One issue for families living in poverty is the availability of child care. Many poor families have young children at home. Hence, in order for the parents to work, they must make provision for their children. This becomes a greater concern in one-parent households. There are a number of factors that parents must weigh when considering how to work and provide for their children simultaneously. They must ask themselves whether it makes sense for them to get a job, given the costs of child care.

This can be illustrated by considering the situation of a mother with two young children. She has been taught by society that it is good to work and to be financially independent. Accepting these values, she looks for a job. Typically, such a mother will have a high-school education or less and therefore not be qualified for professional jobs and the incomes they pay. Instead, she must settle for an unskilled or semiskilled, minimum-wage job that pays just over $200 per week, or under $11,000 per year. Once federal and state taxes have been deducted from her paycheck, she loses around 20 percent of her pay, leaving her with approximately $160. While she is working, she must pay for child care. Typically, child care costs about $60 per week for one child and an additional $30 per week for additional children. After deducting $90 from her paycheck to pay for child care for her two children, she is left with about $70, with which she must pay her rent, food, clothing, electricity, water, and transportation costs. If her rent alone eats up her remaining income, she is faced with the problem of not being able to pay her other bills.

With the push in the late twentieth century to get poor people off welfare, the issue of child care has become crucial. If society wants poor people

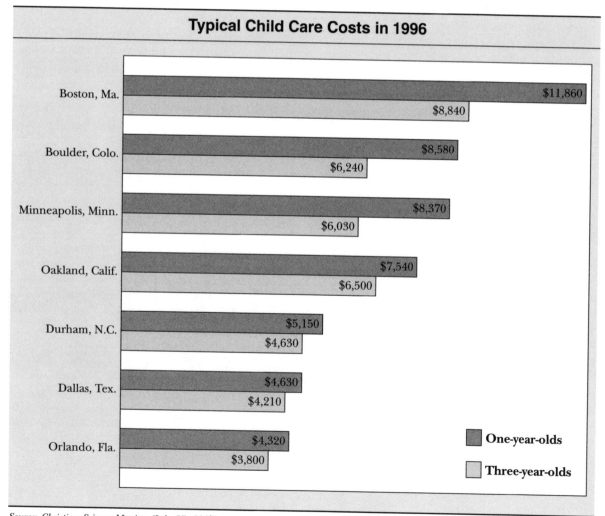

Typical Child Care Costs in 1996

City	One-year-olds	Three-year-olds
Boston, Ma.	$11,860	$8,840
Boulder, Colo.	$8,580	$6,240
Minneapolis, Minn.	$8,370	$6,030
Oakland, Calif.	$7,540	$6,500
Durham, N.C.	$5,150	$4,630
Dallas, Tex.	$4,630	$4,210
Orlando, Fla.	$4,320	$3,800

Source: Christian Science Monitor (July 25, 1997)
Note: Average annual fees charged by licensed child care centers for full-time care.

to work at low-wage jobs, it will have to find some method of financing the cost of child care. If society does not want the cost of child care to act as a disincentive to persons seeking work, it must consider whether it should help subsidize child care for the working poor. This is a key consideration with which society must struggle as it requires that poor people on welfare find jobs. Expecting the poor to work without addressing child care costs is a recipe for disaster. Other related child-care concerns are the safety, accessibility, and developmental opportunities offered by child-care facilities. Parents do not want to take their children to child-care facilities that are unsafe, far away from home, and offer children little or no room for personal development. These issues, too, must be addressed if society wishes to get poor people off welfare and into the workforce.

A key element in helping poor families dig their way out of poverty is to provide them with decent jobs, especially well-paying jobs. Even though the unemployment rate dropped to a relatively low level in the late 1990's, millions of people had no jobs, part-time jobs, or jobs that paid the minimum wage or less. If low-income parents work at minimum-wage jobs and work forty hours a week fifty-two weeks a year, they still earn $2,000 below the poverty level for a family of three. Jobs that pay $6.25 an hour, or $13,000 per year, put a family of three just above the poverty level. Such an income level would not allow families to afford luxuries, but it would meet their basic needs.

Classes in Marriage and Family. Americans see the family as the foundation of society. They see it as important to raising children and having children grow into responsible citizens who contribute to society. It is ironic that while many agree on the importance of the family, little formalized instruction is available on how to raise a family, be married, interact positively, make joint decisions, plan and adhere to a budget, plan when to have children, and raise children in a loving and devel-

The late twentieth century saw an unprecedented rise in homelessness throughout the United States. (Ben Klaffke)

opmentally healthful way. Since society holds the family in such high regard, it may need to consider creating classes to address these concerns.

Health Care. Approximately 40 million people in the United States, many of whom are poor, have no medical insurance. Although Medicaid exists to cover poor people's medical expenses, the poor must usually be on welfare in order to receive Medicaid. Yet, only about one-third of all poor people receive welfare and only about 40 percent receive Medicaid. Besides the majority of poor people who do not receive Medicaid, there are the working poor who do not have health care coverage because their employers do not provide affordable medical insurance. Consequently, millions of poor families live without medical insurance.

Children are especially exposed to illnesses if they go to child-care facilities, in which colds, ear infections, strep throat, and annual influenza strains are typical contagious maladies passed from child to child. Children afflicted with these ailments require medical attention, but medical attention costs money. Thus, low-income parents without medical insurance face a dilemma when their children get sick. They want to care for their children, but they cannot afford to do so. Likewise, when adults in uninsured poor families get sick, they, too, are in a quandary. Because visiting a doctor may place them in debt, they are likely to refrain from seeking medical care. The result is that they can develop more serious health conditions. Thus, they face the choice of either going into debt or hoping that their illnesses will cure themselves. To solve this problem, society must address the question of health care for low-income families.

—*James A. Crone*

BIBLIOGRAPHY

Beeghley, Leonard. *Living Poorly in America.* New York: Praeger, 1983. Discusses definition, rate, and causes of poverty and the relationship of poverty to public assistance and work.

Berger, Peter L., and Thomas Luckmann. *The Social Construction of Reality: A Treatise in the Sociology of Knowledge.* New York: Anchor Books, 1966. Deals with how humans construct their social world and how they use socialization to perpetuate the social structures they have created.

Citro, Constance F., and Robert T. Michael, eds. *Measuring Poverty: A New Approach.* Washington, D.C.: National Academy Press, 1995. Thoroughly examines issues surrounding the measurement of poverty, including defining thresholds and resources, and the use of poverty measures in government assistance programs.

Eitzen, D. Stanley, and Maxine Baca Zinn. *Social Problems.* 7th ed. Boston: Allyn & Bacon, 1997. Addresses the definition, description, causes, and possible solutions of poverty and the family.

Kelso, William A. *Poverty and the Underclass: Changing Perceptions of the Poor in America.* New York: New York University Press, 1994. Provides broad explanations of poverty that focus on both individuals and the economic environment in which they live.

Pressman, Steven. *Poverty in America: An Annotated Bibliography.* Metuchen, N.J.: Scarecrow Press, 1994. Annotates research and analyses by economists, sociologists, and other social scientists on the causes, consequences, and cures of poverty in the United States.

Timmer, Doug A., D. Stanley Eitzen, and Kathryn D. Talley. *Paths to Homelessness: Extreme Poverty and the Urban Housing Crisis.* Boulder, Colo.: Westview Press, 1994. Reports on the homelessness experiences of nine individuals and families in a series of ethnographic studies.

See also Aid to Families with Dependent Children (AFDC); Child abandonment; Culture of poverty theory; Fatherlessness; Feminization of poverty; Head Start; Homeless families; Personal Responsibility and Work Opportunity Reconciliation Act; Single-parent families; Social capital; Social Security; Social workers; Supplemental Nutrition Program for Women, Infants, and Children; Wealth; Welfare.

Pregnancy

RELEVANT ISSUES: Parenting and family relationships; Sociology

SIGNIFICANCE: Pregnancy, while a normal life event, alters the structure of the family system, as boundaries, roles, and duties must be reorganized in anticipation of accommodating new family members

The family is a basic social system that undergoes development, growth, and change. When faced with the physical, social, and psychological challenges that pregnancy brings, pregnancy can be considered a family crisis. It changes the state of the world and families' view of it, and it demands that families readapt by using new methods to resolve the social restructuring. The expected birth of infants reorganizes a two-person pattern into a triangular one and changes only children into siblings. Couples are seldom trained for parenthood, and parenthood's highly romanticized roles often conflict with other social and economic realities. Pregnancy and parenthood also mark persons' final transition into maturity and adult responsibility in society, placing social and economic stress on parents-to-be.

Changes in Understanding Pregnancy. The understanding of pregnancy in North America has gone through dramatic changes since the early 1900's, creating a dynamic shift in the issues facing pregnant families. Before the twentieth century, society viewed pregnancy and childbirth as predominantly women's responsibility. By the 1950's, however, the medical community had characterized pregnancy as a pathological experience and negated family involvement in the process. However, confronted with medical studies and the protests of feminist groups and midwives, hospitals and physicians by the late twentieth century had concluded that women's psychological and physiological health depended women's active participation in pregnancy and childbirth and their families' support during the process. By giving the responsibility for pregnancy and childbirth back to women and their families, the traditional views of male and female roles within the family system were challenged. Expectant fathers were encouraged to play a vital role in an experience from which they had once been excluded. Meanwhile, pregnant women, faced with a society whose feminist movement had steadily devalued motherhood and favored career-oriented roles, questioned their own maternal identity. Society's changing expectations of pregnant couples challenged their marital bonds, the structure of their families, and their individual attainment of maternal and paternal identity.

Pregnant Women. With physical changes and fetal movements as constant reminders, women feel the effects of pregnancy more forcefully than any other family members. During pregnancy, women are faced with psychological tasks that correspond to physiological changes. These tasks include ensuring that they and their fetuses have a safe passage through pregnancy, labor, and delivery; helping their families to accept new members; and creating a maternal bond with their unborn children. Throughout pregnancy, women experience physical changes, making them feel ill, tired, awkward, and vulnerable. This heightens their awareness and concern for their bodies and alters their sense of self. Women's increased physical and emotional dependency on others, particularly their husbands or partners, may leave them struggling with feelings of inferiority even as they look for increasing commitment and cooperation from them.

As pregnant women attempt to develop their new identity as mothers, they may find that they feel unable to achieve their maternal identity because of a lack of knowledge and preparation for that role. Often, they look to their own mothers and their positive or negative relationships for guidance. Pregnant women may also experience a loss of self-esteem as they interrupt their careers for motherhood, as a loss of career is a loss of self for some women. As their own identity begins to change during pregnancy, so does their role within their families. Physically, they may be unable to do housework or work outside the home and will rely more heavily on their partners or children to contribute to the family economy.

Expectant Fathers. Men face their own psychological adjustments when they change from husbands or partners into fathers. In men's evolution as fathers, they evaluate their relationships with their own fathers, which will have helped or hindered them in their understanding of a father's identity. In adjusting to fatherhood, they may feel threatened by their partners' pregnancy, sometimes resulting from their fear of fatherhood and the emotional and economic challenges of child rearing. In response to this perceived threat, they may react by displaying unsupportive behavior, including burying themselves in their work, showing intolerance of their partners' emotional sensitivity, mocking their physical changes, or showing no interest in the pregnancy.

Men can play a variety of roles during pregnancy. They may express themselves as observers: staying emotionally distant and acting as bystand-

Physical exercise is an important element of healthy pregnancies. (Hazel Hankin)

ers to the pregnancy. They may emphasize the tasks to be accomplished during pregnancy and attempt to make all decisions that must be reached. They may also become highly emotionally involved in the pregnancy. Men who are jealous of their partners' pregnancy and unable to experience it may even suffer from what is known as couvade syndrome, which includes physical symptoms of pregnancy such as leg cramps and nausea. Conversely, fathers who have seen themselves in traditional male roles within their families may withdraw, feeling inadequate or fearful of

Stages of Fetal Development

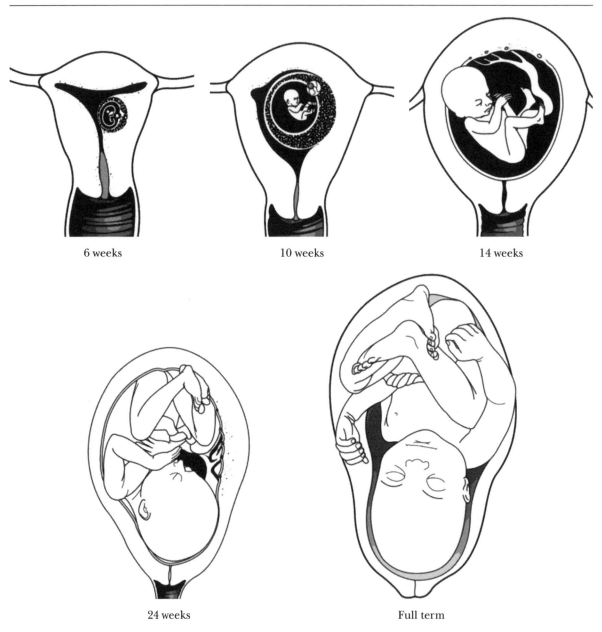

6 weeks

10 weeks

14 weeks

24 weeks

Full term

Pregnancy permanently alters family structures, forcing a reorganization of responsibilities to accommodate new family members. (James L. Shaffer)

attending to their partners' needs during labor and delivery when confronted with a societal emphasis on family activism in pregnancy. Despite the stress that these fears can bring, fathers' participation during childbirth can provide a means of coping with the intense feelings associated with birth and reinforce their identity as parents, leading to more rapid father-infant bonding.

Couples and Pregnancy. The relationship that pregnant women have with their husbands or partners can be the most significant dimension affecting the course of pregnancy. Poor relationships have been associated with premature labor, depression during pregnancy, and maternal postpartum depression. Pregnancy and childbirth can strain relationships that are already in jeopardy and be the decisive event in overturning them. However, if partners become closer and more intimate in sharing pregnancy and their evolving roles as parents, their relationships may mature and broaden as they discover new aspects of each other.

Partners prepare for parenting in similar ways: by reading, planning, fantasizing about the baby and the upcoming change in lifestyle, attending classes, and talking to other fathers and mothers.

They confront the spatial changes that pregnancy and childbirth bring: space within homes must be divided to make room for newcomers. Pregnant women often experience a decreased or increased sexual drive, which affects their husbands or partners sexual function and understanding of their shared sexuality. Families, particularly those with adolescent or older pregnant women, are also affected by pregnant women's nutritional health and physical restrictions. Couples facing an unwanted pregnancy are strained by the difficult decision to terminate it, as they must weigh religious and ethical considerations against the concerns of an extended family or society that may oppose the pregnancy.

Couples benefit from conversing with other pregnant couples, particularly through childbirth preparation courses, which first made their appearance in North America in the 1950's. In such courses, couples may discover people experiencing similar emotional responses, learn techniques to lessen their insecurities and apprehensions, and gain knowledge about the physiological experience of childbirth.

Siblings' Response to Pregnancy. Siblings' influence upon the family can begin even before newborns arrive. Siblings feel parents' anticipation, are sometimes physically affected by their mother's increasing tiredness and awkwardness, and might feel antagonism toward their mothers. The birth of babies may cause sibling reactions ranging from sleep disturbances and frequent crying to emotionalism and regressive behaviors, as siblings reevaluate their place in the family and adjust to their new roles. Societal factors that complicate siblings' adjustment to newborns include working parents, an increased dependence on child care, and other economic changes.

Pregnant families face major structural and functional reorganization as they attempt to accommodate new family members. During pregnancy, the family system is altered: A husband-wife system of interaction must expand to include mother-child and father-child systems. Before infants' birth both partners must adjust to the change from spousal to parental roles. If siblings are involved, they must learn how to accept the unborn children and realize that child order in the family structure will change. Recognizing these psychological adjustments, pregnancy health

care by the late twentieth century included the entire family in an attempt to lessen the stress that pregnancy and childbirth place on families.

—Rebecca Strand Johnson

BIBLIOGRAPHY

Colman, Arthur D., and Libby Lee Colman. *Pregnancy: The Psychological Experience.* New York: Herder and Herder, 1971.

Lederman, Regina P. *Psychosocial Adaptation in Pregnancy: Assessment of Seven Dimensions of Maternal Development.* 2d ed. New York: Springer, 1996.

Lipkin, Gladys B. *Psychological Aspects of Maternal-Child Nursing.* St. Louis: C. V. Mosby, 1974.

Rubin, Reva. *Maternal Identity and the Maternal Experience.* New York: Springer, 1984.

Sherwen, Laurie Nehls. *The Psychosocial Dimensions of the Pregnant Family.* New York: Springer, 1987.

See also Abortion; Birth control; Birth defects; Childbirth; Family crises; Fertility and infertility; Marriage; Multiple births; Postpartum depression; Pregnancy Discrimination Act; Reproductive technologies; Surrogate mothers; Test-tube babies.

Pregnancy Discrimination Act

DATE: Adopted on October 31, 1978
RELEVANT ISSUES: Economics and work; Health and medicine; Law; Parenting and family relationships
SIGNIFICANCE: This act banned various forms of discrimination against pregnant employees

When Congress banned employment discrimination on the basis of gender in Title VII of the Civil Rights Act of 1964, some employers refused to give reasonable accommodation to pregnant women and even fired pregnant employees or canceled their accumulated seniority when they went on unpaid maternity leave. Accordingly, Congress amended Title VII to provide that the terms in the statute "because of sex" or "on the basis of sex" should include "pregnancy, childbirth, or related medical conditions." Abortions, however, were covered only if necessary to protect the lives of mothers. Further protections were later extended under the Americans with Disabilities Act of 1990 and the Family and Medical Leave Act of 1993, including the opportunity under some conditions

The U.S. Congress passed the Pregnancy Discrimination Act in 1978 to protect pregnant workers from being dismissed from their jobs or suffering other unfair treatment because of their condition. (McCrea Adams)

for men to go on leave to assist their pregnant wives and newborn children.

The nondiscrimination requirement does not place any affirmative requirements on employers, who are vaguely instructed to treat pregnancy and childbirth as they would all other medical conditions. In *Troupe v. May Department Stores*, the Seventh Circuit Court ruled in 1994 that the employer was justified in firing a pregnant woman who, as a result of "morning sickness," was repeatedly late to work. —*Michael Haas*

See also Abortion; Americans with Disabilities Act (ADA); Childbirth; Family and Medical Leave Act (FMLA); Men's roles; Pregnancy.

Prenuptial agreements

RELEVANT ISSUES: Divorce; Law; Marriage and dating

SIGNIFICANCE: Prenuptial agreements affect marriages by setting the terms of their dissolution before marriage even occurs

Prenuptial agreements are contracts entered into before marriage. These agreements may address the division of property in the event of divorce, death, or some other event. They also may address alimony, financial support, making of a will, creation of a trust, and other matters. Prenuptial agreements are also called antenuptial agreements, marriage contracts, marital settlement agreements, and premarital agreements.

Postnuptial agreements are similar to prenuptial agreements except they are entered into after marriage. Postnuptial agreements are often treated much the same as prenuptial agreements, both legally and by the parties entering into them.

Development of the Agreement. Prenuptial agreements have the legal status of contracts, but the English common law as brought to America generally did not recognize contracts between husband and wife. Unmarried women had most of the legal rights of men, but the situation for women changed drastically upon marriage, when they gave up legal rights to their husbands, who acted for them. As a result, prenuptial agreements could not be enforced once the couple married. The husband acquired almost total control of the wife's legal affairs and assets.

The harshness of this rule was sometimes miti-

gated, as when the husband abandoned the wife. It was not until the passage of the Married Women's Property Acts in the nineteenth century, however, that wives acquired most of the legal rights of men and unmarried women. Prenuptial agreements became generally enforceable only when these acts became effective.

A prenuptial agreement is a special kind of contract because husband and wife have what the law describes as a confidential relationship. This relationship is much the same as between attorney and client, doctor and patient, and guardian and ward. In such confidential relationships, the parties often owe each other a fiduciary duty. As a result, a court will look more closely at a prenuptial agreement than at an ordinary contract between strangers or people in business.

Most states have statutes governing the creation and operation of at least parts of these agreements. Some states have passed the Uniform Premarital Agreement Act, which provides more detailed legal rules. These statutes provide at a minimum that any prenuptial agreement be in writing and signed by both parties.

Reasons for Prenuptial Agreements. Modern American law looks with favor on prenuptial agreements. Courts favor them as a matter of public policy because they prevent litigation, settle property rights, secure marital peace, and further the welfare of the parties and the purposes of marriage.

Economic and personal factors determine when people will enter into prenuptial agreements. Wealthy people traditionally have used these agreements to keep their fortunes and businesses intact and to keep wealth within a single family. Without such agreements, money and other assets could easily pass into the hands of a spouse who might not have the same loyalty to the family.

Prenuptial agreements have become popular among the middle class, especially professionals. This popularity can be traced to two causes. First, many middle-class individuals own or control more valuable assets than in the past. Second, the increase in divorce followed by second marriages has left many people with children from a first marriage to whom they wish to leave most or all their property. Without a prenuptial agreement, a surviving spouse normally would be entitled under state law to a large share of this property. With

Couples most likely to sign prenuptial agreements are those whose partners enter marriage already owning greatly different amounts of wealth. (Skjold Photographs)

a prenuptial agreement, however, the spouse waives his or her rights to a share of the property of the other spouse. This situation leaves the property free to go to the children of the prior marriage.

Although the terms of prenuptial agreements normally are enforced, there are certain subject areas that they cannot vary or change. A husband and wife owe each other certain marital rights while they are married, such as the right of support. Although a prenuptial agreement may change support obligations after divorce, it cannot change the support obligation while the parties are married. The legal rights of children of the marriage cannot be altered. These rights include the right to support both before and after divorce of the parents, as well as the right of the children to property. A prenuptial agreement also cannot override some state laws on descent and distribution of property upon death of a spouse. The courts and the state legislature must determine which laws are mandatory and which can be altered by agreement.

Court Enforcement of Agreements. Even if a prenuptial agreement addresses a legally accepted subject area, courts may still refuse to enforce a particular agreement. Like all contracts, a prenuptial agreement will not be enforced if it violates public policy or was induced by fraud, misrepresentation, duress, or undue influence. Courts go even further, however, in examining prenuptial agreements because these agreements involve a confidential or fiduciary relationship. Courts often will investigate whether a particular prenuptial agreement is fair, equitable, and reasonable considering the facts and circumstances surrounding the parties and the contract. The purpose behind such close examination is to protect one party from overreaching by the other party. Such overreaching has been found in many prenuptial agreements.

The courts generally impose three requirements when checking the fairness of prenuptial agreements. First, was the agreement signed voluntarily? Second, is the agreement unconscionable? Third, was there complete disclosure?

If a court finds that someone did not voluntarily sign the agreement, it will not be enforced. Fraud, misrepresentation, duress, and undue influence are enough grounds to refuse enforcement. The fact that the person who signed was unwise or gave up substantial assets is irrelevant, because most prenuptial agreements involve giving up something. A court will investigate whether the person had sufficient time and expertise to make a reasoned decision to sign. The age of the person, the time he or she had to consider the consequences of the agreement, his or her access to independent legal counsel, prior business and investment experience, and other factors will be weighed.

Unenforceable Agreements. An unconscionable agreement will almost never be enforced. This kind of agreement must be extreme and gross in its abuse of the affected party. The fact that a spouse gets only a small amount of money or limited assets is by itself not enough to make an agreement unconscionable. Even if the spouse gets a disproportionately small amount or considerably less than without the agreement, a court will still enforce the prenuptial agreement. If a small amount of settlement is accompanied by evidence of overreaching by the other person, however, courts will not enforce the agreement. In addition, an agreement that would leave a spouse destitute or a public charge on welfare will cause a court to refuse enforcement.

Full disclosure also is required. The person seeking to enforce a prenuptial agreement must make full and complete disclosure of his or her financial wealth to the other party at the time of the agreement. The nature and extent of this disclosure varies from state to state. Some states require a detailed listing of all assets and sources of income. Other states require something less and are often satisfied if the parties have a general idea about each other's wealth. Other states impose a duty to inquire and investigate the assets of the other person. If one party fails to make the required disclosure, however, the court will refuse to enforce the prenuptial agreement.

Prenuptial agreements are one way individuals preserve their assets, income, and wealth when getting married. They are a mechanism for passing such wealth to future generations and minimizing interference by a spouse who may not need access to such wealth. Prenuptial agreements also are a source of overreaching when a future spouse is induced to sign an agreement without full disclosure or the benefit of reasoned judgment.

—David E. Paas

BIBLIOGRAPHY

American Bar Association Family Legal Guide. 2d ed. New York: Random House, 1994.

Friedman, Lawrence M. *American Law.* New York: W. W. Norton, 1984.

———. *A History of American Law.* New York: Simon & Schuster, 1973.

Johnson, Daniel. *The Consumer's Guide to Understanding and Using the Law.* Cincinnati, Ohio: Betterway Books, 1994.

See also Alimony; Divorce; Family law; Inheritance and estate law; Marriage; Marriage laws; Wealth.

Primogeniture

RELEVANT ISSUES: Kinship and genealogy; Law
SIGNIFICANCE: Primogeniture is a common form of inheritance that structures family relations around the male line through the oldest son

The concept of primogeniture originated in Roman law. In the Roman Empire the law recognized the male head of the household as *paterfamilias*, who possessed legal jurisdiction over the property of the household and the family members living in it. The *paterfamilias* passed down the patrimony, or estate, of the family to the oldest son. The oldest son did likewise, thus ensuring the union of the estate with an unbroken family line.

In 476 C.E. the Roman Empire collapsed after being invaded by Germanic tribes from northern Europe. Germanic custom divided the patrimony among all the sons of a family, and the tribes that overran the Roman Empire abandoned the practice of primogeniture in their new lands. This further subdivided the patrimony with each succeeding generation. The result of the combination of dividing the patrimony among all the sons of a family and the disappearance of central governmental authority was feudalism, a very localized system of control over increasingly smaller tracts

Under the old system of primogeniture, eldest sons were assured of inheriting most of their fathers' wealth and patriarchal authority. (Wendy Sacket)

of land. Over centuries this system brought disunity and cultural disintegration to the areas in which it prevailed.

The rise of monarchies in Western Europe reversed this process of disintegration. Primogeniture survived in the non-Germanic areas of Europe and later laid the foundation for the appearance of monarchies in the Middle Ages. Significantly, these monarchies first arose in the areas of Western Europe least touched by Germanic influence: in France, England, and Spain. The new monarchies had built up enormous power by 1500 and had strengthened the practice of primogeniture, avoiding the fragmentation prevailing in the Germanic areas. Following the example set by powerful monarchies, primogeniture became a common way of transmitting land ownership not only among kings, but also among ordinary families.

Primogeniture was a more efficient arrangement from both an administrative and an economic perspective than the practice of dividing the patrimony among all the sons of a family. A family with a clear line of authority formed the basis of a patriarchal social structure, and the concentration of family lands in the hands of a single patriarch made for a more efficient social and family economy. Yet, primogeniture had its costs as well. The denial of a share in the family estate compelled the younger sons of the patriarch to seek careers elsewhere, whether in the military, the clergy, or in trade. Primogeniture also completely excluded from inheritance the female members of households. Women, if they possessed any authority over the household at all, did so in case of the death or incapacity of their husbands or fathers only as trustees for their oldest sons until the latter reached maturity.

The practice of primogeniture began to wane in the modern period. In 1870 women in England gained limited rights over family property, thus undermining primogeniture. Also, the legal probation of estates has produced a more equitable division of property within the family. Primogeniture as a legal concept has vanished in the industrialized countries of the Western world, but it still persists in various underdeveloped countries.

—*Aristide Sechandice*

See also Birth order; Equality of children; Family law; Inheritance and estate law; Kinship systems; Marxist critique of the family; Son preference; Wills and bequests.

Prison inmates

RELEVANT ISSUES: Law; Parenting and family relationships; Race and ethnicity; Sociology; Violence

SIGNIFICANCE: Prison inmates, both male and female, often come from negative domestic environments, which are then further disrupted by incarceration

Not only inmates but also the families of inmates, and especially their children, are often adversely affected by inmates' incarceration. Female inmates, although only a small percentage of the total prison population, usually face greater familial problems than male inmates because of their incarceration, which has a greater negative impact on women and their families. Because an extremely disproportionate number of inmates of both genders are ethnic minorities, minority family patterns are highly relevant to the situations of inmates and their families.

Demography. In the late twentieth century there were more than one million prison inmates and more than a half million jail inmates in the United States, and both populations are steadily rising. Approximately half of all inmates belong to minority groups, and most of these are African Americans. Approximately 5 percent are female, although the number of female inmates is gradually on the rise. A large and rapidly growing number of inmates of all backgrounds has been incarcerated for drug-related offenses. The typical prison inmate actually serves about two years of a significantly longer sentence. The typical jail inmate only stays about two weeks, since about half of those in jail have not yet had trials and are often released quickly on bail or their own recognizance. Most prison inmates are in their twenties and thirties, although a gradually increasing number are middle-aged, partly because of mandatory sentences.

The typical inmate, regardless of race or gender, comes from an economically or culturally deprived or dysfunctional family background and tends to have had familial problems at the time of incarceration. These problems have typically been

For many criminal offenders, freedom ends at the moment of arrest. (James L. Shaffer)

By the late 1990's more than a million and a half Americans were incarcerated in prisons and jails—more people than live in many small countries. (Ben Klaffke)

aggravated by other problems, such as unemployment, undereducation, substance abuse, and—especially for females—previous adult or juvenile victimization that has often taken place in domestic settings. At the time of their incarceration, about 75 to 80 percent of female inmates have been de facto custodial parents of children under the age of eighteen. Far fewer male inmates have been custodial parents, although a highly disproportionate number have been absentee or unwed fathers at the time of their incarceration. Only about 20 percent of male inmates have been legally married at the time of their incarceration, and fewer than half of them have ever been legally married. The care and custody of minor children is therefore a much greater area of concern for female than for male inmates, while maintaining contact with their incarcerated fathers is often very problematic for the children of male inmates.

Male Inmates and Their Families. When males are incarcerated, they often become dependent on female family members for information, moral support, and a variety of other tangible or intangible forms of support, including the fiscal and disciplinary responsibility for children in cases in which care and custody were previously shared. This may occasion major role reversals within households. Although women who cope effectively are occasionally strengthened by this experience, family relationships and finances are usually considerably disrupted, while families' collective identity is threatened. Loss of family status in the community is also a frequent problem, both during and after incarceration. Families with relatively strong coping skills can often endure short or moderate incarcerations of up to three years, but families with weak coping skills can rarely endure a year and may disintegrate prior to incarceration, particularly while cases are being handled in the courts.

Married male inmates who retain contact with their families often worry about their partners' sexual fidelity and their own loss of power and status in the family, while their wives tend to have more practical concerns, such as earning money to pay the bills and trying to manage the household in the temporary capacity of single-parent breadwinners. Inmates as well as family members tend to experience a variety of negative emotions, such as fear, loneliness, depression, and guilt. In-

stitutional visitation and furlough programs tend to benefit inmates and their children more than they benefit wives, whose coping mechanisms are often overstretched by the daily needs of economic and personal survival. Conjugal visits are typically appreciated more by male inmates than by their wives, especially if wives must make special arrangements for their children. Many inmates' wives face logistical problems, such as scheduling and transportation, and few correctional institutions have adequate facilities or activities for visiting children.

Upon their release, male inmates often experience difficulty in resuming or reclaiming their former familial roles if other family members have successfully assumed these responsibilities. In extreme cases this may be a factor in males becoming repeat offenders. However, the success of male parolees is usually positively correlated to family ties of almost any meaningful sort. Families that can survive the ordeal of family members' incarceration tend to have something useful to offer to all parties in the relationship and perhaps especially to the former inmates. Studies of this process have inevitably focused on those families that have remained intact, because researchers have found it easier to obtain the cooperation of nonincarcerated relatives, and prison officials may be more sympathetic to researchers studying married inmates than to those studying unmarried inmates.

Given that most male inmates are unmarried at the time of their incarceration, a great deal remains to be learned about the domestic and familial aspects of male inmates' lives and careers. It is known, however, that like their female counterparts male inmates often come from previously adverse domestic situations, including those involving cases of criminality among immediate family members. In fact, previous criminality of male family members, such as fathers or brothers, is one of the most accurate predictors of both crime and delinquency among males, and the lack of a positive male role model within the family is a persistent problem for many boys at risk of delinquency. Many families endure the hardship of simultaneously having several males from the same or successive generations in jail, prison, or juvenile custody.

Female Inmates and Their Families. The first concern of newly incarcerated female inmates is usually the care and custody of their children. In rare cases children's fathers, if available, may be willing and able to help meet this need. However, other family members, such as children's maternal grandparents (and often just their maternal grandmothers), are far more likely to step in and provide temporary domiciles for the children. This is especially likely in those minority subcultures where extended family networks remain stronger than they tend to be in the white, middle-class subculture. If family members cannot house their children, foster care and institutional placement are the most likely alternatives, causing great anxiety to inmates about the possible loss of custody of their children after their release from jail or prison.

Female inmates receive fewer visits and fewer letters from spouses and significant others than male inmates with family ties. They often rely on female relatives, such as mothers or sisters, to maintain contact with their children and other close relatives, about whom they are typically more concerned than most male inmates. Women's prisons are more likely than men's prisons to be geographically distant from inmates' homes, since many states only have one major institution for women. However, to compensate for the loss of familial relationships, female inmates frequently become involved in "play families" within prisons and jails. These simulated extended families often include three "generations," complete with "siblings," "parents," and even "grandparents" of both "genders," as well as occasional "aunts" and "uncles." These simulated extended families are often associated with ongoing homosexual relationships, which tend to be less exploitative and more emotionally positive than comparable homosexual relationships in men's prisons, although a considerable amount of dominance and submission may be involved in both instances.

The male counterpart of the "play family" is the prison gang, which exists more for protection than for companionship, although it does fulfill some of the social functions of extended families. Gangs are much less prevalent in women's prisons, but female gang membership has gradually increased on the street, especially among juveniles and in multigenerational gang families.

Because women inmates in general tend to have been exploited and victimized in dependent or codependent relationships before their incarceration, it is especially difficult for them to get back on their feet emotionally. Some of them have never had adequate self-esteem and have been physical, emotional, or economic victims since early childhood. Positive relationships with children and other family members during incarceration can help them a great deal. However, it is equally important to provide female offenders, most of whose previous economic options have been even more limited than those of male offenders, with significant career alternatives and a measure of economic opportunity. Prison-based programs for female offenders have far too often suffered from inadequate resources and gender stereotyping. Ironically, such programs have also ignored the statistics indicating the incidence of custodial motherhood among female inmates and the psychological importance of family ties.

Family Reunion Program in New York. One good example of an innovative program for male inmates and their families is the Family Reunion Program (FRP) in New York State. Under the FRP, families spend entire weekends together at prisons, uninterrupted by other visitors and relatively unsupervised by correctional officers. Parents work out their own logistical arrangements within the limitations of the rather sterile institutional setting. These are not primarily conjugal visits and may not even involve sexual relations. Both husbands and wives report that activities with their children tend to predominate. Husbands and children report high levels of satisfaction with the program, while wives report that they are moderately satisfied. Problems with the program include the cost to families involved, the inconvenience of scheduling and travel, and the resulting infrequency with which families participate who would otherwise participate more regularly.

If they were combined with inmate home furloughs and family counseling, programs like the FRP could become the cornerstone of successful, family-based rehabilitation programs for inmates of both genders. Resources and facilities for innovative programs will always be a problem as the prisons become increasingly overcrowded and their budgets are stretched to the breaking point. However, part of the administrative burden of such programs—for example, transportation costs of inmates and their families to and from prison,

Female prisoners tend to have fewer visitors from outside and receive fewer letters than their incarcerated male counterparts. (Ben Klaffke)

Despite a trend to provide prisoners with more amenities, incarceration ultimately means severing most contacts with the outside world. (Ben Klaffke)

can be assumed by correctional volunteers. This already occurs to some extent in jurisdictions that have one-on-one sponsor or "buddy" programs, which encourage inmates to develop positive links to community-based volunteers as they prepare for parole. However, such sponsorships need to be extended to include inmates' families whenever possible. At times this may be problematic because of such factors as repeated criminal activity, delinquency, or substance abuse within families, creating an extra burden for volunteers and an added risk for wardens. Often it is merely a case of families not having adequate transportation, gas money, or moral support in dealing with difficult situations.

Nursery and Child Visitation Programs in Nebraska. A good example of an innovative program for female inmates and their children is found at the Nebraska Center for Women in York, Nebraska. This prison houses about 70 percent of the incarcerated adult female felons in the state. Pregnant inmates and those who have recently given birth are permitted to keep their newborns at the prison in private rooms with cribs until they are a year old. Then children up to the age of nine for boys and twelve for girls may visit the prison and stay overnight as many as five nights per month as part of a program called Mother-Offspring Life Development (MOLD). Inmates must pay for their children's meals from their meager savings and arrange for children's transportation. Some transportation duties are performed by volunteers, but most are performed by family members, which is quite difficult for inmates from the western part of the state. Many of the supplies and most of the furniture in the nursery have been donated by private citizens.

Only one other state has a comparable program, which has generated considerable satisfaction among both inmates and the warden. Learning valuable parenting skills and budgeting for visiting children's meals—for example, by cutting back on soft drinks and cigarettes—are considered part of inmates' rehabilitation. The warden has also reported that his concern for the welfare of the children has been a major factor in his decision to continue with the new programs. Except for a few minor injuries to the children on the playground, there has never been a serious problem of implementation.

Furloughs are not granted to Nebraska inmates as often as they are to inmates in many other states, causing some problems with continuity and follow-up. The accessibility of the institutionally-based programs to all inmates with children is another ongoing difficulty because of geography, since York is in a fairly isolated rural area. However, it is located within 100 miles of the state's three largest cities near the interstate highway that connects them, and there is no other maximum- or medium-security facility for women in the state. Part of the geographical difficulty might be overcome by persuading sheriffs in remote western counties to house occasional female felons in their local jails, but it is unlikely that this could easily include all the options for children available at York. Most jails are even more strapped for facilities and resources than prisons, and they are accustomed to a more transient population with less need or opportunity for ongoing rehabilitative efforts. The special needs of women in jail, and especially of pregnant women or women with small children, have long been ignored by the criminal justice system, which has assumed that women are unlikely to be in jail very long.

Conclusions. Lack of programmatic innovation and creativity in the use of community-based resources has hampered correctional efforts to strengthen the family ties of inmates or utilize existing family ties in rehabilitative contexts. Community volunteers and in-kind donations are among the many largely untapped resources for this effort. Although punishment and the protection of the community are clearly among the legitimate manifest functions of jails and prisons, the punishment of inmates' families, and especially their children, clearly is not. Yet, this is often an unintended consequence of the reluctance of correctional officials to take reasonable risks in providing inmates and their families greater access to one another, gradually increasing the availability of special privileges such as furloughs, as inmates get closer to parole.

Starting with small experiments and building toward larger ones would be a wise approach, given the political and economic constraints that any such innovations must face. There are only two hundred incarcerated female felons at any given time in York, Nebraska, and only about half a dozen at any given time care for resident infant children. The entire Canadian prison system incarcerates only a minute fraction of the female inmates found in the United States, and the Canadian government is highly receptive to the special needs of female inmates. This would be an excellent opportunity to expand the Nebraska experiment on a national basis and combine it with more comprehensive use of home furloughs.

—Tom Cook

BIBLIOGRAPHY

Allen, Harry, and Clifford Simonsen. *Corrections in America.* 7th ed. Upper Saddle River, N.J.: Prentice-Hall, 1995. Very comprehensive overview of American corrections, including separate chapters on male and female inmates.

Carlson, Bonnie, and Neil Cervera. *Inmates and Their Wives.* Westport, Conn.: Greenwood Press, 1992. Balanced modern account of the problems of married male inmates from the perspectives of the inmates, their wives, and the prison, including details of the Family Reunion Program in New York.

Clear, Todd, and George Cole. *American Corrections.* 4th ed. Belmont, Calif.: Wadsworth, 1997. Overview of American corrections, including separate chapters on female inmates and race/ethnicity in corrections.

Girschick, Lori. *Soledad Women.* Westport, Conn.: Greenwood Press, 1996. Modern feminist approach to the problems and life situations of the wives of male inmates in Soledad prison, including an excellent bibliography and lengthy quotations from the author's interviews with the participating women.

Hewitt, Bill, Margaret Nelson, and Elizabeth Velez. "Mothers Behind Bars." *People* 46 (November 11, 1996). Modern account of female inmates and their children in Nebraska and Virginia, with details of innovative nursery and visitation programs in Nebraska.

Matthews, Roger, and Peter Francis, eds. *Prisons 2000.* New York: St. Martin's Press, 1996. Modern international perspective on the phenomenon of imprisonment, with recommended reforms.

Schneller, D. P. *The Prisoner's Family.* San Francisco, Calif.: R. and E. Research Associates, 1976. Empirical study of the effects of imprisonment on families of male inmates, including summaries

of former studies dating as far back as the 1920's.

See also African Americans; Alcoholism and drug abuse; Codependency; Dysfunctional families; Father-son relationships; Gangs; Juvenile courts; Juvenile delinquency; Megan's Law; Substitute caregivers; Unwed fathers; Volunteerism.

Privacy

RELEVANT ISSUES: Law; Parenting and family relationships

SIGNIFICANCE: Americans enjoy a great deal of freedom from intrusions into their personal affairs, but this freedom is limited by the need to protect the public welfare and safety

The modern view of privacy, often defined as "the right to be let alone," has its historical roots in respect for private property and liberty. The Anglo-American legal tradition has long emphasized a special zone of privacy within persons' families and homes. Although the U.S. Constitution does not use the word privacy, several provisions in the Bill of Rights protect particular aspects of privacy, such as the Fourth Amendment guarantee against "unreasonable searches and seizures." In the twentieth century, legislatures have passed many statutes and tort laws (laws pertaining to wrongful acts for which relief may be obtained in the form of damages or injunctions) to deter invasions of privacy by government, the press, and others. Since the 1960's the U.S. Supreme Court has explicitly held that the Constitution protects a generic "right to privacy," which includes intimate relationships and personal choices. Canadian law, especially since the 1982 Charter of Rights and Freedoms, has moved in a similar direction.

Fourth Amendment. The Fourth Amendment to the U.S. Constitution requires that police officials have "probable cause" before they conduct a search of private property, and it also suggests that they usually need a search warrant. The framers of the amendment wanted to prevent general searches of all buildings with a Writ of Assistance, and their major goal was to put judicial restraints on how the police might investigate private houses and businesses. In one of first important cases dealing with this amendment, *Boyd v. United States* (1886), the Supreme Court interpreted the amendment broadly so that it applied to any governmental invasion into "the sanctity of a man's home and privacies of life." In the twentieth century the Fourth Amendment became much more significant with the adoption of the exclusionary rule, which requires that any evidence obtained illegally will be excluded from a criminal trial.

The Supreme Court has used an incremental case-by-case approach to interpret the key word "unreasonable" in the Fourth Amendment. Justice Louis Brandeis wrote in 1928 that the amendment prohibited "every unjustifiable intrusion on the privacy of the individual." Most of Brandeis' approach came to fruition in the case of *Katz v. United States* (1967), when the Court announced that the Fourth Amendment must be followed whenever public officials enter into an area with "a reasonable expectation of privacy." This means, for instance, that the police must obtain a warrant to intercept a private telephone conversation, but they do not need a warrant to seize contraband objects in "plain view."

The Fourth Amendment prohibits unreasonable intrusions into the human body. Officials are usually not allowed to order surgery or the use of stomach pumps to obtain evidence of a crime. For less intrusive procedures, such as taking blood to determine if a driver is intoxicated, the police must have probable cause, but they do not need a search warrant because of the time constraints. Government agencies may mandate drug testing for those employees who hold sensitive positions, and public schools are allowed to conduct suspicionless random drug testing of students who participate in interscholastic athletics.

Fifth Amendment. A related form of privacy is the Fifth Amendment right to refuse to incriminate oneself in a criminal case. Interpreted according to the common law, it is incumbent on persons to assert this right, after which judges rule on the validity of their claims. The self-incrimination clause covers only oral testimony, and it provides no protection from submitting to sobriety tests, physical examinations, or mandatory fingerprinting. Since the case of *Miranda v. Arizona* (1966), law officers must inform suspects of their right to remain silent.

Private Choices. In the twentieth century the Supreme Court interpreted the concept of "lib-erty" in the due process clauses of the Fifth and Fourteenth Amendments as protecting substantive rights to make choices about one's private life. In the case of *Pierce v. Society of Sisters* (1925) the Court overturned a state law that prohibited parents from sending their children to private schools, affirming "the liberty of parents and guardians to direct the upbringing and education of children under their control." In the 1960's the Court looked to this and other precedents to recognize a constitutional "right of privacy," especially applicable to reproduction and family relationships.

In the watershed case of *Griswold v. Connecticut* (1965), the Supreme Court overturned a state law that made it illegal to sell or use contraception. Emphasizing the freedom of married couples to decide about procreation, the Court proclaimed that these choices were protected by "a right of privacy older than our Bill of Rights." Seven years later the Court recognized the right of unmarried people to use contraceptives. In *Loving v. Virginia* (1967) the Court declared that a state miscegenation law (a law prohibiting interracial unions) was unconstitutional because it violated the liberty of an individual to choose a marriage partner. In the controversial case of *Roe v. Wade* (1973) the justices voted seven to two to recognize that the right of privacy was "broad enough to encompass a woman's decision whether or not to terminate her pregnancy." The protection of a fetus was judged secondary to women's right of privacy, at least until the fetus attained viability. In later opinions the Court approved many regulations of abortions so long as they did not place an "undue burden" on women's freedom of choice.

The Supreme Court has gradually extended the right to privacy to other questions of personal autonomy. In the case of *More v. East Cleveland* (1977), for example, the Court overturned a city's zoning ordinance which prohibited a grandmother from allowing her grandchildren to live in her single-family home. Justice Lewis Powell declared that "freedom of personal choice in matters of marriage and family life is one of the liberties protected by the Due Process Clause." In the case of *Cruzan v. Director, Missouri Department of Health* (1990) the Court "assumed" that individuals have the right to refuse medical treatment, even when the refusal will result in death.

A common problem in communal homes is a need for extra security to compensate for loss of privacy.
(James L. Shaffer)

At times, the Court has upheld laws that many people believe unnecessarily restrict their autonomy. In 1976 the Court upheld a city regulation that limited the length of policemen's hair, and it has never overturned dress codes in schools. Moreover, in the controversial case of *Bowers v. Hardwick* (1986) the Court voted five to four that the constitutional right of privacy did not include any protected right to engage in homosexual practices, even when such practices occurred in a private bedroom. This decision was based on the idea that the Constitution protected only those kinds of privacy recognized in American "history and traditions."

Privacy in the Private Sector. The Constitution generally does not protect people from invasions of privacy by private individuals or by privately owned businesses, but significant protections are provided by statutes and by the threat of tort suits.

The freedom of the press, guaranteed in the First Amendment, often allows the news media to publish or broadcast information that people would like to keep secret. Sometimes the press can be sued successfully for revealing embarrassing matters strictly of a personal nature, and news reporters also get into trouble if they use fraud or disguise to trespass on private property. In general, however, courts have allowed the media to report true facts if they are "newsworthy," even when the publicity is embarrassing. In the case of *Florida Star v. B.J.F.* (1989) the Court protected the right of the press to give the name of a rape victim when the information came from public records.

Conflicts about privacy frequently occur in the workplace, and such conflicts are sometimes settled in courts of law. Workers have a "legitimate expectation of privacy" in their desks, lockers, or other spaces for private items; all limitations on privacy should be clearly spelled out. Any monitoring of employees must be justified by good business practices. Civil rights laws place a number of restrictions on personal questions that employers can ask of prospective employees, such as the marital status of women. Employers are expected to secure personnel files so that they are not available for public consumption, and the files must be restricted to those with a "need to know." Under the Americans with Disabilities Act, employers must be especially careful to protect the confidentiality of medical records.

Voyeurism is one of the oldest ways of invading personal privacy. Voyeurs, or Peeping Toms, typically spy on people in private places considered secure, such as hotel bedrooms or bathrooms. Voyeurs may make use of peepholes or hidden cameras. The legal cause of action against voyeurs is usually the tort of intrusion, but there can also be criminal penalties in some jurisdictions. Since juries tend to sympathize with the victims of such incidents, legal actions against voyeurs are the most successful of all claims involving invasions of privacy.

—*Thomas T. Lewis*

BIBLIOGRAPHY

Alderman, Ellen, and Caroline Kennedy. *The Right of Privacy.* New York: Alfred A. Knopf, 1995.

Bible, Jon D., and Darien A. McWhirter. *Privacy in the Workplace: A Guide for Human Resource Managers.* New York: Quorum Books, 1990.

Brill, Alida. *Nobody's Business: Paradoxes of Privacy.* Reading, Mass.: Addison-Wesley, 1990.

Decker, Kurt. *Employer Privacy Law and Practice.* New York: John Wiley and Sons, 1987.

Elder, David. *The Law of Privacy.* New York: Clark Boardman, 1991.

Hendricks, Evan, et al. *Your Right to Privacy.* Carbondale, Ill.: Southern Illinois University Press, 1990.

McWhirter, Darien A., and Jon D. Bible. *Privacy as a Constitutional Right: Sex, Drugs, and the Right to Life.* New York: Quorum Books, 1992.

See also Abortion; Americans with Disabilities Act (ADA); Birth control; *Loving v. Virginia*; Megan's Law; News media and families; *Roe v. Wade*; *Wisconsin v. Yoder*.

Private schools

RELEVANT ISSUES: Children and child development; Demographics; Race and ethnicity; Religious beliefs and practices

SIGNIFICANCE: Having prospered in the United States and Canada for more than two centuries, private schools have offered opportunities for instruction in the academic, vocational, and religious subjects that have not been included in traditional public school curricula

Many students in private schools are enrolled in Roman Catholic schools or schools with no religious attachment. Nonreligious private schools that are intended to prepare students for college are often referred to as "prep" schools. Many communities maintain special schools that emphasize ethnic culture, vocational education, distinctive languages, or special artistic activities such as theater, music, dance, painting, and sculpture. In addition to students enrolled in the preceding types of private schools, more than 500,000 students were being home schooled by the late 1990's.

During the early 1990's, private corporations were contracted by school districts in several states to compete with the traditionally administered public schools in those states. The privately managed, public schools run by these corporations were a hybrid between modern models of public and private education.

Vocational Education and Private Schools. Prior to the nineteenth century, schools in the United States were private schools or community schools that had many of the characteristics of private schools, and enrollment in them was limited to a small segment of the school-aged population. During the 1800's, a strong sentiment was expressed for universal public education in both the United States and Canada.

Even as this goal was achieved, however, private schools continued to flourish. Private high schools, referred to originally as academies, were supported because they presented an alternative to the traditional liberal arts curriculum followed in most early high schools. The first of these academies was established in 1751 in Philadelphia by Benjamin Franklin to help students prepare for professional employment. By the middle of the 1880's, more than eighteen hundred academies had been established in the New England states alone.

During the twentieth century, vocational high schools emerged that had objectives similar to the academies. The vocational schools emphasized the skills needed to get and maintain a job in the industrialized cities. Many of these schools and programs were initiated and supported by cities' commercial and industrial employers. Although some of these vocational high schools were public, the spread of public vocational schools was restricted until the 1930's, when federal legislation subsidizing such programs was established.

Religion and Private Schools. Originally, literacy had been considered the primary responsibility of elementary schools because it enabled individuals to read the Bible and use this as a ladder to the development of moral lives. A belief in a critical connection between religion and education was maintained during the 1700's in both the United States and Canada and was largely unchallenged through most of the nineteenth century.

During the late nineteenth century, however, schools became progressively separated from religious teachings. The emergence of scientific thinking was a factor that contributed significantly to the resulting educational secularism. The concepts associated with Charles Darwin's popular theory of evolution did much to propel the acceptance of science and the objective method of inquiry that was linked to the scientific approach to gathering knowledge. Additionally, many progressive thinkers judged that if state and religion were to remain separate, the universal system of public education that was evolving needed to embody this separation as well.

At the beginning of the twentieth century, many politicians supported universal public education because they hoped that education could serve as a transforming experience for the many immigrants who had come to the United States and Canada with distinct languages, customs, and ideas about the role of government. Resisting the political pressures to homogenize them and their children, many immigrants eagerly supported private schools where their children would learn about their parents' religions and cultures. These religious parochial schools, often instructing in languages other than English, were the precursors of the modern system of private, religious schools.

Regulation of Private Schools. Although private schools are subject to regulations, those regulations vary widely throughout the United States. Many private schools have disputed with the states in which they are located about the intrusion of government into matters that the educators in private schools believe to be beyond the appropriate realm of government.

Although regulation is required to ensure the public that private schools are providing quality education, a key characteristic of private schools has been their right to freedom in designating a curriculum, selecting faculty, and admitting students. Many private schools have exercised this freedom by designing curricula that have empha-

Concerns about violence, breakdowns in moral leadership, and declining academic standards in public schools lead many parents to enroll their children in private schools—most of which have religious affiliations. (Dick Hemingway)

Free from the constitutional restrictions on public schools, private schools can provide whatever religious and moral training and activities they wish. (Ben Klaffke)

sized specific cultures, values, or subjects not re-flected in public school curricula. Some private schools have resolved that only students who board at those schools can be eligible for admission. Other schools have insisted that only males or only females are eligible to be students.

State regulation of public schools has focused on general areas such as record-keeping, writing of reports, and the specification of minimal achievements for the licensing or accreditation of the schools. Even a requirement as objective as the specification of a minimum number of hours or days that students must attend school is not universally imposed by all states.

Although curriculum requirements have been set by states, these generally have been extremely broad, sometimes only requiring that children develop skills in general areas such as reading, writing, mathematics, and state history. Other areas to which state regulations often have been extended include health and safety, as well as the eligibility of private schools to receive financial assistance from the government.

The issue of public finance for private schools has been particularly difficult to address, with more than half the states having proposed procedures for supporting the schools and with multiple challenges in the courts from citizens who believed that such funding violated provisions in the Constitution intended to ensure separation of state and religion. In some cases, the intention to fund private schools has been direct—for example, supplying parents with a tax rebate or a voucher to compensate them for the cost of the tuition required by the private schools their children might attend. In other cases, the financial aid has been more circuitous, possibly in the form of services for students with disabilities who attend private schools or transportation that would be shared by public school students and pri-

vate school students who shared a common destination.

Reasons for Sending Children to Private Schools. Private schools generally have been regarded as providing education that is superior to that offered in public schools. Surveys have indicated that this view is typically held by teachers and administrators as well as parents. Reports from the late 1990's compiled by the National Center for Education Statistics indicated that principals and teachers in private schools view themselves as empowered decision makers to a greater extent than

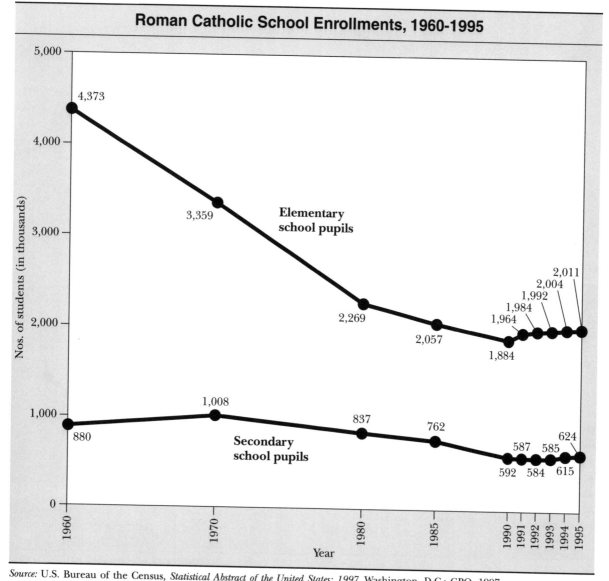

Roman Catholic School Enrollments, 1960-1995

Source: U.S. Bureau of the Census, *Statistical Abstract of the United States: 1997.* Washington, D.C.: GPO, 1997.

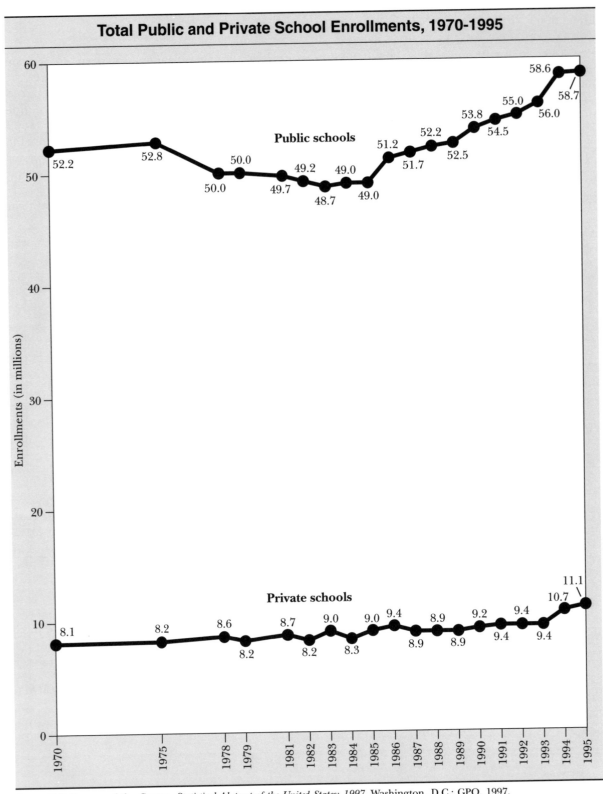

Total Public and Private School Enrollments, 1970-1995

Enrollments (in millions)

Public schools

52.2   52.8   50.0   50.0   49.7   49.2   48.7   49.0   49.0   51.2   51.7   52.2   52.5   53.8   54.5   55.0   56.0   58.6   58.7

Private schools

8.1   8.2   8.6   8.2   8.7   8.2   9.0   8.3   9.0   9.4   8.9   8.9   8.9   9.2   9.4   9.4   9.4   10.7   11.1

1970   1975   1978   1979   1981   1982   1983   1984   1985   1986   1987   1988   1989   1990   1991   1992   1993   1994   1995

Source: U.S. Bureau of the Census, *Statistical Abstract of the United States: 1997.* Washington, D.C.: GPO, 1997.
Note: Figures represent total enrollments in all levels of education, from nursery schools through college.

their counterparts in public schools. Other surveys have indicated that the sense of community among professionals in private schools is dramatically higher than in public schools. Such factors can influence job satisfaction among teachers and then in turn influence the quality of the learning that transpires in schools.

Some of the most famous private schools are those established for children by progressive educators who supported "child-centered" as opposed to "curriculum-centered" approaches to learning. The most famous of the progressive educators was John Dewey, who established an experimental school at the University of Chicago in 1896. Other famous private schools with alternative curricula were the Summerhill School of A. S. Neill in England and the Waldorf-Astoria Schools of Rudolf Steiner in Germany, England, and Switzerland.

Parents sent their children to these schools and many that were patterned after them because they were convinced that their children would learn with educational strategies that were more appropriate than those being employed in the public schools. Additionally, parents hoped that their children would be counseled and disciplined in a manner that would build moral character and ensure safety and health. The prospects of superior academic achievement, safety, and health, when combined with a specialized curriculum that could promote topics such as religion, selective cultures, the arts, or specialized vocational training, are the reasons offered by most parents who send their children to private schools.

—*Gerard Giordano*

BIBLIOGRAPHY

Hakim, Simon, Paul Seidenstat, and Gary W. Bowmen, eds. *Privatizing Education and Educational Choice: Concepts, Plans, and Experiences.* Westport, Conn.: Greenwood Press, 1994.

Kane, Pearl L., ed. *Independent Schools, Independent Thinkers.* San Francisco, Calif.: Jossey-Bass, 1992.

Randall, E. Vance. *Private Schools and Public Power.* New York: Teachers College Press, 1994.

Williams, L. Patricia. *The Regulation of Private Schools in America: A State-by-State Analysis.* Washington, D.C.: U.S. Government Printing Office, 1995.

See also Educating children; Education for All Handicapped Children Act (EHA); Home schooling; Public education; Schools.

Puberty and adolescence

RELEVANT ISSUES: Children and child development; Parenting and family relationships

SIGNIFICANCE: Puberty, a universal stage of development, has a great impact on physical, emotional, and social aspects of life, strongly affecting the relations between adolescents and parents

The most universal biological change that occurs during adolescence is puberty. This term originates from the Latin word *pubescere,* which means to be covered with hair, and is defined as "the attainment of the ability to sexually reproduce." Although puberty may appear to be rather sudden judging from external signs, it is actually a gradual process that begins at conception. Indeed, no new hormones are produced and no new bodily systems are developed at puberty. Rather, at puberty the level of certain hormones changes; that is, increases in some hormones and decreases in others trigger the physical and biological manifestations of "puberty." Although girls begin puberty, on average, two years before boys, both girls and boys mature according to a similar sequence of events, each of which affects their social, emotional, and physical lives.

Sequence of Sexual Maturation. Following menarche—the first menstrual cycle in females—and spermarche—the first ejaculation in males—individuals are sexually mature, or able to reproduce. Many people assume that menarche and spermarche mark the beginning of puberty, but these biological changes actually occur relatively late in the sequence of pubertal development.

As is evident in the table on the next page, the first sign of puberty in both females and males is the development of the secondary sex characteristics. These include breast growth and the appearance of pubic hair in females and the growth of the testes, the scrotal sac, and the appearance of pubic hair in males.

The appearance of secondary sex characteristics is typically followed by an acceleration in height and weight. Physical growth during puberty is referred to as "asynchronous," meaning that different areas of the body grow at different rates. Because of asynchronous development, many youth appear gawky and awkward during the pubertal period, whereby some body parts (such as legs) seem out of proportion with the rest of the body (such as the torso).

The rapid acceleration in growth usually lasts about two and a half years. Females typically gain less height than males; females tend to grow about eight to ten inches and males about twelve to thirteen. Noticeable changes are also evident in body composition. Both males and females experience an increase in muscle and fat tissue. However, in males the proportion of muscle to fat tends to increase at a rate of three to one, while it tends to increase at a rate of five to four in females. Additionally, muscle and fat are distributed differently between males and females. A greater portion of fat tissue tends to accumulate around the hips of females, giving them an "hourglass" figure. In contrast, given the significant increase in muscle tissue, the shoulders of males are typically larger than their hips, resulting in an inverted "triangular" shape.

About the time the growth spurt occurs, the primary sex characteristics, including the penis in males and the ovaries in females, begin to develop. During this time, females typically experience their first menstrual cycle and males experience spermarche. Following these occurrences, males and females are biologically ready to sexually reproduce. This does not mean, however, that they are socially or emotionally prepared for parenthood. During the final stages of puberty, both females and males experience growth of underarm hair and production in the oil and sweat glands, particularly in the facial regions, which may cause the appearance and development of acne.

Affective, Behavioral, and Cognitive Changes. Laurence Sternberg contends that beginning in early adolescence and with the onset of puberty adolescents experience significant affective (emotional), behavioral, and cognitive changes, which necessarily have an impact on the parent-child relationship. He notes further that "realignment" across each of the affective, behavioral, and cognitive domains is a necessary and healthy developmental process for parents and their adolescent children. Realignment is best understood as a process of renegotiation and compromise between parents and their developing children and a time when parents and children begin developing new expectations about each other.

Parents and their pubertal children experience affective transformations, or changes in the way they feel about each other. Examples of affective issues are those dealing with conflict resolution and feelings of intimacy between individuals. Although many believe that parents and their adolescent children experience intense and frequent

Physical Changes in Boys and Girls During Puberty

BOYS		GIRLS	
Characteristic	Age at first appearance (years)	Characteristic	Age at first appearance (years)
Testes and scrotal sac develop	10-13½	Breasts develop	8-13
Pubic hair appears	10-15	Pubic hair grows	8-14
Body size increases rapidly	10½-16	Body size increases rapidly	9½-14½
Penis size increases	11-14½	Menarche begins	10-16½
Facial and underarm hair appears	Two years after pubic hair	Underarm hair grows	Two years after pubic hair
Oil- and sweat-producing glands	Same time as underarm hair	Oil- and sweat-producing glands	Same time as underarm hair
Voice changes (growth in larynx)	Time of penis growth		

During the 1950's James Dean's and Natalie Woods's portrayals of troubled teenagers in Rebel Without a Cause *(1955) caught the imaginations of teenagers throughout the world.* (Museum of Modern Art, Film Stills Archive)

Many adolescents respond to the physical and emotional changes through which they are going with anxious perplexity. (James L. Shaffer)

conflict, investigators have demonstrated that overt conflict and rebellion are not omnipresent in the majority of families during the adolescent period. Only a small minority of families, approximately 5 to 10 percent, report consistent conflict during this stage of development. It is normal, however, for families to experience mild forms of conflict and disagreement; conflicts tend to reach a peak during the early adolescent years, when pubertal changes are visibly noticeable. Typically, however, conflicts are not intense and do not indicate a diminished sense of affection between adolescents and their parents.

Moreover, most conflicts between early adolescents and their parents center on mundane, day-to-day activities or events. The most frequently mentioned areas of conflict include disagreements over dress (such as what is "proper"), dating, and grades. When questioned, both adolescents and their parents agree about the primary topics of disagreement. Interestingly, mother-daughter conflicts tend to last longer and to occur more frequently than conflicts between mothers and sons, fathers and sons, or fathers and daughters. Parents and teenagers tend to agree that after conflicts have begun, they usually end with the teenagers following the wishes of their parents. In only 18 percent of cases do conflicts end with parents following the wishes of their teenagers, and only 13 percent of conflicts end with joint discussions and equal compromises. It appears, therefore, that when conflicts arise, early adolescents acquiesce to the wishes of their parents. Finally, teenagers typically report more overt conflicts with their siblings than with their parents.

Other research examining affective changes in parent-child relationships during puberty find that, in general, adolescents and their parents remain intimate throughout the adolescent period. However, teenagers going through puberty spend significantly more time with their friends or alone than with their parents. Indeed, these adolescents spend as little as 5 percent of their time exclusively with their parents, even though they report that they need them. Results from studies indicate, for example, that the greatest fear among 60 percent of adolescents between the ages of thirteen and eighteen is that something will happen to their parents or that they will lose them.

Although the early adolescent period places affective demands on the family system, most families adjust to the changes quite well. Authoritative families, those who make compromises and allow their children to be involved in the decision-making process and who have a history of flexibility, appear well equipped to weather the affective changes that occur during the pubertal period, much more so than families who resist change.

With the advent of puberty and continuing throughout much of the adolescent period, the behavioral domain of the parent-child relationship also undergoes a period of restructuring or renegotiation. The behavioral domain comprises the ways in which individuals behave toward each other and includes, for example, issues relating to decision making, autonomy, and privacy. Typically, research reveals that as adolescents mature they gain influence in family decision making. Although fathers generally remain as influential as they were before, mothers' decision-making influence on their pubertal children appears to wane. Moreover, due to increasing maturation and their

need for independence, adolescents and their parents may experience temporary bouts of strife, anxiety, and conflict until new behavioral rules and expectations have been established. Whereas youths' lives prior to the onset of puberty and adolescence were structured and monitored by their parents, following puberty and throughout the adolescent period youth develop an increasing need for autonomy. They desire freedom to come and go, to manage their own money, and to be increasingly responsible for their actions and decisions. Over time, adolescents are increasingly required to monitor their own behavior and to make decisions on their own.

When tensions and conflicts centering on behavioral issues emerge within families, they most often take one of two forms. They occur either in cases of excessive parental authoritarianism, as a result of which parents are reluctant to allow their adolescents the autonomy they really need and want, or in cases of excessive parental permissiveness, causing parents to appear not to care one way or the other about what their teenagers do, with whom they do it, or when they do it. Parenting that is either authoritarian or permissive may create tensions, because teenagers, although they need more autonomy than they did as children, still need and want rules and family structure. Tensions and conflicts also occur if adolescents exhibit either excessive opposition to authority, whereby they disregard all rules and regulations set by their parents or other guardians, or excessive dependency on their parents or guardians, when they reject independence and autonomy.

Some families are better at negotiating this behavioral realignment than others. Difficulties are most likely to occur when adolescents' interest in, or need for, autonomous behavior is out of step with parents' willingness to grant it. This most typically occurs when adolescents want more freedom and independence than their parents are willing to allow. It occurs less frequently that parents want their adolescents to be more independent than the latter want to be. Families with a history of flexibility and adaptability tend to adjust more easily to behavioral changes during early adolescence than either authoritarian or permissive families.

Cognitive growth and development during puberty cause changes in the parent-child relationship. Cognitive issues involve the way people think about each other and about their relationships in the family. Beginning with puberty and early adolescence, family members alter their views about each other and their mutual relationships, necessitating a "restructuring" of the parent-child relationship and the functioning of the family. Cognitive changes, with the potential for parent-child conflict, occur when parents and adolescents develop new expectations about each other. Research suggests that their expectations are based on their history together (their previous behavior and what they know about each other on a personal level) and their expectations of how "typical" adolescents or parents should be. Conflicts in parent-child relationships arise when these expectations are violated, when either parents or adolescents deviate from expectations or fail to meet them.

Cognitive changes in the parents of pubertal adolescents may also create tension in the parent-child relationship. As children age and mature, their parents age and mature as well. Researchers have increasingly recognized that adolescence is a time of change not only for teenagers but also for their parents, and that as their children mature and become more independent parents must redefine themselves and their parental role to better reflect reality and their children's developing autonomy. Thus, cognitive redefinition involves parents' perceptions of themselves; parents must adjust their own behavior and beliefs about their role as "parents" as their children become increasingly responsible for themselves and rely less on their parents to meet their needs. Moreover, as children enter adolescence, their parents often enter middle adulthood, forcing many to reflect on their own lives and futures. These cognitive changes appear to differ between mothers and fathers.

It may be especially difficult for parents—and especially mothers—to redefine and adjust their behavior, because they have invested much in their roles as parents and continue to define themselves through their children. Yet women who are involved in activities outside the home, such as those who are employed, and redefine their parental roles as their children age and mature, may adjust more easily to their children's maturity than those whose sole identity revolves around parent-

ing. The adolescent period may be difficult for fathers as well. Research suggests that fathers may look back over the years, wishing they had been more involved with their children and with child rearing while their children were younger. Yet, it is often during adolescence, when their children desire less parental authority and attention, that parents—and especially fathers—may feel the need to be closer to their children.

Results of Previous Work. Research indicates that puberty exerts an impact on family relationships. In essence, parent-child relationships become transformed when adolescents go through puberty. This transformation is particularly noticeable in the way parents and their pubertal children feel about each other (the affective domain), behave toward each other (the behavioral domain), and think about each other (the cognitive domain). Whereas parents exhibited nearly total control over their children prior to puberty, with age and maturity and the onset of puberty children gain independence and autonomy. Many investigators have also found that puberty increases the distance between adolescents and their parents and intensifies conflicts. Although "negative" emotions, communications, and behaviors, such as complaining, anger, and conflict, increase, "positive" emotions, communications, and behaviors (such as support, smiling, and laughter) do not appear to similarly decrease. Research indicates that following the adolescent growth spurt, the negative exchanges between adolescents and their parents begin to diminish.

Despite frequent discussion about negative changes in the parent-child relationship when adolescents reach puberty, much research has examined the positive changes as well. Parents continue to be significant in their adolescents' lives throughout puberty and the adolescent period. Although peers tend to influence each other strongly in mundane issues such as clothing and hairstyles, parents tend to have greater influence on their adolescent children in making major decisions and life choices, such as in their political affiliations, educational goals, and career choices. J. Youniss and J. Smollar describe the transformation between parents and their adolescent children as moving from unilateral relationships, in which parents exert total or nearly total control, to peerlike relationships, in which mutual respect develops and in which parents and their adolescent children develop a friendship not previously experienced.

Teenagers' Reactions to Puberty. In addition to these expected and normative, or typical, changes in the parent-adolescent child relationship beginning near puberty, teenagers' reactions to puberty may also exert a significant impact on their social and emotional selves, which in turn may affect their family relationships.

Research reveals that boys and girls often react quite differently to the timing of puberty, or when it begins in relation to one's peers. Individuals who begin puberty before their age peers are re-

ferred to as early maturers; those who reach puberty at approximately the same time as their peers are said to be on-time maturers; and those who begin puberty later are said to be late maturers. The timing of physical maturation varies depending on several factors, including nutrition, health status, ethnicity (with African Americans tending to mature earlier than whites), genetic factors, environmental stress, and exercise level.

Early maturing males appear to have an advantage during adolescence because their physical appearance, or physique, tends to fit the "ideal" image of the American male. They are bigger, stronger, and more adultlike than males who have

During adolescence teenagers encounter one of life's great natural forces: peer pressure. (James L. Shaffer)

not yet physically developed. Early maturing males are typically very outgoing and popular among their peers; they tend to hold leadership positions and to be extremely self-confident. However, despite their physical appearance and subsequent social advantages, early maturation may place some males at a disadvantage. Because they look like adults, early maturing males may be pressured to be responsible, take jobs, and live up to adult expectations. Moreover, early maturing males may develop associations with older peers, peers who may pressure them to become involved in drug and alcohol use, delinquency, or other situations they are not equipped to handle. Just because persons appear physically mature does not necessarily mean that they are also cognitively and emotionally mature or able to handle responsibility or high-pressure situations.

Late maturing males, in contrast, are often more dependent and childish and less mature and self-conscious than early or on-time maturers, and they are less likely to be viewed as leaders among their peers. As adults, however, late maturing males appear to be more insightful, creative, and inventive than either on-time or early maturing males. Some researchers contend that this is so because they were not pushed into adult roles as adolescents before they were emotionally ready, but rather were allowed time to develop their creative and intellectual talents. Thus, although early maturing males appear to be advantaged during adolescence because of their physical appearance, late maturing males may be advantaged as adults.

As with boys, differences in pubertal timing among girls also has an impact on their social, emotional, and physical lives. Unlike early maturing males who enjoy a social advantage, early maturing females appear to be at a social disadvantage during adolescence. They tend to be less popular, more submissive, withdrawn, and self-conscious than late maturing females. Early maturing females are physically distinct from their peers; not only do they mature earlier than other females, but they also mature before males the same age. Thus, early maturing females are taller and heavier than other girls and boys their age. Unlike early maturing males, whose physiques American society desires, the bodies of early maturing girls are not considered desirable. In societies that consider thinness physically attractive,

such as the United States, Canada, and the European countries, early maturation may cause females to dislike and be embarrassed by their bodies. Research tends to confirm this; early maturing females are more likely to have negative self-images and to report emotional disturbances and depression at greater rates than either late or on-time maturing females. Early maturing females are also more likely than their on-time and late maturing peers to engage in delinquent activities and to engage in drug use, alcohol, and early sexuality. This may largely be accounted for because older youth, and particularly older males, are often attracted to early maturing females; early maturing females who become involved with older groups of peers may experience social pressure to engage in activities that they are not cognitively or emotionally prepared to handle.

In contrast, females who mature later than their peers may experience social advantages. Late maturers tend to remain thinner longer and maintain figures that more closely match Western societies' conception of the "ideal" body type. Research indicates that, on average, late maturing girls are more outgoing, popular, and confident than their early maturing peers.

Impact of Pubertal Timing on Family Relationships. Regardless of pubertal timing, sons report increased distance between themselves and their parents during adolescence. Early maturing sons, however, report less frequent calm communication with their fathers and view them as less accepting than do less physically mature boys. Early maturing males also report more intense, but not more frequent, conflicts with both their mothers and fathers than on-time maturers, while late maturers report less intense conflicts with their fathers. Pubertal maturation also appears to increase sons' autonomy from their parents. Physically mature boys report that their parents are more permissive, allowing them more autonomy, than parents of boys who are less physically mature.

As with boys, pubertal timing may also have an impact on the parent-child relationships among girls. Early maturing girls report less calm communication with their mothers and tend to view their mothers as less accepting of them than the mothers of either on-time or late maturing girls. Early maturers also report more intense, but not more

In addition to the sexual maturation that characterizes their physical changes, adolescents experience the first stirrings of mature romantic attraction. (James L. Shaffer)

frequent, conflicts with their mothers than do other girls. Late maturing girls tend to report fewer conflicts with their mothers than early maturing girls. Given that early maturing females may become involved with older groups of peers and engage in delinquent activities or activities of which their parents do not approve, conflicts in the parent-child relationship may ensue. Interestingly, mothers of late maturing girls have also reported less frequent conflicts with their daughters than other mothers. As with boys, the timing of puberty appears to have little impact on girls' closeness with their mothers or fathers. Although both male and female pubertal adolescents report greater conflicts with their parents, they do not report feeling more distant from them during adolescence than they did when they were younger.

—*Rochelle L. Dalla*

BIBLIOGRAPHY

Cobb, Nancy J. *Adolescence: Continuity, Change, and Diversity.* 2d ed. Mountain View, Calif.: Mayfield, 1995. An extended discussion of the manifestations of adolescence, including the physical, cognitive, and emotional changes that occur during this developmental period.

Montemayor, Raymond, Gerald R. Adams, and Thomas P. Gullotta, eds. *From Childhood to Adolescence: A Transitional Period?* Newbury Park, Calif.: Sage Publications, 1990. Considers various areas of physical, social, and social-cognitive development in adolescence, written by experts in the field.

Paikoff, Roberta L., and Jeanne Brooks-Gunn. "Do Parent-Child Relationships Change During Puberty?" *Psychological Bulletin* 110 (1991). Describes changes in the parent-child relationship during puberty, paying particular attention to variables that have an impact on those relationships, such as parental growth and maturation and changes in adolescents' peer groups.

Sternberg, Laurence. *Adolescence.* 4th ed. New York: McGraw-Hill, 1996. Provides a detailed discussion of adolescence, examining the fundamental changes of adolescence, contexts of adolescence, and psychosocial development during adolescence.

_____. "Impact of Puberty on Family Relations: Effects of Pubertal Status and Pubertal Timing." *Developmental Psychology* 23 (1987). Examines pubertal status and pubertal timing in relation to family relationships, focusing on the positive as well as negative changes that frequently occur between parents and their adolescent children.

_____. "Reciprocal Relations Between Parent-Child Distance and Pubertal Maturation." *Developmental Psychology* 24 (1988). Examines the relationship between pubertal maturation among youth and their need for autonomy and independence.

Voydanoff, Patricia, and Brenda W. Donnelly. *Adolescent Sexuality and Pregnancy.* Newbury Park, Calif.: Sage Publications, 1990. Examines factors that have an impact on adolescent sexual activity, determinants of nonmarital adolescent pregnancy, factors associated with pregnancy resolutions, consequences of teenage childbearing, and intervention strategies.

Youniss, J., and J. Smollar. *Adolescents' Relations with Mothers, Fathers, and Friends.* Chicago: University of Chicago Press, 1985. Describes changes in adolescents' relationships with significant social contacts, including their mothers, fathers, and peers.

See also Bar Mitzvahs and Bas Mitzvahs; Behavior disorders; Childhood history; Circumcision; Eating disorders; Erikson, Erik H.; Generational relationships; Hall, G. Stanley; Mother-daughter relationships; Rites of passage; Sex education; Siblings; Teen mothers.

Public education

RELEVANT ISSUES: Education; Law; Sociology
SIGNIFICANCE: Changes in society influenced the evolution of public education, including the adoption of compulsory education policies, and changes in public education influenced the roles and expectations of family members

Public education is a system of education that provides each child the opportunity to be educated at public expense. State and local governments are responsible for financing and regulating public education. All fifty states of the United States and all Canadian provinces have their own public school systems. Public school systems generally comprise elementary schools, junior high or middle schools, high schools, and, in some cases, preschool programs. Throughout its history, public

Public School Enrollment Rates in the United States in 1995

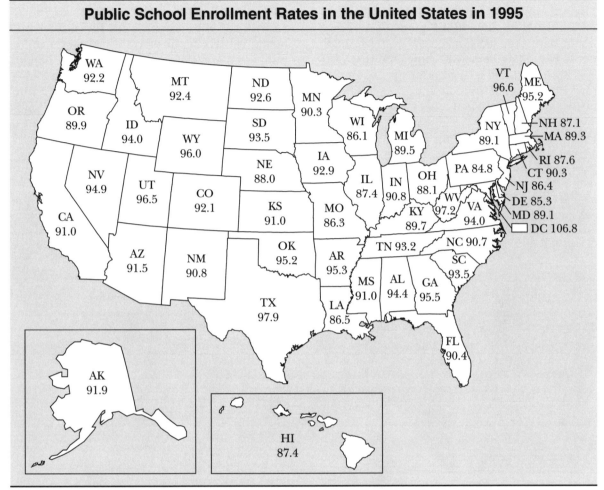

Source: U.S. Bureau of the Census, *Statistical Abstract of the United States: 1997.* Washington, D.C.: GPO, 1997.

Note: Figures are based on percentages of residents aged five through seventeen in each state. High percentages may reflect out-of-state enrollments; low percentages may reflect high private-school enrollments.

education, and specifically compulsory public education, has been labeled as both the cause and solution to various problems affecting families, communities, and society.

Compulsory education refers to mandatory school attendance. Both the United States and Canada have compulsory education laws at the state or provincial level. The laws, although they may vary among the states, tend to apply to children between the ages of six and sixteen. Attending private or parochial schools instead of public schools may satisfy compulsory education laws.

Public Education in the United States. The adoption of public education followed a similar process in both the United States and Canada.

However, major efforts to establish public schools began earlier in the United States than in Canada. During the colonial period in the United States, the New England colonies had more homogenous populations than colonies in other areas, allowing for the establishment of schools acceptable to the entire community. It was in New England, and specifically Massachusetts, that the earliest trends toward public schooling developed. In 1646 Massachusetts demonstrated its support for education by passing the Oulde Deluder Law, which mandated public financial support for elementary and secondary education.

Just after the conclusion of the Revolutionary War, in 1779, Thomas Jefferson proposed a law in

Virginia supporting limited public education. His Bill for the More General Diffusion of Knowledge would have supplied public funds for educating needy boys. Representatives of wealthy land owners defeated his bill in the Virginia legislature because they believed that educating the poor would upset the prevailing social system.

Major steps toward the development of public education in the United States occurred in the 1820's and 1830's. In Massachusetts, Horace Mann, the first Secretary of the Massachusetts State Board of Education, used his research and public reports to further the establishment of common schools in that state. In 1827 Massachusetts became the first state to legislate public schooling. It was also the first state to adopt compulsory education laws in 1852. All northern states had compulsory laws by 1860. Compulsory education requirements increased among the states as they became more industrialized and urbanized.

The idea that government should provide free education to its youths is a relatively late historical development that did not take hold in the United States until after the 1830's. (Hazel Hankin)

The southern states were much slower in adopting compulsory education laws because of their more rural, less affluent populations. Mississippi was the last state to adopt some form of compulsory education in 1918.

According to the Tenth Amendment to the U.S. Constitution, the power to create and regulate schools was reserved to the state governments. However, the federal government has historically and significantly influenced public education. The first example of federal involvement in education occurred with the passage of the Land Ordinance of 1785, which set aside each sixteenth section of every township for the benefit of public schools. The Northwest Ordinance of 1787 further established the federal government's commitment to the education of its citizens by stating that "schools and the means of education shall forever be encouraged."

Public Education in Canada. In Canada, Jesuits and Recollects established missionary schools in the early 1600's. Religiously based schools flourished in Canada, and the government was not involved with the schools until the 1760's. The movement for government regulation of education began in 1766, when Nova Scotia passed a law calling for local clergy to examine teachers. The following year, leaders on Prince Edward Island reserved land for building schools. Quebec became the first province to provide financial support to its schools with the passage of the "Act for Free Schools" in 1801. Other provinces followed Quebec's example throughout the nineteenth century and, in 1889, Alberta and Saskatchewan became the first provinces to pass compulsory education laws.

In 1867 the Federation government, established to unite the provinces, passed the British North America Act. This act reserved complete control of the schools to the provinces. Despite this restriction of power, the federal government has had influence on Canadian schools, especially during the twentieth century. Although there is no national Minister of Education, the federal government provides money and resources to the schools through its other agencies. In 1944 Canada's governing body passed the Family Allowances Act, which provided a monthly allowance to school age children who attended school regularly and met certain performance requirements.

Struggles for Influence and Control. The goals, responsibilities, and merits of public education have been a source of contention among the public and lawmakers since the establishment of public schools. Some critics believe that public schools accept too many responsibilities or set unacceptable goals. They feel that, in some instances, the schools undermine the authority and influence of parents. Of particular concern to some persons are curricula such as sex education, family life education, and "values clarification." Services that the schools are involved in, such as guidance and counseling, mental health, lunch and breakfast programs, and medical, family, and social referrals also cause concerns. On the other side, people argue that schools must do more to prepare students for the changing demands of adulthood and the world of work. Additionally, as communities become more diverse, controversy has continued around the appropriateness of religious activities in schools and the question of "separation of church and state."

Public vs. Private Schools. Parents have a certain degree of legal control over the education of their children, although limitations exist. Parents who object to public education may send their children to private schools to fulfill the requirements of compulsory school attendance laws. Officials often grant such exemptions when compulsory attendance laws are in violation of First and Fourteenth Amendment protections. The first major U.S. Supreme Court case concerning compulsory attendance laws was *Pierce v. Society of Sisters* (1925). In 1922 Oregon passed a compulsory education law requiring that all children attend a public school in their district. The law rejected private and parochial schools as unacceptable alternatives to public schooling. Referring to the Fourteenth Amendment, the Supreme Court overturned the Oregon law but ruled that private schools could be required to meet the same stipulations as public schools. In a later case, *Wisconsin v. Yoder* (1972), the Supreme Court ruled that the State of Wisconsin could not force parents to send their children to public schools if the parents believed that public education was detrimental to their religion and way of life.

Parents and their children also retain some rights when they participate in public education. In *Meyer v. Nebraska* (1919) the Supreme Court

Although public schools are run by city and county governments, ultimate responsibility for them rests with the states. In 1995 the state of New Jersey exercised that responsibility directly by taking over Newark's schools because of the local school board's poor performance. (AP/Wide World Photos)

ruled against a Nebraska law that mandated that all subjects be taught in English. The Court ruled against the law on the grounds that the teacher has the "right to teach" as desired by the parents of the schoolchildren. Also, students have rights in the school setting, but they may not enjoy all the rights of adult citizens who are not in school. Teachers legally serve in place of parents or guardians in exercising responsibility for ensuring the welfare of children under their supervision. Parents and guardians may obtain their children's public and private records from schools and challenge their contents. They may restrict their chil-

dren's participation in some school activities and courses.

Public and compulsory education have influenced family life by requiring families to address the issue of the education of their children. This requirement has not only increased the educational level of the citizenry but has also influenced the dynamics of family life. Families must send their children, who meet age and other requirements of the states, to public or private schools or respond to the state and local governing bodies concerning their reasons for not doing so. At the same time, parents or guardians can influence the nature of the education their children receive. They can influence public education by voting in elections of school and governing officials and by participating in meetings involving public education policies. They may choose to send their children to private schools or teach them at home. Thus, public education and family life have greatly influenced each other.   *—Alvin M. Pettus*

BIBLIOGRAPHY

Clabaugh, Gary K., and Edward G. Rozycki. *Understanding Schools: The Foundations of Education.* New York: Harper & Row, 1990.

Hunt, Thomas C., ed. *Society, Culture, and Schools: An American Approach.* Garrett Park, Md.: Garrett Park Press, 1979.

Katz, Joseph. *Education in Canada.* Hamden, Conn.: Archon Books, 1974.

Selakovich, Daniel. *Schooling in America: Social Foundations of Education.* New York: Longman, 1984.

Spring, Joel. *American Education: An Introduction to Social and Political Aspects.* New York: Longman, 1978.

See also Children's rights; Educating children; Family values; Home schooling; Private schools; Schools; *Wisconsin v. Yoder.*

Quakers

RELEVANT ISSUES: Parenting and family relationships; Religious beliefs and practices

SIGNIFICANCE: Both the structure of Quaker families and Quaker attitudes concerning family-related issues closely mirror beliefs and practices found in the Quaker act of worship and in the organization of the Quaker religion

The Religious Society of Friends (Quakers), a religious denomination whose origins can be traced back to the preaching of the Englishman George Fox in the mid-seventeenth century, is known for its distinctive worship service and its practice of decision making through consensus.

Quaker Meetings and Families. Acting under the conviction that there is "that of God in every person," Quakers who meet for worship sit quietly with each other, listening for the voice of what they call the "Inner Light": the power of God as revealed to a person within. Such traditional Quaker meetings involve no ordained priests or ministers to lead services and reflect the deep-seated Quaker belief in the equal worth of all individuals in the eyes of God. This belief is also reflected in the Quaker meeting for business, where members gather to make decisions of importance to the group as a whole. The clerk or leader of such meetings has no more authority than the other participants, and no votes are taken to decide issues. Rather, those present aim for consensus: a shared agreement on the truth of a matter reached through open discussion, in which each person feels equally free to participate.

These values of equality, community, and respect for individual freedom highlight the Quaker family itself. In their activities and practices, Quaker families are a microcosm of Quaker meetings. Conversely, the spirit of cooperation and interdependence found in Quaker meetings, together with members' concern for considering individual members as having equal standing and for treating them with equal respect, have led many to observe that Quaker meetings are them-

selves a macrocosm of the smaller unit of the Quaker family.

Quaker Marriage and Divorce. Perhaps no other practice better symbolizes Quaker values than Quaker wedding ceremonies, events marked by a distinctive absence of ceremony and ritual. Because Quaker weddings take place within the context of meetings for worship, neither ministers nor priests perform them. Rather, in becoming husband and wife, two people marry each other. In front of the others present, who act as witnesses to the wedding, a bride and groom promise that with God's help they will be committed to each other for life as husband and wife. Because the value of simplicity is among the primary values of Quakerism, there is no "ring ceremony" in Quaker weddings, as in most other Christian wedding services. Should those who marry wish to exchange rings with each other, they may do so after the ceremony at which the marriage certificate is signed.

While many present-day Quakers believe that only men and women have the right to form families through Quaker marriage, others believe that gays and lesbians have this right as well. As a result, some Quaker congregations in the United States permit gays and lesbians to marry each other within the meetinghouse, even though such marriages do not have legal standing. In addition, Quakers do not condemn those who live together out of wedlock, recognizing that values such as mutual respect, trust, and integrity are the essential binding elements in personal relationships. Whether couples should or should not marry is for Quakerism a matter of individual conscience.

Once couples are married, however, Quakerism counsels that if their marriages should falter, couples should make every effort to remain together rather than terminate their relationships through divorce. For Quakerism, divorce represents a violation of the lifetime commitment couples make to each other in their wedding vows and is thus contrary to Quaker belief and practice. There is, however, no policy explicitly forbidding Quakers to divorce, and those who do so are still welcome as members within the meeting for worship.

Structure of Quaker Families. There is no "head of household" in Quaker families. Just as Quakers deny patriarchal authority in their religious organization, they also reject patriarchy as a natural form of family organization. From the beginning Quakers recognized that women as well as men had the authority to preach the word of God. Within the household, Quakers accept both husband and wife as equal partners, with equal rights to explore and develop their own self-potential. Emily Jennings Stowe, a Quaker woman regarded as Canada's first physician, was an example of how the commitment to equal rights for members of both sexes provided Quaker women with a measure of freedom to express their own opinions and to pursue interests outside the home, freedom that was often not enjoyed by their non-Quaker counterparts. Not surprisingly, some Quaker women became leaders in the early women's movement in the United States, including Lucretia Mott and Susan B. Anthony. In her efforts to bring about social change, Anthony worked to extend the property rights of women and to give women the right to have custody of their children following divorce.

Unlike some denominations, Quakerism does not emphasize the importance of having large families, and there is no church teaching on contraception to control family size, the use of which is left up to individual couples. From the beginning, children are raised so as to feel that they are a significant part of the community created by those attending particular meetings for worship. Loving Quaker parents strive to raise their children not to accept Quaker beliefs at face value but, if they commit to them at all, to do so only after careful consideration and questioning. Quaker parents also aim to give their children a sense of self-worth disassociated from gender and to treat girls and boys with equal consideration while educating them in the Quaker values of equality, simplicity, and tolerance for others.

A Quaker school classroom in Brooklyn, New York. (Hazel Hankin)

Quaker Families and Modern Social Issues. Traditionally, Quakers have been opposed to all forms of social injustice and oppression and to participating in violent activities. This includes warfare, which Quakers view as dehumanizing and contrary to the idea that because of the presence of God within, all humans are to be treated with respect. Thus, Quakers are united in opposing all forms of domestic violence. On other family-related issues of social importance, however, no particular consensus among Quakers exists.

In the light of fundamental Quaker beliefs, it is perhaps not surprising that there is no official Quaker teaching on abortion. Concern that having unwanted children might in some cases further the oppression of women could lead some Quakers to support legalized abortion, while concern that abortion represents a form of violence against human beings could lead other Quakers to seek different solutions to the problem of unwanted pregnancies, such as adoption. Other beginning-of-life issues, such as whether the use of surrogate mothers and in vitro fertilization are morally justified, are also left up to the conscience of individual Quakers.

With respect to end-of-life issues, there is no clear-cut consensus among Quakers as to whether euthanasia or physician-assisted suicide is justified. In general, the elderly are treated by Quakers with the same respect accorded to all other persons. Unlike many others in American society, Quakers do not view the coming of old age as akin to the onset of an illness. For those who experience suffering at the end of their lives, some Quakers recommend that family members seek care and pain relief that permits them to continue to live with dignity. Other Quakers, however, would say that if persons request assistance specifically to end their lives, such assistance should be provided out of respect for their individual autonomy.

Just as persons might discuss particularly troublesome issues with members of their own families in order to achieve understanding, Quakers believe that in order to seek a consensus it is important to talk within the "family" of the meeting about issues on which there is no general agreement. While Quakers are quite supportive of equal rights for women and racial minorities, there is no clear-cut consensus among Quakers concerning gay and lesbian rights, and discussions on this topic take place in many modern Quaker meetings. —*Diane P. Michelfelder*

BIBLIOGRAPHY

Bacon, Margaret Hope. *Mothers of Feminism: The Story of Quaker Women in America.* New York: Walker, 1980.

_____. *The Quiet Rebels: The Story of Quakers in America.* Philadelphia: New Society Publishers, 1985.

Barbour, Hugh, and J. William Frost. *The Quakers.* Westport, Conn.: Greenwood Press, 1988.

Brinton, Howard. *Friends for Three Hundred Years.* Wallingford, Pa.: Pendle Hill Publications, 1952.

Fager, Chuck. *Without Apology: The Heroes, the Heritage, and the Hope of Liberal Quakerism.* Media, Pa.: Kimo Press, 1996.

See also Couples; Gay and lesbian families; Marriage; Religion; Weddings.

Quinceañera

RELEVANT ISSUES: Marriage and dating; Parenting and family relationships

SIGNIFICANCE: The quinceañera is a ceremony for fifteen-year-old women in Latino society that signifies the passage from girlhood to womanhood

The quinceañera is a very significant aspect of Hispanic culture in Mexico, Central and South America, and in Latino communities in the United States. The origin of the quinceañera is somewhat unclear. Although it may long ago have originated in Spain, the quinceañera has not been notable in Spanish society since the beginning of the twentieth century.

The structure of the quinceañera ceremony reflects the intimate bond between family and community in Latino culture. Mothers and fathers present their daughters at large festivals that closely resemble wedding ceremonies in terms of cost and energy. Young women celebrating their quinceañeras dress lavishly in expensive clothes as do their mothers and fathers. Moreover, music and food are provided for guests. Although they are not exactly religious ceremonies, quinceañera festivals often take place within church meeting halls and are occasionally presided over by neighborhood priests. The quinceañera attracts great atten-

Quinceañeras resemble weddings in their ornateness, cost, and social significance. (James L. Shaffer)

tion in urban as well as rural Latino communities in the United States.

The communal aspects of the quinceañera tradition are also notable. Most prominent among the benefactors of the quinceañera are young women's godparents. These godparents are expected to assume significant responsibility for the expenses of the celebration. For example, one *padrino* (godparent) may be responsible for arranging the music, another for arranging the food, and yet another for arranging beverages. These *padrinos* are announced soon after the festivities begin. Parents acknowledge proudly the cheers and salutations of the gathering when a

master of ceremonies presents them to the assembled guests. Close friends who have also played a role in the lives of the family are also acknowledged. Thus, the quinceañera tradition reunites the family in a close and intimate gathering that also strengthens communal bonds.

The quinceañera celebration resembles the type of debutante ball or ceremony that is still practiced among upper-middle- and upper-class American families. However, a major difference between debutante balls and quinceañera celebrations is that quinceañera celebrations are not confined to the affluent. Like affluent Latino families, Latino families with few economic resources hold lavish ceremonies. Poor Latino families may pawn their possessions and borrow money from neighbors and extended family in order to hold quinceañera celebrations. At quinceañera celebrations participants listen to robust music, dance, and enthusiastically eat traditional Latino foods. In contrast, debutante balls are reserved and formal. The music at quinceañera festivals is often boisterous and unrestrained, while at debutante balls it usually serves as a background ornament. At both types of events, however, those attending are expected to dress formally.

While the quinceañera emphasizes that young women can now be courted by interested men, young women are not expected to leave the family home or sever their ties to their godparents. To the contrary, the quinceañera is a formal opportunity for young women to acknowledge those attachments in which they have a serious interest.

—*Douglas W. Richmond*

See also Age of consent; Bar Mitzvahs and Bas Mitzvahs; Courting rituals; Latinos; Rites of passage.

Recovery programs

RELEVANT ISSUES: Children and child development; Health and medicine; Parenting and family relationships; Sociology

SIGNIFICANCE: Recovery programs allow dysfunctional families to regain their health and vitality

Recovery programs originated with the founding of Alcoholics Anonymous (AA), which promotes a twelve-step recovery program. AA, founded in 1935 by Robert Smith and William G. "Bill" Wilson, has helped millions of people overcome the destructive effects of alcoholism. By the 1990's, the organization included more than 93,000 groups in 131 countries, with an estimated membership of more than two million.

Drug users are among those who have been helped by attending meetings of Alcoholics Anonymous and its offshoot, Narcotics Anonymous. Other recovery programs, such as Overeaters Anonymous (O-Anon), Gamblers Anonymous (Gam-Anon), and Sex Addicts Anonymous, have adopted the twelve-step spiritual philosophy developed by AA. Adjunct groups such as Al-Anon, Alateen, Adult Children of Alcoholics, and Codependents Anonymous (CoDA) have sprung up to aid those affected by the addictions and behaviors of relatives and loved ones.

Growing Recovery Movement. The growth of these organizations—all based on the concept that individuals can recover from addictive compulsions—and their accompanying twelve-step program of spirituality constitute the social phenomenon known as the recovery movement. These programs have no dues or fees; the only requirement for membership is that an individual desires to become free of addictions and compulsions.

Alcoholics, substance abusers, and others whose lives have become unmanageable because of addictive and compulsive behaviors attend meetings in which they share their experiences and hopes with others who have been in similar situations. This sharing of stories and life experiences is one of the cornerstones of the twelve-step recovery process.

The first recovery step involves an admission of powerlessness over a substance or behavior, whether it is alcohol, drugs, sex, gambling, food, or work. Next, individuals in recovery are encouraged to examine their past experiences closely in an effort to take responsibility for and accept the consequences of past actions. Other steps encourage personal spiritual growth and a policy of reaching out to assist others who have similar troubles. As members work through the necessary steps of the program (not necessarily in a particular chronological order), they are said to be "recovering" from, rather than "cured" of, addictive compulsions.

Alcoholism (considered to be the primary addiction) and substance abuse affect more families than do other addictions. More than ten million Americans are estimated to be alcoholics. An estimated 75 percent of alcoholics are male. Alcoholism is found among people of all ages and cultural and socioeconomic backgrounds.

The Family Disease. Addiction is considered a family disease, and dysfunctional family behavior is likely to persist unless the entire family receives treatment. Generally, the term "dysfunctional" means that the family does not function according to customary social norms. For example, parental roles are reversed when children of addicted parents take on caretaking responsibilities for their parents. Although they may not realize it, family members often allow or "enable" the person with a compulsive disorder to continue a pattern of destructive behavior.

In the early 1980's, counselors and therapists began to notice that as problem drinkers began to recover and regain many things they had lost as a result of alcoholism, problems in their families persisted and often intensified. Behavioral research has shown that although addicted individuals improve physically and mentally as they remain clean and sober, their families do not experience similar improvement.

One of the primary reasons why families should participate in recovery programs is that such programs foster an awareness of the pervasive consequences of addiction, particularly addictions involving dependence on chemical substances such as alcohol and drugs. Research has indicated that alcoholism seems to be prevalent along family lines. Although conclusive evidence has yet to be found, studies have shown that between 50 and 80 percent of all alcoholics have a close relative who suffered from alcoholism. Such findings appear to validate the theory that some individuals have an inherited predisposition to addiction. Some research suggests that alcoholism may be linked in part to the presence of a particular gene on chromosome eleven in human beings.

Alcoholism and other addictions can involve emotional problems, particularly related to depression and manic-depressive behavior. Social problems also play a role in addiction. In the 1990's, it was estimated that one in every three families in the United States was affected in some way by a drinking problem.

Children of alcoholics and problem drug-users may be affected by a parent's disease in several ways. Having an addicted parent increases children's risk of becoming addicted themselves. Problems associated with children of alcoholic parents include speech disorders, low academic performance, hyperactivity, psychosomatic complaints, drug use, and problem behaviors such as aggression, impulsiveness, and failure to take direction from authority figures. On the positive side, some children of alcoholic parents choose to avoid drinking as a result of unpleasant childhood experiences.

Treatment for Families. Families have several options for addiction treatment. Some choose to enter family counseling, others participate in self-help recovery groups, and still others choose to become involved in a combination of counseling sessions and self-help groups. In family counseling, family members have the chance to talk about their problems in a safe environment, without shame or blame, under the guidance of an objective, caring therapist. Individuals can examine past behaviors as well as modern family problems, and establish goals in working together to ensure a happier future. Psychologists and counselors have found that the best time for families to undergo counseling as a whole is while the addicted family member is undergoing rehabilitation as part of an in-house program at a medical facility or an outpatient treatment program, both of which usually require active participation in twelve-step programs.

Substance addictions are complex disorders that may require a combination of treatments for recovery. In the acute phase of their disease, alcoholics or drug addicts may suffer from medical complications and serious health problems that require hospital treatment. Such health problems may be part of the first step toward recovery. A comprehensive treatment plan involves family participation and family counseling. Family members can telephone a local hospital or a local chapter of Alcoholics Anonymous or another recovery program to learn about other options for getting help.

Although treatment is most beneficial when the entire family is involved, sometimes this option is not possible. Active alcoholics or drug addicts may not be ready to enter a recovery program. Family members may seek assistance to improve the quality of their own lives even though the addicted family member does not participate.

By consulting with a therapist, family members can learn how they may inadvertently be contributing to a larger family problem. Through awareness instead of denial, they can learn how to avoid supporting an addict's detrimental drinking or drug-related behavior. If the addict is a gambler, family members may learn how to care for themselves despite limited financial resources or other money problems.

When individuals with compulsive disorders find less support as a result of such changes within their families, they may become inclined to change and accept a program of recovery themselves. Through counseling, family members can acquire the tools and the commitment to aid the progress of an addict's recovery.

Twelve-Step Recovery Programs. In addition to AA and Narcotics Anonymous, which are designed to assist recovering alcoholics and drug addicts, there are a variety of recovery programs tailored to the needs of family members. Al-Anon and Alateen, for example, provide support to the families and teenage children of alcoholics.

In Al-Anon, spouses and other family members are welcomed by people who have experienced similar problems in living with individuals suffer-

Recovery programs are designed to help people whose lives have become unmanageable because of problems such as alcoholism. (Don Franklin)

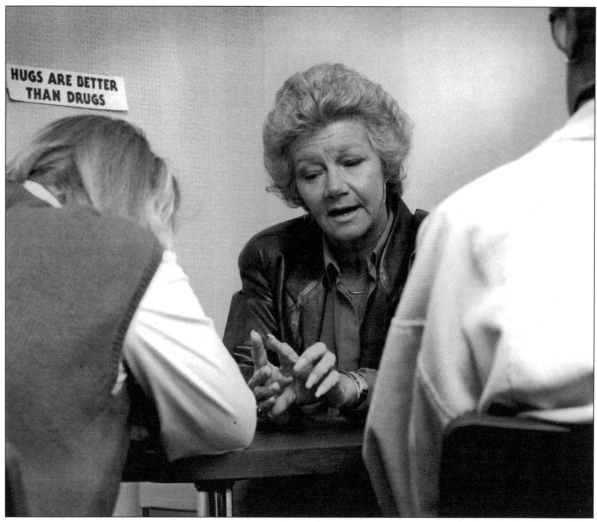

The success of any recovery program rests on the willingness of people with serious problems to seek outside help. (James L. Shaffer)

ing from alcoholism. Such contact alleviates the feeling of isolation and separation from the community that is common among families of alcoholics. New members of Al-Anon are encouraged to elect sponsors, someone who is available any hour of the day to help the newcomer over immediate hurdles.

In Alateen, teenagers come together to share their experiences. The intense shame associated with having an addicted parent is something all members have experienced. In this support group, teenagers are free to talk and express emotions that may have been suppressed for years.

Overeaters Anonymous welcomes people with various eating disorders, undereaters and bulimics as well as overeaters. Although participants are not placed on diets, they are encouraged to share nutritional information and reach appropriate weight goals by sponsors who have had success. O-Anon is for individuals, particularly family members, who have been affected by others' eating disorders. Such individuals may become compulsive themselves in their efforts to control the behavior of another person who has an eating disorder.

Types of Recovery Programs. Narcotics Anonymous helps people recover from chemical dependency, and Families Anonymous is available to assist people concerned about chemical dependency in relatives or friends. Members of Smokers Anonymous meet to support each other through the process of quitting cigarettes. Gamblers Anonymous works with people who want to stop compulsive gambling, and Gam-Anon is available for people affected by the behavior of gamblers. Sex Addicts Anonymous deals with compulsive sexual behavior, and Co-Dependents of Sex Addicts (COSA) supports people affected by the sexual conduct of such addicts.

Parents Anonymous is open to parents who are abusive or are afraid of becoming abusive toward their children. The organization also works with teenagers who have been or are current victims of parental abuse. Other twelve-step programs include Sexual Abusers Anonymous, Depressives Anonymous, Emotions Anonymous, Cocaine Anonymous, Overachievers Anonymous, Native American Children of Alcoholics, Shoplifters Anonymous, Agoraphobics Anonymous, Schizophrenics Anonymous, and Prostitutes Anonymous. Some chapters of Alcoholics Anonymous have established special programs for gays, lesbians, and nonsmokers.

All twelve-step recovery programs follow the basic tenets and spiritual philosophy underlying Alcoholics Anonymous. At meetings, people use only their first names to extend an atmosphere of trust for those who prefer anonymity. As their common goal, these programs attempt to teach people how to live. They attempt to bring peace and happiness to the lives of addicts and their families, and they promote healing.

Codependency. In her best-selling work *Codependent No More*, Melody Beattie developed the recovery concept of codependency. Beattie illustrated how people who are personally involved with individuals who are chemically dependent or have addictive personalities become compulsively disordered themselves. Such people may take on characteristics of hostile control and manipulation, constantly giving to others but not knowing how to receive. In Beattie's estimation, the conditions that make such individuals feel victimized make them more disordered than their addicted significant others. She strongly advocates that such people seek recovery through the twelve-step program known as Codependents Anonymous (CoDA).

Adult Children of Alcoholics (ACoA). This twelve-step program assists adult children of alcoholics who find themselves playing out roles and behaviors that became ingrained when they were children growing up in alcoholic homes. Sharon Wegscheider-Cruse describes the following rigid roles adopted by adult children of alcoholics: the enabler, the hero, the scapegoat, the lost child, and the mascot.

The enabler takes on responsibilities that allow compulsive or addicted individuals to continue in their detrimental behavior. For example, by calling in sick for a family member suffering from a hangover, an enabler may inadvertently contribute to an alcoholic's continued pattern of excessive drinking. A deep sense of shame and the desire to cover up for another's mistakes leads to a process popularly referred to as denial.

The hero, who is usually the oldest child and a high achiever, is predisposed to workaholism in adult life. The job of such children is to "cure" the family, often at the price of their own health.

The scapegoat, who is commonly the next child in line chronologically, is the family member who receives the blame for all family problems. By focusing on this child, the family overlooks the behavior of the addicted individual. The scapegoat often internalizes this blame-taking role, becoming the so-called black sheep of the family in adulthood.

The lost child role falls upon younger middle children who become lost in the crowd in an alcoholic home. Such children receive very little, if any, attention and suffer extreme loneliness, pain, and isolation later in life. These lost children find it almost impossible to enter into long-lasting relationships.

Individuals who act as mascots in the family serve as a catalyst for comic relief through their irresponsible behavior. Behind this comic mask, however, lies sadness and pain. As adults, mascots find it difficult to be taken seriously. Although they were cut-ups in class as children, mascots have difficulty focusing on and completing tasks as adults.

Through intervention, counseling, and participation in twelve-step groups such as ACoA, these painful family roles can be recognized and discarded. Information regarding twelve-step groups is available in public libraries and on the Internet.

Many such programs are listed in local telephone directories, and some of these programs have toll-free hotlines that provide information and advice twenty-four hours a day.   —*M. Casey Diana*

BIBLIOGRAPHY
Bailey, Covert. *Fit or Fat.* Boston: Houghton Mifflin, 1977. Subscribes to the twelve-step recovery program as a permanent means of achieving weight control.
Beattie, Melody. *Codependent No More.* New York: Harper & Row, 1987. This best-selling classic of the recovery movement discusses options for people who exhibit compulsive behavior themselves as a result of their relationships with addicted people.
Casey, Karen. *If Only I Could Quit: Becoming a Non-Smoker.* Center City, Minn.: Hazelden Educational Materials, 1987. Adapts the twelve-step approach for those wishing to recover from an addiction to tobacco smoking.
Cork, Margaret. *The Forgotten Children.* Toronto: PaperJackson Association/Addiction Research Foundation, 1969. A forerunner of the recovery movement, this work addresses the various effects that addiction has on children.
Durse, Joseph. *Painful Affairs: Looking for Love Through Addiction and Co-Dependency.* Deerfield Beach, Fla.: Health Communications, 1989. Discusses how some individuals turn to destructive relationships for comfort and prescribes a program of treatment and recovery.
Maxwell, Milton. *The A.A. Experience.* New York: McGraw-Hill, 1984. Although this book was written for professionals in the recovery movement, it is easily read and provides in-depth information regarding Alcoholics Anonymous and its twelve-step program.
Satir, Virginia. *Conjoint Family Therapy.* 3d ed. Palo Alto, Calif.: Science and Behavior Books, 1983. Written by a renowned behavioral scientist, this work provides a scientific explanation for much of the recovery movement's impetus.
Wegscheider-Cruse, Sharon. *Another Chance: Hope and Health for the Alcoholic Family.* Palo Alto, Calif.: Science and Behavior Books, 1981. Written by a leading figure in the treatment of adult children of alcoholics, this book describes the effects of addiction on each family member and provides solid steps toward recovery.

See also Al-Anon; Alateen; Alcoholism and drug abuse; Behavior disorders; Codependency; Dysfunctional families; Eating disorders; Family counseling; Family therapy; Shelters; Support groups.

Recreation

RELEVANT ISSUES: Children and child development; Marriage and dating; Parenting and family relationships

SIGNIFICANCE: Engaging in fun activities together as spouses, as parents and children, and as families and extended families is one of the best ways to strengthen family relationships and provide children and other family members with a sense of well-being and stability

The importance of families spending recreation time together has not always been accepted in America. In colonial times, what little time families had for recreation tended to involve the family as a whole. Yet, with the coming of urbanization and the Industrial Revolution in the mid-and late nineteenth century, recreation moved out of the home. One study of a typical American city in the 1920's found that clubs and other organizations were replacing family gatherings and that whole-family parties had almost totally disappeared and were replaced by gatherings of same-age, nonrelated groups, such as adults socializing with other adults and teenagers with other teenagers. By the 1930's a renowned family sociologist claimed that families had lost their recreational function to agencies and groups outside the family. Time, however, has proven him wrong. In the mid- and late twentieth century, having fun for most people involved being with their whole family or family members.

Importance of Family Recreation. Research has shown that most family members, with the possible exception of adolescents and young adults, devote most of their leisure time to the family. Eight out of ten of the most frequent recreational activities are performed with one or more family members. Spending time with their families is the top-ranked leisure time objective for Americans. Two-thirds of all preferred recreational activities occur at home, and of those that occur outside the home 60 percent occur with family members. Yet, many persons do not feel that they spend enough time together as families.

Among one sample of American married couples, 40 percent felt they did not spend enough time together talking and doing fun things. Almost half of all parents felt that they did not spend enough time with their children, and many children reported that they would like to spend more time with their parents. One-third of teenagers felt they did not spend enough time with their fathers, but most felt that they did spend enough time with their mothers. More than half of these teenagers wanted to engage in more family activities. Even among those teenagers who said they frequently spent time in family recreation, half wanted more family activities. Only 6 percent wanted to engage in fewer activities with their families. Even though family recreation is important to most people, not every family member enjoys the time they spend together with their families. One study found that

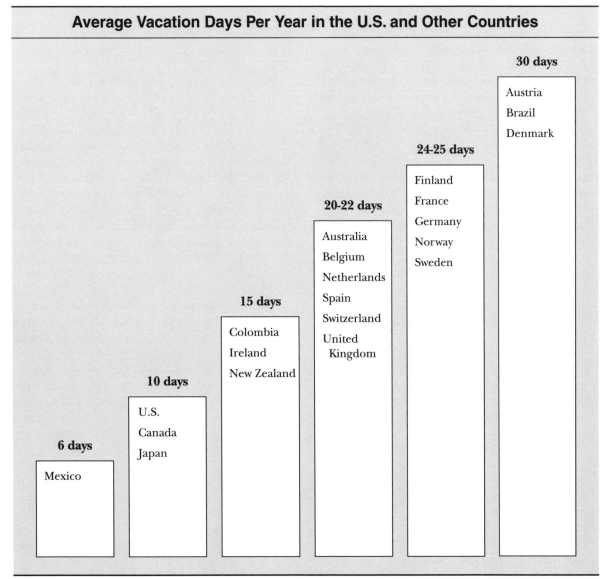

Average Vacation Days Per Year in the U.S. and Other Countries

6 days
Mexico

10 days
U.S.
Canada
Japan

15 days
Colombia
Ireland
New Zealand

20-22 days
Australia
Belgium
Netherlands
Spain
Switzerland
United Kingdom

24-25 days
Finland
France
Germany
Norway
Sweden

30 days
Austria
Brazil
Denmark

Source: Christian Science Monitor (June 3, 1997)

Note: The amounts of time parents have to spend with their families vary greatly among industrialized nations, but North American nations all rank low. This chart summarizes the average number of vacation days that workers receive in each country after one year on their jobs.

while 80 percent of elementary school-age children enjoyed performing recreational activities with their parents, only a minority of parents, especially fathers, felt that such activities were fun.

Family Influences on Recreational Activity. Several aspects of family life affect recreation. What families do depends to a large extent on what stage of the family life cycle they are at, the presence of children, spousal and parental employment, and the number of parents in the home. Although teenagers and single young adults are the least likely to participate in family recreational activities, getting married and having children moves most leisure activities back into the family. When couples are without children, husbands may take charge of planning recreation for themselves and their wives. When preschoolers are in the home, however, mothers usually take charge of family recreational activities. Once the children are older, fathers take over again. Moreover, the ages of the children influence the types of activities in which families participate. For example, when there are preschool children in the home, parents play less golf and tennis, spending more time at the swimming pool and doing other activities that adults and children can perform together. Families with young children and school age children are the most likely to have family vacations. When children reach their teens, family vacations tend to cease unless parents allow their teenage children to help plan vacations and allow them to bring friends along.

Another factor that affects family recreation is parents' employment. When fathers and mothers work long hours, the time families have for recreation together is lessened. Since parents in most one- and dual-parent families work, families have to be creative in finding the time and resources for engaging in recreational activities together. Two parental incomes has its advantages and disadvantages. Increased income allows families to do more things, especially away from home, but working parents often have less time for family activities.

Recreation's Effects on Marriages. Research has shown that the more time persons spend at recreational activities without their spouses, the more unhappy their marriages are. Yet, simply being together is not enough. Studies have shown that spouses who spend much recreational time together while communicating poorly with each other have found that their marriages deteriorate. Spouses who spend much time engaging in recreational activities together while communicating well with each other have found that their marriages improve. Wives suffering from stress are happier with their marriages if they communicate well with their husbands while engaging in leisure activities. Some husbands, however, experience the opposite effect. If they suffer greatly from stress, they are less satisfied with their marriages if they spent much leisure time together with their wives. It may be that participating in recreational activities adds to the stress that husbands feel over work or other matters.

Disagreements over how to spend leisure time is also a predictor of marital problems, while agreements over how to spend leisure time strengthens marital relations. Although spouses may strengthen their marriages by performing recreational activities together, if one spouse feels "forced" into having "fun," joint leisure time can backfire and lead to spousal resentment. Couples' favorite activities together include playing sports, hiking, camping, having sexual relations, eating out, visiting with friends, and going on drives. The actual activity is not nearly as important as that both partners want to engage in them together and that they have a good time.

Effect of Recreation on Families. Most people have heard the saying, "The family that plays together stays together." A characteristic of strong, happy families is having plenty of time together to play, talk, laugh, and share. One study of strong, happy families found that their favorite activities included vacations, outdoor activities like camping and hiking, eating together, and playing sports and games together. Family counselors also agree that spending time together doing fun, uplifting, recreational activities strengthens family solidarity. For many families the most frequent activity is watching television. Many people assume that watching television is generally bad. Yet, when families watch television together in moderation and discuss what they are watching, television can promote discussions of issues and values important to the family. They can discuss how families solve problems, how anger is to be handled, the consequences of inappropriate expressions of anger in the family, and the meaning of sexuality

During the 1950's the rapid spread of televisions and the growing amount of programming revolutionized family recreational habits. (AP/Wide World Photos)

Family-life professionals recommend that parents regularly work with their children in activities such as crafts. (Mary LaSalle)

A recreational activity loved by most children, swimming is also an activity that usually requires close parental involvement because of the need for vigilant supervision. (Lynn Abigail)

for the family. Television watching that divides family members, is engaged in excessively, and leads to arguments rather than discussions is inappropriate.

Organized and Spontaneous Family Activities. Although most family members feel the need for family recreation, they sometimes want more or less of it and sometimes enjoy it or consider it a burden or duty. It often helps if families learn to balance the leisure time they spend together between organized, even routine, activities and spontaneous activities. Most families benefit from having a certain number of regular family activities. Some activities that help strengthen families include regular weekly "family nights," scheduled team sports with some or all family members either participating or watching, regular large family gatherings such as a family reunions at holi-

day time, and annual trips to favorite family destinations.

Without regularly scheduling time together, most families do not spend as much time together as they want or need to in order to strengthen family relations. Weekly family nights, for example, have been recommended by family-life professionals as a time to play in the yard, play board games, wrestle, work with arts and crafts, and build models. Such family nights also afford families the time to formally or informally hold "family councils" to discuss rules and plan for outings. Some families actually have short "lessons" on family values such as honesty and helpfulness, but many find it useful to "teach" family values as they arise in the course of family activity. What seems to be most important is that such family nights are held regularly, that they are fun, and that they do not

Family games are most likely to provide fun for all members without provoking ill feelings if they are based more on chance than on skill or knowledge. (James L. Shaffer)

last too long or interfere with other family obligations, such as household chores. Creative families find ways to turn regular household chores into enjoyable games and activities. Chores become "fun" when they are performed jointly, when they build relationships, and when parents are flexible about how they are to be performed.

Families must be able to engage in fun activities at the spur of the moment without much previous planning. In fact, some of the best and most memorable family activities are often spontaneous and unplanned. Spontaneous activities that many couples or families enjoy include quick strolls around the neighborhood, bike rides to the park,

or a game of touch football. A spontaneous "Do you want to go play catch?" from a big brother to a younger brother can be a great way to have fun, relieve boredom, and cement a relationship.

Balancing Time with Different Family Members. Balancing planned, organized activities with unplanned, spontaneous activities is not the only balancing that helps families enjoy and benefit from recreation. Parents employed full-time outside the home often find that to balance between employment, household duties, and family recreation they must forgo pursuing some of their own favorite activities. All family members must learn to balance time between several different family groups for maximum benefit to family and individual well-being. Family members must have time alone or be able to engage in pleasant non-family-related activities, such as computer games, biking with friends, reading a book, or jogging.

It is important for spouses to spend one-on-one time together, for each individual parent to spend time alone with each individual child, for brothers and sisters to have time together without parents' supervision, for the whole family to engage in activities together, and for extended families to meet occasionally. Too much or too little time with these groups can be detrimental to family well-being. Each family and its members must decide the right amount through communication and negotiation. When resentment is a common feature of attempts to increase or decrease family time together, this is a good indication that a re-evaluation of priorities must be undertaken.

Competition in Families. Recreation can be a hindrance rather than a help to families if recreational activities become too competitive. Family fights may erupt over a "friendly" game of one-on-one basketball or Monopoly. Families can prevent recreation from getting out of hand and becoming too competitive by establishing clear rules to which all agree. For example, if one-on-one basketball must be won by two baskets, this should be clear from the start. Participation should be voluntary. If family members do not want to engage in a particular activity, they should not be forced to do so or be made to feel they are not a part of the family if they choose not to play. It is a good idea to have rules that "level the playing field." For example, if families play baseball, they should play with sponge balls so that younger children have as good a chance to score a hit as their older siblings. Families should play games where physical or mental maturity is of little or no consequence, such as games of chance. They should also play games in which winning is not the object.

Family Recreation in the Future. Given how wrong family commentators were in the 1920's and 1930's about the future of family recreation, it may be foolhardy to predict the future of family recreation. However, some trends seem worth mentioning. Technology will certainly continue to have an effect on family recreation. Ninety-five percent of all technology since the early use of primitive tools was developed in the period from 1972 to 1997. There is no indication that this trend will not continue apace. One only has to look at how modern forms of transportation, such as automobiles and airplanes, and modern electronics, such as television, computers, and the Internet, have influenced where families can go, what they can do, and when they can engage in recreational activities. While it may not be possible to predict how continuing changes in transportation, housing, computer technology, and other technologies will affect family recreation, it is clear that families will continue to make use of these technological advances to have fun.

—*Thomas B. Holman*

BIBLIOGRAPHY

Curran, Dolores. *Traits of a Healthy Family.* Minneapolis, Minn: Winston Press, 1983. Describes fifteen traits shared by healthy families, including having a sense of play and humor, a balance of interaction among members, and shared leisure time.

Holman, Thomas B., and Mark Chamberlain. *Family Together Workbook.* Bountiful, Utah: John Harmer Associates and the Marriage Study Consortium, 1996. Includes five lessons with accompanying activities for creating strong, happy, healthy families.

Holman, Thomas B., and Arlin Epperson. "Family and Leisure: A Review of the Literature with Research Implications." *Journal of Leisure Research* 16 (1984). Reviews research on the effects of family life cycle, size, and income on family leisure activities and research on how engaging in leisure activities affects families.

Nutt, Grady. *Familytime: A Revolutionary, Old Idea.* Washington, D.C.: American Family Society, 1977. Written to help family members talk with one another constructively, wisely, compassionately, well, often, and regularly by helping them discover ways to engage in fun activities together.

Pappas, Michael G. *Prime Time for Families.* Minneapolis, Minn: Winston Press, 1980. Provides more than fifty activities, games, and exercises for personal and family growth.

See also Computer recreation; Couples; Entertainment; Family gatherings and reunions; Family unity; Holidays; Parenting; Youth sports.

Reed v. Reed

DATE: Decided on November 22, 1971
RELEVANT ISSUES: Law; Parenting and family relationships
SIGNIFICANCE: The U.S. Supreme Court determined in *Reed v. Reed* that state laws preferring one family member over another on the basis of sex may violate the Equal Protection Clause of the U.S. Constitution

Throughout American history family relations have been regulated by state laws, which often reflected stereotypical views about the appropriate roles of men and women. Such laws were occasionally challenged in the Supreme Court, but until *Reed v. Reed* they were consistently upheld.

Sally and Cecil Reed were divorced parents. Each wanted to administer the estate of their adoptive son, Richard. Cecil Reed was appointed because Idaho law allowed both men and women to administer estates but gave automatic preference to men. Sally Reed appealed Cecil's appointment, arguing that Idaho's male preference violated the equal protection clause of the U.S. Constitution. Historically, American courts had treated sex discrimination as constitutionally permissible as long as it had a "rational basis," such as Idaho's presumption in this case that men generally know more about business.

Breaking with established precedent, a unanimous Supreme Court declared that "To give a mandatory preference to members of either sex over members of the other, merely [for administrative convenience] is to make the very kind of arbitrary legislative choice forbidden by the Equal Protection Clause. . ." As a result of this and subsequent decisions, state laws regulating marriage, divorce, child custody, alimony, child support, property, and inheritance are now constitutionally suspect if they treat men and women differently.

—Craig W. Allin

See also Gender inequality.

Religion

RELEVANT ISSUES: Marriage and dating; Parenting and family relationships; Religious beliefs and practices; Violence
SIGNIFICANCE: Religion significantly influences the family by helping to determine its structure, identity, behavior, and psychological health

The family and religion are inseparable and mutually influential. According to sociologist Carl Zimmerman, "the most sacred or divine aspect of society is considered to be the family system and being religious is tantamount to being a good husband, a good wife, or a good parent." This is especially true of Judaism, in which the family is divinely ordained by the first commandment of the Torah: "You shall be fruitful and multiply." Not to marry is to violate divine law.

Religion has a decisive impact on the domestic life, the behavior, and the family relationships of persons in every culture. It determines the very structure of the family and the pattern of relations among its members. Religious rituals, myths, and symbols serve to bind the family into a cohesive unit and fosters among its members a sense of identity and permanence. Religious beliefs and values play a critical role in the moral formation of children and the moral conduct of parents, and in this way it shapes the moral habits of the larger society. Finally, religion helps sustain the psychological health of families through pastoral counseling and other therapeutic means.

Religion and Family Structure. For practical purposes "family" may be adequately defined as a household with at least one parent and one child who may be related by blood to its parent(s) or legally adopted. The term "religion" is notoriously difficult to define. However, Edgar S. Brightman's definition of religion is representative and serviceable: "Religion is concern about experiences which are regarded as of supreme value; devotion toward a power or powers believed to originate, increase, and conserve these values; and some suitable expression of this concern and devotion, whether through symbolic rites or through other individual and social conduct."

Religious beliefs and values help form the distinctive structure of the family and govern the interrelationships of family members. Gordon Allport distinguished two basic types of religious persons: the "extrinsically" religious person, who uses religion as a means to personal ends like security, consolation, social status, and friendship, and the "intrinsically" religious person, who understands religion to be the chief end or purpose of life, orienting all of life's other activities. James Anthony added two other religious orientations to Allport's fundamental pair: the "questing" religious personality, who is not afraid to address the perennial philosophical questions of life, and the "orthodox" person, who scrupulously follows traditional doctrines, rules, and rituals.

Melvyn C. Raider collected evidence showing that some of these religious orientations are associated with certain types of family organization. Thus, adults with either an orthodox or extrinsic religious orientation tend to form "closed" families. Such families value loyalty and sincerity in their members and provide them with a strong sense of belonging. Paternal authority is exercised and strict discipline maintained in the interest of building good moral character in children. By contrast, adults with a more intrinsic religious orientation tend to form "open" or "random" families. Open families are especially sensitive to their members' needs, encourage the expression of emotions, and foster intimacy among their members. Decision making is democratic, persuasion is preferred over coercion, and the virtues of tolerance and rationality are cultivated. Families of the random type are similar in some ways to the open variety, but they are particularly characterized by spontaneity, creativity, and tolerance of their members' diverse viewpoints. In such families discipline is relaxed and children's freedom of choice is encouraged.

Rules Governing Family Life. Religions universally prescribe precise rules for every aspect of family life and establish the pattern of intrafamily relationships; there are religious laws governing marriage, divorce, contraception, abortion, procreation, gender roles, and extramarital sexuality.

For Orthodox Judaism, these laws are found in the sacred texts of the Torah, Talmud, and Mishnah. They prescribe that husbands are the heads of households and the owners of property and that family member-

ship depends on blood, legal ties such as marriage, and geographical location. Talmudic family values include purity, which is manifest in premarital chastity; fidelity within marriage; procreation and companionship between husbands and wives; and children's honoring of parents.

In Roman Catholicism the rules for ordering family life are found in the encyclical *Casti Connubii* (1933) and the document *Educational Guidance in Human Love* (1983). These texts specify that procreation is the chief purpose of marriage, conjugal love is an important end of marriage, periodic abstinence is the only permissible means of birth control, and marriage is a Sacrament dissoluble only through annulment and death.

Conservative Protestants regulate families according to the following principles: The love between husbands and wives is the primary relationship, serving as a model for children to emulate; the disciplining of children must be firm but lov-

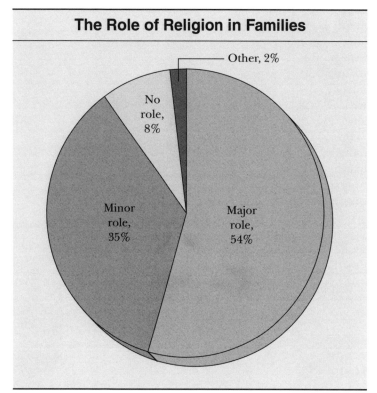

The Role of Religion in Families

Other, 2%

No role, 8%

Minor role, 35%

Major role, 54%

Source: Parentsroom website

Note: In early 1998 Parentsroom conducted an informal poll among visitors to its website, asking them how big a role religion played in their family life and child rearing. This chart summarizes the responses. Percentages are rounded to the nearest whole number.

ing; husbands are the heads of households, but they must respect their wives and be unselfish and generous in their actions.

Religion and the Family Bond. Religious rituals, a form of repetitive behavior in which family members participate, nurture faith by keeping alive the memory of vital myths and symbols and suppressing information that might weaken it. Rituals such as Christian baptism or the Jewish rite of passage called Bar and Bas Mitzvah help bind families into cohesive units and foster among their members a sense of identity and continuity over time. Families with a questing religious orientation tend to

engage in fewer rituals than families with an intrinsic orientation. In contrast to families with an intrinsic orientation, extrinsically oriented families are likely to perform rituals mechanically with little sense of their meaning.

Religious doctrines may also strengthen the family bond by reinforcing moral behavior. Evelyn Kaye spoke of the "Coalition with God" technique to enforce obedience. Thus, in strict religious families, parents may seek to control the unobserved behavior of their children by warning them that any infractions, although not punished by them, will almost certainly be punished by God. Kaye

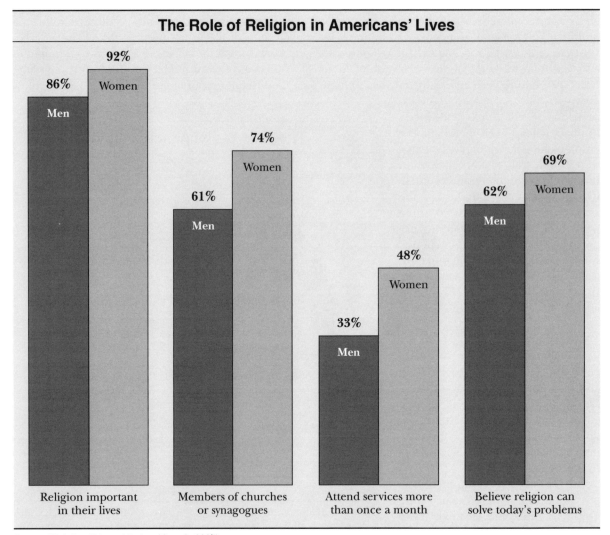

The Role of Religion in Americans' Lives

	Men	Women
Religion important in their lives	86%	92%
Members of churches or synagogues	61%	74%
Attend services more than once a month	33%	48%
Believe religion can solve today's problems	62%	69%

Source: *Christian Science Monitor* (Oct. 6, 1997)

Note: In 1997 the Gallup Poll surveyed a cross-section of Americans to learn how they see religion in their lives. This chart summarizes the responses of men and women.

Religion has a pervasive impact on families in almost every culture in the world. (James L. Shaffer)

cited studies showing that this technique has the effect of strengthening family bonds by turning children's resentment of behavioral restrictions inward toward themselves rather than outward toward parents, thereby preserving family peace. However, there is a danger that adolescents may question this technique of behavior control and decide to reject their parents' religious beliefs.

Family crises in strict religious families typically spring from the sexual awakening of adolescents who experience a conflict between their newly stirring sexual desires and the moralistic religious teachings of their parents. Moreover, fear of sex because of its perceived inherent sinfulness is common in such families. Children who absorb this attitude may encounter psychological difficulties in adulthood. As adults, they may repress certain urges because of moralistic indoctrination from childhood and consequently suffer from impotence, frigidity, and psychosis.

Jesus Christ's teaching that one should love all humanity has a profound impact on Christian views of family.
(James L. Shaffer)

Religion and Family Values. Members of religious families, in their behavior both toward one another and toward persons outside the family circle, exemplify distinctive moral values derived from their religion. One such value—the central one in Christian households—is unconditional love for all humanity as expressed in acts of personal self-sacrifice for the sake of the public good. Religious families put altruism, or love for others, before egoism, or love for oneself. A second value particularly of closed religious families, whose religious orientation is either extrinsic or orthodox, is respect for duly and legitimately constituted authority, whether human or divine. Fathers, who typically have authority in closed families, must never use it arbitrarily or abuse it for selfish reasons; rather, they must exercise it lovingly and responsibly toward their subordinates.

Religious beliefs and values learned by children in the home persist, even if only in the form of emotional attachments to them, throughout their whole lives. Kaye compares these beliefs and values to persons' native language, which cannot be lost even when other languages may be learned later.

A Crisis in Religious Family Values. The increasing modernization of the United States has resulted in the dominance of secular values that disrupt traditional family and religious ties and undermine the authority of religion in family life. One such value is individualism, which takes social, political, and economic forms. The ethos of individualism spawns attitudes and behavior that are not only opposed to the traditional moral values espoused by religion but also weaken the family bond and impair family structure. Examples of such individualism are sexual permissiveness, the acceptance of divorce, the legalization of abortion, the use of artificial methods of birth control, the tolerance of homosexuality, single-parent families, and women working outside the home.

It has been found that when secular and religious values conflict, even religious families typically opt to follow the secular. This was especially true of many Roman Catholic families who, since the early 1960's, drifted away from the traditional teachings of their church regarding family and marriage. There was, for example, widespread disagreement between the laity and clergy over artificial birth control and abortion. By 1983, 85 per-

cent of Roman Catholics had rejected the Church's authority to legislate in personal matters such as birth control. In 1978 the divorce rate among Roman Catholics was only three percent lower than that among Protestants.

Among immigrant groups, Jews achieved the greatest degree of adaptation and assimilation into the secular ethos of American society. However, the price they paid for this assimilation was a loss of their religious identity and a weakening of their family ties, as indicated in the 1980's by lower fertility rates, higher divorce rates, and higher rates of interfaith marriage than among members of other religious denominations. Thus, in 1980 it was estimated that about one-third of all Jewish marriages involved non-Jewish spouses.

Religious institutions generally responded to this crisis in one of two ways. Christian fundamentalists and other conservative religious groups directly condemned the secularization of the family and sought to restore the type of family that existed before 1930: namely, the "closed" type of family built around patriarchal authority, traditional gender roles, and the strict disciplining of children. Since the early 1980's these groups attempted to further their goals politically, coalescing into quasipolitical movements such as the Moral Majority and, in the 1990's, the Christian Right. The 1990's also saw the emergence of the Promise Keepers, a fast-growing and influential evangelical movement of Christian men, which enjoined its members to follow Biblical principles in their roles as husbands and fathers. The group was controversial because of its Fundamentalist character and the perception that it sought to subjugate women.

By contrast, liberal religious groups, such as mainline Protestant denominations, sought to accommodate and adapt to secular trends. Rather than seeking to control families, as do religious conservatives, liberal Protestants have worked to offer them support in weathering these trends. Rather than condemning outright such practices as divorce, abortion, and premarital sexual activity, they have offered pastoral counseling and support to members of their congregations who have engaged in such practices.

Religious Support for Families. Religion plays an important role in sustaining the psychological health of families, particularly in the form of fam-

Most American private schools have religious affiliations and include religious education in their curricula. (James L. Shaffer)

ily therapy practiced by clergy trained in pastoral counseling. Religion has unique resources to help families cope with bereavement, loss, and the sometimes traumatic unpredictableness of life and to provide them with confidence and hope in order to face an uncertain future. A fundamental part of a therapist's job is to be hospitable and to put sufferers at ease, which should come naturally to religious therapists. Hospitality is an obligation in many major religions. For example, Jewish law prescribes hospitality toward strangers, and early Christian religious orders established sanctuaries and "hospitals" for the afflicted. Moreover, religious therapists must exercise compassion, a virtue in Judaism and Christianity.

Religious-based therapy has certain advantages over secular therapy. Christian or Jewish therapists can refer to the Bible for effective models of mutual caring among family members. Therapists can exploit the religious faith of family members that typically fosters in them hope, openness to change, and responsibility for one another. There is evidence that religious couples are less likely to divorce and more willing to commit themselves to salvaging weak marriages. Third, organized religion can provide a network of support for ailing families. Finally, religious-based therapy differs from secular varieties because it recognizes that suffering itself has value by offering persons a unique opportunity for spiritual growth; because it conceives of its therapeutic goal not as clients' comfort and security, but rather their joy, freedom, and inner peace or serenity; because it seeks to give clients a deeper and richer sense of the meaning and mystery of existence; and because it conceives of therapy as more than clinically and objectively applying scientific techniques to control behavior, but fundamentally as an act of love, which Allport considered "incomparably the greatest psychotherapeutic agent."

Loyalty Toward Marriage. Americans have remained loyal to the institution of marriage, and they number among the most religious peoples in the world. In 1980 it was estimated that more than half of all Americans (around 131 million) were church members; about 40 percent of American adults attended religious services during a typical week, as compared to 20 percent of English adults. This bears out Alexis de Tocqueville's characterization of the United States as a nation with the soul of a church. Family and religious organizations have the effect of humanizing an increasingly impersonal and harsh society resulting from massive industrialization and urbanization and of buffering vulnerable individuals from social reality. Religious institutions function as a buffer zone between families and the larger social environment. —*Richard A. S. Hall*

BIBLIOGRAPHY

Allport, Gordon W. *The Individual and His Religion: A Psychological Interpretation.* New York: Macmillan, 1950. Allport, a distinguished American psychologist, considers the place of religious sentiment in the mature human personality, arguing that this sentiment can be healthy insofar as it helps integrate the personality and provides it with meaning.

Brightman, Edgar S. *A Philosophy of Religion.* Englewood Cliffs, N.J.: Prentice-Hall, 1940. Brightman, one of America's foremost thinkers in the Personalist school, concentrates on religion as a form of experience, interprets that experience, and relates it to the whole of human life, consequently considering religion from multiple standpoints—philosophy, psychology, and sociology.

Burton, Laurel A., ed. *Religion and the Family: When God Helps.* New York: The Haworth Pastoral Press, 1992. Collection of articles by different authors on the critical role played by religion in family therapy that deals with such issues as the integration of religion into therapeutic practice and the distinctive characteristics of religious-based therapy.

D'Antonio, William V., and Joan Aldous, eds. *Families and Religions: Conflict and Change in Modern Society.* Beverly Hills, Calif.: Sage Publications, 1983. Collection of articles by different authors on how the forces of modernization in the United States have resulted in an ethos of rampant individualism that has eroded traditional religious control of and support for families.

Kaye, Evelyn. *Cross-Currents: Children, Families, and Religion.* New York: Clarkson N. Potter, 1980. Kaye discusses the impact of religion on families, particularly its effect on marriage and children of parents of different faiths, concluding that the decisive factor in the religious education of children is their parents.

Trent, John, et al. *Go the Distance: The Making of a Promise Keeper.* Colorado Springs, Colo.: Focus on the Family Publishing, 1996. Book by members and advocates of the Promise Keepers movement who clearly lay out its goals, one of which is "building strong marriages and families through love, protection, and biblical values."

See also Baptismal rites; Bar Mitzvahs and Bas Mitzvahs; Family unity; Family values; Hinduism; Hutterites; Jews; Mennonites and Amish; Moral education; Mormons; Quakers; Roman Catholics.

Remarriage

RELEVANT ISSUES: Demographics; Law; Parenting and family relationships

SIGNIFICANCE: The majority of remarriages include persons who are divorced rather than widowed, and most remarriages include children from previous marriages, resulting in a profusion of stepfamily relationships

The United States has the highest remarriage rate in the world. In 1994, 40 percent of all marriages involved a remarriage for at least one of the spouses. Beginning in colonial America until the 1920's, almost all remarriages involved widowed persons, but by 1987, 91 percent of remarriages involved divorced men and women and only 9 percent included widows or widowers.

An estimated six in ten marriages in the United States and four in ten marriages in Canada are expected to end in divorce. Some divorced individuals experience several remarriages and divorces, but the majority of remarriages are second marriages. Remarriages are somewhat less stable than first marriages. They have a 20 percent greater likelihood of ending in divorce than first marriages; however, it has been projected by some scholars that divorce rates for first and subsequent marriages eventually will converge.

Demographic Characteristics. Approximately two-thirds of all divorced persons in the United States eventually remarry. Approximately 60 percent of divorced persons cohabit with their future spouse prior to remarrying. Beginning in the 1970's, the rate of remarriage declined in the United States and Canada. One explanation for this decline is the increase in postmarital cohabitation after divorce. Although women are less likely to remarry than men, they are just as likely to cohabit as men. It has been conjectured that lower rates of remarriage for women may be the result of increasing numbers of women choosing to cohabit with a partner rather than enter a remarriage.

The average person who remarries does so within three years following a divorce. For divorced men, the median age at remarriage is thirty-seven years; for women, it is thirty-four years. The median age of widowers who remarry is sixty-three, and the median age for widows is fifty-four. Divorced women are more likely to remarry than widowed women of the same age, and divorced men are more than twice as likely to enter a new marriage as are single, never-married men.

Probability of Remarriage. The probability of remarriage for women drops markedly with age. Divorced women who are older than forty are less likely than younger women to remarry. Less than 20 percent of divorced women in their forties and fifties remarry, and less than 5 percent of divorced women in their sixties remarry. Age does not affect a man's likelihood of remarriage. Peo-

A high proportion of marriages among older couples are remarriages for one or both partners. (James L. Shaffer)

ple who remarry prior to the age of thirty are more likely to marry someone who has never married, whereas those who remarry between the ages of thirty and sixty-four are more likely to marry a divorced person.

Other factors such as race, income, education, and the presence of dependent children also affect the probability of remarriage. Whites have the highest remarriage rate of all racial groups. African Americans remarry less frequently than whites, and less than 50 percent of divorced African American women remarry, compared to 75 percent of white women. Hispanic women have a lower probability of remarriage than African American women and approximately half the remarriage rate of white women.

Men with middle or high incomes are more likely to remarry than other men. Women with lower incomes are more likely to remarry than women with higher incomes. The rate of remarriage drops for women as their income and level of education increase. Educational level is not a factor in the rate of remarriage for men.

Remarriage is more likely if a person has no children or a small number of children from a previous marriage. Having three or more dependent children reduces the probability of remarriage for divorced women.

Blended Families. Blended families, also referred to as stepfamilies, remarried families, binuclear families, and reconstituted families, are the fastest growing family type in the United States. A blended family consists of the newly married spouses and the children of at least one spouse from a previous marriage. Approximately 40 percent of blended families include one or more stepchildren under the age of eighteen. Most of these children are the biological children of the mother and stepchildren of the father. In a small number of blended families, both spouses are stepparents to their spouse's biological children.

Blended families differ structurally from first-married families in several ways. First, one biologi-

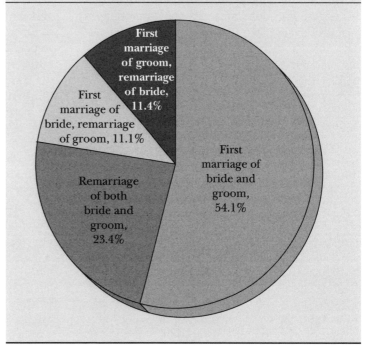

First Marriages and Remarriages of U.S. Couples in 1998

First marriage of groom, remarriage of bride, 11.4%

First marriage of bride, remarriage of groom, 11.1%

First marriage of bride and groom, 54.1%

Remarriage of both bride and groom, 23.4%

Source: U.S. Bureau of the Census, *Statistical Abstract of the United States: 1997.* Washington, D.C.: GPO, 1997.

cal/adoptive parent lives outside the family household. Second, the parent-child relationship predates the formation of the marriage and the marital relationship with a new spouse. Third, there is no legal relationship that binds stepchildren and stepparents. Federal and state laws do not clearly specify the legal rights and responsibilities between stepparents and stepchildren in such areas as economic support, custody after divorce, visitation rights, and inheritance.

Various structural differences of blended families have the potential to produce boundary ambiguity, such as the uncertainty of who is included in the family and who is not, and who is responsible for specific roles and tasks within the family. This lack of clarity regarding family boundaries has the potential to increase family stress and the risk of behavioral problems in children. More boundary ambiguity exists in stepmother families than in stepfather families, and children in these families are considered to be at increased risk for behavioral problems.

Remarriage has been called an incomplete institution because of the fact that social norms and social roles are not as clearly defined as in first marriages. There are no clearly stated guidelines for how to relate to a former spouse, the stepparent's role in disciplining children, or what words and names to use for the various relationships that arise in blended families.

Stepparenting. A basic problem in blended families is that the role of stepparent is neither clearly defined nor well understood. Negative stereotypes that portray stepmothers as cruel and uncaring and stepfathers as physically or sexually abusive increase the levels of family stress and hinder the development of positive family relationships. The role of stepmother may be more difficult than the role of stepfather because the mother is more directly involved in care of the children. Particular points of difficulty for stepmothers include accepting and being accepted by the new spouse's children, accepting the bond between the stepchild and the stepchild's biological mother, being a part-time or weekend stepmother, and a spouse's continued relationship with his former wife.

There is evidence that stepmother-stepchildren relationships are more problematic than stepfather-stepchildren relationships, and that stepmother families tend to involve more conflict and poorer adjustment than stepfather families. Stepmothers who reside in the same household with their stepchildren seem to experience higher levels of stress and more dissatisfaction with their lives than stepfathers who reside with their stepchildren.

Stepfathers often are unsure about their relationship with their stepchildren and about what is expected of them in the stepfather role. Stepfathers tend to view themselves as less adequate and less competent than biological fathers view themselves. Stepfathers tend to have more difficulty relating to girls than to boys, and to be more distant and detached than stepmothers. Most stepfathers are concerned that they will not be accepted by their stepchildren and fear being compared with the children's biological father. Stepfathers who also are biological fathers are more apt to successfully fulfill the stepfather role. This is especially the case when the oldest stepchild is relatively young, less than eight years of age.

Disciplining stepchildren is a common problem in blended families, especially for stepfathers. It can be difficult for stepfathers to enforce rules and achieve discipline while simultaneously trying to maintain a close and friendly relationship with stepchildren. Some stepchildren may resist a stepfather's discipline and the assumption of the father role, and many mothers become protective of their children in matters pertaining to discipline by a stepfather. More positive relationships between stepparents and stepchildren are more likely to develop if stepparents become friends to their stepchildren prior to assuming the role of disciplinarian.

Half Brothers, Half Sisters, and Stepsiblings. Half brothers and half sisters have one parent in common, either the father or mother, and are biologically related. A mutual child of the couple is more likely to be born in a stepfather-biological mother marriage if the stepfather is younger and has no biological children. Approximately two-thirds of white women and one-half of African American women have another child after remarriage.

When each spouse in a remarriage has children from a previous marriage, the children are called stepsiblings. Stepsiblings have no biological or legal relationship to one another. Not much is known about the relationships of stepsiblings. Available information suggests that stepsiblings usually are not as close as siblings but that they tend to get along well after an adjustment period to the new family and are likely to form feelings of attachment.
—*Marie Saracino*

BIBLIOGRAPHY

Belovitch, Jeanne. *Making Remarriage Work.* Lexington, Mass.: Lexington Books, 1987.

Berman, Claire. *Making It as a Stepparent.* Updated ed. New York: Harper & Row, 1986.

Einstein, Elizabeth. *The Stepfamily.* Boston: Shambala, 1985.

Lofas, Jeannette, and Dawn B. Sova. *Stepparenting.* New York: Kensington, 1990.

Savage, Karen, and Patricia Adams. *The Good Stepmother.* New York: Avon Books, 1988.

Smoke, Jim. *Growing in Remarriage.* Grand Rapids, Mich.: Revell, 1995.

See also Baby-boom generation; Blended families; Displaced homemakers; Family demographics; Marriage; Serial monogamy; Stepfamilies; Widowhood.

Reproductive technologies

RELEVANT ISSUES: Health and medicine; Parenting and family relationships

SIGNIFICANCE: New medical technologies and procedures have challenged the biological limitation that human reproduction is related to sex and that children are related to their mothers

Research beginning in the 1950's, primarily centered around hormonal controls of the menstrual cycle and ovulation, led to effective oral drugs for birth control. The birth control "pill" provided an effective female contraceptive that separated sex from pregnancy and is generally recognized as a major contributor to the 1970's era of sexual freedom. While the advent of acquired immunodeficiency syndrome (AIDS) in the 1980's dampened this freedom for individuals who were sexually active outside the framework of monogamous relationships, advances in drug implants and "morning-after pills," including RU-486, continued to make birth control increasingly reliable.

Reproductive technology accelerated as equipment and techniques were developed to treat the

Americans gathered outside the French embassy in Washington, D.C., in June, 1993, to both protest against and support the French-produced drug RU-486, popularly known as the "abortion pill." (AP/Wide World Photos)

one in seven women who are infertile. While artificial insemination had been in use for decades, the first test-tube baby was born in the United States in December 1981. First developed in Australia, in vitro fertilization uses a laparoscope to retrieve eggs from women who are unable to conceive directly. The eggs fertilized in glassware are either reimplanted or frozen using protective cryoprotectant chemicals. This technique became effective with the development of drugs that stimulate the ovulation of many eggs. A surrogate mother can receive the fertilized embryo and carry the pregnancy to term on behalf of the donor. Reversing this procedure, it is possible to artificially inseminate egg donors and then flush out the embryos five days later and implant them into mothers who have intact uteruses but defective ovaries. Derived from established agricultural practices, the first case of human embryo transfer in the United States occurred in 1984. This increases the potential number of "parents" to five: the donor father and mother, the surrogate mother, and the adoptive father and mother. As with earlier artificial insemination, human embryo transfer separates reproduction from sex.

Following implantation, additional technologies allow parents to make decisions on the status of fetuses. Amniocentesis is a traditional diagnostic technique whereby amniotic fluid is withdrawn from the uterus and cells sloughed from fetuses are tested for genetic defects, including Down syndrome. Newer techniques can sift fetal cells from a mother's bloodstream, eliminating the risk of miscarriage associated with amniocentesis. While amniocentesis is only effective after the end of the fourth month of pregnancy, chorionic villi sampling (CVS) can be used by the eighth week. A small sample is drawn from the chorionic membrane, which the embryo contributes to the placenta, and the cells are analyzed. Original CVS research was conducted in China until it was evident that this was being used for sex selection. Meanwhile, Landrum Shettles and colleagues promoted techniques that allowed couples to heighten their chances of having boys or girls on demand. While science has been effective in producing technologies that allow couples to prevent, produce, or select children, society has found it far more difficult to decide the extent to which these technologies should be commercialized, to determine the status of embryos, and to define motherhood and family. —*John Richard Schrock*

Types of Contraceptive Devices

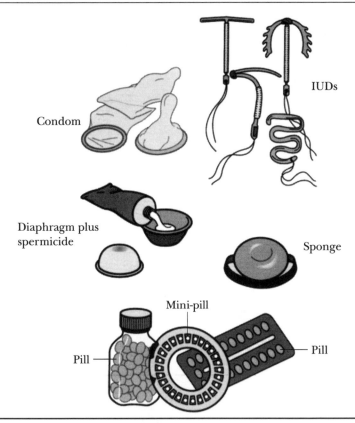

Condom

IUDs

Diaphragm plus spermicide

Sponge

Mini-pill

Pill

Pill

Many different kinds of devices have been designed to prevent pregnancy, from barrier methods such as condoms and diaphragms to hormonal methods such as birth control pills. Each method has its own advantages, disadvantages, and failure rates.

See also Abortion; Birth control; Eugenics; Fertility and infertility; Multiple births; Planned

Parenthood Federation of America (PPFA); Sterilization; Surrogate mothers; Test-tube babies; Zero Population Growth movement.

Retirement

RELEVANT ISSUES: Aging; Demographics; Economics and work

SIGNIFICANCE: Retirement, a rite of passage from employment to work separation, often accompanies other critical life decisions and thus has broad consequences for both retired persons and their families

Because of demographics and longer life spans, a revolution has occurred, especially in the developed world, in the relationship between age and employment and in the growing number of retirees. In early America, mandatory retirement at a fixed age was rare, and not until the 1800's did retirement in private and public employment become common in many occupations. Eventually, as industrial life took hold, workers started to retire earlier as they became unable to keep up with the speed of the modern assembly line or refused to accept demotion after they had supposedly passed their peak. Unions in the United States contributed to this trend by fighting for employee retirement programs. Whereas in 1890 the labor force participation rate for males sixty-five and older was 68.3 percent, by 1970 the corresponding rate was 26.8 percent.

Paradoxically, despite the increase in the average life span, the negative mystique about age persists, and older workers, rightly or wrongly, have been stereotyped as beyond the point of being able to make a major contribution to their employers or society. Accordingly, whether by subtle or more obvious pressure or the offer of irresistible incentive packages, many workers, despite their own best judgment or protective laws, move from employed to retired status.

Retiring is at times classified as having a honeymoon phase, focusing on persons' sense of liberation from the work routine; a disenchantment or depression phase, during which retirees' fantasies are not met; a reorientation phase, during which persons undergo some kind of reality check; and at times a termination phase, during which the retirement status becomes irrelevant, because persons either return to employment or become sick or disabled, so that the retirement role is exchanged for a new one.

Preparation for Retirement. Retirement is a process. As retirement approaches, men and women often anticipate it as they gradually disengage themselves from their work roles. Such disengagement prepares some for their actual retirement so that disengagement becomes less painful.

By the close of the twentieth century in the United States there has paradoxically been a trend toward early retirement, especially in the nonprofessional occupations, despite the protection of the Age Discrimination in Employment Act (ADEA) of 1967, which banned mandatory retirement in most occupations at any particular age. Early retirement reflects improvements in private pension plans and U.S. Social Security retirement benefits, or, increasingly, buyout programs and other employer inducements to workers to retire. However, it also evidences the greater value workers assign to leisure time. Thus, by 1990 three-fourths of men and four-fifths of women were voluntarily collecting smaller early Social Security retirement benefits between the ages of sixty-two and sixty-five, after which "normal" retirement benefits go into effect. Only about fifteen percent of men and under ten percent of women were still working beyond that age.

Gender Differences. Because the occupational role has been more central to men's self-concept than to women's, men tend to respond more negatively to the loss of this essential part of their identity than women and generally find it more difficult to adjust to retirement. Women experience more dramatic changes than men during maternal "retirement," because with their longer life expectancy mothers spend more and more years suffering from the empty nest syndrome following the departure of their last child. Thus, while women's social interaction decreases, their solitary existence, especially following widowhood, increases.

In the last analysis, the significance of retirement for both men and women depends on the importance and meaning of work for them. With increasing numbers of women in professional careers in the late twentieth century, women's investment of self-concept in their work may be no smaller than that of men. However, women retir-

Despite the fact that increased longevity has also meant that older people have more years of being productive, negative stereotypes about advanced age have tended to persist. (James L. Shaffer)

ees may still suffer less of an identity crisis than men, because many of them have played important family roles as wives, homemakers, mothers, and even grandmothers.

With a few exceptions, retirement does not seriously alter the preretirement allocation of household chores along traditional gender lines. Wives remain primarily responsible for housework, despite the fact that they often expect greater help from their husbands. However, in some cases the division of labor becomes more egalitarian as couples approach retirement age, especially if wives remain employed or are in poor health.

Whether retirement brings an increase, decrease, or no change in the quality of marriage depends on factors internal and external to spousal relationships. Internally, both partners must redefine themselves and their mates in light of the changes that retirement brings. External factors, especially the possible loss of income and declining lifestyle, may place strains on couples. Although the change in external roles may pose a challenge to individual self-esteem, spouses may rely more on each other for support.

Especially in the case of the upper-middle and upper classes, retired couples are little different in terms of self-confidence, goal orientation, or empowerment than before. Good health is especially important to a satisfying marital relationship, as are financial security, social contact with family and others, a sense of purpose allowing further self-development, and the ability to structure life meaningfully. Continuity is evident: Those who have had vital, rewarding marriages are likely to enjoy continued marital satisfaction, whereas those who have experienced unsatisfying marital relationships are likely to experience continued marital dissatisfaction. More generally, the idea that retirement seriously impacts on the quality of marriages one way or another is unsubstantiated. This does not mean that couples will not experience temporary transition problems while adjusting from one status to another. However, along the way, both marriage partners may discover pleasure from their release from work responsibilities and their increased freedom of mobility.

Retirement and Income. Together with retiree's health, income will significantly determine individuals' postretirement decisions. For example, retirees may have to decide whether they will opt to remain at their current residences, whether they will move to more modest accommodations or to more comfortable climate zones, or whether they will reside in retirement communities or age-segregated housing. Some may even decide to return to their countries of origin or move abroad. Postretirement activities and, more generally, postretirement lifestyles will depend largely on persons' incomes.

In developed countries pension programs (still usually vestigial in the developing world) are of two kinds: private programs, often employer- or union-sponsored; and public programs. In the United States the first private pension plan was begun by the American Express Company in 1875. Germany pioneered social security legislation in the 1880's, mandating old-age, sickness, and disability insurance. The first general federal government retirement program in the United States was the Social Security system—now Old Age, Survivors, and Disability Insurance (OASDI)—established in 1935. The Great Depression of the 1930's made it evident that the average worker or employee did not have sufficient individual means to enjoy anything close to comfortable retirement when there were relatively few employer- or union-sponsored pension plans and usually insignificant personal savings. OASDI, with retirement benefits at its core, is financed by equal contributions from employees and their employers. By the 1990's, after several expansions of coverage, some 95 percent of jobs involving more than forty million beneficiaries were in the program. Even at that time, some two-thirds of Americans older than sixty-five relied on such benefits for more than half their retirement income.

OASDI benefits were raised in a series of amendments to approximate "income security" standards. A cost-of-living allowance (COLA), allowing benefits to keep pace with the officially declared inflation index, was established in 1972. Whereas in the United States early retirement Social Security benefits are payable at age sixty-two for both men and women, in Canada the corresponding age for both is sixty. "Normal," or standard, retirement age in the two countries is sixty-five.

After the unions abandoned their earlier opposition to private pension plans, such plans began to proliferate in the United States in the 1950's.

Private pension plans came into existence not only because of management's greater sense of obligation toward workers, but also because management discovered that good retirement benefits could be used to attract good workers and could lead to higher employee morale and thus greater productivity. Accordingly, private pensions, now protected by the Employee Retirement Income Security Act (ERISA) of 1974, are no longer viewed as a gift, but rather as deferred wages for which pension funds or employers themselves are responsible.

In Canada, an old-age pension system was created in 1927. The test of eligibility was at first based on means. However, beginning in 1965 means-tested benefits were modified by the addition of a second, earnings-related, pension component.

The U.S. Social Security system is in part based on social insurance (with current workers funding current retirees) and in part on public assistance. All those insured receive benefits as an entitlement, but many collect more than they have ever paid into the system. This imbalance is projected to cause a deficit crisis in the twenty-first century, when the ratio of those working and contributing to the support of retirees—mostly the post-World War II baby-boom generation born between 1946 and 1964—will drop to below two to one from 16.5 to one in 1950. Thus, the law has already raised the "normal" retirement age to sixty-seven by 2027, and it is widely expected that additional measures to increase contributions, decrease benefits, or both will have to be enacted to keep the system viable. In the meantime, with improved benefits, the number of American retirees below the poverty line has decreased significantly.

Overall, the determinants of postretirement income are the same as preretirement income. Education, occupation, and marital status (whether or not retirees' spouses are still working or also collecting retirement income) are significant factors influencing persons' income levels following retirement. Workers without additional—or any—retirement benefits suffer in a perverse way, moving from poor to even poorer when they cease working.

Retirement and Family. Persons time their retirement according to such factors as health, pensions, and occupational characteristics, but, im-

portantly, they also time retirement according to their marital and family status. Married men tend to retire later than nonmarried men, because the former have greater economic needs than the latter, forcing them to continue working into later life. Nonmarried and especially divorced women are inclined to delay retirement longer than married women, reflecting their more precarious financial positions. Married women frequently adjust their timing of retirement to that of their typically older husbands, thus ending work relatively early. The fact that women often care for relatives may also affect the timing of their retirement. Generally, married persons experience more positive retirement attitudes, greater retirement satisfaction, and better postretirement adaptation than nonmarried persons. However, it also appears that the more married couples are incorporated into a broader kin network, the less likely it is that they will experience closeness and the sharing of activities with their partners. Nevertheless, kinship ties tend to be strengthened after persons retire, as they have more free time for their families, even as other social ties—for example, with former work colleagues—may decline.

Whatever forms of support retired persons enjoy, illness or death makes spouses—especially men—more vulnerable than they were before reaching retirement age. Other life events can have an important impact on the pre- and postretirement condition. Husbands consider dual retirement the most satisfying condition, because retired wives provide retired husbands with a sense of consensual validation. In contrast, the situation of retired husbands with working wives runs counter to traditional gender roles, rendering some form of maladjustment common.

Conclusion. Despite overall improvements in the health and financial security of retirees in the developed countries, society has not managed to solve the inherent conflict that age—and thus work performance—affects individuals differently. Thus, mandatory retirement, where it occurs strictly on the basis of age, often runs against the interests of both individuals and society. In contrast, for those who dislike their jobs and for whom retirement represents a release from the misery and drudgery of working life, society has not found an institutional solution either.

Indeed, innovative phased retirement, which al-

Western societies have continued to undervalue the contributions that older persons are capable of making. (James L. Shaffer)

Increased longevity has meant many more years of retirement for many people. (Dick Hemingway)

lows persons to ease out gradually by working fewer days, engage in part-time work or job-sharing, or participate in job redesigning to better suit older workers, is still the exception rather than the rule in the late twentieth century. In their public policies, governments have been equally ambivalent. Some encourage retirement by virtue of their pension laws. Others discourage it by various measures. Still others, such as the U.S. government, do both. The United States provides optional early retirement under Social Security while favoring the continued employment of older

workers by enacting age discrimination laws against mandatory retirement or even by encouraging the hiring of lower-income individuals older than fifty-five years of age under Title V of the Older Americans Act of 1965. Subsidies to senior centers and other programs may also be relevant.

Society has not found a way to reconcile the needs and expectations of younger workers for access to jobs and upward mobility with the wishes of older workers not to be forcibly retired. This problem may be eased by a growing economy able to generate additional jobs and a new form of education that places work and leisure in their proper perspectives, instead of merely promoting a culture venerating productivity and the need for individuals to contribute maximally to it.

In the meantime, interest groups such as the American Association of Retired Persons (AARP) have strived to improve the lot of both older workers (fifty-five years of age and older) and retirees. This private voluntary organization, founded by Ethel Percy Andrus in 1958, lobbies government on matters of concern to elderly and retired workers such as adequate Social Security and cost-of-living allowances; encourages members to become more directly involved in politics; and provides such services as preretirement, tax, health, housing, and legal counseling. In sum, the problem of providing some kind of meaningful life during the lengthened period between retirement and death, a result of longer average life span, is one which individuals, employers, private voluntary organizations, and governments must still address.

—*Peter B. Heller*

BIBLIOGRAPHY

Friedan, Betty. "The Retirement Paradox." In *The Fountain of Age.* New York: Simon & Schuster, 1993. Explains how many persons experience the trauma of retirement and illustrates it with human interest vignettes.

Richardson, Virginia E. *Retirement Counseling: A Handbook for Gerontology Practitioners.* New York: Springer Publishing, 1993. Focuses specifically on women, African American, and Latino retirees.

Sterns, Harvey L., et al. "Work and Retirement." In *Gerontology: Perspectives and Issues,* edited by Kenneth F. Ferraro. New York: Springer Publishing, 1990. Focuses on the extensive ramifications and the opportunities offered by retirement.

Szinovacz, Maximiliane, et al., eds. *Families and Retirement.* Newbury Park, Calif.: Sage Publications, 1992. Details how marriage, divorce, and kin are related to the retirement experience.

Szinovacz, Maximiliane, and David J. Eckert. "Families and Retirement." In *Handbook of Aging and the Family,* edited by Rosemary Blieszner and Victoria H. Bedford. Westport, Conn.: Greenwood Press, 1995. Details the effects of retirement on marital and family relationships and the effects of marital and family relationships

on retirement, with examples of the links between them.

Williamson, Robert C., et al. *Early Retirement: Promises and Pitfalls.* New York: Plenum Press, 1992. Result of a survey based on questionnaires and interviews among mostly middle-aged, downsized workers and employees, with individual profiles focusing on their adjustment to retirement.

See also Aging and elderly care; Baby boomers; Employee Retirement Income Security Act (ERISA); Friend networks; Gender longevity; Inheritance and estate law; Intergenerational income transfer; Older Americans Act (OAA); Retirement communities; Senior citizen centers; Social Security; Wealth; Work.

Retirement communities

RELEVANT ISSUES: Aging; Demographics; Parenting and family relationships

SIGNIFICANCE: Retirement communities are a relatively new alternative for older citizens, who now can live in an age-segregated environment while receiving a varying range of services

Some people have described retirement communities as halfway stations between pre-retirement residences and nursing homes, but formal definitions of these communities are as varied as the services they provide. Retirement communities differ greatly in terms of their physical characteristics, organization, amenities and recreation opportunities, fee structure, and other aspects.

Variety. The breakdown of retirement communities into categories often includes retirement towns and villages, retirement subdivisions, retirement residences, and continuing care retirement communities (CCRCs). The type of ownership also can be used a basis for classification. Some are owned by residents and others rented by residents. In one hybrid form, residents buy their dwellings, but ownership reverts back to the corporate owner upon their death.

Many of these settlements have developed an autonomous community life, but others depend to varying degrees on the services of the outside community. A retirement community may take the form of a service-oriented mobile home park, a series of detached residences, or a high-rise public housing project, or even extend to an entire leisure community or a full-service continuing care retirement community.

Services provided may include housing, housekeeping services, recreation, therapy, sit-down meals (including those for special diets), social services, transportation, storage, parking, and, most important, medical care if necessary. In the more modest communities, the services may be limited to housing and one or two meals a day served cafeteria style. Fees would be correspondingly lower. In CCRCs, there is often an entrance fee, part of which may be refundable upon the resident's relocation or demise (payable to the estate) in addition to the customary, usually high, monthly fee. Some of the newer CCRCs are based on the concept of owner equity, somewhat like a cooperative or condominium. In short, the variety is impressive.

So are the numbers. It is estimated that by the year 2000, there will be about fifteen hundred CCRCs in the United States with about half a million residents. That population will come out of more than three million elderly—about 10 percent of those older than sixty-five—who live in congregate residential facilities. Half of that population will live in nursing homes. Unlike nursing home patients, members of retirement communities are expected to be in fairly good health and sufficiently active to participate in community events.

Communities offer a variety of programming for residents. A typical week's activities at one community that emphasizes an active social life for residents includes such organized events as church services, exercise classes, bingo, cinema, barbecues, ice cream socials, piano instruction, sing-alongs, crafts classes, baking instruction, lunch out, social night, and shopping and banking expeditions. Clubs might be organized around activities, such as a walking club to combine socialization with exercise.

Origins. Although California had a statute as early as 1939, most of the other states that regulate retirement communities at all enacted their legislation between 1975 and 1986. Existing statutes vary widely in purpose, coverage, certification or registration requirements, disclosure provisions, contract content, and enforcement agencies (if any).

Retirement communities started as real estate developments planned somewhat off-handedly by public and private sponsors for an elderly clientele. Sponsors have included government agencies, fraternal lodges, labor unions, religious groups, voluntary associations, and real estate developers. In some way or another, the above were responding to the expressed desire of some older people to live with others of similar age and stage of life, often in warmer climates such as those of Florida and California. The mobility of older citizens in the automobile age, their willingness to relocate, and their desire to live in a special age-segregated environment also help to explain the acceptance and spectacular growth of these communities.

Subsequently, retirement communities were established in northern states—for example, New Jersey and Pennsylvania—as well as in Canada, where they are usually smaller than in the United States but otherwise do not differ in any systematic way. Retirement communities arose in these locations because some older adults preferred to remain in familiar surroundings.

Pros and Cons. Criticisms of retirement communities, where they occur, are principally focused on the fact that the relatively homogeneous age groups—and often racial, social, religious, and income groups—create an artificial environment. Anthropologist Margaret Mead characterized retirement communities as "golden ghettos" untypical of the natural world. Other critics have stressed the stultifying atmosphere that a group of bored or listless senior citizens leading a hedonistic life in pursuit of happiness can generate. Most observers, however, view a retirement community as a unique opportunity to remain physically and socially active and to be relieved of many household responsibilities.

Other reasons for the success and growth of these communities are the increasing pool of elderly in both the United States and Canada, their longer life expectancy, and their better financial standing, which makes retirement facilities more affordable. The latter is a result of increased government Social Security and Medicare payments as well as the increasing prevalence and benefits of pension plans and personal retirement savings options. The elderly of the late twentieth century will be among the last Americans to be able to rely to any significant degree on pensions for their retire-

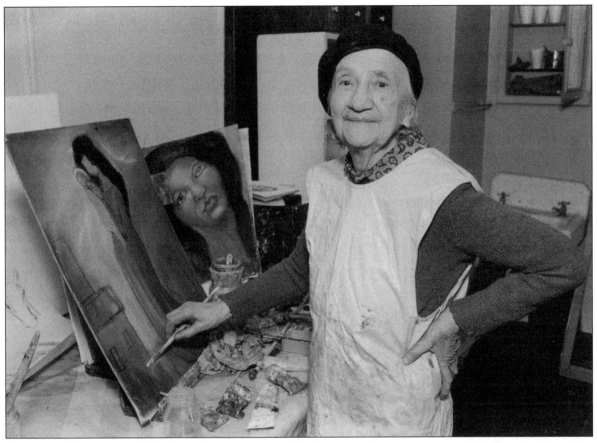

For many older persons, living in retirement communities has made it easier to accomplish long-standing goals. (Hazel Hankin)

ment, but the elderly of the future have been warned, and many are saving to pay for a comfortable retirement.

Relationships. The tradition of elderly parents moving in with their children or even grandchildren upon retirement or when they become unable to care for themselves is no longer as strong. There may be other "push" factors encouraging the growth of retirement communities, such as the deterioration of the elderly's earlier residential neighborhoods, the loss of their friends through relocation or death, or even an excessive number of children in their vicinity. Finally, developers have found the establishment of such communities—especially at the upper end of the scale—very lucrative.

Various polls and anecdotal reports suggest that retirement community residents tend to be satisfied with them, especially because of the socializ-ing possibilities such congregate living affords. Malcontents tend to compare the services of staff unfavorably with the personalized touch of family members. In addition, sometimes the type of retirement community selected may not be tailored to meet the needs and desires of particular residents.

Staff often fulfill a surrogate family role, as do other residents and peers, through socializing and support. Family assistance, support, or merely presence often is unavailable because of estranged relations, lack of sustained contact with family over many years, distance, or simply personal preference. With loners excepted, those who are thus unattached must rely on on-site support systems. Even when the younger family members live nearby, the prevalence of working couples makes it difficult for the younger set to care for older relatives.

Case Study. Pine Woods is an adult home community in central Florida covering some three hundred acres of land. The site was purchased by an insurance company in 1972 because of its mild climate, rolling hills, woodlands, waterways, and isolation from congested areas. The community was deliberately planned to be relatively small to maximize a friendly village atmosphere. In 1992, Pine Woods had nearly two thousand residents.

A sixteen-hundred-seat auditorium in the clubhouse is the hub of social and recreational life. The facility has covered shuffleboard courts, a swimming pool, saunas, whirlpools, and a marina with access to a lake for boating and fishing. Other activities take place in smaller meeting rooms. The retirement community has a closed-circuit television system, cable television, paved and lighted streets, an around-the-clock security system and security gate, and a call-button system linking residents to security for emergencies.

A residents' cooperative association board of directors is responsible for overall policy and financial arrangements. A general manager has day-to-day responsibility for the community and for the paid staff, including a recreation director. In the course of its life cycle, new and younger residents move in as some older settlers move out or die, thus helping to energize the facility and take over voluntary leadership roles. Other types of retirement communities with older clienteles would tend to focus more on health services rather than recreation, or at least on those activities that require less physical exertion. —*Peter B. Heller*

BIBLIOGRAPHY

Beesley, Kenneth B. *Social Well Being in Planned Retirement Communities: A Review and Pilot Study.* Peterborough, Ontario, Canada: Trent University, 1989.

Down, Ivy M., and Lorraine Schnurr. *Between Home and Nursing Home: The Board and Care Alternative.* Buffalo: Prometheus, 1991.

Moss, Rudolf H., and Sonne Lemke. *Group Residences for Older Adults.* New York: Oxford University Press, 1994.

Osgood, Nancy J. *Senior Settlers: Social Integration in Retirement Communities.* New York: Praeger, 1982.

Sherwood, Sylvia, et al. *Continuing Care Retirement Communities.* Baltimore: Johns Hopkins University Press, 1997.

Smithers, Janice A. *Determined Survivors: Community Life Among the Urban Elderly.* New Brunswick, N.J.: Rutgers University Press, 1985.

Teski, Marea. *Living Together: An Ethnography of a Retirement Hotel.* Washington, D.C.: University Press of America, 1981.

See also Aging and elderly care; Communities; Gender longevity; Home sharing; Institutional families; Mead, Margaret; Nursing and convalescent homes; Retirement; Senior citizen centers.

Rites of passage

RELEVANT ISSUES: Children and child development; Education; Religious beliefs and practices; Sociology

SIGNIFICANCE: Rites of passage integrate persons into their culture, society, or vocation through some sort of formal or semiformal initiation and ceremony

In a primitive society, typically a tribe in a complex of villages, rites of passage involve the three stages of separation, indoctrination, and reintegration. Typically, pubescent or adolescent boys and girls judged ready by parents, elders, or shamans or priests are separated from their families and billeted in dormitories adjacent to the village but physically separated and off limits to outsiders. The family may go through a symbolic mourning because the separation signifies the death of childhood. The initiates, held in seclusion in their separate dormitories, are in a symbolic state of being out of the world for the weeks or months of the initiation period.

The indoctrination is carefully controlled by adults, who teach the initiates the lore of their culture through myths, legends, songs, and dances, often with symbolic meanings that they must interpret themselves. There may be physical and psychological challenges. There may be a test of strength, skill, and courage, such as killing a lion. There may be fasting and a vision quest in which the initiates seek communion with the spirit world.

Sexual Play. The program for girls is likely to have several differences from the boys' program. There may be some ritualized flirting and sexualized play between the boys and the girls, carefully controlled by the adults. The purpose is to expand the initiate's reference from the family and clan to the whole society and prepare the initiates to be functioning adult members of their culture. The village also may go through a special period of religious practice and ritual during this time. When the program is finished, the initiates are welcomed back and accepted as adults. They may even thereafter live in their own separate huts.

Traditional, preindustrial India was a much more complex society than an illiterate hunting and gathering, pastoral, or subsistence agricultural society. It became the custom to separate a Hindu boy from his parents around the age of ten and send him to a guru school for a religiously oriented education until around the age of twenty. This program continues, although it is less widely practiced than in the past.

As with the primitive initiation program, and unlike the Western practice, the spiritual, aesthetic, and sensory are valued as much as the intellectual. The object is to teach the youth to reason and to become an integrated human being as well as to impart knowledge.

Universal or General Rites of Passage. High school is a virtually universal experience in the United States and Canada, and although not ev-

Among North Americans, high school graduation is one of the few nearly universal rites of passage. (Hazel Hankin)

eryone graduates, there is a formal graduation ceremony. The graduates are to a greater or lesser extent regarded as adults. High school students are mostly the passive recipients of information and generally are emotionally distant from the school administration in the abstract, although relations with some teachers may be warm.

College traditionally involves separation from the family and close interactions with peers in dormitories and fraternity houses. Adult guidance generally is minimal, and the emphasis is more on acquiring knowledge than becoming an integrated human being. College is often a place of experimentation with and learning about romantic relationships.

Coming out parties signify that a young woman is ready to come out into society, usually at the age of seventeen or eighteen. These affairs involve extensive preparation, including several semiformal and informal social events in which mothers and experienced women guide the debutantes. There is little spiritual component to this initiation.

The quinceañera is a celebration of a girl's fifteenth birthday in Latin American countries and communities. It is common in Mexican American communities in the United States. The celebration, involving a girl's family and friends, symbolizes entry into adult society, and in the United States it is an affirmation of ethnic culture. There is a strong religious component.

Religious Rites of Passage. The purpose of a religious confirmation rite is to confirm individuals as functioning members of their religion. Among Jews, boys and girls are confirmed through the Bar and Bas Mitzvah ceremonies at the age of thirteen. A boy is then regarded as a man for religious purposes and can be part of a minyan, the minimum number of men needed for religious services. Although they are accepted as adults, boys still are not generally treated fully as adults by parents, teachers, or society.

In the Catholic communion, the rite of confirmation has had different practices and meanings over the centuries. For most of the twentieth century, it typically involved an entire parochial class, with some children a year younger or a year older than the norm, a year after the rite of first communion. In the third quarter of the twentieth century it became, like first communion, more of an individual than group rite. Various Protestant denominations also have confirmation ceremonies.

In the Church of Jesus Christ of Latter-day Saints (Mormon religion), boys generally become deacons at the age of twelve and holders of the Aaronic priesthood at the age

Even so minor an achievement as graduation from kindergarten may be perceived as a significant rite of passage by those involved. (Arkent Archive)

Religious ceremonies such as confirmation rites and Bar Mitzvahs are rites of passage vitally important to members of the religions involved but often unknown or misunderstood by outsiders. (Mary LaSalle)

of sixteen. Religious and social duties are carefully designed to fit their level of maturity.

Military Service and Scouting. The U.S. military, like other military services, has been an integrating force for young men of various ethnic, religious, racial, and regional backgrounds. The threat or actuality of combat, along with rigorous train-

ing and harsh discipline, toughened men's characters. Reintegration into society seemed to go fairly smoothly after the two world wars and during the Cold War period until the Vietnam War.

Israel's military system is nearly universal among citizens and is a strong socializing component. Nearly all men and the majority of women are called to military service, and after active duty, men serve in the reserves until the age of fifty. In addition to military training, Israeli men and women are taught the history and lore of the modern state of Israel and the Israeli army.

In the United States, the Boy Scouts, Girl Scouts, and Campfire Girls are sponsored by civic organizations and churches and have a loose ideology. They aim to develop citizenship, leadership, and character, but they have had limited impact as rites of passage organizations.

Vocational Rites of Passage. Under the traditional apprentice system, a boy would apprentice to a master at the age of fourteen, often boarding in the master's household for his seven-year apprenticeship. At the age of twenty-one, he would become a journeyman, undertaking a geographical rite of passage by journeying to other towns to obtain work assignments and be certified by resident masters. Then he would be able to support himself, get married, and eventually become a master with apprentices of his own.

This system demonstrates the three principles of separation, indoctrination, and reintegration, as well as a personalized system of instruction by an elder. A 1992 Department of Labor report on work skills identified five key complexes of expertise, one of which was a set of interpersonal skills of working well with others, teamwork, customer service, negotiation, and leadership. Development of these skills is consistent with the apprentice system.

The U.S. Coast Guard, in a type of apprentice system, operates a sailing bark with twenty-two sails for cadets because sailing ships are more challenging than motorized ships and because they require intensive teamwork. Many occupations have entry-level jobs through which employees must pass before being recognized as fully qualified practitioners. Medical residency for doctors in training is one of the clearest examples.

Modern Versions. In the past, and more rarely now, Australian aborigine boys would be sent on a six-month endurance test in the wilderness known as a "walkabout." An Australian film of that title inspired several programs using that name in the United States and Canada during the 1970's, intended to facilitate the transition from school to life. These programs often made use of a background of relevant academic study and empha-

sized relationships and networking. Programs were designed so that participants could learn from experience, presenting opportunities for decision making and chances to test limitations. One Canadian program uses canoe and camping trips in Ontario and Quebec.

Some programs recognize that the transitional journey essentially is an inward journey to achieve psychic transformation. One such program uses guided imagery, drawing, masks, and improvisational games.

Outward Bound originated as survival training for merchant seamen during World War II. Years later, it became a popular inner quest program for adults of all ages. It has inspired other programs based on hiking, climbing, boating, and camping activities but is oriented toward building teamwork and promoting inner growth.

—*William L. Reinshagen*

BIBLIOGRAPHY

Greenberg, Joanne. *Rites of Passage.* New York: Holt, Rinehart and Winston, 1979.

Kett, Joseph F. *Rites of Passage.* New York: Basic Books, 1977.

Mahdi, Louise Carus, Nancy Geyer, and Michael Meade, eds. *Crossroads: The Quest for Contemporary Rites of Passage.* Chicago: Open Court, 1996.

Mead, Margaret. *Coming of Age in Samoa.* New York: Morrow Quill, 1928.

Turnbull, Colin M. *The Human Society.* New York: Simon & Schuster, 1983.

See also Bar Mitzvahs and Bas Mitzvahs; Circumcision; Communities; Enculturation; Gangs; Moral education; Puberty and adolescence; Quinceañera.

Rockwell, Norman

BORN: February 3, 1894, New York, N.Y.
DIED: November 8, 1978, Stockbridge, Mass.
AREA OF ACHIEVEMENT: Art and the media
SIGNIFICANCE: Norman Rockwell's nostalgic paintings of family life, which graced the covers of widely read magazines from 1916 to 1970, made him popular with generations of Americans who were amused by his humorous portrayals of everyday events

Norman Rockwell's work enjoyed great popular success during his lifetime, but after his death in

Norman Rockwell at work. (Archive Photos)

1978 art critics came to realize that he was also a very skilled craftsman. A Norman Rockwell museum was built in Philadelphia to display the original paintings, which were reproduced on the covers of magazines such as *The Saturday Evening Post, Look,* and the *Literary Digest.* This collection of numerous paintings by Rockwell in a single museum has enabled people to appreciate the wonderful evolution in theme and quality of this unassuming artist.

Rockwell was born in New York City on February 3, 1894. His early work was highly sentimental and evoked the Victorian era. The models in his magazine covers from the 1910's to the late 1920's wore clothing that had been in fashion twenty to thirty years earlier. There was no reference to the profound recent social changes that had taken place in America. Rockwell did, however, portray nostalgic scenes with humor. A famous example of his mixture of wit and nostalgia can be seen on the cover of the March 9, 1929, issue of *The Saturday Evening Post,* depicting an elderly doctor putting a young patient at ease by first placing his stethoscope on her doll before listening to her heartbeat. Even during the Great Depression in the 1930's, there was still no social commentary in Rockwell's covers for *The Saturday Evening Post,* because the editors of this weekly magazine were conservative Republicans opposed to the political changes implemented by President Franklin D. Roosevelt.

During World War II Rockwell began to treat a wider variety of themes. In 1943 he painted a series of four paintings that are almost universally considered to be his masterpieces. In these four paintings, first reproduced in *The Saturday Evening Post,* Rockwell used ordinary people to represent Freedom of Speech, Freedom of Worship, Freedom from Want, and Freedom from Fear. Millions of copies of these paintings were distributed throughout America during World War II. After the war Rockwell continued to treat social and political themes, including racism. In a touching painting entitled *New Kids in the Neighborhood,* which appeared on the May 16, 1967, cover of *Look,* Rockwell portrayed two African American children meeting three white children in their new neighborhood. Rockwell suggests that racism makes no sense, because these five children will simply learn to live together in harmony, as adults

also should. Rockwell was a highly skilled artist who developed from a nostalgic and sentimental illustrator into a gifted social commentator.

—*Edmund J. Campion*

See also Art and iconography; Cassatt, Mary; Emotional expression; Family values; Grandparents.

Roe v. Wade

DATE: Ruling issued on January 22, 1973
RELEVANT ISSUES: Health and medicine; Law; Parenting and family relationships
SIGNIFICANCE: This Supreme Court case established that a pregnant woman has a constitutional right to an abortion on demand in the first trimester of pregnancy

Roe v. Wade sprang from the attempt of "Jane Roe" (Roe's real name was Norma Jane McCorvey) to terminate her pregnancy by means of abortion in Texas in 1970. Texas law forbade abortion except "for the purpose of saving the life of the mother." Roe's life was not endangered by her pregnancy. With the encouragement of her attorney, Sarah Weddington, Roe decided to challenge the Texas statute on constitutional grounds. A federal district court suit was brought against Henry Wade, the district attorney of Dallas County, asking that he be enjoined from enforcing the Texas abortion statute on the grounds that it unconstitutionally interfered with pregnant women's rights to personal privacy. The district court agreed with Roe, and Texas appealed to the U.S. Supreme Court. The case was first argued on December 13, 1971, reargued on October 11, 1972, and decided by the Court on January 22, 1973.

The fundamental issue in *Roe v. Wade* is whether "personal privacy" rights pertain to a woman's decision to have an abortion. By 1971 the Supreme Court had extended the idea of "liberty" protected under the due process clause of the U.S. Constitution to include some marital and personal privacy rights. The most important precedent was *Griswold v. Connecticut* (1965), in which the Court held that persons have a right to receive and use contraceptive devices and information. The same right was extended to unmarried persons in *Eisenstadt v. Baird* (1972). In these cases the Court assumed for the first time that there is a "zone of privacy" that protects private family and sexual decisions.

The Court's seven to two decision in *Roe v. Wade* was written by Justice Harry Blackmun. The decision held that a pregnant woman has the right to an abortion on demand in the first trimester of pregnancy. In the second trimester the state is free to place some restrictions on the right to protect the health of the mother. In the third trimester, after the fetus has "quickened," the state may have the power to prohibit abortion altogether. This Court opinion balanced the interests of state governments against the personal privacy rights of women. The state's interest is to protect unborn life and the safety and health of pregnant women. Roe's interest was what the Court called "the fundamental right of single women and married persons to choose whether to have children." By tying persons' right to an abortion to their right to choose whether to have children, Blackmun brought the case more squarely within the precedent established by *Griswold v. Connecticut* and substantially increased women's autonomy both within and outside the family.

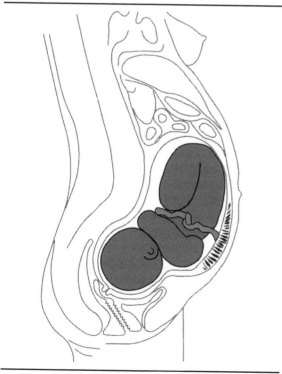

Cross-section of a pregnant woman in the third trimester, when abortion is illegal under Roe v. Wade.

The Supreme Court's *Roe v. Wade* decision has continued to generate enormous controversy. Since the case was decided, there have been constant efforts by its opponents to overturn it and by its supporters to protect the rights it established. The passions raised by this case have occasionally resulted in violence, and the issue is almost constantly before the Supreme Court in one form or another. Because the decision in the case appeared to many people to be political rather than judicial in character, there have been many demonstrations in front of the Court itself.

—*Robert Jacobs*

See also Abortion; Birth control; Planned Parenthood Federation of America (PPFA); Privacy.

Roman Catholics

RELEVANT ISSUES: Marriage and dating; Parenting and family relationships; Religious beliefs and practices

SIGNIFICANCE: Roman Catholics have traditionally stressed the dignity of human life as a reflection of the life of Jesus Christ; this belief has influenced their attitude toward birth control, abortion, and sexual ethics

In the mid-1990's there were approximately seventy-five million Roman Catholics in North America. Believing that the life of Jesus Christ would be best nurtured in a monogamous family setting, the Roman Catholic Church, with its center in the Vatican, has established the Sacrament of marriage. Because marriage is considered sacred, it is also thought to be permanent. Therefore divorce and remarriage are discouraged. Women are venerated for their motherhood and are thus encouraged to add to their glory by having children. Catholics think that these children benefit best by growing up in traditional families.

Changes in cultural viewpoints and practices have affected traditional Roman Catholic beliefs regarding the family. Catholics, both lay and clergy, are challenged by the issue of adaptation to the changing culture. If the Church changes too much to accommodate the culture, it risks losing its identity as Roman Catholic. If it does not adapt to the culture, it risks losing relevance to its members. Modern theologians attempt to bridge this gap to stay loyal to their tradition but at the same

Roman Catholicism is both the largest Christian denomination in the world and the church with the most diverse membership. (James L. Shaffer)

Roman Catholicism differs from other Christian faiths by its adherence to the Sacramental system. (James L. Shaffer)

time to make Catholic family doctrine more relevant to the changing times.

Entrance into the Family and the Family of God. Roman Catholics are distinguished from other Christian denominations by their adherence to the sacramental system. They believe that God calls them into a relationship from the moment of baptism. This relationship is nourished and intensified by the reception of the other Sacraments. The initial Sacrament that allows access to the other Sacraments is baptism, because it incorporates Roman Catholics into the graced life of God and into the family of the Church community.

Community—the community of the family and the larger community of the Church—is especially stressed by the Church. In the view of Catholics,

the life of infants is made sacred and imbued with the dignity of children of God. Respect for life is essential for those who are so loved by God that the life of Christ is communicated to them. The ritual of baptism stresses the responsibility of parents to educate their children in the beliefs and practices of the Church. Siblings are encouraged to attend the baptism of infant brothers and sisters and welcome the newly baptized children into the family. Because infants who have not reached the age of reason cannot make an intelligent commitment to the faith, another Sacrament is received later in life. When children reach the age of reason, or more likely at puberty, they ratify the baptismal commitment by receiving confirmation. For those baptized as infants, confirmation provides

Roman Catholicism is especially prevalent among Italian Americans, Irish Americans, and Latinos. (Hazel Hankin)

them with the opportunity to ratify freely and deliberately the commitment that was made for them at baptism.

Permanence of Marriage. The marriage between men and women is sacramentalized according to the Catholic view, because it reflects the covenanted relationship between God and the people of Israel. According to the New Testament, Jesus insisted that this covenanted relationship between a man and woman consists of a oneness that is to be permanent. When the Pharisees asked him about divorce, Jesus answered, "Have you not read that the Creator from the beginning made them male and female, and he said, 'This is why a man leaves his mother and father and becomes at-

tached to his wife, and the two become one flesh'?" (Matt. 19:5) He speaks strongly against divorce and says that a man who marries a divorced woman commits adultery. This statement by Jesus has led many people to believe that Catholics prohibit divorce. Actually the words of Jesus refer to remarriage after divorce. "Now I say to you; anyone who divorces his wife and marries another is guilty of adultery." (Matt. 19:9)

Roman Catholics recognize that there are many legitimate reasons for married couples to divorce, such as abuse of children or spouses, monetary conflicts, or incompatibility. Divorce in the eyes of Catholics does not destroy a marriage; divorced couples live apart, but the Sacrament of matrimony they received at their marriage ceremony still stands. Marriages are not terminated until one member of a couple attempts to remarry while the other is still alive. Such persons are considered adulterers.

If a person's first marriage is declared null and void by Church authorities, either partner can attempt a valid second marriage. The annulment does not cause any embarrassment to the children of the first marriage, because it states that the sacred covenant agreed upon at the Sacrament of matrimony had an impediment that made it impossible for a valid Sacramental marriage. Church annulments do not call children "illegitimate." Examples of such impediments include consensual defects that affect any contract negotiation. If persons are underage, they cannot make a valid contract and cannot enter into the Sacrament of mar-

riage. Concealment of past pertinent information, such as previous commitment to a mental hospital or a prison record, the inability to have children, a drug background, or any other forms of deception hamper one's ability to make an intelligent commitment to marriage. Since both partners to a marriage must consent fully to marrying, priests converse with them separately before the wedding to ask if either party has been coerced into marrying because of such factors as unwanted pregnancies or pressure from parents.

If persons who first marry in a Roman Catholic Church wish to have a second Catholic wedding, they must secure a Church annulment along with a civil divorce decree. If Catholics wish to marry persons who have already had Catholic weddings, an annulment must be secured if they wish to have another Catholic wedding. If they marry persons

The Roman Catholic Church operates the largest private school system in North America. (James L. Shaffer)

before a justice of the peace or in non-Roman Catholic ceremonies, an annulment is not necessary. Although such persons are not considered practicing Catholics and are not able to receive the Sacraments, they are encouraged to attend Mass and other rituals, because they are still members of the Church. They must obtain a Church annulment along with civil divorce decrees. If the persons they desire to marry have been previously married and the latter's partners are alive, they must secure an annulment from the Roman Catholic Church in order to have subsequent Church weddings.

The Church's emphasis on the permanence of marriage and its discouragement of remarriage is rooted in Paul's letter to the Ephesians, in which marriage is portrayed as a symbol of Christ's union with his church. The union of man and woman in marriage is actually based on the union of Christ with the Church. When husbands love their wives as their own flesh, they act as Christ does with the Church. Marriage is a Sacrament signifying on Earth the future unity of God's people in heaven.

The Purpose of Marriage. The second Vatican Council, held in the early 1960's, changed the distinction made between the primary and secondary purposes of marriage. Previously, the Church had taught that the primary goal of marriage was the begetting of children and the secondary end the mutual love of husband and wife. The bishops of the council said that while not making the other ends of marriage of less value, the true practice of conjugal love and the whole nature of family life resulting from it tend to dispose spouses to cooperate courageously and, through the love of God and Jesus Christ, enrich their families.

This new theology of marriage is best shown in the revised ritual for the Sacrament of matrimony. The covenantal nature of the marriage bond is compared to the union of Christ with his church. The essential element of mutual affection in body and mind is stressed and the importance of procreation and the education of children is mentioned. The celebrant speaks of the necessity for the virtue of faith for the Sacrament and the significance of the Eucharistic setting for marriage. Brides and grooms are allowed some freedom in the expression of their vows, but they must always include the dimension of permanence using the words "all the days of my life."

Reproduction and Sexuality. Because one of the purposes of marriage is the procreation of children, Catholics had been encouraged to have large families. In agrarian societies, children help with the farm work, but in consumer societies, large families can be financial and emotional burdens on parents. The 1965 Vatican Council introduced the concept of responsible parenthood, in which married couples, when planning their families, "should thoughtfully take into account both their own welfare and that of their children, those already born and those which may be foreseen." The council fathers encouraged spouses to practice conjugal chastity, whereby couples were counseled to avoid artificial means of birth control in regulating births. Natural family planning, sometimes referred to as the rhythm method, was recommended.

The Vatican documents on sexual ethics stressed the basic teaching regarding genital sexual activity, which finds its true meaning in marriage. Sexual union is only legitimate if a definitive community of life such as marriage has been established between men and women. The problem associated with premarital sexual activity is that in the demand for responsible parenthood the act must be contraceptive. Since intercourse during premarital sex occurs outside a Sacramental love union, it is not a love relationship publicly proclaimed nor does it reflect God's love for God's people. Premarital sexual acts violate the act of mutual self-giving, by means of which two people express their willingness to assume permanently unconditional responsibility for each other.

The second Vatican Council condemned abortion by stating that "infanticide and abortion are abominable crimes." This declaration was based on the premise that the right to life is the primordial right of humans. Thus, every human life must be respected from the moment the process of generation begins—that is, when the egg is fertilized. The fertilized egg is looked upon as a potential human being, because a new genetic package develops with its characteristic traits already fixed. The council based its arguments on the premise that "he who will become a human being is already a human being." Although the Church acknowledges the impossibility of deciding the moment at which life begins, it acts as if human life were present from the moment of fertiliza-

The Catholic Church's rigid opposition to all forms of birth control has provoked a powerful dissident movement among devout Catholics who advocate birth control and a woman's right to choose abortion. (Betty Lane)

tion. This reasoning is based on the doubt of fact: Since it is uncertain when life begins, the safe course is to regard human life as starting at fertilization.

Family and Society. Catholics believe that the family, which exists at the heart of society, is the most basic community of human membership. Pope John Paul II said that the future of humanity passes by way of the family. The early Church referred to the family as the house or domestic church where the presence of God was experienced in a loving community. Family relationships require fidelity, which involves hurt and forgiveness, sacrifice and failure, joy and happiness. Parents who stand by their children even when they seem to reject their families' values, grandparents who help to raise their grandchildren when the parents are unable to do so, single parents who go to great lengths to raise and nurture their children without the benefit of their partners, children who care for ill and elderly parents are all examples of faithful lives that require Church support.

The Church addresses the need for the extended family. It is impossible to raise children effectively solely in the nuclear family. All families, even those with two parents, need a wider circle of uncles and aunts, grandparents, and godparents. Elders enrich the lives of families. Pope John Paul II said that they should be cherished, not merely tolerated, for they are a witness to the past and a source of wisdom for the young and for the future.

When both parents work outside the home, flexible roles for children and parents are necessary. This can appear difficult if families do not value the model that household duties must be shared. However, each generation is challenged to leave the world a more beautiful and beneficial place than the one it inherited. Older family members are encouraged to pass on their wisdom and faith in the Church, providing countercultural messages about poverty, consumerism, sexuality, and racial justice.

Roman Catholic bishops have said that the Catholic community is called upon to become a persistent, informed, and committed voice for children and families, urging all American institutions "to put our children first." They have stated that as a community we are called upon to draw attention to the hostility and danger present in our society, which attacks family values and negatively affects our children. The Church should assist in developing policies and programs that help families protect children's lives and overcome the moral, social, and economic forces that threaten their future. The bishops continued to emphasize the dignity of children, who should be treated with respect in the family and given responsibilities for each family member's welfare.

Families are encouraged to share in the mission of the Church by caring for the poor, infirm, and elderly. They can give time, energy, or money to help care for the less fortunate. Christian life includes obligations beyond the family circle; children learn the joy of contributing to the common good in the home, neighborhood, church, and society.

Pope John Paul II stated that there are some people who live in extreme poverty, in which promiscuity, lack of housing, unstable relationships, and extreme lack of education make it impossible for them to speak of a true family. There are others who, for various reasons, have been left alone in the world. "For these people, the doors of the great family which is the church—concretely the parish and the diocese—must be opened even wider." The Roman Catholic Church endeavors to care for families and try to build the community of faith.

—*Marianne Ferguson*

BIBLIOGRAPHY

Ferguson, Marianne. "Catholic Attitudes Toward Sexuality." In *Human Sexuality: An Encyclopedia*, edited by Verne L. Bullough and Bonnie Bullough. New York: Garland, 1994. Discusses the views and attitudes of the Roman Catholic Church toward various aspects of human sexual practice.

John Paul II. *The Apostolic Exhortation on the Family: Familiaris Consortio.* Hales Corner, Wis.: Priests of the Sacred Heart, 1981. Apostolic exhortation on the nature and tasks of the Christian family and the scope of pastoral care needed by families.

McBrien, Richard. *Catholicism.* San Francisco, Calif.: Harper, 1994. Recent update on most of the basic Roman Catholic teachings.

U.S. Catholic Conference. *Putting Children and Families First: A Challenge for Our Church, Nation, and World.* Washington, D.C.: U.S. Catholic Conference, 1991. Pastoral statement examining the social conditions of children and the moral and religious dimension caring for them.

Vatican Council II. *Pastoral Constitution on the Church in the Modern World.* Washington, D.C.: U.S. Catholic Conference, 1965. Teaching on the dignity of marriage, the role of the family, and the duty of society and the Church to support families.

See also Abortion; Annulment; Baptismal rites; Birth control; Cultural influences; Divorce; Godparents; Interfaith marriages; Latinos; Marriage; Parenting; Religion; Remarriage.

Salk, Jonas

BORN: October 28, 1914, New York, N.Y.
DIED: June 23, 1995, La Jolla, Calif.
AREA OF ACHIEVEMENT: Health and medicine
SIGNIFICANCE: An American research scientist in preventive medicine, Salk developed the first effective vaccine against poliomyelitis (polio or infantile paralysis)

After graduating from the New York University School of Medicine in 1939, Salk went to the University of Michigan, at which he became an assistant professor of epidemiology and worked on the

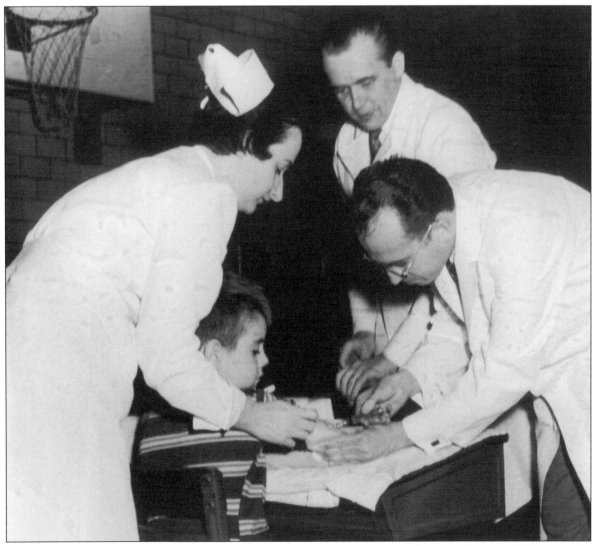

Jonas Salk administering a polio vaccine injection into a Pittsburgh, Pennsylvania, schoolboy in 1954 in the first large-scale test of the serum he discovered. (AP/Wide World Photos)

development of influenza vaccines. In 1947 he became head of the Virus Research Laboratory at the University of Pittsburgh, at which he taught microbiology and preventive medicine for seventeen years and at which he began his research on a vaccine for polio in 1949.

In the 1940's and 1950's polio had become one of the most feared diseases in the world, often occurring in epidemics, especially during summer months in temperate zones. Polio is an acute communicable disease caused by viruses that attack and produce inflammation of the gray matter of the brain and spinal cord, often leaving victims with paralysis. Since the majority of polio cases occurred in children between the ages of four and sixteen years old and paralytic cases were found most often in preschool-age children, the protection of children from this devastating, long-lasting disease had become a high medical priority by the 1950's. In 1952 Salk and his associates had developed an inactivated virus vaccine that provided immunity against polio. In 1953 he announced the development of a trial vaccine, and some of the first people to receive it were Salk, his wife, and their three sons.

Sponsored by the National Foundation for Infantile Paralysis (the March of Dimes Foundation), massive field tests were successfully conducted in 1953 and 1954. The vaccine came into wide use in 1955. Unfortunately, due to the rush of activity caused by the public excitement over the possibility of finally controlling the dreaded disease, some poorly prepared vaccine samples led to some fatalities. However, Salk's vaccine was used thereafter with great success. In fact, with a policy of infant immunization, polio has been virtually eradicated from the United States and other developed countries. It still remains a major public health problem, however, in much of Africa, Asia, and Southern Europe.

After the Salk polio vaccine was pronounced safe and effective in April, 1955, Salk received many honors, including a citation from President Dwight D. Eisenhower and a Congressional gold medal for his significant achievements in medicine. However, Salk refused to accept any cash awards for his work and continued his research to improve the vaccine. In 1960 an effective oral polio vaccine was introduced by Albert Bruce Sabin. In 1963 the Salk Institute of Biological Studies was established in La Jolla, California, and Salk served as director of the institute for eighteen years. Salk withdrew from biological research in 1985, but he later returned to spend some time working on the development of a vaccine against acquired immunodeficiency syndrome (AIDS). —*Alvin K. Benson*

See also Acquired immunodeficiency syndrome (AIDS); Health of children; Health problems.

Sandwich generation

RELEVANT ISSUES: Aging; Parenting and family relationships
SIGNIFICANCE: As longevity has increased in late twentieth century North America, adults have been increasingly obliged to care for two generations, their parents and children, contributing to the growth of the sandwich generation

In late twentieth century North America people are living longer and having fewer children. This has changed the age composition of the North American population. The "graying" of the population is a major factor contributing to the growing number of sandwich generation families. The expanding proportion of older persons is bringing with it dramatic changes in family structure. People are giving more thought to the nature and extent of services necessary to support older persons and to their views on the respective roles of family and society in providing for these needs.

Caring for Two Generations. As persons live longer, the aged have a greater need for assistance from their families. The term "sandwich generation" refers to adults who provide financial or task assistance to their parents while also caring for their own dependent children. Adults may assist their parents by providing them with emotional support, financial assistance, transportation, shopping and cleaning, meal preparation, and personal hygiene. At the same time, they may assist their children financially and emotionally and even care for grandchildren. Thus, members of the sandwich generation serve as a support system for both their aging parents and their dependent children. They are, in essence, "sandwiched" between the needs of two generations, balancing the needs of their children, the needs of their parents, and their own needs, obligations, and ambitions in the home and workplace.

Members of the so-called sandwich generation find themselves having to care for both their parents and their own children. (Dick Hemingway)

With longer life spans and later child bearing, more middle-aged persons find themselves sandwiched between providing child and elder care. Estimates of the percentage of sandwiched persons vary widely. Corporate studies suggest that as many as 40 percent of the population belong to this category, while other studies suggest that the figure is only 6 percent. In 1986 the huge corporation IBM reported that 6.3 percent of its employees were responsible for both their children and parents. By 1991 this figure had risen to 11 percent. Regardless of the actual percentage, experts agree that in the twenty-first century there will be greater numbers of sandwiched persons.

Financial Responsibilities of Sandwiched Families. The financial choices facing sandwiched families are difficult. Even if parents are healthy, sandwiched persons still have to juggle between parents' eventual needs and their responsibilities to their children. Compromises are inevitable. The parents of sandwiched persons require much more financial support than the children of sandwiched persons. Sandwiched families that do not have the financial resources to help parents may bring their parents into their communities or households or offer them nonmonetary assistance.

Because there is no national health care program in the United States as there is in Canada, the U.S. government is quick to stress the financial responsibility of families for the health care and other needs of aged family members. In thirty states, Supplemental Security Income (SSI), which assists low income older persons, requires of children who are financially capable that they help support their parents. However, this law is rarely enforced. As a result of the proposed health care reforms that were under debate in the U.S. Congress in the 1990's, families may be asked or even required to shoulder ever-increasing responsibility for elderly family members. Limiting persons' access to nursing home care and reducing support services may become policy. Proposed reforms may include increased community-based supportive services and mandated assistance from families. Regardless of the outcome, the growing message has been that families must bear responsibility for aged parents and children. In the United States, this may result in nursing homes for the very rich or the totally destitute, leaving most elderly people in the care of their families.

Helping Children. One trend contributing to the financial burden on the sandwich generation is the prolonged financial dependence of children. In 1990, 23 percent of the U.S. population between the ages of twenty-five and thirty-four lived with their parents—an increase of 45 percent since 1970. A combination of attitudes, economics, and demographics underlies this phenomenon. Adult children have begun to marry and establish their careers later in life. In a 1990 *Newsweek* special issue on "Families in the Twenty-First Century," one article stated that American youth, in a sharp reversal of historical trends, were

taking longer to mature. Although more young people were enrolled in college than previously, fewer graduated and many took longer to get their degrees.

Some researchers have blamed the economy for the prolonged dependency of young adults on their parents. In the 1990's the younger half of the baby-boom generation—that is, adults in their mid-twenties to mid-thirties—seemed to have taken the brunt of economic downturns. Many young adults have joined the labor force at a time of stagnant wage growth and have been trapped in a rental market that has seen apartment rents increase at double the inflation rate since 1970. Higher rents have meant that the adults in this age group have been less able than older age cohorts to save for down payments on homes. Unable or unwilling to establish their own households, many young adults have lived longer with their parents. The phenomenon of adult children leaving home and returning several times for brief periods because of economic difficulties or changes in marital status has been called the "boomerang effect." As a result, typical young adults of the 1990's lived with their parents for a total of twenty-four to twenty-six years.

Helping Parents. It is believed that one out of six parents or spouses age sixty-five or older will require some form of assistance—either from their children or other sources. Daughters and daughters-in-law provide care more often than sons. In the United States the average sandwiched caregiver in the late 1990's was a woman in her forties with a family income of less than $40,000. Parents most frequently required assistance with shopping, transportation, and household chores, such as meal preparation, housecleaning, and laundry. More daughters (69 percent) than sons (59 percent) assisted their parents with personal functions such as eating, toileting, and dressing. Often daughters have helped their parents to use the telephone, make visits, and to perform household tasks.

Overall, caregiving daughters have spent an average of 4.0 hours per day and sons 3.5 hours per day on caregiving tasks. Yet, sons have been more likely than daughters to help parents financially in writing checks, paying bills, and assisting in the preparation of income tax returns. Sons have also helped more often than daughters with home

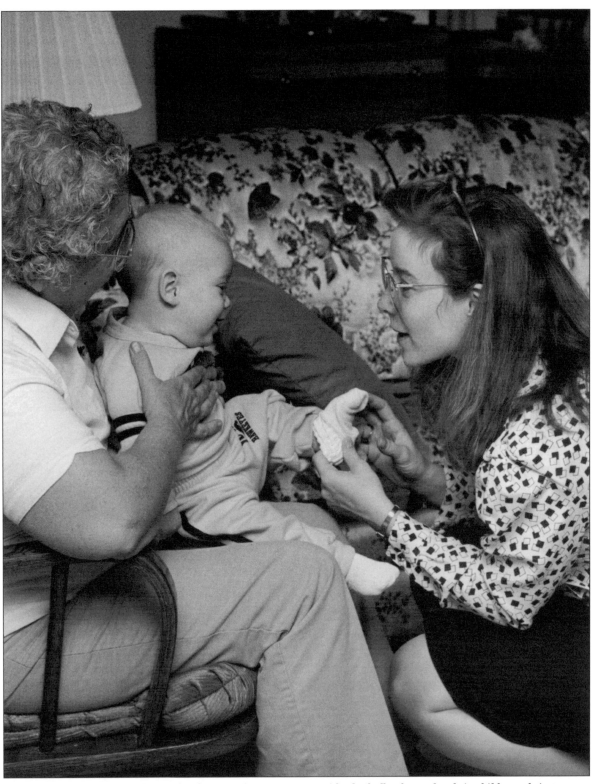

Among couples caught in the sandwich generation, women provide the bulk of care for their children, their parents, and their in-laws. (James L. Shaffer)

maintenance. As aging persons have fewer adult children and perhaps no daughters, sons may be required to provide help with a wider variety of tasks than has previously been the case.

One-third of all women above the age of eighteen will care for both children and parents during their lifetimes. Many will spend more years helping a parent than in raising their own children. Half of caregivers provide care for two to five years, but only 6 percent provide it for more than five years. Women's roles as caregivers remain entrenched in the expectations of society and individual families. Caregiving tasks are often viewed as the responsibility of females. Women are the most likely to have little intergenerational support during their middle years. This phenomenon is called the "generational squeeze," because women in the middle generation give significantly more support than they receive.

Effects on Work. The 1982 Informal Caregivers Survey revealed that 44 percent of caregiving daughters and 55 percent of caregiving sons were in the workforce. Within these two groups, about 25 percent of working daughters and sons reported conflicts between work and caregiving responsibilities. For many, the conflict forced them to cut back on work hours, change their work schedules, or take time off from work without pay. The strains on women have shown up at the workplace: Of caregivers to the elderly, most of whom are women, some 14 percent have switched from full-time to part-time jobs, another 28 percent have considered quitting their jobs, and 12 percent have left the workforce because of caregiving responsibilities.

Looking to the Future. Longer life spans will continue to put more middle-aged and older family members in the position of providing care to elderly relatives. The chances are increasing that a retired person will also have a living parent who needs care. As a result, care for the disabled elderly may increasingly fall on those who are old themselves.

What the future holds in store for sandwiched persons is an open question. Intergenerational support and cooperation will be more critical. Older persons may help younger relatives with child care when they are able, and as they age, the persons whom they help may provide reciprocal care for them. Parents will probably rely more on friends and volunteers because fewer family members will be able to provide assistance. Communities may need to provide more services to support the independence of older persons when families cannot provide support. With families, friends, and communities working together to balance their needs, older persons will be able to live with dignity and their younger relatives will be able to meet the demands of their own busy lives.

—*Virginia W. Junk*

BIBLIOGRAPHY

Durity, A. "The Sandwich Generation Feels the Squeeze." *Management Review* 80 (1991).

Junk, Virginia, Laurie A. Stenberg, and Carol A. Anderson. "Retirement Planning for the Sandwich Generation." *Journal of Home Economics* 85 (Summer, 1993).

Schurenberg, Eric. "The Crunch of Caring for Both Parents and Kids." *Money* 18 (March, 1989).

VanCaspel, V. *Money Dynamics for the 1990's.* New York: Simon & Schuster, 1988.

Woodward, Kenneth L. "Young Beyond Their Years." *Newsweek Special Issue: Families in the Twenty-First Century* 114 (Winter-Spring, 1990).

See also Aging and elderly care; Baby-boom generation; Baby boomers; Family caregiving; Family life cycle; Family life education; Life expectancy; Work.

Sanger, Margaret

BORN: September 14, 1879, Corning, N.Y.
DIED: September 6, 1966, Tucson, Ariz.
AREA OF ACHIEVEMENT: Health and medicine
SIGNIFICANCE: Margaret Sanger worked to provide American women with safe, effective birth control devices and family-planning information

As a young woman, Margaret Sanger trained as a nurse at White Plains Hospital. She frequently assisted physicians who delivered infants in the poverty stricken tenements of New York City and was often asked by new mothers how to prevent future pregnancies. Unless women's health was in danger, it was against the law to provide such information. Sanger became convinced that frequent pregnancies not only endangered the lives of mothers and their children but also contributed to their poor living conditions. She believed that women had the right to control the rate at which they conceive children, devoting her life to making "every child a wanted child."

Margaret Sanger educated herself on the various types of birth control methods then available, including condoms, diaphragms, and the rhythm method. In 1912 she wrote a series of articles on birth control for the New York socialist newspaper the *Call* entitled "What Every Girl Should Know." The articles, which instructed women on various devices and their usage, were quickly banned by postal authorities. Sanger began her own newspaper, *Woman Rebel*, in 1914 and wrote a birth control handbook called *Family Limitations*. Within a few

months she was arrested for violation of the Comstock Law. Passed in 1873, the Comstock Law prohibited the mailing or dissemination of information on birth control. Such information was defined as "obscene," "lewd," and "lascivious." The case against Sanger was later dismissed.

In 1916 Sanger opened the Brownsville Clinic, the first American birth control clinic, in Brooklyn, New York. That same year she began publication of *Birth Control Review*. In October, the Brownsville Clinic was raided by police. Sanger was arrested and served thirty days in the workhouse, but she continued to work for repeal of the Comstock Law upon her release.

Sanger wrote *Woman and the New Race* (1920), in which she charged that poverty, crime, war, and famine were the result of overpopulation and that the repeal of the Comstock Law would reduce the effects of these scourges. The book sold more than 200,000 copies. She founded the American Birth Control League and served as its president from 1921 to 1928. As a result of Sanger's work, the birth control movement continued to grow, and additional birth control clinics were opened across the country. State clinics began operation in 1937.

By World War II there were 539 birth control centers across the country. Sanger traveled the world on speaking engagements to promote the greater acceptability of family planning. She later authored *The Pivot of Civilization* (1922), *Happiness in Marriage* (1926), *Motherhood in Bondage* (1928), and two autobiographies, *My Fight for Birth Control* (1931) and *Margaret Sanger: An Autobiography* (1938). Sanger continued writing and speaking out about family planning until her death in 1966.

—*Leslie Stricker*

See also Birth control; Eugenics; Planned Parenthood Federation of America (PPFA); Sex education; Wattleton, Faye.

Margaret Sanger in 1952. (AP/Wide World Photos)

Schools

RELEVANT ISSUES: Education; Parenting and family relationships

SIGNIFICANCE: Although many child-rearing and educational tasks have shifted from families to schools, the educational experiences of students continue to depend heavily on family background, parental involvement in schools, parenting styles, and the decisions and sacrifices of parents

Until the late nineteenth and early twentieth centuries, the home was the center of most economic and educational activities. With industrialization, however, economic activities moved steadily from family farms and shops to offices and factories. Moreover, women in both Canada and the United States entered the paid labor force in increasing numbers throughout the twentieth century, so that by 1995 three-quarters of American women with children worked outside the home. Under these circumstances, much of the task of education moved from families to formal institutions.

The growth of public schooling accompanied the movement of work away from the home. Horace Mann, who is known as "the father of American public education," argued in the mid-nineteenth century that education was the responsibility of the community and the state, not simply a family obligation. By 1900 public schooling for children through the high school years had become nearly universal in America.

The shifting of education from families to schools has lessened the direct involvement of families in education, and schools have come to play an increasing role in child care. Nevertheless, families do continue to have a great deal of influence on schooling by affecting the quality of education available to their children, by shaping their children's capacities for learning and attitudes toward learning, and by choosing schools and making educational plans for their children.

Family Socioeconomic Status and Schooling. Family socioeconomic status consists of the income level a family enjoys, the amount of prestige generally accorded to the occupations of the parents, and parents' educational levels. Researchers have consistently found that students from higher socioeconomic backgrounds tend to perform bet-ter in school, to have greater educational aspirations, and to complete more years of schooling than students from lower socioeconomic backgrounds. In 1991 U.S. students from families with yearly incomes of $10,000 to $20,000 had an average score of 379 on the verbal part of the Scholastic Aptitude Test (SAT), a nationwide test of school achievement. By contrast, those with yearly family incomes of $50,000 to $60,000 had an average score of 440. Those with family incomes above $70,000 had an average score well over 500.

Socioeconomic differences in families' plans for their children's future education become evident as early as the ninth grade. The more affluent and better educated parents are, the more likely their children are to plan on finishing high school, attending college, and completing graduate or professional training beyond college. These plans are related, in turn, to actual years of school completed. According to an article in the August 15, 1994, issue of *Business Week* magazine, about three-fourths of those born into families in the highest income quarter of American families obtained at least bachelor's degrees. Among those from families in the lowest income quarter, only about 1 in 20 graduated from college.

Social scientists have most often offered two general types of explanations for the relationship between family socioeconomic status and success in schooling: economic explanations and cultural explanations. Economic explanations are perhaps among the most obvious. Wealthier families can afford to send their children to better schools and they can give children greater financial support through more years of schooling. Even when children attend public schools, public schools in wealthier neighborhoods generally have greater funding than those in poorer neighborhoods.

Cultural explanations of socioeconomic differences in educational success concentrate on variations in child-rearing practices, attitudes, and expectations. Middle-class parents are more likely than low-income parents to read to small children and to have educational materials in their homes. Since relatively well-to-do, well-educated parents have more experience with educational systems than do poorer parents, the more advantaged parents are often better able to prepare their children for school. Furthermore, mothers and fathers in professional jobs owe their livelihoods to their

The more affluent and educated parents are, the more likely their children will be to finish high school and attend college. (Ben Klaffke)

own educational qualifications, and they therefore tend to emphasize the importance of education to their children. Since parents generally expect their children to achieve levels of education at least equal to their own, middle-class and wealthy parents tend to hold high expectations regarding their children's educational achievement, and they make these expectations known.

Education and Family Composition. Family composition refers to family size and family structure. In general, children from larger families show weaker school performance and complete fewer years of school than children from smaller families. This may be partly due to socioeconomic influences: Poorer people tend to have more children than wealthier people. However, even when one takes the major background characteristics of parents into consideration, children in small families are more likely than children in large families to complete high school and college. The reasons for this are not clear, but one possible explanation is that the fewer the children in a family, the more time and child-rearing effort parents can devote to each child.

The influence of family structure on schooling became a matter of great concern over the course of the late twentieth century, as one-parent families became increasingly common. In 1960, according to U.S. Census data, only 9 percent of U.S. families were headed by single parents. By 1990 the percentage of single-parent families had tripled, reaching 27 percent. The overwhelming majority of these one-parent families were headed by mothers. During the 1980's researchers began to look at the effects of mother-only families on the schooling of children. Those investigating these issues consistently found that children from mother-only families achieve lower levels of education and are more likely to drop out of school than children from dual-parent families. These effects are greater for boys than for girls. Furthermore, children from one-parent families are more likely to be discipline problems in school than children from dual-parent families, and girls from single-parent families are more likely to become teen mothers than girls from dual-parent families. Each of these factors can affect schooling.

The consequences for schooling of living in single-parent families appear, to some extent, to be the result of poverty. Families headed by single women in North America have a poverty rate six times that of other families. However, most researchers have found that children from single-parent families show weaker educational performance than other children even after income is taken into consideration. One of the most likely explanations for this finding is that the demands of being a parent are too much for one person alone. Some educators have also maintained that children with only one parent are deprived of an important role model, typically the father.

Parental Involvement. Even though parents are not as directly involved in the education of their children as they were when most education took place at home, parents continue to exercise a strong influence on schooling. The more that parents are involved in the schooling of their children, through providing volunteer services, being active in fund-raising activities, talking to teachers, or simply keeping track of their children's studies, the better their children perform and adjust. Since both parents and schools now play major roles in rearing children, children fare best when these two elements work together in close communication. In order to overcome the educational disadvantages associated with relatively low family socioeconomic status, it is particularly important that lower-income parents be involved with schools.

Head Start, a U.S. government preschool program for low-income children, emphasizes the involvement of parents. Many Head Start schools place parents on advisory committees and policy boards to give them a place in decision making. The program stresses that parents should serve as volunteers. In public schools, Parent-Teacher Organizations (PTOs) or Parent and Teacher Associations (PTAs) are focal points for the school activities of parents. Some of the national organizations that promote parental involvement in schools are the National Parent and Teacher Association, the Home and School Institute, Parents as Teachers National Center, and the National Coalition for Parent Involvement in Education. A full list of these and other parent involvement organizations, with addresses, may be found in *Innovations in Parent and Family Involvement* (1993) by J. William Rioux and Nancy Berla.

Styles of Parenting. According to Laurence Steinberg, a professor of psychology interested in education, the three dimensions of parenting that most affect children's learning are acceptance, firmness, and autonomy. Acceptance refers to how much parents express love and support for their children. Firmness refers to the limits and rules that parents place on the behavior of children. Autonomy refers to how much parents allow and encourage children to express individuality.

Combinations of these three dimensions create parenting styles. Parents who emphasize firmness excessively are "authoritarian" and can hinder the educational development of children by stifling independent thought or by provoking the children to rebel. Parents who place too much emphasis on acceptance of their children are labeled "permissive" or "indulgent." This results in children receiving too little direction in schoolwork. Psychologists believe that "authoritative" parents, those who are firm with their children while providing them with emotional support and opportunities for self-expression, make the greatest contributions to their children's educations. Steinberg identifies a fourth style of parenting, "disengagement," which is practiced by about one-quarter of the parents he studied. Disengagement refers to a lack of interest or involvement in children. Steinberg maintains that students with disengaged parents are the most likely to perform poorly in school and to drop out of high school.

Parental Decisions About Schools. Parents make two kinds of decisions about where their children will attend school. First, they decide what type of school their children will attend: a public school, a private school, or a parochial (Roman Catholic) or other religious school. Second, even when children attend public schools, parents can decide where their children will attend school by choosing to live in some school districts rather than in others.

Family income, tradition, religion, and the social environment of nearby public schools are major factors affecting parents' decisions about where to send their children to school. Parents with high incomes can afford to make a wide variety of choices about their children's schooling, and they can send their children to expensive private schools. Parents who have attended private or religiously oriented schools are much more likely than other parents to send their children to such schools. Those with strong religious beliefs often want to send their children to schools that will emphasize religious teachings.

Religion is sometimes connected to political views that affect family choices about schools. Parents may see public schools as actually irreligious and as undermining values that the parents hold dear. As schools have taken up child-rearing activities that used to be reserved for parents alone, such as teaching children about sex, many mothers and fathers have felt that educators are attempting to take control of children away from families. In response, some deeply religious parents have established their own Christian schools, or schools of other faiths, and some have turned to home schooling to ensure that their children learn a desired set of values and beliefs.

Perhaps the most critical influence on the decisions of parents is the social environment of local public schools. The greater the number of low-income students in a school district and the greater the problems with discipline, violence, or drugs, the more likely parents are to sacrifice income to send children to a private, religious, or other type of school. The social environment in schools in different districts also appears to influence families' decisions about where to live.

Parents whose children are to attend public schools obtain information about the schools in the areas to which they plan to move. Those who are able to choose their neighborhoods will avoid neighborhoods where their children would attend school with large numbers of low-income students. Some parents may also move if they feel uncomfortable with the changing racial make-up of the schools. Some educators and social scientists have argued that the practice of busing, of bringing children to schools away from their own neighborhoods to achieve racial integration, has contributed to "white flight," the movement of white, middle-class families away from cities to suburbs where busing is less common.

One of the most difficult decisions regarding schooling is the decision about whether and where young people will attend college. The importance of a college degree has grown. In the 1960's the average college graduate earned about 18 percent more than the average high-school graduate. By the 1990's the average college graduate earned 43 percent more. At the same time, however, college educations became much more

*Among families able to choose where to send their children to school, considerations about schools'
social environments tend to take precedence.* (Ben Klaffke)

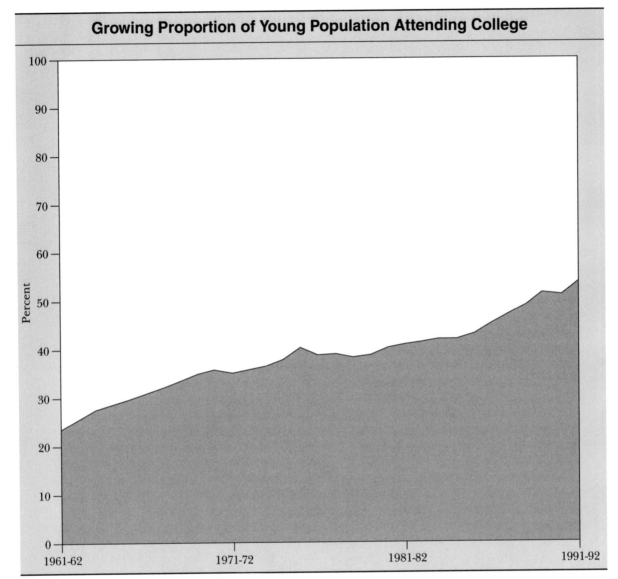

Growing Proportion of Young Population Attending College

Source: *Christian Science Monitor* (Aug. 8, 1997)

expensive: From 1980 to 1996 costs at public universities grew by 256 percent and costs at private universities by 219 percent. These growing costs and benefits posed an additional problem: While children received the increased benefits of college degrees, most of the costs were paid by their parents.

Many middle-class parents have attempted to deal with these rising costs through long-term planning and sacrifice, skimping on their own entertainment and luxuries throughout their children's lifetime to save money. Others have taken out additional mortgages on their homes or depleted retirement savings to pay for college, steps that economists generally say are unwise, since they endanger parents' own futures. The 1990's also saw a decline in enrollment at costly private liberal arts colleges, as parents turned increasingly to lower-cost public universities.

—Carl L. Bankston III

BIBLIOGRAPHY

Berger, Eugenia Hepworth. *Parents as Partners in Education: The School and Home Working Together.*

New York: Maxwell Macmillan, 1991. Intended as a textbook, this considers the interaction between parents and schools from historical, psychological, sociological, and other perspectives.

Coleman, James S. *Equality and Achievement in Education.* Boulder, Colo.: Westview Press, 1990. Collection of essays dealing with inequalities among students and with academic achievement, several of which focus on the role of family background and on family decision making about schooling.

_____. *Parental Involvement in Education.* Washington, D.C.: U.S. Department of Education, 1991. Discusses the importance of parental in-

volvement in education and describes possible programs and policies for improving parental involvement.

Lareau, Annette. *Home Advantage: Social Class and Parental Intervention in Elementary Education.* Philadelphia: Falmer Press, 1989. Presents interviews with parents to examine how middle-class parents prepare children for school more effectively than do working-class parents.

Rioux, J. William, and Nancy Berla. *Innovations in Parent and Family Involvement.* Princeton, N.J.: Eye on Education, 1993. Provides a wide range of information about programs that promote parental involvement in education, and offers a

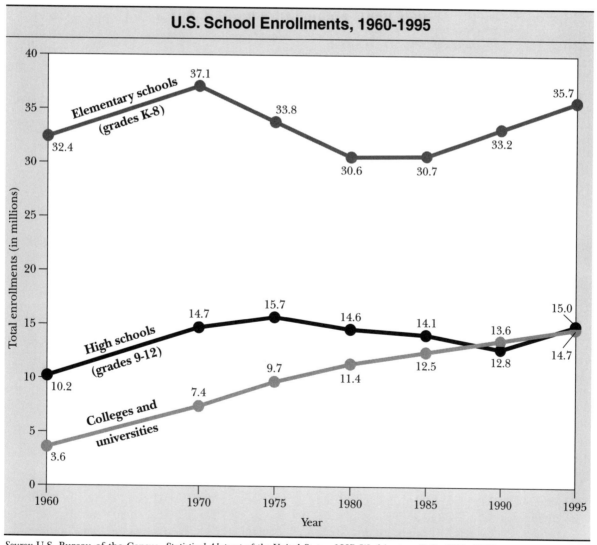

U.S. School Enrollments, 1960-1995

Source: U.S. Bureau of the Census, *Statistical Abstract of the United States: 1997.* Washington, D.C.: GPO, 1997.

summary of research on parental involvement in schools.

Steinberg, Laurence D. *Beyond the Classroom: Why School Reform Has Failed and What Parents Need to Do*. New York: Simon & Schuster, 1996. Provides evidence that the attitudes of students toward education shape their school performance and sees family life as a major influence on these attitudes.

See also Children's rights; Educating children; Home schooling; Parenting; Private schools; Public education.

Second shift

RELEVANT ISSUES: Economics and work; Parenting and family relationships; Sociology

SIGNIFICANCE: The increase in dual-earner families has challenged individuals to create a balance between the needs of families and the demands of work, changing the way families provide for their basic needs

In *The Second Shift: Working Parents and the Revolution at Home* (1989), Arlie Russell Hochschild and Anne Machung explored what parents thought about how they managed their time and energy each day before and after paid employment. The longitudinal study focused on the activities of fifty couples, each with at least one child under the age of six. Hochschild and Machung discovered that women worked approximately fifteen hours longer than men each week caring for families and households.

Stalled Revolution. Hochschild concedes that women have always worked. What was new in the 1970's and 1980's was the numbers of women who became wage earners, spawning child care for pay, the massive spread of the second shift, and the struggle within marriages to equalize the load at home. In the nineteenth century men's power base shifted from the land to wages and the accumulation of money. In the late twentieth century, when women increasingly worked for wages outside the home, there was no one left behind the scenes to maintain the household infrastructure. Simultaneously, the workplace remained inflexible, inadequately accommodating family demands on workers. Hochschild called the strain between the change in women's roles and the

absence of change in business, government, and men's roles in the home the "stalled revolution."

The 1950's Standard. In the late twentieth century role expectations for women swung from one extreme to another, making the stalled revolution particularly stressful. During the nineteenth and early twentieth centuries educational opportunities for women had increased, the age of first marriages gradually rose, and fertility rates decreased. Following World War II many of these trends reversed as a result of a unique and temporary conjuncture of economic, social, and political factors. First, during the war families' savings were three times higher than before or after. Following the war government expanded services, such as educational benefits, housing loans, and highway and sewer construction, while the private sector created housing in the suburbs. All of this combined with the American economic competitive advantage to fuel a tremendous expansion of the middle-class and a lifestyle that many households could support with one paycheck. As a result, the pendulum swung to one side, as the perceived ideal role for women was to stay home, have babies, care for the children, shop, cook, launder the clothes, and clean the house. Studies from the 1950's show that these tasks took more time than ever before to complete, even with new "labor saving" devices, partially because the middle-class homemaker worked without the benefit of servants.

In the 1970's and 1980's the pendulum swung in the opposite direction, as women reverted to the earlier pattern of maintaining smaller families while entering the workforce in greater numbers than ever before. However, role expectations were often based on the 1950's model. Thus, women were expected to work the "second shift" at home after completing a full day of paid employment. Depending on the couples, men sometimes assisted their wives with some of the tasks of the second shift, but most of the time women were forced to bear this responsibility alone. Hochschild and Machung report in *The Second Shift* that the sharing of household and child care responsibilities improved marriages, regardless of the degree of egalitarianism that the partners preferred. Although family size shrank, there was still much to do. By 1993 married women working full time contributed to 41 percent of their families' income. Single women had to bear full financial

One of the most outstanding social developments of the late twentieth century was a huge increase in the number of wives and mothers working outside of their homes. (James L. Shaffer)

responsibility by themselves. Clearly, women were working to meet basic needs, not just for frills.

Family-Friendly Policies Emerge. *The Second Shift* concluded that most individuals felt they were doing all they personally could to balance the needs of family life and the demands of work and career. As a result, Hochschild and Machung called for restructuring the workplace and society to better accommodate the needs of families, especially those with young children. Other researchers and scholars concurred that job structures, work policies, and government services needed to be reorganized to make them more compatible with family life.

The media began to focus attention on companies that provided on-site child care, flexible work hours, compressed work schedules, and family-leave policies. The Family and Medical Leave Act of 1993 was passed requiring employers to allow their employees to take time-limited unpaid leaves for personal or family illnesses or the birth of children.

Attention also turned toward changes that were occurring in men's roles. Many researchers reported that men were accepting more responsibility for child care, often equally sharing parenting roles with their wives. Articles and books, such as *Wait a Minute, You Can Have It All* (1993) by Shirley Sloan Fader and *He Works, She Works: Successful Strategies for Working Couples* (1995) by Jaine Carter and James Carter, emerged to provide suggestions and guidance to couples struggling to solve the problem of a fair division of household responsibility. Demographics reinforced these changes, as sons and daughters of dual-earner couples grew up and established their own families. These younger couples tended to share housework and child care, viewing shared responsibilities as the norm.

The Way We Never Were. A discussion of family values engaged society in the 1990's. In *The Way We Never Were: American Families and the Nostalgia Trap* (1992) family historian Stephanie Coontz warned against nostalgia for a largely mythical past filled with gender separated roles and extended families. She identified ways that families could eliminate guilt or blame for unmet expectations. Rosalind C. Barnett and Caryl Rivers in *She Works/He Works: How Two-Income Families Are Happier, Healthier, and Better-Off* (1996) documented how both men and women were happier when both partners were wage earners.

As family-friendly policies became more prevalent, discussion centered on the needs of different family forms. Hochschild's *The Time Bind: When Work Becomes Home and Home Becomes Work* (1997) studied employees at every career level at a large midwestern corporation and their family members to discover time priorities. She noted a trend that the "first shift" seemed to be taking more time, causing the second shift to be more hurried. In order to cope, families were buying more time-saving goods and services when they could afford them. They also seemed to minimize children's need to spend time with their families.

Even though family-friendly work policies were available, Hochschild observed that workers chose not to take advantage of existing benefits. Their reasons were numerous, including their need for extra pay, their concern about jeopardizing jobs and promotions, their love for their jobs, and the fact that jobs served as a haven from family troubles. In Hochschild's study, work seemed to capture the emotional allegiance of many people. She concluded that for many persons work was more rewarding and had greater importance than the family. Hochschild speculates that this is primarily a result of the emphasis on work as personal identity and of the devaluing of families by society.

The Future. Workplace experts agree that a major change is taking place in North America as to the meaning and location of work. Factors such as increased workplace participation of women, falling real wages, downsizing, flexible work hours, telecommuting, and increased self-employment have blurred the boundaries between work and family life. The personal accommodations that families have established may provide a stopgap measure, but what is required is further societal change.

Coontz argues that it is necessary to dispense with the misconceptions about the "traditional" family and recognize that the division of work between men and women in the United States was just a temporary situation. It is also necessary to recognize and promote the strengths of all family types, including two-parent, single-parent, dual-earner, or single-earner families. She agrees with other family life experts who advocate a better balance between market activities, such as work, business, and government, and nonmarket activities in the family and community spheres. Services to all types of families regardless of their economic class must be increased. Family-friendly policies must be established and people must feel free and comfortable to take advantage of them. In the late twentieth century, the second shift continued to be a topic of discussion and a problem that many individuals were attempting to solve.

—*Joann Driggers*

BIBLIOGRAPHY

Barnett, Rosalind C., and Caryl Rivers. *She Works/He Works: How Two-Income Families Are Happier, Healthier, and Better-Off.* New York: HarperCollins, 1996.

Carter, Jaine, and James Carter. *He Works, She Works: Successful Strategies for Working Couples.* New York: Amacom, 1995.

Coontz, Stephanie. *The Way We Never Were: American Families and the Nostalgia Trap.* New York: Basic Books, 1992.

_____. *The Way We Really Are: Coming to Terms with America's Changing Families.* New York: Basic Books, 1997.

Fader, Shirley Sloan. *Wait a Minute, You Can Have It All.* New York: G. P. Putnam's Sons, 1993.

Hochschild, Arlie Russell. *The Time Bind: When Work Becomes Home and Home Becomes Work.* New York: Metropolitan Books, 1997.

Hochschild, Arlie Russell, and Anne Machung. *The Second Shift: Working Parents and the Revolution at Home.* New York: Viking, 1989.

McKenna, Elizabeth Perle. *When Work Doesn't Work Anymore.* New York: Delacorte, 1997.

Morris, Betsy. "Is Your Family Wrecking Your Career?" *Fortune* 135 (March 17, 1997).

Schor, Juliet B. *The Overworked American: The Unexpected Decline of Leisure.* New York: Basic Books, 1992.

See also Dual-earner families; Family: concept and history; Family economics; Hochschild, Arlie Russell; Mommy track; Women's roles; Work.

Senior citizen centers

RELEVANT ISSUES: Aging; Demographics; Parenting and family relationships

SIGNIFICANCE: As increasing life expectancy has created a larger elderly population and chang-

ing family structures have minimized extended families, many elderly people have their social and service needs met through alternate sources

In 1965, the groundwork was laid for the provision of a variety of social services for the elderly in the United States with the passage of the Older Americans Act (OAA). This legislation provided funding for many programs, including senior citizen centers, which tended to take the form of social clubs for the aged. These centers were needed, to some extent, because of an increase in the population of older persons.

The Aging of North America. In 1995, persons sixty-five years of age or older constituted 13 percent of the U.S. population and 12 percent of the Canadian population. By the year 2030, when most of the baby-boom generation will have retired, it is expected that 21 percent of the United States population will be age sixty-five or older, along with 20 percent of the Canadian population.

In ageist societies, retirees often are excluded from much social participation with those other than age peers. Social isolation, although detrimental to persons of all ages, has been shown to be especially problematic to those in late life. Thus, a place for older people to gather had become important. There were approximately 450 of these seniors' clubs in the United States in 1965.

In slightly more than a decade, however, it became clear that more than just a club-type setting was required. In 1978, amendments to the reauthorization of the OAA called for the creation and support of multipurpose senior centers. This change was the result of recognition that many older persons had a variety of needs that were not being met adequately under other circumstances.

For various reasons, older persons are less likely to live with extended family members than in the past, and even if they do, they may not have someone with them in the home as much as they want or need. Many older persons therefore might have to rely on outsiders to meet some of these needs. Multipurpose senior centers developed as community focal points where elderly people could come together for services and activities to help support their independence.

Types of Available Services. The services available at these centers typically include transportation, legal assistance, health screening, congregate dining, and "meals on wheels" delivered to those unable to get to the senior center. Activities may include regular dances, arts and crafts training, exercise programs, and board or card games.

As many as 15 percent of the elderly population, or more than five million people, may have participated in some programs at a U.S. senior center in the 1990's. In 1997, more than two hundred centers and clubs were registered with the Canadian Senior Citizens Information and Service Center.

By the late 1980's, a prominent researcher on senior centers estimated that there were as many as thirteen thousand senior centers in the United States. By the late 1980's, however, the Administration on Aging had ruled that allocations under the OAA no longer could be used to support the administration of these senior centers. Consequently, most of them have had to resort to seeking operating capital through the support of foundations and holding various kinds of fundraisers.

Adult Day Care. Many multipurpose centers offer what is sometimes referred to as respite care or adult day care (ADC). This service is designed to provide the primary caregivers—usually family members—time off so that they do not suffer unduly from the burden of caregiving, which can

Many residents of senior citizen centers fill their time with activities such as games and crafts. (AP/Wide World Photos)

Dances are regular activities at many centers. (Mary LaSalle)

become a twenty-four-hour-a-day job. Provided on a more long-term basis, it may also enable the primary caregiver—often an adult daughter or daughter-in-law of the elderly person—to return to the work for pay she may have left so that she could provide this care.

ADC centers are often attached to long-term care (LTC) facilities, even though ADC is designed to delay the older person's entry into LTC. In Canada, eligibility for ADC is established along the same lines as for LTC, and it is almost invariably provided by nonprofit organizations. In the United States, ADC is available in some senior residential facilities, some hospitals (nonprofit or otherwise), and some churches.

Wherever ADC services are provided, they enable elders to continue living at home while getting the supervision, assistance, and interaction they need during the day. ADC services may include physical rehabilitation, nursing, and transportation. This latter service may include home pickup and return. Overall, 90 percent of ADC users in the United States live within an hour of the center providing service to them.

About 70 percent of ADC participants are women. Most live with family: 29 percent with children, 20 percent with a spouse, and 13 percent with other relatives or friends. One-fifth live alone.

Need for Advanced Services. In the late 1980's, 23 percent of U.S. elders living in the community had health-related difficulties with at least one of the activities of daily living (ADL), including dressing, bathing, and eating. Twenty-eight percent of them had difficulty with at least one of the instrumental activities of daily living (IADL), such as laundering, cooking, or housekeeping. Less than half of those with ADL difficulty were receiving some sort of help, but most of those with IADL difficulty were receiving assistance. Most ADC center users indicate at least mild levels of the age and disease-related confusion commonly called senility.

The U.S. National Center for Health Statistics indicates that rates of impairment of one sort or another vary by region. This variance leads to a differential incidence of need for ADC services. These different levels of physical need are one factor in the level of demand relative to capacity. Forty-three percent of ADC centers in the South had waiting lists, whereas only 15 percent of such

centers in the Midwest had waiting lists. Other factors in demand include marital dissolution rates, which are considerably higher in the South than in the Midwest. Spouses are a significant source of care, and lack of a spouse may increase the need for outside caregiving.

ADC centers date back to 1947 in the United States, with one begun at the Menninger Clinic in Kansas. Their growth had been curtailed until recently by the introduction of Medicare and Medicaid legislation, which provided only for payment of medical services rendered by physicians, hospitals, and LTC facilities. With increased efforts at containing costs and finding options that provide for more independence and dignity for elders, health service providers have looked more closely at ADC as an option.

Some organizations have begun to explore novel ways of combining child and adult day care services, which may allow young children and their grandparents or great-grandparents to spend more time together, being cared for in proximate or even interrelated facilities. This could be a great boon to the parents of these children, members of the so-called sandwich generation that has the responsibility of caring for both their children and their parents. —*Scott Magnuson-Martinson*

BIBLIOGRAPHY

Heide, Julie, and Linda C. Webb. *Day Care Programs and Services for Elders in Rural America.* Kansas City, Mo.: National Center for Rural Elderly, 1991.

Kirwin, Patricia M. *Adult Day Care: The Relationship of Formal and Informal Systems of Day Care.* New York: Garland Press, 1991.

Krout, John A. *The Organization, Operation, and Programming of Senior Centers: A Seven Year Follow Up.* Fredonia: Dept. of Sociology and Anthropology, State University of New York, College of Fredonia, 1990.

_____. *Senior Centers in America.* Westport, Conn.: Greenwood Press, 1989.

Myerhoff, Barbara. *Number Our Days.* New York: E. P. Dutton, 1978.

Siler, Cinda. "Finding Day Care for Your Aging Parent." *Money* (December, 1987).

Weissert, William G., et al. *Adult Day Care: Findings from a National Survey.* Baltimore: Johns Hopkins University Press, 1990.

See also Ageism; Aging and elderly care; Extended families; Life expectancy; Nursing and convalescent homes; Older Americans Act (OAA); Retirement; Retirement communities; Sandwich generation; Social Security; Widowhood.

Separation anxiety

RELEVANT ISSUES: Children and child development; Parenting and family relationships

SIGNIFICANCE: Separation anxiety is experienced by most young children and adolescents at certain stages, and although it can affect family life, in most cases it is developmentally appropriate

Separation anxiety exists on a continuum, with varying degrees of distress, impairment in functioning, or interference that differentiate between what is "normal" and what is problematic. At the normal (or "developmentally appropriate") end of the continuum is the mild anxiety that the majority of young children between the ages of one and two exhibit when they are separated from their parents. This separation anxiety typically becomes prominent again in children between the ages of four and six, when they begin nursery and primary school. Importantly, young adults also often experience separation problems or "homesickness" at certain developmental stages. These problems appear to be most relevant during young adults' first year at college, when many freshmen live away from home for the first time. These forms of separation anxiety are common, typically short-lived, and normal.

At the other end of the continuum is Separation Anxiety Disorder (SAD). In the fourth edition of the American Psychiatric Association's *Diagnostic and Statistical Manual of Mental Disorders* (1994), SAD is defined as undue anxiety because of separation from the home or separation from significant figures in children's lives. SAD is one of the most common and serious mental health problems affecting children. Interestingly, although the term "separation anxiety" has long been part of clinical lore in the field of child development, it has only been since 1980, with the publication of the third edition of the American Psychiatric Association's *Diagnostic and Statistical Manual of Mental Disorders*, that SAD has been recognized as a distinct clinical disorder.

Leaving a child at a child-care center or school, especially for the first time, can be stressful for both the child and the parent. (James L. Shaffer)

Separation anxiety can affect many aspects of family life. One of the most common triggers for separation anxiety in young children is being left with baby-sitters or other caregivers (for example, child-care workers). In modern society, in which most parents work, the issue of child care is particularly relevant. The experience of leaving children with caregivers is often extremely stressful not only for children, but also for parents. Parents must often physically disentangle themselves from their children, leaving them in distress. Most parents find this experience intensely upsetting. Indeed, in some cases parents make significant adjustments to their own social and professional lives in order to avoid leaving their children with baby-sitters or child caregivers. While parents' efforts to organize family life around their children's separation anxiety may be effective in the short term, in the long term this strategy appears to prolong children's anxiety and encourage dependence. This in turn results in further difficulties for children. Thus, if separation issues are not overcome, children will find it extremely difficult to form new relationships and settle into new environments at school or child-care centers. —*Vanessa E. Cobham*

See also Behavior disorders; Bonding and attachment; Childhood fears and anxieties; Emotional abuse; Freudian psychology; Parenting; Stranger anxiety.

Serial monogamy

RELEVANT ISSUES: Divorce; Marriage and dating; Sociology

SIGNIFICANCE: A form of marriage in which a divorced man or woman remarries repeatedly, the incidence of serial monogamy has increased greatly in late twentieth century America as a result of the high divorce rate

The term "serial monogamy" was first coined in 1950 by Hortense Powdermaker in her book *Hollywood, The Dream Factory*, a well-researched anthropological explanation of the influence and effects of the film industry upon the changing morals of the American public. Her book essentially accused Hollywood of mass production of prefabricated daydreams that appealed to the public's frustration and offered encouragement to their fantasies. However, she also felt that the daily publicized personal accounts of actors and actresses ingenuously redefined traditional folk and culture heroes and effectively portrayed hedonistic lifestyles and deteriorating morals that condoned divorce, particularly repetitive divorce, while glorifying behavior that was once not socially acceptable.

Serial monogamy has been defined as repetitive marriage in which a divorced man or woman remarries but is never legally married to more than one spouse at the same time. Since the mid-1990's sociologists and anthropologists have also used such terms as binuclear families, stepfamilies, and even pluralistic families to define what has become a definite shift from the once traditional intact, lifetime, monogamous, nuclear family system to the more common forms of extended pluralistic marital arrangements. A major consequence of serial monogamy, divorce and remarriage, is the creation of stepfamilies; approximately 60 percent of remarriages include a parent with physical custody of one or more children.

Statistically, divorce and remarriage percentages are significant, for more than half of all marriages in the United States are marriages in which at least one partner has been previously married, 61 percent will remarry other divorced men and women, and about one-third marry never-married individuals. Remarriage is common for divorced persons, and divorced men are more likely to remarry than are divorced women. Remarriage courtships are invariably brief; approximately one-third of divorced individuals marry usually one year after their divorces and approximately 50 percent of all divorced women remarry within seven months of separation. Among those who remarry between the ages of twenty-four and thirty-four years of age, the time between divorce and remarriage is usually about three years. It is well documented that ethnicity affects remarriage rates; approximately 55 percent of white women and 42 percent of African American women remarry, whereas Latinos are less likely to remarry than these other groups.

Although the number of single-parent families has increased throughout the world, within the United States they are the fastest-growing type of family. Persons have more than a 65 percent chance of divorcing, remarrying, or living in a single-parent family or stepfamily as a child or parent sometime during their lives. In fact, some

The most famous serial monogamists are actors, such as Elizabeth Taylor, pictured here with her eighth husband, Larry Fortensky. (AP/Wide World Photos)

sociologists think that the situation of an evolving pluralistic family system has become a natural part of the modern United States because of shifting social values and because the atmosphere of intimacy, effective socialization of children, and the assignment of proper social roles and statuses can often be fulfilled by these new family structures.

—*John Alan Ross*

See also Blended families; Couples; Divorce; Marriage; Monogamy; Nuclear family; Stepfamilies.

Settlement houses

RELEVANT ISSUES: Economics and work; Law
SIGNIFICANCE: Settlement houses played an important role in protecting and aiding immigrant families in the early twentieth century in their attempts to adjust to their new urban environment

In the fifty years following the end of the Civil War, the United States changed from a society that was mainly agricultural and rural to one that was predominantly industrial and urban. Accompanying that change were other changes, among the most significant of which was the magnitude and nature of the "new immigration" to the United States.

Origins. The number of immigrants reaching the United States between the mid-1860's and the 1910's was twice as high as that which came to the United States in the preceding fifty years. Even more momentous, the waves of immigrants who inundated the eastern seaboard of the United States in the late nineteenth and early twentieth centuries were from central, eastern, and southeastern Europe and were considered by many as

European immigrants arriving at Ellis Island in the early twentieth century. (AP/Wide World Photos)

more difficult to assimilate than previous immigrants. The emergence of social settlements in the United States should be examined in the context of these changes.

The idea of settlement houses or social settlements did not originate in the United States: A group of Christian Socialists helped to establish the Working Men's College in London in the mid-nineteenth century. Led by John Ruskin, an art professor at Oxford and a committed social reformer, young men and women became residents in working-class districts, hoping to eradicate the evils brought by industrialization. They were ill prepared.

In 1884, Samuel A. Barnett, vicar of what was called the worst parish in London, inspired several young men to establish a university settlement (named Toynbee Hall after a student who had died while attempting to serve the workingmen) in London. The goals of the students who resided at Toynbee Hall were simple: to reduce class antagonisms, to live among the people, and to use Toynbee Hall as an outpost of culture and education.

Settlement Houses in the United States. The university settlement idea practiced in Great Britain soon caught on in the United States. In 1886, several students of Amherst and Andover Theological Seminary created a Neighborhood Guild in New York City's Lower East Side. In 1887, students from Smith, Wellesley, Vassar, Bryn Mawr, and Radcliffe established chapters of what would become the College Settlement Association. Two years later, they opened their first settlement in New York.

Shortly after College Settlement was founded, Jane Addams and Ellen Gates Starr opened Hull House in Chicago. It would soon become the most famous social settlement in the United States. Hull House was followed by the creation, under the leadership of Lillian Wald, of Henry Street Settlement in New York in 1893. By 1910, there were more than four hundred social settlements in the United States.

There were several differences between English and American social settlements. English settlements usually had a religious connection, but most social settlements in United States avoided identification as a religious mission. American settlements worked with immigrants, most of whom were unfamiliar with the English language and the Anglo-Saxon culture, whereas English settlements dealt with the English working class. English settlements believed that reform had to begin with the individual, but American settlement workers soon came to believe that true reform could come only after the social environment was improved. There was one characteristic shared by the English and the American settlements: The belief that settlement workers must reside in the neighborhood that they were attempting to help.

Settlement Houses and the Family. Settlement houses performed several functions that were only peripherally associated with family life. They sponsored art exhibitions, organized community improvement associations and housing reform groups, promoted a variety of educational programs (including kindergartens), worked closely with labor unions, advocated the establishment of playgrounds and better recreational opportunities, sponsored and conducted numerous social research investigations, and (in the case of Hull House) became actively involved in city ward politics.

The strains of modern urban life on the family were paramount, however, and child labor was one of the problems with which a settlement house first had to contend. Starr and Addams at Hull House recognized that child labor reforms could not be achieved unless there was a body of social statistics to support claims concerning the hardships of child labor.

The opportunity to conduct social research studies came in 1891, when Florence Kelley, an experienced social investigator, came to Hull House as a resident. Kelley was soon appointed by the governor of Illinois as a special investigator for the Illinois State Bureau of Labor; later, she served as a factory inspector. Twelve years later, Illinois passed a child-labor law that became a model for other states. Kelley, who had moved to the Henry Street Settlement in 1899, continued her work for child labor reform.

State officials, however, often failed to comply with or enforce child-labor laws, and Kelley, Addams, Wald, and others helped to form the National Child Labor Committee in 1904. The committee could not get a federal child-labor law passed but was instrumental in getting the courts to recognize and address the more blatant evils associated with child labor. The committee also was successful, after a vigorous eight-year battle, in getting a Children's Bureau established in the U.S. government.

Condition of Working Women. In 1904, the same year that the National Child Labor Committee was established, several settlement house workers began to pressure President Theodore Roosevelt and Congress to create legislation that would require the Department of Commerce and Labor to investigate the conditions of working women in the United States. The law was passed in 1907, and nineteen volumes of the findings of the investigation were published between 1910 and 1913.

One of the by-products of this investigation was the discovery of a direct relationship among low wages, the low level of education of women, and the existence of prostitution in the urban centers of the United States. Addams and other settlement workers hoped that public awareness of and exposure to such information would lead to at least an amelioration of the worst aspects of prostitution.

Although labor unions were at first suspicious of the motives of the settlement workers, they soon discovered that settlement houses were valuable allies, particularly in the attempts to help women organize. They were active in the formation of the National Women's Trade Union League in 1903, and they continued to campaign for laws that protected women and children.

Useful and Useless Programs. In the area of family life, both the settlement houses and the neighborhoods they served profited from early programs. Settlement workers, given their university and middle-class origins, initially provided a series of educational programs for the immigrant neighborhoods. They discovered that the kindergarten and day care programs they provided for children involved them in educational programs for adults that ranged from cooking and sewing classes to classes in budget management and shopping techniques.

Some programs were discovered to be useless, such as teaching the proper way to serve tea, but others, such as the establishment of model flats and housekeeping centers where settlement workers could teach in a more realistic setting, proved to be rewarding. The experiences gained from these programs were later reproduced by public schools and some governmental agencies.

The settlement house movement reached its peak in the second decade of the twentieth century and was in several ways undermined by its own success. Their demise was in part a reaction to social experimentation in the 1920's. In addition, settlement workers became disillusioned with their inability to reform more fully the communities they served. By the beginning of World War II, however, many of the family-related programs initiated and promoted by the settlement houses and their residents had been incorporated in city, state, and federal agencies.   —*Robert L. Patterson*

BIBLIOGRAPHY

Addams, Jane. *Twenty Years at Hull-House, with Autobiographical Notes.* New York: Macmillan, 1910.

Davis, Allen Freeman. *Spearheads for Reform: The Social Settlements and the Progressive Movement, 1890-1914.* New York: Oxford University Press, 1967.

Frankel, Noralee, and Nancy S. Dye, eds. *Gender, Class, Race, and Reform in the Progressive Era.* Lexington: University Press of Kentucky, 1991.

Stebner, Eleanor J. *The Women of Hull House: A Study in Spirituality, Vocation, and Friendship.* Albany: State University of New York Press, 1997.

Trolander, Judith Ann. *Professionalism and Social Change: From the Settlement House Movement to Neighborhood Centers, 1886 to the Present.* New York: Columbia University Press, 1987.

Wald, Lillian D. *Windows on Henry Street.* Boston: Little, Brown, 1934.

Yans-McLaughlin, Virginia, ed. *Immigration Reconsidered: History, Sociology, and Politics.* New York: Oxford University Press, 1990.

See also Addams, Jane; Community programs for children; Day care; Hull House; Juvenile delinquency; Lathrop, Julia C.; Social workers; Volunteerism.

Sex education

RELEVANT ISSUES: Education; Health and medicine; Marriage and dating

SIGNIFICANCE: The 1980's and 1990's were marked by a sharp conflict between advocates of sex education, who believed that students in the public schools should receive a broad knowledge of human sexuality, and opponents, whose agendas led to the dismantling of sex-education programs in several states

The first movement formally to add sex education to U.S. public school curricula made only minor progress in the 1960's and 1970's. In the late 1980's, the perception of acquired immunodeficiency syndrome (AIDS) as a fatal sexually transmitted disease compelled most states to develop guidelines and require sexuality education, an effort that focused on disease prevention and behavior modification. While sex education has remained a consistent part of the standard curriculum in Canada, American educational reform efforts have defused most state-mandated sex-education programs.

Early Efforts. American society long relied on parents to provide their children with the basic "facts of life." By the 1960's the complexity of new medical technologies and basic biological knowledge rendered most parents incapable of answering questions about sex. Increases in divorce rates, single-parent families, the availability of birth control pills, and more open discussion gave the appearance of a sexual revolution. Before World War II there had been little bona fide sex education in public schools or colleges; Alfred Kinsey's elective sex-education course for undergraduates at Indiana University in the late 1930's was an exception. In the new atmosphere of the 1960's, formal educational programs at both colleges and public schools were allowed in some regions. The first human sexuality text was by James Leslie McCary, a University of Houston psychology professor who started with 185 students in his first class and filled his university's largest lecture hall with more than 1,100 students four semesters later.

Well-trained secondary-level biology teachers often covered human reproductive biology on par with other aspects of the human body in required coeducational classes. In family-life education classes primarily for girls, home economics teachers detailed childbirth, child care, menstruation, birth control, and even sexual response. Health education was usually part of physical education; sex education was usually handled by coaches or physical-education teachers in cursory, single-sex sessions in locker rooms, where films were shown and questions answered.

Parents and Their Teenage Children

In the interest of promoting frank discussion about sex within families, Parenting Without Pressure sponsors National Talk with Your Teen About Sex Month every March. During this annual event the organization encourages parents to give their children up-to-date and accurate information on sex and to keep lines of communication open. The event's overall goal is to reduce misinformation and help teenagers make their own responsible decisions about sex.

Early sex education focused on reproductive biology. Some educators expressed disdain for focusing on "mere plumbing." Later sex education evolved into "sexuality education" with decreasing emphasis on biology and substantial coverage of culture, psychology, health, personal skills, and relationships. However, sex education as a separate and distinct topic made school officials uneasy and met with opposition from religious and conservative elements. As a result, only Maryland actually mandated sex education by the early 1980's. Most states also permitted students to opt out of sex-education class sessions on religious grounds. The movement away from sexual freedom and toward more conservative values in the United States in the late 1970's and early 1980's made sex education a forgotten curriculum.

AIDS Makes Sex Education Urgent. The discovery of acquired immunodeficiency syndrome (AIDS) in the 1980's dramatically altered public perceptions of the need for sex education. Since AIDS was an incurable disease transmitted by both homosexual and heterosexual contact, a sense of urgency led many state school boards to risk controversy and mandate some level of sexuality education, including information on how to prevent the transmission of AIDS. By 1986 New Jersey, Kansas, and the District of Columbia had joined Maryland in mandating sexuality education. By 1993, seventeen states required sexuality education and thirty more encouraged it with recommended guidelines.

Sex Education Advocates. Supporters of sex education have contended that it should be covered just as thoroughly and naturally as other so-

Expectant parents attending a pregnancy education class. (James L. Shaffer)

cial and biological topics. Advocates have also claimed that the quality of students' lives has risen when they understand their sexuality, arguing that abortion levels, unwanted pregnancy, and sexually transmitted diseases would substantially increase without sex-education programs. In reply to criticism that sex education belonged at home, they have pointed out that the knowledge of sex needed in the late twentieth century far exceeds the basics most parents understand and that knowledgeable parents have failed to provide their children with sex education. Advocates have presented data indicating that nine out of ten parents want their children to receive sex education in the schools. In addition, advisory committees have been established in thirty states to review sex-education materials and programs, providing community input and support while reducing resistance to sex education.

Sex-Education Problems. Opponents have contended that the quality of school sex-education programs varies so widely that surveys of their effectiveness have been unlikely to show clear-cut differences. Educators have noted that most states do not require coverage of sexual behavior, abortion, condoms, masturbation, sexual identity and orientation, and sexuality and religion. Sex educators have advocated far more coverage at earlier ages, contending that much sex education has come too late, while opponents have objected to exposing younger children to such a mature topic. State guidelines have usually omitted controversial topics, including those that are vital for students such as abortion and birth control methods. Local school administrators have diluted such guidelines to avoid local controversy, but they have almost never exceeded them. Sex educators have noted that teachers of sex education are rarely certified and that only nine states have required specific training. Few states have monitored schools to assure that state regulations are implemented. With these limitations, supporters have contended that it is difficult to assess the effectiveness of sex education.

Sex-Education Opponents. Opponents of sex education have been political conservatives or religious fundamentalists. Most have contended that parents have prime responsibility for educating their children, dismissing the need for a detailed understanding of anatomy, disease symptoms, or cultural attitudes that differ from Judeo-Christian norms. They have viewed advisory committees as liberal efforts to force sex education on communities.

Opponents have asserted that classroom teaching and discussion of sexual topics encourages premarital sex, arguing that premarital sex, childbirth out of wedlock, and sexually transmitted diseases have increased despite sex-education programs. In those states where sexuality education has been mandated, opponents have often promoted "Sex Respect" programs which concentrate on reinforcing just-say-no abstinence while containing little information on sexual anatomy, birth control, or practices to avoid contracting AIDS and other sexually transmitted diseases.

Six states have prohibited specific sex-education topics, including Louisiana, which bars sex instruction in early grades; South Carolina, which prohibits discussion of premarital sex or topics unrelated to reproduction; and Utah, which does not permit advocacy or acceptance of homosexuality, birth control for unmarried minors, or details about sexual intercourse. Virtually all states have given parents the option of excusing their children from sex-education classes, in whole or in part. This parental opt-out was written into sex-education mandates to defuse opposition and gain acceptance. A shift to more conservative and religious values in the mid-1990's, combined with lessening concern over the AIDS epidemic, has led several states to dismantle their sexuality-education mandates. —*John Richard Schrock*

BIBLIOGRAPHY

Boston Women's Cooperative. *The New Our Bodies, Ourselves.* New York: Simon & Schuster, 1992.

Burt, John J., and Linda Brower Meeks. *Education for Sexuality: Concepts and Programs for Teaching.* 3d ed. New York: CBS College Publishing, 1985.

McCary, James Leslie. *Human Sexuality.* New York: Van Nostrand Reinhold, 1967.

Money, John, and Anke A. Ehrhardt. *Man and Woman, Boy and Girl.* Baltimore: Johns Hopkins University Press, 1972.

Sex Information and Education Council of the United States. *Guidelines for Comprehensive Sexuality Education, K-12.* New York: Author, 1991.

_____. *Unfinished Business: A SIECUS Assessment of State Sexuality Education Programs.* New York: Author, 1995.

See also Acquired immunodeficiency syndrome (AIDS); Birth control; Ellis, Albert; Family life education; Masters, William H., and Virginia E. Johnson; Moral education; Planned Parenthood Federation of America (PPFA); Puberty and adolescence; Public education; Reproductive technologies; Sanger, Margaret; Sexuality and sexual taboos.

Sexual revolution

RELEVANT ISSUES: Divorce; Marriage and dating; Parenting and family relationships

SIGNIFICANCE: Shifting attitudes from the 1960's to the 1980's led to greater societal acceptance of sexuality and sexual behavior

"Sexual revolution" is a term that was first used in the 1960's to describe what many perceive to be a dramatic shift in sexual attitudes and behaviors.

Experts disagree, however, as to whether this shift was so much a "revolution" as a stage in a cycle of change in attitudes toward sexual matters, a sexual "renaissance," or the continuation of a much longer, gradual shift in attitudes and behaviors. Many people assume that this so-called sexual revolution was a sudden rebellion against the Victorian mores that characterized the mid- to late nineteenth century and against associated negative attitude toward sexual expression. Whether due to revolution or evolution, the sexual mores of

Typical of sexually inhibited films of its era, The Marrying Kind *(1952) depicted a married couple sleeping in separate beds.* (Museum of Modern Art, Film Stills Archive)

the 1960's to the 1980's certainly represented a dramatic shift away from those of a century earlier.

Victorian Attitudes Toward Sex. The Victorians separated love and sex, with love being the romantic foundation for marriage. Sex was permissible within marriage, but only in moderation. Respectable women had to take care not to do or say anything that might inflame the lust of men; they certainly were not expected to enjoy sexual activity themselves. As early as the late 1800's, however, attitudes toward sex within marriage were becoming more positive, and gradually the emphasis changed to sexual activity as a means of expressing love. Major changes that occurred during the 1960's and 1970's included the possibility of reliably separating sex from reproduction (thanks to the development of the oral contraceptive pill and increased access to legal abortion), the belief that sex could be separated from love, an emphasis on women's enjoyment of sex, and an increasing openness toward same-sex activities. "Gay liberation" is another term that dates from this time. This era also saw an increase in sex education, the beginnings of modern scientific research on human sexual functioning, and the advent of sexual therapy.

Some researchers believe that the outcomes related to these changes were a more widespread belief in persons' right to choose how they wish to behave sexually, a greater tolerance of premarital sexual activity, a willingness to participate in sexual acts previously considered unacceptable, and an awareness of sexual interest among people such as the elderly and the physically handicapped, who were previously assumed to lack sexual interests and needs. A number of studies indicate that attitudes toward other aspects of human sexuality, such as pornography and homosexuality, have not changed significantly from previous decades. Some persons believe that the so-called "sexual revolution" represents a state of degeneracy and that various social controls must be reinstated to direct people's behavior back to a more moral focus.

Broad Social Transformations. It is difficult to sort out the changes brought about by the sexual revolution and those brought about by a great many other social changes that occurred simultaneously. More liberal divorce laws, the concept of "victimless crimes," legal challenges to the regula-

tion of behavior between consulting adults, an increase in the numbers of women (and especially of mothers) in the workforce, advertising that increasingly used sex to sell products of all kinds, increased leisure, greater affluence, and increased access to news and information because of technological changes have all played a part in creating societal problems often blamed exclusively on the sexual revolution.

These social changes, including the sexual revolution, have had an important impact on families, although whether this impact is seen as positive or negative depends largely on individuals' perspective. The separation of sexual activity from reproduction has led, in part, to a new definition of family. No longer is the norm two parents with children. Adults who choose not to have children or adults of the same sex may form families.

Marriage, Cohabitation, and Divorce. While the vast majority of Americans marry eventually, cohabitation has become more common since the sexual revolution. The U.S. Census Bureau has even created a designation for this: POSSLQ (person of opposite sex sharing living quarters). Cohabitors fall roughly into two equal-sized groups: college students and persons previously married. Some young people regard cohabitation as a prelude to marriage, but cohabiting does not necessarily lead either to marriage or to a lasting marriage. To minimize the legal problems associated with breaking up, some previously married persons choose to cohabit rather than to remarry, while others live together to avoid "marriage penalties" in the tax code or to avoid a decrease in retirement income that sometimes comes with remarriage.

The family is also affected by changes in attitudes toward monogamy. Sexual fidelity to one's partner is widely held to be the ideal, even by those who engage in sexual intercourse outside their primary relationship. Much research was done in the 1970's and 1980's about various forms of so-called "open marriage." This took a number of forms, from polygamy to consensual recreational adultery ("swinging" or "wife swapping"). Possibly due to concerns about acquired immunodeficiency syndrome (AIDS) and other sexually transmitted diseases, more people in the 1990's report having had only one sexual partner in the preceding year.

The sexual revolution made possible public forms of romantic behavior that would have been unthinkable in earlier eras. (James L. Shaffer)

Some people blame the increased divorce rate on the sexual revolution. Divorce certainly has a major emotional and financial impact on families. However, those who support liberalized divorce laws point to the negative impact on the family of unhappy and unfulfilling marriages. More conservative thinkers believe that existing laws should be changed to make divorce more difficult, while more liberal thinkers believe that divorced families require more social, psychological, and financial support. Efforts to force noncustodial parents to pay court-ordered child support is an example of helping diminish the burden of divorce on the family.

Sex Education and Medical Advances. The sexual revolution was accompanied by an increased role for the schools in teaching about human sexuality. This has removed some of the parental responsibility for providing their children with information and guidance. Opponents of sex education see this as depriving parents of their rights, while proponents point to numerous studies indicating that many parents fail to fulfill this important role for their children. Both sides cite the unfortunate consequences of sexual activity, such as teenage pregnancy and sexually transmitted diseases, as evidence that there is either too much or too little sex education in the schools.

Increased research on human sexuality has improved the understanding of sexual functioning and led to the development of medical and psychological treatments for conditions that might previously have gone undiagnosed. Men suffering from diabetes, for example, may suffer from impotence due to disease-related changes in their blood vessels. This condition may be successfully treated with a variety of medical and surgical techniques. Sexual therapists can successfully treat anorgasmia, or the inability to reach orgasm. The sexuality of aging people, the mentally or physically handicapped, and children has become more fully understood in the late twentieth century than it was previously.

Increased awareness and more open discussion of sexuality has led to changes in how the problems of rape, sexual abuse, and incest are approached. New laws, better enforcement, more sensitivity to victims, and improved therapies for both victims and perpetrators exist. Along with these more positive changes are important ethical and legal challenges involving "false memory" allegations and the right of persons accused of sex crimes to confront their accusers (especially if accusers are children). Debate has also centered on the best course for families when sexual abuse is discovered. Is it best to remove children from the family? Is foster care for children the best alternative? If perpetrators are required to leave home, how will this affect family finances, stability, and the emotional health of family members? Laws about marital rape also have important ramifications for the family. Granting women the right to refuse sexual intercourse certainly alters the power structure within the family.

Shifting Views of Sexual Norms. Another important change accompanying the sexual revolution is that sexual activity has tended to become viewed as the norm. People who wish to remain celibate may find little social support for their position. Indeed, they may be pitied or ridiculed. Some women also feel that the sexual revolution has put them in a position in which they are more, rather than less, vulnerable to sexual exploitation. They feel that they have fewer reasons to refuse sexual activity if women in general are expected to enjoy and participate in sex. Certainly the portrayal of sex in the movies, on television, in print, and in advertising does not support celibacy, substantiating the view that humans are sexually active.

The decade of the 1990's saw what some people have called a counterrevolution. Skyrocketing rates of sexually transmitted disease, ongoing debate about the morality of abortion, social problems caused by teenage pregnancy, and other problems associated with a more relaxed attitude toward human sexuality have led to a reevaluation of beliefs and attitudes. Some are calling for a return to more restrictive laws and social constraints, while others wish to preserve the positive aspects of a more liberal view of human sexuality while placing greater emphasis on personal and societal responsibility. —*Rebecca Lovell Scott*

BIBLIOGRAPHY

Boston Women's Health Book Collective. *The New Our Bodies, Ourselves.* New York: Simon & Schuster, 1992.

Cline, S. *Women, Passion, and Celibacy.* New York: Carol Southern Books, 1993.

Cozic, C. P., ed. *Sexual Values: Opposing Viewpoints.* San Diego, Calif.: Greenhaven Press, 1995.

D'Emilio, J. D., and E. B. Freeman. *Intimate Matters: A History of Sexuality in America.* New York: Harper & Row, 1988.

Janus, S. S., and C. L. Janus. *The Janus Report on Sexual Behavior.* New York: John Wiley and Sons, 1993.

Kelly, G. F. *Sexuality Today: The Human Perspective.* 4th ed. Guilford, Conn.: Dushkin Publishing Group, 1994.

See also Acquired immunodeficiency syndrome (AIDS); Adultery; Couples; Marriage; Masters, William H., and Virginia E. Johnson; Open marriage; Sex education; Sexuality and sexual taboos.

Sexuality and sexual taboos

RELEVANT ISSUES: Children and child development; Health and medicine; Kinship and genealogy; Law; Marriage and dating; Parenting and family relationships; Religious beliefs and practices; Sociology

SIGNIFICANCE: With their deep historical roots in Judaism, medieval Christianity, and Puritanism, American values have shaped social attitudes toward sex, mores, taboos, and sexual practices

To understand American attitudes toward sexuality and the relevance of these attitudes for American family life, it is necessary to place them in historical and cultural context. The religious roots of American sexual values extend far back to ancient Judaism, early Christianity, medieval theology, and Puritanism.

Judaism. Jews believed that the primary purpose of sex was procreation, not pleasure. Given their unique social and historical position as a relatively small, persecuted tribe surrounded by hostile neighbors, their preoccupation with procreation is understandable. The Hebrews had to multiply their numbers in order to defend themselves against outside attacks. The biblical commandment "Be fruitful, and multiply" reflected this concern for reproduction. The Hebrews took the command quite seriously. Sex was understood as nothing other than the procreative act. Fruitfulness in marriage was deemed a divine blessing, while infertility amounted to a curse. When they reached the age of physical maturity, Hebrew men and women were expected to marry and reproduce.

The Jews cultivated a positive and joyous attitude toward sex. Since intercourse was the fulfillment of a divine command, it was customary for them to celebrate religious feasts and Sabbath by engaging in intercourse with their spouses. However, the commandment to procreate was not taken as a law binding on every Jew. Although early Judaism did not encourage a celibate life, later Judaism spawned sects such as the Essenes, who voluntarily renounced marriage and family life. The Essenes may have served as a model for the first cenobite monks of early Christianity.

Christianity. Notable contrasts exist between Christian and Jewish attitudes toward sex. Early Christians believed that they were the elect of God who spiritually replaced Jews as God's chosen people. They viewed themselves as the eschatological people, the people of the last days. Awaiting the Second Coming of Christ, which they believed was imminent, they showed little interest in worldly affairs, including starting new families. Many of them sold their possessions, severed their family ties, and formed communes.

When it appeared that the end of the world was not to occur immediately, Christians began to marry and establish families. Nevertheless, as a small and insecure minority they maintained an otherworldly orientation. The church fathers and early theologians reinforced this eschatological orientation by teaching that carnal pleasures were fundamentally evil. Many of the church fathers were influenced by Manichaenism, the dualistic metaphysics that viewed the world in terms of two ultimate principles constantly at war with each other: good and evil. They urged the Christians to join forces with the good and fight against evil. In their view, the forces of evil were led by Satan, who used human sexual desires as tools to divert Christians away from their spiritual destiny. In sharp contrast to Judaism, such a view resulted in a theological devaluation of sex.

The church fathers cited Saint Paul's example and teachings to convince the Christians that it was better to remain single than to remarry. Marriage was for the emotionally weak, for those who were unable to resist the temptations of the flesh. Sex was viewed as a necessary evil, grudgingly permitted only within the context of a monogamous, heterosexual marriage whose sole purpose was procreation. In contrast to the Jewish practice of celebrating sex, the Roman Catholic Church advocated abstinence from sex on religious holidays. Abstinence was particularly recommended during Lent. Origen, Tertullian, Saint Jerome, Saint Augustine, and a host of other Christian theologians consistently taught that a life of celibacy was spiritually superior to married life. Interestingly, some of these men had "sinful" pasts before they became ardent advocates of celibacy and renunciation.

Augustine, in particular, believed that one could not perform any form of sex without committing at least a venial sin. To avoid committing serious sin, couples were advised to approach their marital duty with prayer, clearly keeping in mind the procreative intent of the sexual act. The pleasure that accompanied sexual intercourse was not to be enjoyed for its own sake. Married persons, no less than those who had renounced marriage, were taught that they had an obligation to be chaste within marriage. Augustine's teaching that lust was a consequence of original sin became widely accepted. Ever since Augustine, the notion of chastity within marriage became a basic idea in the Christian theology of marriage.

Thomas Aquinas, the most prominent theologian of the High Middle Ages, appealed to natural law to buttress the belief that the sole purpose of sex was procreation and the continuation of the human race. Monastic orders that had already been founded in the fourth century C.E. grew and multiplied during the Middle Ages. In the eleventh century Pope Gregory VII issued a decree prohibiting all priests from marrying. With the establishment of celibacy as a requirement for priesthood, the Church left no doubt in the minds of the faithful that a celibate life was clearly superior to married life. The medieval Church created a variety of sex sins that required people to atone through fasting and penance. Nocturnal emission, masturbation, oral sex, anal sex, *coitus interruptus*, contraception, fornication, adultery, incest, homosexuality, sodomy, and bestiality were among them. After the Reformation, medieval theology became the official theology of the Roman Catholic Church. In an attempt to defend clerical celibacy, monks and priests reinterpreted the Bible to make celibacy central to Christian theology.

Mary's immaculate conception, the virgin birth of Jesus Christ, and his life as a single man became subjects of voluminous writings.

Sexuality and Protestantism. As part of the rebellion against the pope, Protestant reformers, including Martin Luther and John Calvin, rejected clerical celibacy and the vow of chastity. However, they were unable to shake themselves loose from the Augustinian view of sex as sinful.

Puritans, the dominant settlers of New England, were strict Calvinists who sought to lead a simple, pure, and devout life in a new land, free from the corruption and sin that had plagued their native England. Puritans believed in a strict sexual morality as part of the disciplined and conservative society that they sought to found in the New World. They abhorred adultery, homosexuality, fornication, and incest. However, the asceticism they espoused in theory did not always translate into practice. Many of them fell into the same corruption that they had fled as they had opportunities to take mistresses from the Native Americans they captured and the indentured servants they acquired. As the settlement spread from east to west, trading glass beads, guns, knives, and other goods for native women became common practice.

Victorian Morality. Nineteenth century Europe and America experienced a conservative cultural ethos known as Victorianism. Victorianism depicted women as gentle, delicate, submissive, and innocent. Open discussion of sex was taboo both within the family and in public. Women were expected to react to the sexual initiatives of their husbands with shock and disgust. Men were taught to believe that imposing their sexual desires upon their fragile and angelic wives any more than was absolutely necessary amounted to abusing them and turning them into prostitutes. Women were never expected to initiate sex. Sex during menstruation and pregnancy was forbidden because it was considered to be defiling and did not serve its primary purpose: procreation.

The public sexual morality of the Victorians, however, contradicted their private sexual behavior. The Victorian period was in reality a time of sexual hypocrisy rather than sexual restraint. It is estimated that in the nineteenth century prostitution was more widespread than at any other time in history. This was partly due to the fact that men felt safer in expressing their forbidden sexual de-

The first screen kiss in film history was considered sensational when this film was released in 1896. (Museum of Modern Art, Film Stills Archive)

sires in anonymous sexual encounters with prostitutes than with their supposedly innocent wives. The unprecedented proliferation of prostitution contributed to the spread of syphilis and gonorrhea, resulting in a public health disaster in Europe and America. The myth that the only effective cure for these venereal diseases was sex with a virgin added to the tragedy. Large numbers of young girls from poor backgrounds were bought and sold as prostitutes.

Twentieth Century Attitudes. The twentieth century saw the naturalization and demystification of sex. Several factors contributed to the acceptance of sex as a fact of life. American men were exposed to the freedom and adventures of mingling with foreign women in the relatively more open societies of Europe during World War I, while American women were forced to work outside the home to replace men in the service. Women's massive entry into the workforce not only created a need for more practical clothing that revealed more of the female body, but also decreased the social distance between men and women. The years immediately after World War I saw accelerated momentum in the Suffrage Movement, culminating in 1920 when women were granted the right to vote. The granting of universal suffrage brought women a step closer to gender equality. In the 1920's and 1930's the availability of automobiles provided young people with a greater opportunity for sexual experimentation. It was during this period that Sigmund Freud's ideas about the pervasive power of sexuality gained popularity in the United States.

World War II further eroded traditional values and exposed sexual hypocrisy. The Kinsey Report of 1948 shockingly revealed that 70 percent of men had contacts with prostitutes and 40 percent had committed adultery. Further, 37 percent of men and 19 percent of women had experienced homosexual relations. Many men and women had experimented with a variety of deviant sexual acts, including bestiality. The availability of effective and cheap birth control methods made it possible for ordinary people to approach sex recreationally rather than solely as an act of procreation. These massive social changes that occurred during the first half of the twentieth century, coupled with

William H. Masters and Virginia Johnson, whose 1966 book Human Sexual Response *helped revolutionize modern views of sexuality.* (AP/Wide World Photos)

Public displays of physical affection, once largely taboo, have become commonplace. (James L. Shaffer)

the explosion of youth culture in the 1960's, ushered in a sexual revolution that was to sweep away many of the footholds of sexual orthodoxy.

Sexual Taboos. The Polynesian word "taboo" refers to the prohibition against specific actions or against contact with specific objects. The word was introduced into the English language in the eighteenth century by European explorers who became aware of the existence of such prohibitions among the island peoples of the South Pacific. Soon after the introduction of the word into English, Westerners realized that taboos were found in all known societies, including their own. It is not always fully understood why objects or actions become taboos. Perhaps people believe that prohibited objects are unclean or sacred and that prohibited actions must strictly be controlled to prevent them from causing harm to the whole of society.

Sexuality and its expressions form a large part of the taboos found in any society. The Jews regarded certain forms of sex as taboos at all times and others only at certain times. For example, the Jews, like all other known cultures, regarded incest as taboo. It was a violation of the incest taboo to have sex with one's blood relatives and kin by marriage. Incest was punishable by flagellation or even death. An exception to the incest taboo were levirate marriages, under which widows could demand of their deceased husbands' surviving brothers that they have sexual intercourse with them in order to beget children. The Bible mentions and condemns instances of father-son incest and father-daughter incest. Anthropologists have noted that the foundation of the incest taboo is not genetics, but a need to maintain a stable family structure with distinct roles and statuses assigned to all family members. Patriarchal values, on which the traditional Judeo-Christian family are erected, demand that male family members abide by the implied contract not to infringe upon one another's sexual rights.

Sex during menstruation was another taboo for the ancient Hebrews. The reason for this prohibition derived from the significance of blood in the Jewish religion. For Jews, blood is the essence of life. To control shedding and using blood, Jewish law and tradition developed various blood taboos. The blood of slaughtered animals, for example, had to be completely removed before meat could

be eaten. Consumption of blood or any blood product was forbidden. Sexual contact with menstruating women was a taboo because of the possibility of coming into contact with blood. Moreover, the Hebrews believed that menstrual blood was unclean and that sex with menstruating women was defiling. Because its purpose was unknown, menstrual blood evoked fear and anxiety. Some argue that the origin of the prohibition against Jewish women becoming rabbis and women in most Christian denominations becoming priests stems from the ancient belief that menstruation is impure.

The blood that is lost during childbirth was also considered impure. It defiled women and their babies. Only after performing ritual purification forty days after childbirth were Jewish women permitted to enter temples. The ritual of "churching" still found among traditional Christians, which requires that prayers and rites of purification be performed before women who have undergone childbirth may enter churches, has its origin in this ancient Jewish practice.

Homosexuality. All "unnatural" forms of sex are considered taboo by Jews and Christians, including homosexuality and bestiality (sex with animals). The Bible condemns these forms of sex because they result in wasting semen. The New Testament condemns homosexuality as a heinous sin. For ancient Jews homosexuality was a crime punishable by death. Bestiality, which was not an infrequent practice among pastoral peoples, was also a capital crime.

The modern term sodomy has its origin in a wrong interpretation of what actually happened in the city of Sodom. Biblical scholars deny that the passage about Sodom's destruction mentioned in the nineteenth chapter of the Book of Genesis was related to the practice of homosexuality. The notion that homosexuality was the sin committed in Sodom was based on a later interpretation of the ambiguous term "to know." While in certain contexts this term as used in the Bible means carnal knowledge, it also has other meanings, including a literal one. The cities of Sodom and Gomorrah were probably destroyed by an earthquake. According to the prophet Ezekiel, the sins of Sodom included pride, sloth, and neglect of the poor and the needy. Nevertheless, in England and America the term sodomy has come to mean the homosexual act, bestiality, and a variety of "unnatural" sexual practices including anal and oral sex.

The acceptance of Christianity by the Roman Empire in the fourth century led to the enactment of laws prohibiting sodomy. Roman law provided for the imposition of the death penalty on those convicted of sodomy. During the Middle Ages homosexuals were treated with the same disgust and hatred as were heretics. Like heretics, homosexuals were sometimes burned at the stake. Sometimes they were also regarded as worse than murderers, because they supposedly posed a threat to the survival of the human race itself.

Sodomy laws still exist in the criminal codes of most of the American states. They are so broadly defined that they prohibit virtually every form of nonvaginal sex between men and women. Although such laws are seldom implemented and most people ignore them, the fact that they exist on the books testifies to the continuing influence of Judeo-Christian values on American culture. Although Jewish law made lesbianism a crime, lesbianism was hardly ever punished. In late twentieth century America, lesbianism has been viewed less seriously than homosexuality.

Masturbation. The term "onanism" is misapplied to refer to masturbation. The sin of Onan, son of Judah, did not involve masturbation, but his refusal to fulfill his obligation to his brother's widow. Onan did perform intercourse with his brother's widow as required by law, but rather than consummating the act, he let his semen spill on the ground. Such interruption is known as *coitus interruptus*. Onan committed *coitus interruptus* in order to avoid producing offspring for his brother, so that he himself could inherit his brother's wealth.

In Christian tradition the term "onanism" came to mean masturbation. Masturbation was considered a sin and the cause of many physical and psychological ailments. In the eighteenth century an unknown English preacher in Boston published a treatise claiming that masturbation caused mental illness and infertility. Some medical practitioners supported the Christian teaching that the wasting of sperm through masturbation would result in degeneracy or a weakening of body and mind. Maladies ranging from baldness to schizophrenia were attributed to masturbation. *Onania: Or, a Treatise on the Disorders Produced by Masturbation* by

the physician S. A. D. Tissot (1728-1787) was widely accepted as a scientific work. Although the theory of degeneracy is no longer held to be valid, the cultural and religious disapproval of masturbation still persists.

Birth Control. Any form of sex other than heterosexual sex engaged in for the sole purpose of procreation was denounced by Jewish and Christian thinkers. According to Jewish tradition, men were allowed to waste their seed only when it was deemed necessary to avoid harming fetuses. Thus, men were allowed to have intercourse with pregnant women provided they did not ejaculate into their vaginas. Persons who knowingly harmed pregnant women committed a crime punishable by death. Similarly, any attempt to interfere with a man's reproductive capacity was also severely punished. Thus, if women grabbed men's testicles while fighting with them, their hands and, in some cases their breasts or nipples, were also cut off. Reproduction of offspring was so important for the tribe that newlywed couples were permitted a year off from work to help them start their families without delay. The modern practice of the honeymoon probably has its origin in this Jewish practice of giving newlyweds time off from work.

The Jews considered infertility a curse. In cases where wives were infertile, husbands were expected to take in concubines to bear their children. This practice is illustrated by the story of Sarah, Abraham's wife, who begged her husband to find a concubine to bear him a male child.

Interracial Marriage. Commonly known as miscegenation, interracial marriage is a relatively new taboo. Historically, various races have always intermingled to the point that no single existing race can be considered pure. The mixing of peoples with various skin colors, hair textures, and facial features was not a taboo prior to the sixteenth century, when Europeans began their world voyages of exploration. Portuguese and Spanish explorers freely mixed with the native peoples they encountered, and the offspring of these unions were identified under the new racial categories of mulattos and Creoles.

For reasons still poorly understood, race mixing through marriage has long been a problem for the peoples of the English-speaking world. Some believe that this taboo has a religious basis, insofar as white Europeans found it difficult to accept Afri-

WHAT MISCEGENATION IS!

—AND—

WHAT WE ARE TO EXPECT

Now that Mr. Lincoln is Re-elected.

By L. SEAMAN, LL. D.

WALLER & WILLETTS, Publishers,

NEW YORK.

One of the most powerful sexual taboos throughout U.S. history was race "mixing." (Library of Congress)

cans and other dark-skinned races as fully human. Others believe that the prohibition against race mixing was a form of racist ideology that was consciously promoted to justify slavery. Marrying those who were defined as inferior was prohibited because it served to erode the very ideological basis of oppression. Despite social and legal strictures prohibiting marriage between whites and African Americans, many white males chose to exploit African American female slaves sexually by producing children with them. Such children have never been considered white.

Pornography. Although considered to be taboo, pornography as the portrayal of sexual fantasy for prurient purposes has existed in every known civilization. The nature of pornography is such that it is not only intended to appeal to persons' erotic interests, but it is also meant to challenge sexual taboos. The open, mundane, and casual violation of sexual taboos portrayed in pornography such as incest, adultery, group sex, sex on the job, sex between professionals and their clients, and every imaginable form of deviant sex makes pornography what it is. It depicts forbidden fantasies as attainable and invites viewers to think the unthinkable without guilt. It also suggests that sex and love are not necessarily linked and that monogamous relationships are not necessary for the enjoyment of sex. Pornography flouts the Judeo-Christian view that the purpose of sex is procreation.

Abortion. The taboo against abortion is rooted in the Judeo-Christian concept of the purpose of sex and the definition of what constitutes human beings. Abortion as a method of contraception militates against the basic biblical commandment to reproduce. A major unresolved aspect of the abortion issue is the question of when life begins. Ancient Jewish law did not recognize the fetus as a human being. Prior to birth, a fetus did not enjoy the legal status of a human being because it did not enjoy independent existence. The notion that life begins at conception is a product of late nineteenth century Christian theology. Until then, most Christians believed that abortion was not a sin until the fetus moved within the uterus (quickening). English common law also permitted abortion prior to quickening.

Beginning in the nineteenth century, various American states passed antiabortion laws, forcing women to resort to illegal and unsafe means to terminate unwanted pregnancies. Under pressure from women's groups, medical professionals, and various advocacy groups, states began to liberalize their abortion laws. It took the landmark 1973 Supreme Court ruling in *Roe v. Wade* to make abortion legal in all fifty states. Since 1973, antiabortion activists, with the support of conservative politicians and Christian lobbyists championing "family values," have carried on a sustained campaign to overturn the Supreme Court's ruling. Although it has not been overturned by the late 1990's, such groups have succeeded in limiting women's access to abortion. Restrictive laws have been enacted stipulating that women must receive their husbands' consent in order to abort, that minors must obtain their parents' consent, and that women must endure specified waiting periods before having abortions.

Patriarchy and Sexuality. Consistent with the cultural traditions of pastoral peoples, the organization of the Hebrew family was patriarchal and matrilineal. Men had absolute and final authority in their households. Women were married into their husbands' families, and children inherited their fathers' names. The Hebrews preferred male children, because they were more useful than females for hard, pastoral work and warfare. In the words of the Psalms, "As arrows are in the hand of a mighty man; so are children of the youth. Happy is the man that hath his quiver full of them." Women's primary role was to be men's helpmates. Unlike the women of other ancient Middle Eastern societies such as the Egyptians, Akkadians, and Sumerians, Hebrew women rarely rose to positions of power. No female Hebrew rulers are mentioned in history.

Patriarchy, rooted in the pastoral values of the ancient Hebrews, has come to dominate Western attitudes toward sexuality and the family. Women in patriarchal cultures are considered men's property. Because of the chattel status of women in such cultures, men and women who have violated the same taboo may be guilty of different crimes. According to Jewish jurisprudence, men who committed adultery were guilty of stealing other men's property, which was not a capital offense, whereas women accused of committing adultery were punishable by death. Rape was also treated as an aspect of property law. The expression "taking it" to refer to forcible sex with women is a reminder of how deeply embedded modern society is in the culture of patriarchy.

Women's sexuality was desired and feared simultaneously. It was feared because of the mythical linkage between females and the powers of Satan. The witch-hunts and trials that occurred in Salem, Massachusetts, in 1692, in which nineteen women were hanged, attests to the persistence of the centuries-old belief in the evil powers of female sexuality. Nineteenth century Victorianism, which transformed the image of women as evil seductresses into the image of them as helpless, delicate, angelic, and almost sexless creatures did nothing to balance the scales of sexual standards. On the contrary, this image provided a new ideological justification for the isolation and segregation of women from public life.

The sexual revolution of the 1960's and 1970's, while definitely removing the Victorian sexual constraints on women, did not alleviate their inequality in the domestic and public spheres. The 1980's and 1990's saw a new stage in the women's movement that focused on the assertion of womanhood in nonsexual rather than Victorian asexual terms. Sexual harassment laws have provided women with the right to be free from being treated as sex objects at the workplace, while marital rape laws have helped secure their sexual freedom at home. These legal and cultural changes have been viewed by many as pathways to sexual equality.

—*Mathew J. Kanjirathinkal*

BIBLIOGRAPHY

Bullough, Vern L. *Sex, Society, and History.* New York: Science History Publications, 1976. A well-researched historical study of the linkages between sexuality and society.

Bullough, Vern L., and James A. Brundage, eds. *Handbook of Medieval Sexuality.* New York: Garland, 1996. A collection of well-researched studies dealing with the medieval approach to sexual issues, including marriage, homosexuality, gender roles, and contraception.

Davis, Nigel. *The Rampant God: Eros Throughout the World.* New York: William Morrow, 1984. Places sex in a global perspective, arguing that there is much to be learned from the practices of other cultures.

Feldman, D. M. *Marital Relations, Birth Control, and Abortion in Jewish Law.* New York: New York University Press, 1968. Contains a wealth of information on Jewish law pertaining to birth control and abortion.

Mosher, Clelia Duel Mosher. *The Mosher Survey: Sexual Attitudes of Forty-five Victorian Women.* New York: Arno Press, 1980. Presents a wide range of information gathered on the basis of a questionnaire completed between 1892 and 1920 about the personal and sexual lives of women in the nineteenth century.

Schur, Edwin M. *The Americanization of Sex.* Philadelphia: Temple University Press, 1988. Places an understanding of the role of sexuality in the context of America's unique social and cultural contexts.

Smith, Bradley. *The American Way of Sex: An Informal Illustrated History.* New York: Gemini Smith, 1978. A highly readable, illustrated work that explores the history of sexual norms and practices in the United States from pre-Columbian times to the 1970's.

Tannahill, Reay. *Sex in History.* New York: Stein & Day, 1982. A thought-provoking, historical overview of sexuality as understood by the world's major civilizations.

See also Abortion; Birth control; Gay and lesbian families; Gender inequality; Incest; Interracial families; Marital rape; Marriage; Masters, William H., and Virginia E. Johnson; Polyandry; Polygyny; Roman Catholics; Sexual revolution.

Shakers

RELEVANT ISSUES: Parenting and family relationships; Religious beliefs and practices

SIGNIFICANCE: Since the Shaker religion believes in celibacy, the term "Shaker families" does not refer to biological relationships, but rather to living arrangements within Shaker villages

The Shakers, officially called the United Society of Believers, require all new members to forsake the worldly concept of family and join a larger, communal family of fellow believers. At its height in the 1820's, Shakerism had established nineteen such communal villages in New England, New York, Ohio, Indiana, and Kentucky. In the 1820's the Shaker villages at New Lebanon, New York, and Union Village, Ohio, each had more than five hundred inhabitants. By the 1990's only one Shaker

The dance for which Shakers became famous. (Archive Photos)

village, at Sabbathday Lake, Maine, remained active, and only eight inhabitants kept the faith.

The sect was founded by Ann Lee, who fled persecution in England and arrived in New York in 1774. Lee, known to the faithful as Mother Ann, was the source of the Shaker prohibition against sexual relations, probably arising out of her unhappy marriage to Abraham Standerin and the stillbirths or early-infant deaths of her four children. She was also the originator of the ecstatic visions and trembling displays of religious insights that was the origin of the name "Shaking Quakers," or "Shakers." It was Lee's successors, however, who established the communal lifestyle and the more ritualized whirling dance for which the sect is famous. Instrumental in both these developments were Joseph Meacham, who led the Shakers in the late 1780's and early 1790's, and Lucy Wright, who directed Shakerism from 1796 until 1821 and who was the first of many prominent female Shaker leaders.

In 1787 at New Lebanon, New York, Meacham instituted policies for sharing responsibility and property, which other Shaker communities basically followed for the next two centuries. In each village, members (or believers as they called themselves) were housed in family units and usually given geographical labels such as West Family or North Family. New converts lived in one family and were acquainted with Shaker religious doctrine by the two elders and two elderesses who guided the religious and secular life of each family. Women and men lived in separate quarters, which were most often on opposite sides of the same dwelling. These dwellings were equipped with distinctive dual doors and staircases so that the two sexes could be separated from one another as they came and went.

In each Shaker family daily tasks were assigned along fairly traditional gender lines: Sisters cooked, cleaned, and washed while brethren farmed, built, and engaged in craft making. Family journals record, however, that in times of need sisters helped with the harvest and brethren with the canning of ripening fruit. Moreover, many mothers who brought young children with them into the society were freed from the burden of daily child rearing, except when their monthly duties assigned them to the family nursery. Such shared responsibility helped make most Shaker families and villages financial successes in their heyday. —*Richard M. Marshall*

See also Communal living; Hutterites; Mennonites and Amish; Mormons; Religion; Sexuality and sexual taboos.

Sheehy, Gail

BORN: November 27, 1937, Mamaroneck, N.Y.
AREA OF ACHIEVEMENT: Sociology
SIGNIFICANCE: Sheehy extended developmental psychology to adulthood, discerning and later exploring predictable stages of adult growth

Sheehy, a graduate of the University of Vermont, received a fellowship to study under Margaret Mead at Columbia University in 1970. In 1974 she was awarded a grant from the Alicia Patterson Foundation for further studies in adult development. From these studies several of her later works evolved. *Passages: Predictable Crises of Adult Life* (1976) met with immediate critical and popular success, remaining on *The New York Times* best-seller list for three years and eventually being translated into twenty-eight languages. *Pathfinders* (1981) drew upon the experiences of sixty thousand American men and women who had emerged victorious from crises in their lives. Other significant works dealing with distinct stages in adult growth include *The Silent Passage: Menopause* (1992) and *New Passages: Mapping Your Life Across Time* (1995), in which she argues that there is a second phase of adulthood that occurs in middle life.

Sheehy is also a well-known jour-

nalist and editor and often appears as a social commentator on television news programs. Among her other works are the novel *Lovesounds* (1970); *Gorbachev: The Man Who Changed the World* (1990), for which she won the Washington Journalism Review Award in 1991; and the play *Maggie and Misha* (1991), a political satire. —*Christine R. Catron*

See also Empty nest syndrome; Family life cycle; Mead, Margaret; Menopause; Midlife crises.

Shelters

RELEVANT ISSUES: Marriage and dating; Parenting and family relationships; Violence
SIGNIFICANCE: In response to the growing disclosures of wife abuse in Canada and the United States, shelters or transition houses have been established in local communities as a temporary refuge for women and children seeking to flee violent homes and abusive partners

Author Gail Sheehy in 1988. (AP/Wide World Photos)

Wife abuse is a problem of enormous magnitude. Researchers who study family violence argue that one woman in six in Canada and the United States has been the victim of a violent act from a husband within a given year. One in four has experienced a husband's violence at some point in her marriage. For millions of women and children, home life is marked by fear and tension. From this perspective, going home can be dangerous.

Need for Transition Houses. Wife abuse is not a problem linked to inner cities, nor is it a direct result of poverty, alcoholism, or periods of unemployment. While violence against wives is not a new problem, disclosures of abuse are on the increase. For many years shame, embarrassment, and fear kept women from telling friends or health care professionals about their experiences of physical or emotional abuse. They blamed themselves for being poor wives or mothers. They hoped that by trying harder to please their abusive husbands the violence would stop.

While deliberate acts of physical violence tend to be what is most commonly identified as family violence, other forms of abusive behavior can include willful neglect; emotional, financial, or sexual abuse; or the threats of such intended acts. Many children witness the violence that is directed against their mothers, and others are victims of parental rage themselves. The consequences of violence are varied and enduring, and the journey toward healing and wholeness can be long and arduous. One of the most important steps for abused women is to remove themselves from the home environment that endangers their physical and emotional health. The question is posed as to where women and their children can go when violence permeates the family home.

Establishment of Women's Shelters. Leaving abusive husbands is very difficult for most women. Fear, a sense of powerlessness, and economic dependency keep many battered wives in homes where their physical and mental health cannot be assured. Many abused women have nowhere to go but shelters when their own lives and the lives of their children are endangered.

Safe houses, shelters, or transition houses offer temporary housing to women and their children who flee abusive husbands. In 1995 Statistics Canada reported that there were 405 women's shelters located across the country, including transition houses, second-stage houses, and other emergency refuge centers. In addition to the provision of temporary housing, these facilities often provide individual and group counseling for abused women and their children, while some houses also sponsor child-care and parenting skills programs. According to data reported by Statistics Canada, almost 100,000 women and children sought refuge in transition facilities in the period from 1994 to 1995.

The first shelter for battered women in the United States was opened in St. Paul, Minnesota, in the late 1970's. By the late twentieth century, there were 1,500 shelters for battered women. Some researchers have argued that wife abuse is one of the main factors behind homelessness in America. Each year scores of women and their children are turned away from shelters because there are no available beds; many facilities have long waiting lists. The exact location of transition houses is kept confidential, for many abusive men try to find and revictimize their wives or girlfriends who have sought shelter there. Nonetheless, phone numbers of transition houses are widely publicized, and women can call them at any time seeking information or addresses.

Functions of Shelters. The primary goal of domestic violence shelters is to offer women and their children safe housing for thirty and sometimes ninety days. During this time abused women are put into contact with other agencies and resources that may assist them as they seek to establish a new life free from the abuse of the past. Women and their children may also receive individual or group counseling. Often there are programs at shelters that increase the networking opportunities for resident women, and by participating in these programs battered wives can begin to combat the loneliness and isolation they experience in the aftermath of abuse. Second-stage housing, on the other hand, offers battered women longer-term accommodations (from six months to two years) to bridge the gap between the temporary refuge of transition houses and the establishment of a permanent life free from abusers.

Despite the need for temporary shelters, most transition houses are poorly funded, relying in large measure on voluntary donations, corporate donors, or yearly government grants to keep their

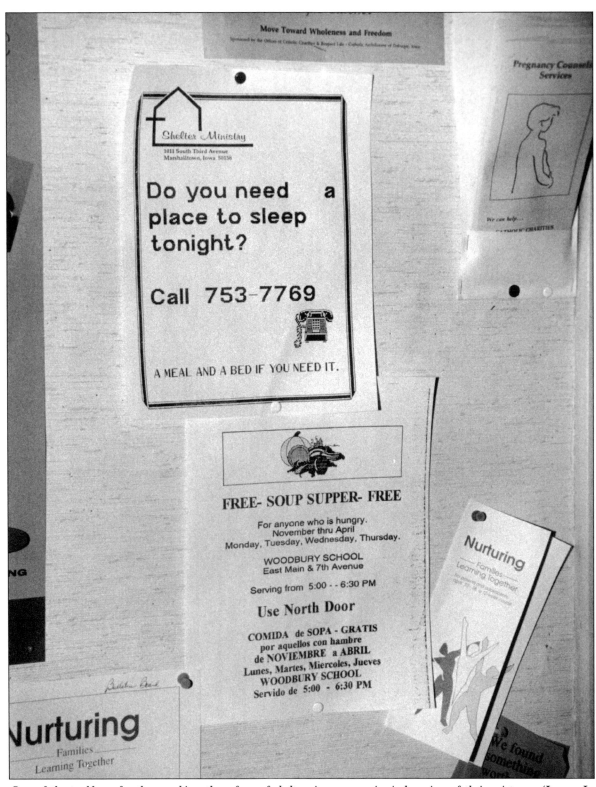

One of the problems for those seeking the refuge of shelters in emergencies is learning of their existence. (James L. Shaffer)

When persons seeking a shelter do not know where else to go, they are likely to turn to churches. (Skjold Photographs)

doors open. In consequence, excessive staff time is directed toward fund-raising activities and successive grant applications. While few people challenge the need for transition houses in every community across North America, governments seem reluctant to offer them adequate and consistent funding.

Given the temporary nature of shelters and the lack of social structural support for battered wives, many women return to their abusive partners. The reality of revictimized women has led most shelter workers to be pessimistic about the chances for change in the lives of batterers, despite their promises to cease being violent. Peace and tranquillity are often short-lived in abusive homes. Often women flee to shelters and return to abusive husbands many times before they finally terminate such relationships forever.

Link Between Feminism and Shelters for Women. The recognition of the prevalence and seriousness of wife abuse can be linked to grassroots feminists active in what is commonly known as the transition house movement. Their message has been threefold: to reveal the extent of male violence against women, to challenge traditional responses to women who have been victims, and to establish profeminist services for female survivors. From a feminist standpoint, violence against women is a specific example of male power and control, which includes encouraging women to be economically dependent on their husbands. Feminists who have been involved in the establishment of shelters for battered wives have wanted to give women the opportunity to flee dangerous home environments. They have also sought to ensure that women are empowered to make choices that end wife abuse forever and offer them a future free from the risk or reality of violence. Thus, transition houses have not been simply temporary shelters for women but also resource centers that could offer women counseling and acquaint them with resources available in their local communities.

As transition houses have become more numerous, their feminist base has weakened. As a result, some researchers believe that the political struggle to highlight the gendered nature of wife abuse has been lost. Many transition house workers and those who lobby on their behalf believe that society still treats wife abuse as a personal problem rather than as a political issue of male power and control. For this reason, some believe that shelters, safe houses, and sanctuaries for women simply place a Band-Aid on a problem that requires radical surgery. To be sure, the response to male battery against women should be a transformed society in which violence is neither tolerated nor glamorized. In the meantime, however, transition houses offer a refuge to women and children running for their lives.

—*Nancy Nason-Clark and Danielle Irving*

BIBLIOGRAPHY
Roberts, Allert R., ed. *Helping Battered Women: New Perspectives and Remedies.* New York: Oxford University Press, 1996.
Statistics Canada, 1994-1995. Transition Home Survey, Data tables 1-20. Ottawa, Canada: 1995.
Straus, Murray, Richard Gelles, and Susan Steinmetz. *Behind Closed Doors: Violence in the American Family.* New York: Doubleday, 1980.
Thorne-Finch, R. *Ending the Silence: The Origins and Treatment of Male Violence Against Women.* Toronto: University of Toronto Press, 1992.
Timmins, Leslie, ed. *Listening to the Thunder: Advocates Talk About the Battered Women's Movement.* Vancouver, British Columbia: Women's Research Centre, 1995.
Walker, Gillian. *Family Violence and the Women's Movement: The Conceptual Politics of Struggle.* Toronto: University of Toronto Press, 1990.

See also Cycle of violence theory; Domestic violence; Family crises; Family Violence Prevention and Services Act; Gender inequality; Homeless families; Recovery programs; Violence Against Women Act; Volunteerism.

Siblings

RELEVANT ISSUES: Children and child development; Parenting and family relationships
SIGNIFICANCE: The quality of relationships between siblings influences the social and personality development of children, affects all members of the family, and serves as a source of distress or support even into later life

The relationship between siblings has been the subject of numerous legends. The Egyptian story of Osiris and his sister Isis was one of the earliest.

Sister-sister relationships are less likely to be aggressive than brother-brother or brother-sister relationships. (Arkent Archive)

Child and family researchers, however, did not give the subject much attention until the 1980's.

Sibling life has a sense of its own. It can be somewhat secretive, outside the view of parents. Adult children often describe events in which they were involved together of which their parents had been totally unaware. One aspect of which parents are unaware or ignore is physical abuse between siblings. This most commonly takes the form of stronger siblings hitting, kicking, or slapping weaker siblings. Society often minimizes such violence, and parents are tolerant not knowing what to do. Even with such intense sibling rivalry, brothers and sisters feel bonded to one another in a way that affects them for good or bad during their entire lives.

Sibling Relationships in Early Childhood. In preschool siblings, older children exhibit more aggressive and more nurturing behavior in their relationships than do their younger siblings. Older siblings initiate antagonistic behavior 80 percent of the time, and younger siblings are more likely to submit rather than to counterattack. On rare occasions, when young siblings start fights, older brothers and sisters are likely to retaliate physically. In brother-brother relationships physical aggression occurs more frequently than in sister-sister relationships at this age. In mixed sex relationships both sisters and brothers are likely to be aggressive.

Older siblings are also more likely to initiate nurturing and social behavior than younger siblings. Older sisters are more likely to be kind and nurturing than older brothers regardless of the sex of the younger siblings. When relationships between siblings are friendly and cooperative, the ability of sisters as well as brothers to understand the emotional perspective of others increases as they move into middle childhood.

The quality of sibling relationships in early childhood is greatly affected by parents' relationships to their children. When parents treat one sibling more favorably than another, conflict between siblings increases. The conflict is more intense when mothers show differential treatment. When all siblings feel securely attached to their parents, they are more likely to form secure attachments to one another. There is a relationship between the amount of conflict between siblings and the frequency of parent intervention in sibling conflicts. The more parents intervene the more conflict there is between siblings. The quality of the parents' marriage is also related to the quality of sibling relationships. When parents are satisfied with their marriage, conflict between siblings decreases. When parents are divorced, however, siblings often turn toward each other for support and security.

In early childhood, stepbrothers and stepsisters are usually cooperative with each other. Their relationships are influenced by the conflict that may exist between the parent with whom they live and the parent who visits. Provided these relationships are relatively free of tension, there is no reason that relationships between stepchildren cannot be cooperative and close in early childhood.

Sibling Relationships in Middle Childhood. During middle childhood the influence of older siblings on the development of younger ones is stronger than the influence of younger siblings on the development of older ones. It also appears that male siblings have more developmental influence on females than female siblings on males.

The amount of time siblings spend with peers increases dramatically in middle childhood. Often older siblings play the role of introducing peer groups to younger siblings. This can occur intentionally or inadvertently, as when friends come to the home and happen to meet younger siblings. The presence of siblings appears to promote interaction with peers during middle childhood.

Brothers and sisters during middle childhood spend most of their time watching television together and about equal amounts of time in playing with toys or in reading and playing drama. They spend the least amount of their time, 5 to 10 percent, in games and noncompetitive physical activities. In brother-brother relationships much time is spent in competitive physical activities, but in sister-sister and sister-brother relationships very little time is spent in such activities. Older sisters in particular are likely to assume teaching behavior toward their younger sisters but not toward their younger brothers.

Conflict in sibling relationships generally declines with age. In middle childhood, as younger siblings become more mature, there is an increase in their verbal aggression toward their older siblings, but they also begin to exhibit more cooperative behavior. If rivalry exists it appears to remain about the same during this period.

In most sibling relationships there is an increase in closeness and companionship during the school-age years. It is possible that association with peers influences the development of social skills in siblings and that they bring these social skills into their sibling relationships. Siblings begin to disclose more to each other than to their parents. This bond of confidentiality, if kept, serves to solidify their sibling bond. If broken, it can cause intense sibling conflict.

In middle childhood mothers' marital satisfaction influences the quality of sibling relationships. When mothers appear to be happily married, brothers and sisters appear to have better family relationships.

As siblings grow older, the amount of nuturance they give each other tends to diminish. (James L. Shaffer)

Older sisters are more likely to be nurturing than older brothers. (James L. Shaffer)

Relationships between stepbrothers and stepsisters are usually characterized by greater conflict if their parents remarry when the children are in middle childhood. Children's competition for parents' affection, the increased possibility of differential parental treatment of siblings, and competition set the stage for conflict. Parents who are aware of these issues can help to foster cooperation between stepchildren by emphasizing the talents and contributions of each child and by using democratic parenting styles.

Sibling Relationships in Adolescence. Less is known about what happens to sibling relationships during adolescence than in any other period. Same-gender siblings report greater closeness and warmth during this period than opposite-gender siblings. Nevertheless, siblings of both genders report a decrease in trust, enjoyment, and understanding in their relationships with one another, with the greatest decrease occurring in sister-sister relationships. At about the age of twelve, the amount of nurturance siblings give to other siblings decreases. If rivalry and conflict exist, they often peak in early adolescence and then taper off by late adolescence, as siblings learn better ways of managing conflict. The closer the age of the siblings, the greater the conflict. Siblings report less interaction with one another during adolescence because of their increased interaction with their peers.

During adolescence, older siblings serve as important agents of socialization for younger ones. In matters such as school course and teacher choices, extracurricular involvement, and dating experience, siblings influence one another. Socialization in sexuality occurs in adolescent sibling relationships. In this aspect brothers are more likely to affect brothers and sisters more likely to affect sisters. Same-gender siblings are more likely to discuss sexual behavior with each other than with their parents. The sexual behavior of older siblings and their discussions of it impacts younger siblings, who will either be inclined to imitate their behavior or will be repulsed and avoid it when they reach that age. Brother-sister relationships serve as safe laboratories in which both can practice flirting and interaction with the opposite gender. Opposite-sex siblings of similar ages often serve as sources of information about who is attracted to their sibling counterparts.

Relationships between adolescent stepchildren are either very supportive or highly antagonistic. If stepchildren are of the same gender and close in age, there is greater chance for rivalry. If they are opposite in gender and of similar age, they are less prohibited in being sexually attracted to each other because of the lack of family blood ties. Both of these conditions create potential for conflict, arguing, and fighting. In some cases, however, stepchildren support each other during adolescence in their discussions about their relationships with divorced parents.

Sibling Relationships in Adulthood. Relationships between siblings change in various ways when they reach adulthood. Marriage and family life, careers, and separate living arrangements usually mean that siblings have less time for interaction with one another. Yet, siblings remain powerful influences on one another during adulthood, even when they are not as physically present as they were during childhood.

Whether or not siblings are close to one another as adults depends largely on what family experiences they had when they were younger. Families that stress harmony, lack of parental favoritism, and recognition of individual talents and contributions create a context for close sibling relationships in adulthood. From time to time siblings give power to their shared experiences by getting together and discussing commonly shared activities they experienced as children, such as vacations, school events, games, church attendance, or shared crises. These stories, when retold, tend to strengthen the bonds and renew siblings' closeness to one another. Family reunions, joint vacations, birthdays celebrations, and letter writing do much to maintain closeness between siblings during adulthood. The additional factor of the growth of the extended family and the relationships between cousins continues to cement the bond between siblings.

Parents also serve as conduits of information about the family between one sibling and another. Of course, the ways in which parents frame this information influences the feelings of one sibling toward another. If parents talk about a sibling to another adult child in a negative way, that person will most likely also develop negative feelings toward the sibling.

Most people assume that sibling relationships

Relationships between stepbrothers or stepsisters are typically closest in early childhood. (Arkent Archive)

are permanent. They go on even when there is little opportunity for direct contact and even when there is anger and hostility. The family bond is ingrained in people even when their family experiences have been unpleasant.

Sibling rivalry in adulthood begins in childhood and is initiated more often by brothers than by sisters. In most cases the rivalry is fueled by parents treating siblings differently. When brothers and sisters marry, they carry their attitudes to their marital partners and their children, and the rivalry becomes entrenched in the larger extended family. Despite some presence of sibling rivalry in adulthood, most people report that they have developed ways of interacting that avoid conflict and overt rivalry. Conflict is higher in relationships with stepchildren than in relationships with full siblings.

Three major events in adulthood seem to affect sibling relationships: marriage and having children, divorce and widowhood, and poor health or the death of family members. For example, siblings are often required to cooperate to take care of aging parents. The sense of caring evoked by a crisis such as death or divorce provides an opportunity for sibling contact and instills greater mutual appreciation between siblings.

Sibling Relationships in Later Life. The importance of sibling relationships seems to grow during later life. The existence of siblings, either sisters or brothers, seems to affect the well-being of both aging men and women. Elderly men with siblings have a greater sense of emotional security than those without siblings. Elderly women with siblings feel more stimulated by life and enjoy their roles more than those without siblings. Among older widows and widowers, the quality of sibling social support is a predictor of better positive outcomes. Older people who have close bonds to their siblings report less depression than older people who lack close bonds to siblings. After the death of mothers, older sisters often assume their mothers' role of looking after their brothers. Following the death of a brother's wife, many sisters become their brothers' caretakers. Brothers may also assume a deceased husband's role for a widowed sister, but not to the same degree as sisters for their brothers.

Reminiscing about earlier times becomes more frequent among older people. Reviewing life is an important task for people in later life, and an important part of life is one's relationship with siblings. Sharing recollections of childhood experiences seems to be a source of comfort and even pride for older people. They are more likely to reminisce about their childhood with their siblings than with their adult children. This reminiscing helps siblings put their current relationships into context. It provides further meaning to the important contribution of the relationship.

Relationships with sisters appear to be particularly important in later life, regardless of whether the sibling pair consists of two sisters or a brother and sister. Brothers appear to initiate contact as frequently as sisters in old age, but elderly people ascribe more positive influence to their relationships with sisters than with brothers. Of people more than 60 years of age, 53 percent report having an extremely close relationship with their sisters and another 30 percent report having a close relationship with their sisters. It is safe to say that sibling relationships continue to change even in old age, and brothers and sisters may still grow closer to each other in the last decades of life. They share common parents who often have died or require care themselves, serving to increase cooperation and closeness between siblings.

Even after a sibling dies, the sibling relationship still has an impact on living brothers and sisters. If the sibling relationship was filled with conflict and rivalry, feelings of bitterness and estrangement live on. If the relationship was cooperative and close, the deceased sibling can be further idealized.

—*James M. Harper*

BIBLIOGRAPHY

Bank, Stephen P., and Michael D. Kahn. *The Sibling Bond.* New York: Basic Books, 1982. Discusses identification, caring, conflict, and sexuality between siblings.

Boer, Fritz. *Sibling Relationships in Middle Childhood.* Leiden, the Netherlands: DSWO Press, University of Leiden, 1990. Reports the research findings of two large studies investigating relationships between siblings between the ages of six and thirteen.

Boer, Fritz, and Judy Dunn. *Children's Sibling Relationships: Developmental and Clinical Issues.* Hillsdale, N.J.: Lawrence Erlbaum, 1992. Examines the role of sibling relationships in common problems of childhood and explores implications for parents.

Cicirelli, Victor G. *Sibling Relationships Across the Life Span.* New York: Plenum, 1995. Discusses research findings about sibling relationships in early childhood, adolescence, adulthood, and old age.

Fishel, Elizabeth. *Sisters: Love and Rivalry Inside the Family and Beyond.* New York: William Morrow, 1979. Discusses the relationship between sisters from childhood to old age.

Greer, Jane, and Edward Myers. *Adult Sibling Rivalry: Understanding the Legacy of Childhood.* New York: Crown, 1992. Discusses what happens between siblings when there is conflict and tension and at various family events such as marriage or the death of a parent.

Hetherington, E. Mavis, David Reiss, and Robert Plomin. *Separate Social Worlds of Siblings.* Hillsdale, N.J.: Lawrence Erlbaum, 1994. Examines why siblings experience the same family differently.

Kahn, Michael D., and Karen G. Lewis. *Siblings in Therapy: Life Span and Clinical Issues.* New York: W. W. Norton, 1988. Discusses the dynamics of normal and clinical sibling relationships from infancy through late life.

Lamb, Michael E., and Brian Sutton-Smith. *Sibling Relationships: Their Nature and Significance Across the Lifespan.* Hillsdale, N.J.: Lawrence Erlbaum, 1982. Looks at the lifelong influences of siblings on one another.

See also Attachment theory; Birth order; Blended families; Child rearing; Disciplining children; Family caregiving; Family size; Favoritism; Multiple births; Only children; Twins.

Single life

RELEVANT ISSUES: Aging; Children and child development; Demographics; Economics and work; Parenting and family relationships

SIGNIFICANCE: As society, demographics, and the understanding of family have changed, single life has become an option for many and a part of the social and familial fabric of the United States

The description of single life depends upon the set of lenses through which one sees family. If the lenses are legal ones, then marriage or blood ties determine family, while the absence of marriage determines singleness. Until the final quarter of the twentieth century most people considered single life as simply an unmarried state, whether or not singleness was a matter of choice. The most common expectation was that one would marry, remain married for life, and raise a nuclear family. Within that legal framework, persons were either single because they never married, because they were married and divorced, or because they were married and survived a spouse. If one considers singleness as simply an unmarried state according to legal contracts or religious rituals, those who have been involved in new or alternative families not based on marriage are simply single. For example, women or men who are members of Roman Catholic religious orders would be considered single.

Single Status as Alternative Lifestyle. If one describes single as "alone," the picture changes. Single could be considered without relational ties of commitment or support. Within such a framework unmarried members of intentional communities, either traditional or new, and couples not legally married, including same-sex couples, would not be considered single. As persons mutually responsible for the continuation of a shared life, including those who raise children, these would be considered alternative forms of family. Some examples of such families are communities of nuns or monks and communities of nonreligious persons living together in mutual support and gathered for a common goal, such as for social justice or education. Such groups may have members with relational or economic ties to one another and may comprise married or unmarried persons. Clearly, as social understanding has shifted, it is progressively difficult to speak with logical exclusivity about single life.

Given changing demographics, the U.S. Census has recorded an increase in single-person dwellings. Changes in gender equality and economics have made single life more possible and more accepted than it once was. Advances in technology, such as reproductive technology, and changed social sensibilities, such as the acceptance of having children out of wedlock, have brought to single life some experiences that were formerly the preserve of married life. Choosing to have and

Married and Unmarried Americans, 1950-1995

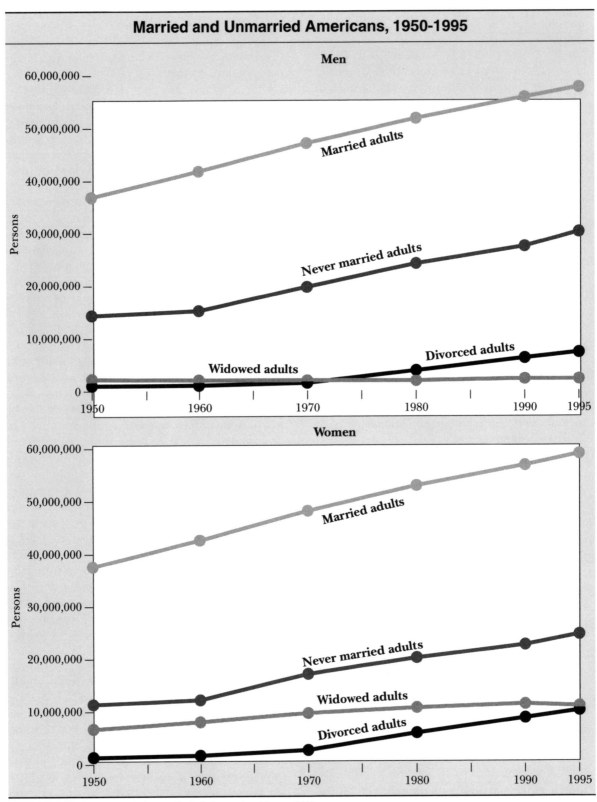

Source: *The Time Almanac 1998.* New York: Information Please, 1997.

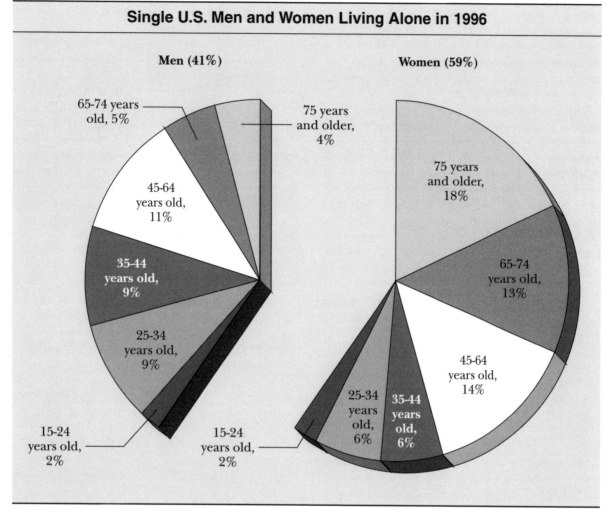

Single U.S. Men and Women Living Alone in 1996

Men (41%)

65-74 years old, 5%

75 years and older, 4%

45-64 years old, 11%

35-44 years old, 9%

25-34 years old, 9%

15-24 years old, 2%

15-24 years old, 2%

Women (59%)

75 years and older, 18%

65-74 years old, 13%

45-64 years old, 14%

25-34 years old, 6%

35-44 years old, 6%

Source: U.S. Bureau of the Census, *Statistical Abstract of the United States: 1997.* Washington, D.C.: GPO, 1997.
Note: In 1996 approximately 24,900,000 Americans aged 15 years and up were single and living alone. Percentages are rounded to the nearest whole number.

raise children has become an option for single persons desiring to remain single and for persons considered legally single who live in committed relationships, including same-sex ones. Many singles rely on friends, colleagues, and extended family, much as others formerly relied and still rely on the nuclear family. The ties that singles have chosen or forged serve to provide the support once expected primarily of persons related by blood or marriage ties. Such ties include the growing number of singles' social situations, friendship and work networks, and relational support groups.

Single vs. Unmarried. As the number of "alone" singles increases, it seems that resourceful and

resilient singleness is a positive choice rather than an absence of marriage. In fact, some who see "single" as not synonymous or interchangeable with "unmarried" speak of "ever single" rather than "never married" when considering stable singles. Such singles decide to remain unattached, free, and active in their careers and friendships, considering themselves to be complete rather than incomplete, societal gifts rather than societal problems. Some studies show that ever-single women show higher life satisfaction than their male counterparts and divorced women. They are often more satisfied than married women, possibly because of their particular life purpose and connections. Within the realm of "ever single," co-habitation, which formerly was compared to marriage, may be considered a new form of relationship that has much in common with singlehood and represents an alternative to more conventional forms of being single.

The number of single parents has increased as chosen single motherhood has become increasingly acceptable and as separation, widowhood, and divorce have increased the numbers of both stable and temporary singles who are parents. The fact that financial independence is no longer the preserve of males, and that the choice of motherhood, both socially and technologically, is no longer essentially tied to marriage, challenges the assumption that single mothers are incomplete and that the care they provide their children is inadequate.

Some Pertinent Issues. Myriad issues were posed for those considered single in late twentieth century America. Given the history of the patriarchal nuclear family, which has been the norm in the United States, and the social and economic structures most aptly suited to the nuclear family, most issues facing singles are relational or economic in nature. How these issues affect different persons can be seen by investigating elderly widows and nuns.

Given women's greater longevity and the economic inequalities they face, including lower or no Social Security, the loss of long-term partners can cause emotional as well as financial problems. Older women's greater need for health care coupled with less access to it can cause great limitations and isolation. Because single persons are accorded less social acknowledgment than couples, social pain can heighten economic insecurity. The situation of persons rendered single by the loss of long-term partners can be particularly stressful when such loss is not publicly acknowledged, as in the case of many elderly same-sex partners. Some widows and other senior women have approached these issues by gathering in shared living situations; they seek housemates or enter into communal living arrangements. These arrangements can provide the relational and economic benefits they need. Some widows and widowers choose to seek new mates without legally marrying, deriving the benefits of companionship and support without the legal, financial, and rela-tional encumbrances that are associated with the institution of marriage.

Those legally seen as single who actually have family-style commitments sometimes deal with issues that seem more attached to nuclear family situations. For example, nuns deal with relational and economic commitments to their elderly relatives and to those still actively involved in work outside their family households. Because of their decreasing numbers in twentieth century America, their increasing median age, and their expanding health care and retirement needs, active nuns are a double variation of the sandwich generation. They are committed to caring for the economic, emotional, and health needs of their biological parents and their aging sisters.

Since singles in late twentieth century America and internationally are a heterogeneous group, simple categorizations are not possible in discussing their experiences of single life. The rapid increase in singleness in the United States is due not only to women's opting for autonomy and independence, but also to social, structural, and technological changes. Single life supports itself through friendship and networking, through ties with families of origin and extended families, through circles of teachers, mentors, and companion singles. What seems clear is that single life can no longer be equated with being unmarried or emotionally isolated.

—*Frances R. Belmonte*

BIBLIOGRAPHY

Doress, Paula Brown, Diana Laskin Siegal, and The Midlife and Older Women Book Project, in cooperation with The Boston Women's Health Book Collective. *Ourselves Growing Older: Women Aging with Knowledge and Power.* New York: Simon and Schuster, 1987.

Dreman, Solly, ed., *The Family on the Threshold of the Twenty-first Century: Trends and Implications.* Mahwah, N.J.: Lawrence Erlbaum, 1997.

Gordon, Tuula. *Single Women: On the Margins?* New York: New York University Press, 1994.

Miller, Dorothy C. *Women and Social Welfare: A Feminist Analysis.* New York: Praeger, 1990.

See also Alternative family types; Child care; Dating; Divorce; Familism; Home sharing; Kinship systems; Welfare; Widowhood.